ENGLISH WORDS
AND THEIR BACKGROUND

ENGLISH WORDS AND THEIR BACKGROUND

By
GEORGE HARLEY McKNIGHT, PH.D.

GORDIAN PRESS
New York
1969

Originally Published 1923
Reprinted 1969

Copyright © 1951 by
GEORGE H. McKNIGHT
Published by Gordian Press, Inc., By Arrangement
with Appleton-Century-Crofts

Library of Congress Catalog Card Number: 69-20052

PREFACE

THIS book aims to introduce the reader to what has been called "the interesting World of Words." The study of words is not exclusively a study of roots and stems, of prefixes and suffixes, as is too frequently supposed. On the contrary its range of interest is as wide as life itself. It may be made to illustrate the cultural progress of the race, not only the development of the material elements of civilization, but the progress in knowledge and the changes that have affected modes of thought. But, above all, words are interesting on account of the human nature revealed. In the creation and use of words there appears not only the sense of beauty and the sense of humor, but a human fallibility exhibited in inexactness of knowledge and in seemingly capricious modes of procedure. In fact the variety of interest to be found in words corresponds with the variety of interest in complex human nature. All in all, the history of words introduces so much of the unexpected and strange that the subject matter becomes often less that of science than of romance.

But along with the interest and entertainment richly afforded by word-study as a science, there is a practical side, a side of value to one interested in language as an art. In order to operate an instrument efficiently one must be acquainted with the nature of its mechanism. In the same way in order to have an effective command of the resources of the English vocabulary, one must know about the materials of which the vocabulary is composed and the processes by which its words have reached their present meanings.

The customary method of studying synonyms and questions of purity and propriety is but a superficial one. A satisfactory understanding of the nature of words may best be reached through a knowledge of the underlying causes and the ability to answer the question, Why?

In one other way the subject of words challenges attention at the present time. There are now under way remarkable changes in the use of words, changes which reflect the changing conditions in the modern world. These modern features of the subject are made prominent in the present work, not only on account of their own interest, but because of the belief that the general principles that govern the use of words may best be observed in present-day, living language. Throughout, accordingly, an emphasis is thrown on the tendencies apparent in the language of our own time. The changes that are going on under one's own eyes are made to serve in the explanation of features in the language of periods more remote.

In the preparation of this work my obligations have been many. In its chapters will be found many a twice-told tale. To the stimulating works of Archbishop Trench, now more than half a century old, every student of words is indebted. To the remarkably sane work of Greenough and Kittredge I am indebted in ways which even the many references to that work fail fully to indicate. To the admirable works of Weekley, not least of all his *Etymological Dictionary,* my debt has been heavy. Mencken's *The American Language* and L. P. Smith's *The English Language,* and the various works of Skeat, Jespersen, Emerson, Hirt, Schrader, Bradley, and Brander Matthews have provided much material for which I wish to acknowledge indebtedness. All of the great English dictionaries have yielded information, but particularly the Oxford Dictionary, without which the present work could hardly have been composed.

Finally, I wish to make grateful acknowledgment for aid from several of my friends and colleagues. Professors G. M. Bolling and M. Percival have read much of this work while in manuscript, and Professors J. V. Denney, G. M. Bolling, and R. E. Rockwood have read several of the chapters in proof. For many helpful suggestions received from them I wish to record my thanks.

G. H. McK.

CONTENTS

CHAPTER		PAGE
	Preface	v
I.	Standard English	1
II.	Dialect	12
III.	American English	23
IV.	Slang	37
V.	Technical Words	70
VI.	The Native Element in the English Vocabulary	81
VII.	Borrowed Teutonic Elements	99
VIII.	Classical Element	106
IX.	The French Element	122
X.	Varied Sources	138
XI.	Blending of the Various Elements	152
XII.	New Creations and Compounds	163
XIII.	Folk-Etymology	180
XIV.	Some Figures of Syntax	191
XV.	Tropes	202
XVI.	Figures of Similarity	217
XVII.	Figures of Contiguity	232
XVIII.	Generalization and Specialization	248
XIX.	Euphemism and Hyperbole	265
XX.	Degeneration and Elevation	280

CONTENTS

CHAPTER		PAGE
XXI.	Words and Archæology	293
XXII.	Words and Culture History	312
XXIII.	Words and Romance	341
XXIV.	Place-Names	358
XXV.	Personal Names	377
XXVI.	Choice of Words	393
XXVII.	Words Past and Present	412
	Word Index	431
	Subject Index	441

ENGLISH WORDS
AND THEIR BACKGROUND

ENGLISH WORDS
AND THEIR BACKGROUND

CHAPTER I

STANDARD ENGLISH

No cultivated ear is required to distinguish different English-speaking peoples by their manner of speech. An Irishman, an Englishman, a Scotchman, or an American may be distinguished by speech more readily than by manner or appearance. With literary English the case is different. Cultivated Scotchmen from Hume to Stevenson, cultivated Irishmen from Swift to Shaw, cultivated Americans from Cotton Mather to Henry James, have written in a language hardly to be distinguished from that of contemporary cultivated Englishmen. A literary language with few deviations from uniformity belongs not only to England, but to the various parts of the English-speaking world.

The history of the rise of this standard form of English makes an interesting story. A search for beginnings leads one back more than five hundred years, to the second half of the fourteenth century, the time of Wycliffe and Chaucer. Long before the time of Chaucer, to be sure, as early as the ninth century, in the Anglo-Saxon period, a literary standard had been formed. Largely due to the literary activities of Alfred the Great and the political supremacy reached by his kingdom of Wessex, in the South of England, the language of Wessex became accepted as the standard form of language in literary composition. Even works composed at an earlier date in other parts of England, such as the *Beowulf* and the poetry of Caedmon and Cynewulf, composed in the North, have come down to us in the standard language of the Old English period, the Southern dialect of Wessex.

The Norman Conquest, however, soon led to the loss of this English standard of speech. Following the Conquest, the English-speaking element in the population became so reduced in station that the English language had little literary importance. The real literary language of England was not English, but French, or Latin. For three centuries little was written in English, and the little produced was written in the form of speech natural to the writer and varying, therefore, with the section of the country to which the writer belonged. There was entire absence of controlling standard. In the matter of language, anarchy prevailed.

The development of the standard languages of the world closely accompanies the development of national feeling. In England the growth in national feeling, that becomes more and more apparent in the victorious reigns of Edward I and Edward III, was accompanied by development of feeling hostile to the use of French then firmly established in the use of the ruling and the cultivated classes of England, and favorable to the renewed use of the native English language then occupying a lowly station. The result was that in the second half of the fourteenth century the English language came once more to its own, into use not only in Parliament and the law courts and in schools, but in the literary productions composed for English cultured society.

In the revival of literature in the English language, the form of language adopted was the dialect of the East Midland district at that time not above the level of other dialects of England. A variety of reasons led to this choice. This dialect served as an effective compromise between its neighboring dialects on the north and on the south. It was the dialect of centers of culture such as Oxford and Cambridge. It was the dialect of London, the metropolis and the center of official life. Finally, as the dialect of London, it was the form of speech native to Chaucer, the first great literary artist to write in English for more than four centuries. As the language of Oxford, it was used by Wycliffe in preference to his native Yorkshire dialect. As the dialect of London and the English court, it was used by Chaucer's contemporary, Gower, in preference to his native Kentish dialect. The influence of Chaucer and Gower led to its use by their disciples, Occleve and Lydgate, and the influence of the language of this school of writers is apparent in practically all of the writers of the following century. The second half of the fourteenth century, therefore, in the time of the beginning of Standard English, a beginning made when the East Midland dialect, that of London, became fixed on as the form of English for general literary use. It is from this dialect of English, once used only in a comparatively small part of England, that in the course of several centuries developed the cultivated language now the standard for literary use throughout the English-speaking world.

An important element in the charm of Chaucer is the colloquial freshness of his language. The language of literature was not far removed from that in colloquial use. The spelling adopted was not, like that of modern English, determined by any rule or tradition, but was governed by the desire to represent by means of letters the natural pronunciation. In other words the spelling was in general phonetic. The constructions used, also, were not artificial ones imposed by grammatical law, but were for the most part those of natural usage. A consequence of the absence of grammars and dictionaries and spelling books was that the language underwent rapid change. A hundred years later, when Caxton was confronted with the problem of determining the form of English to be used in the printed books now for the first time issuing from his press, he found that the English of his time was much changed from that used in the writings of Chaucer and his contemporaries. The necessity of adopting a form of English intelligible to his fifteenth-century readers, led Caxton in his printed books to conform to the mode of speech current in his time. The literary language in this way kept pace with the progress in colloquial speech.

In the following century, however, a combination of causes contributed to check the rapid change in the language. In the first place the influence of the books, now printed for the first time, and issued in relatively large editions, aided in fixing the form of the language. A second influence contributing toward the same effect was the activity, springing from the Reformation, in translating the Bible into English. The language of the Authorized Version of King James, issued in 1611, is in general that determined by the translators of the first half of the sixteenth century. The invention of printing, then, and the translation of the Bible, did much toward determining the final form of literary English.

The language of the sixteenth century, however, was by no means as definitely fixed as that of the present day. Its lack of regularity in spelling, in vocabulary, and in grammar was perhaps more than compensated for by the freedom enjoyed by writers of that period in the adoption of new words and the combination of existing words in word-compound and in phrase. The expressive power of present-day English owes an incalculable amount to the phrase-making power of Shakespeare and his contemporaries in a period when the language was in a more fluid state.

The order and regularity lacking in sixteenth-century

English, was contributed in the course of the two following centuries. In the seventeenth century the words so freely imported and manufactured in the preceding century were subjected to a sifting process, and most of the words that survived to the end of this century have remained permanently in the language. In the eighteenth century, especially near the end, the influence of grammars and dictionaries made itself fully felt. Words admissible into literary use were registered with their meanings in dictionaries, which also more and more undertook to indicate the pronunciation. English grammar became a subject for school study, and conformity to the use authorized by dictionary and grammar became the test of cultivation in language.

Such, briefly told, is the story of the rise of Standard English. One of several vulgar dialects of the fourteenth century has, by cultivation, been raised to the position of the literary language of the English-speaking world.

In the nature of its origin and development the English standard language is not exceptional. Its history is paralleled in the case of most of the other great literary languages of the modern world. Literary German is called High German because developed from the speech native to Southern or High Germany. The elevation of this dialect gained at the same time literary and religious sanction through its adoption by Luther for his Bible translation in the sixteenth century. In the same way literary French is developed from the speech native to that part of northern France of which Paris is a center. The speech of the South of France offered a certain amount of rivalry. This Provençal speech was effectively developed for literary use in the Troubadour poetry of the twelfth century, and in our own day has served as the literary instrument for Mistral, one of the most eminent of modern French poets. The prevailing form of literary French, however, is that based on the dialect of the northern district, the *langue d'oïl* as distinguished from the Provençal *langue d'oc*.

In Spain again it is the dialect of the kingdom of Castile, of which Madrid is the center, at one time only one of several independent Spanish kingdoms, that has come to serve as the literary language of the entire nation. In Italy it is the dialect of Tuscany, the district including Florence and Sienna, that has been thus elevated. Dante and Petrarch, who only a short time before Chaucer began to write in London English, adopted the Tuscan dialect for Italian literary use, contributed greatly toward developing the literary value of this dialect and giving to it prestige. In Holland a literary language was formed from the various Low German dialects of the Netherlands, with the Frankish element, however, dominating. This standard form of speech not only serves as the literary language for Holland and its colonial settlements in South Africa and the East Indies, but in the nineteenth century, in the face of much opposition from supporters of local dialects, became adopted as the official language for the Flemish element in the population of Belgium.

Considerably more recent in its development is the literary language of Russia. In earlier times the literary language of Russia was a compromise between old Slavonic and Russian.[1] The break with the past came at the end of the eighteenth century, when the literary language now in use was formed with the current spoken language as its basis. The direct reflection of the Russian spirit and of Russian life which distinguishes modern Russian romance, is said to be due to the close relation of the literary language to everyday speech.

A still more recent instance of the rise of a new literary language is to be found in Norway and is explained, as in almost all instances, by a rise of the spirit of nationalism.

---

[1] Meillet, p. 228.

In Norway the growth of nationalism in the nineteenth century, which led to the separation from Sweden, also led to a revolt from the use of Danish, the language hitherto used by Norwegian writers, including the world-famed Björnson and Ibsen, and the language used in the social intercourse of cultivated people. The new spirit of nationalism led to the recreation of a national Norwegian language, called the *landsmaal*, "country speech," which now shares with the Danish language the place as official language of the country. This new Norwegian national language, however, differs from the other national languages in that it does not come from the elevation of a single one of the native dialects officially recognized, but is supposed to be a reconstruction of the original Norwegian language from elements derived from the many separate dialects native to the isolated districts of that sparsely settled country.

Even in our own day, we are told, in the country with the most ancient civilization, in China, there is in process of formation a new standard language. This language is intended to provide a common linguistic medium for the various people of that vast country now separated from each other by difference of dialect. It is also intended to absorb names for features of Western civilization unprovided with names in older Chinese.

In estimating the value of the different literary languages, an important matter to be considered is the relation of the literary standard to everyday speech. In the case of Russian, it has been pointed out that this relation is exceptionally close. The case of Modern Greek will illustrate the reverse situation. In the formation of the modern literary language of that country it is natural that there should have been felt sentimental consideration for the Greek past. In consequence the Romaic, or modern Greek, used in literature is closely related to classical

Greek. One acquainted with ancient Greek can without great difficulty read a modern Greek newspaper. In the case of the everyday speech of the modern Greek the situation is different, and in consequence there is wide divergence between the written and the spoken form of modern Greek. The cultured term in use for bread, for example, is *artos*. In order, however, to make oneself understood at a bakery, in asking for bread, one needs to use the vernacular term *psumé*. The name *hudor*, for water, which goes back to classical Greek, appears on the labels of water bottles, but in asking a waiter for water, one needs to use the vulgar term *nero*.[2]

Not unlike is the divergence which, in later stages of English, has come about between the cultivated literary language and the mode of speech natural among uncultivated people. Let us take by way of illustration a bit of colloquial American of the kind everywhere to be heard on the lips of unschooled American youth. *Them guys ain't got no pep.* The expression belongs to the language of the street, or, as some may prefer to say, of the gutter. At the same time it is straightforward speech; its meaning is plain and unambiguous. The objection to it is that it does not conform to the tests applied to Standard English. The first word is ungrammatical; the second, slang; the third, bad grammar again; the fourth, redundant and colloquial; the fifth, illogical; the sixth, slang once more. To sum up, judged by accepted standard, not one word is left of six monosyllables in a sentence the meaning of which is clearly and forcefully conveyed.

Obviously there is a deep chasm between standard English and certain forms of popular speech. Standard English, like standard modern Greek, is an artificial product. It stands aloof from the popular elements that appear in uncultivated speech. New words such as

---

[2] G. H. Moses, *National Geographic Magazine*, October, 1915.

STANDARD ENGLISH

josh, v., *jolly,* v., *spiel, stunt, jay, jazz,* are branded as slang. Homely old words such as *chuck,* v., *chunk, chore, peek,* v., *bust,* v. are condemned as dialectal or provincial. Pronunciations such as *bile* (for boil), *restin* (for resting), *nater* (for nature,), *tay* (for tea), *chayney* (for China), *wownd* (for wound), in preceding centuries accepted more or less in cultivated use, are rated by the modern censor of speech as vulgar, or at least old-fashioned. Spellings such as *licour, ayre, floare, musick,* are condemned as grossly incorrect, although these four words thus spelled appear in the writings respectively of Chaucer, Shakespeare, Milton, and Samuel Johnson. Much of the energy devoted to the cultivation of so-called ''Good English'' is devoted to the task of eliminating features like those cited above, which do not conform with the artificial standard, a prodigious task in dealing with persons not reared in surroundings where the cultivated standard speech naturally prevails.

It is, perhaps, not the part of wisdom to minimize the advantages accruing from the uniformity and regularity the lack of which was felt in earlier periods. That in the course of the last centuries the English language has gained in precision, will hardly be denied. It must not be lost sight of that language is not created for the single individual, but is a social instrument for communication between many individuals. It is important that the language medium should offer as little as possible resistance to the thought current, and this end is attained only when the symbols of language are ones that convey precisely the same meaning to all who use the language.

There is, however, reason for questioning the limits to which the process of standardization may profitably be carried. In the language of Shakespeare, it has been clearly shown, the popular speech of the time has everywhere given the pattern. In the cultivated language of to-day, the reverse is often true; effort is made to have the standard language of literature give the pattern for colloquial use. Can the English of to-day be said to be a more effective means of expression than that used by Shakespeare?

Objections to the imposition of fetters on language have been voiced at different stages in the history of modern English. In the sixteenth century a writer as mindful of good form, as devoted to classical rule, as Sir Philip Sidney, called it "a peece of the Tower of Babilon's curse that a man should be put to schoole to learne his mother tongue." In our own time of radical change, the spirit of revolt[3] in language finds expression in the careless humor of the student phrase, "What's grammar among friends?" as well as in the more coolly reflective review article entitled, "Is Grammar Useless?"[4] an article which aroused many echoes from the American press.

For the formation of a just opinion regarding the value of a rigid standard of language, the history of Latin offers valuable suggestion. In the hands of Cicero the Latin language reached a perfection of form which was regarded as final. Ciceronian Latin came to serve as an absolute standard of correctness in cultivated speech. The importance, however, of a fixed standard was shown by the prevalence of vulgar forms of Latin in various provinces of the Roman Empire. The divergence from the Ciceronian standard increased with time, and after several centuries, the different forms of Vulgar Latin developed in France and Spain and Italy, in their turn, were adopted in literary composition and served as the beginnings from which developed modern French and Spanish and Italian.

---

[3] The same spirit of revolt is alive in France. Anatole France speaks of the "writers who still obey the laws of grammar, and the *Jeunes* who are deliberately false to them." *Living Age*, January 7, 1922.

[4] *North American Review*, July, 1920.

The lesson to be drawn is obvious. A language may not be completely standardized and live. Fixity in the form of a language gives immobility to the national thought expressed. Ideas inherited from the past, to be sure, may find adequate expression in the fixed idiom of the past. The shifting, developing forms assumed by living thought, however, demand the plastic medium of a living language.

Fortunately, English is not yet a dead language like Latin. "The circle of the English language," said Sir James Murray, "has a well-defined centre, but no discernible circumference." On its outer bounds Standard English maintains contact with living forms of speech from which its vital forces are constantly renewed. On the one side it draws intellectual sustenance from the technical terms created by ever expanding scientific knowledge. On the other side it derives new life from the homely word-stores of the popular dialects and from the constantly renewed elements in colloquial speech covered by the name slang.

REFERENCES FOR FURTHER READING

GREENOUGH and KITTREDGE, *Words and their Ways in English Speech* (New York, 1901), Ch. vii.

O. F. EMERSON, *History of the English Language* (New York, 1894).

STRONG, LOGEMAN, and WHEELER, *The History of Language* London, 1891), Ch. xxiii.

A. MEILLET, *Les Langues dans l'Europe Nouvelle* (Paris, 1918).

CHAPTER II

DIALECT

Of the sources from which Standard English renews its energies we may first take under consideration the popular dialects. It should be held in mind that Standard English was itself in its origin but one of many dialects of the Middle English period. When, in the fourteenth century, the East Midland dialect emerged as the standard form for literary English, it overshadowed the rival dialects, but by no means smothered them out of existence. Among the uneducated folk, who formed a majority of the population, the influence of the literary standard was comparatively little felt, and the dialectal modes of speech native to various parts of the country have persisted to our day in the illiterate speech of the country folk. In fact, a dialect map of Great Britain is more complex in its divisions to-day than it would have been five centuries ago. In addition to the broad lines which in the fourteenth century marked the boundaries between the dialects of the North, the Midland, and the South, there have come into existence minor boundary lines marking a number of dialect districts in the British Isles almost as numerous as the county divisions, though not coinciding entirely with these. In the classification of dialects by Skeat there are distinguished nine dialect groups in Scotland, three in Ireland, and thirty in England and Wales.

The wealth of words in the different local dialects of Scotland has been made too familiar by such writers as Burns and Scott, to need illustration here. The local vocabularies of other parts of Great Britain offer a comparable supply of words less exploited as yet. Baedeker, in his guidebook for Great Britain, regarded it as serviceable to the tourist to give a list of local names in use in the Lake District of northwestern England. He offers the following list with standard English equivalents: *beck*, 'brook'; *combe*, 'hollow'; *dodd*, 'spur of a mountain'; *fell*, 'mountain'; *force*, 'waterfall'; *gill*, 'gorge'; *hause*, 'top of a pass'; *holme*, 'island'; *how*, 'moundlike hill'; *nab*, 'projecting rock'; *pike*, 'peak'; *raise*, 'top of a ridge'; *scar*, 'wall of rock'; *scree*, 'steep slope of loose stones'; *thwaite*, 'clearing.'

Shifting to the South of England, one finds in the Isle of Wight such words as *straddlebob* and *dumbledore* for 'beetle'; *nammut*, 'luncheon'; *zote*, 'soft,' 'silly'; *lowz*, 'allows'; *gurt*, 'great'; and in East Sussex: *call over*, 'abuse'; *clocksmith*, 'watchmaker'; *cocker-up*, 'spoil'; *kiddle*, 'tickle'; *lawyer*, 'thorny bramble'; *sarment*, 'sermon'; *tot*, 'bush,' 'tuft of grass'; *twort*, 'pert and saucy'; *winterpicks*, 'blackthorn berries'; *winterproud*, 'cold.'[1]

From the East Midland district, the home district of Standard English, Professor Skeat prints a specimen of English dialect which is hardly intelligible at all unless translated.

Norfolk Dialect	*Translation*
Rabbin—Tibby, d' ye know how the knacker's mawther Nutty du?	Stephen, do you know how the collar-maker's daughter Ursula is?
Tibby—Why i' facks, Rabbin, she's nation cothy; by Goms, she is so snasty that I think she is will-led.	Why, in fact, Robin, she is extremely sick; by ——, she is so snarlish, that I think she's out of her mind.

---

[1] Skeat, *Our English Dialects*, pp. 129-132.

Rabbin—She's a fate mawther, but ollas in dibles wi' the knacker and thackster; she is ollas a-ating o' thapes and dodmans. The fogger sa, she ha the black sap; but the grosher sa, she have an ill dent.

She's a clever girl, but always in troubles with the collarmaker and thatcher; she is always eating gooseberries and snails. The man at the chandler's shop says she has a consumption; but the grocer says she's out of her senses.

This passage reveals in striking fashion the wealth of expressive words in English, seemingly crude because of their unfamiliarity, but undeniably rich in expressive power, which have not been admitted into standard literary use. The recorded store of such words is an enormous one. The *English Dialect Dictionary*, compiled by Dr. Joseph Wright, is in six large volumes and contains more than a hundred thousand of these unappropriated words.

The character of dialect words, like those in standard English, is varied. Many of them are good old words which have been rejected by Standard English. Words of this class are *fain*, 'glad' (O. E. *fægen*); *fey*, 'fated' (O. E. *fǣge*); bide, 'wait' (O. E. *bīdan*); *thole*, 'endure' (O. E. *tholian*); *nesh*, 'delicate' (O. E. *hnesce*); *kemp*, 'fighter' (O. E. *cempa*); *speer*, 'inquire' (O. E. *spyrian*); *bairn*, 'child' (O. E. *bearn*); *stee*, 'ladder' (O. E. *stige*); *dree*, 'suffer' (O. E. *drēogan*); *weird*, 'fate' (O. E. *wierd*). The fiery old Laird of Auchinleck, when he exclaimed regarding Cromwell, "God, sir, he gart kings ken that there was a lith in their neck," brought into service from older English three fine words, *gart*, *ken*, and *lith*, which have not found a place in Standard English.

Many dialect words, however, have not so legitimate a line of descent. Among the few illustrative examples cited above, will be observed a number of words springing from a perversion of words familiar in standard English. To this class belong *nammut* (noon meat), *lowz* (allows), *sarment* (sermon), *gurt* (great), *ollas* (always). Hardly, if at all, lower in dignity than the English *much* and *uncouth* are the northern dialectal variants appearing in the Scotch *mickle* and *unco*.

In other instances these words are foreign words admitted into dialectal use but not into Standard English. To this class belong most of the special names used in the Lake District, most of them of Scandinavian extraction, and Scotch words such as *bonnie, achet* (plate), *douce, fash, dour, tass* (glass), derived from French.

Still another class of dialect words is composed of local creations such as *winterpicks, winterproud, will-led, black sap, beergood,* and their like.

If one turns one's attention to conditions more near at hand, to the local variations in the language in different parts of America, one will easily reach a realization of the way difference in dialect comes into being. The language of America has not only, as remains to be seen, become differentiated in many respects from that of Great Britain, but local variations in vocabulary are everywhere in evidence, some of them dialectal variations imported into America, others having their origin in fresh creation of names varying in different localities. In words of literary character and, therefore, subject to the standardizing influence of schools, the variation is relatively little, but in names of things outside the sphere of schools and literature the tendency toward variation is strikingly apparent. The following parallel lists of names for common things in districts as close together as northwestern New York (Wayne County) and central Ohio will serve to illustrate the tendency toward dialectal differentiation:

New York (Wayne County)	*Central Ohio*
Woodchuck	Ground-hog
Golden robin	Oriole
Hell-diver	Devil-diver

New York (Wayne County)	Central Ohio
High-hole	Flicker
Shag-poke	Mud-hen
Dove	Pigeon
Pigeon	Dove
Yellow-bird	Goldfinch
Wild canary	Yellow-bird
Bullhead	Catfish
Bitternut	Pignut
Walnut	Hickory nut
Black walnut	Walnut
Hard maple	Sugar maple
Maple sap	Sugar water
Blacklongberry	Blackberry
Blackcap	Black raspberry
Pail	Bucket
Spider	Skillet
Pit, or Stone (of peach)	Seed
Fried-cake	Doughnut
Husk (corn)	Shuck (corn)
Bundles (of grain)	Sheaves
Cultivate	Plough
Drag	Harrow
Wagon-box	Wagon-bed
End-board (of wagon)	End-gate or (Tail-gate)
Nut (of bolt)	Burr
Shucks (of peanuts)	Shells
Paris green	Poison green
Kerosene	Coal oil
Rubbers	Gum shoes

In the case of a number of the words in the above lists, compiled about twenty years ago, both forms may be known in one or both of the sections of country, due to the rapid mingling of dialects in modern times, caused either by a common literature or by the close personal communication among members of different communities, but the lists nevertheless afford illustration of the constant tendency toward differentiation in the vocabularies of different communities.

DIALECT

Striking products of this tendency are the synonymous names for many plants and trees. For example, take the names *Virginia creeper* and *woodbine,* *steeple bush* and *hard-hack,* *mullen* and *velvet plant,* *spotted boneset* and *spotted joe-pye weed,* *chicory* and *blue sailors,* *Jack-in-the-pulpit* and *Indian turnip,* *yarrow* and *milfoil,* *butter and eggs* and *yellow toad-flax.* The *mountain ash* is variously named *rowan, quickbeam, dogberry, wicken,* and *wicky.* The varied names for *winter green* and *peanut* are cited in the following chapters.

In bird names the same variation is to be encountered. Take the bobolink, for example. From the Chesapeake Bay to Florida he is known as the *redbird.* In the South he also has the names *ricebird* and *skunk blackbird.* In Jamaica he is the *butter-bird.* In southern Canada and the northern United States he has the name *meadow-wink.* William Cullen Bryant conferred on him still another name, the not unmerited title, *Robert of Lincoln.* The Baltimore oriole has a comparable variety of names, including *golden oriole, golden robin, English robin, firebird, hangbird,* and *hangnest.* In America probably no other bird has a longer list of names than the flicker. From various parts of the country have been cited the following list: *golden-winged woodpecker, pigeon woodpecker, yellow-hammer, clape, high-hole, high-holer, high-holder, yarup, wake-up, nicker, yucker, tucker, yellow-shafted woodpecker.* But even this list is exceeded by the list of synonyms cited by Archbishop Trench for the English woodpecker as follows: *specht, woodspick, woodsprite, woodhack, awlbird, pickatree, treegobber, thewhole, rainfowl, woodwall, yaffingale, hecco, green-peak, eatbee, rainbird, yaffle.*[2]

If variation in the names for things appears within a country, it is to be expected that in the widely separated parts of the English-speaking world the same phenomenon

---
[2] Trench, *English Past and Present,* p. 205.

should appear. A few examples will suffice. American *candy* is called in English *sweets,* in Australian and Anglo-Indian *lollies* or *sweets*. American sheep-*ranch* is Australian sheep-*run,* English sheep-*walk*. American *up-country* and *farmer* are Australian *bush* and *bushman*. American *tramp* or *hobo* is Australian *sundowner*. American *alfalfa* is Australian *lucerne*. American *grub,* 'something to eat,' is Australian *tucker,* Anglo-Indian and South African *scoff*.

Since the function of language is the communication of thought from one mind to another, there is obvious advantage in a uniformity in the symbols of thought. A lack of uniformity is often the source of confusion and misunderstanding. When an Englishman speaks of a *row,* he means 'noise' and 'commotion'; when an American speaks of a *row,* he means a 'quarrel' or a 'fight.' To *pull one's leg* to an Englishman means 'to fool' or 'deceive'; to an American it usually means 'to cajole' or 'curry favor.' During the war the different meanings attached to the words *nervy* and *nervous* by the American troops on the one hand, and by the English and Australian troops on the other, proved a frequent source of misunderstanding and friction. An English boy in Australia caused consternation in his family at home by announcing his marriage to a girl from the *bush*. The family, unfamiliar with the Australian use of the word *bush,* naturally wondered if the bride were white or black or yellow.

The variety of names for one thing in many instances proves to be an embarrassment of riches. Shall one say coal *hod* or *scuttle* or *bucket* or *pail?* On an Ohio golf course how shall one name the small stream that provides so many of the natural hazards? Among caddies and players usage varies between *creek* and *run* and *branch* and *brook*.

The inconvenience resulting from dialectal lack of uniformity is apparent. On the other hand, the disadvantages of standardization carried too far, are not less obvious. The effect of a standardization of language is to reduce to one mold. Its disadvantage is that it restricts the formative powers of language. It excludes fresh compounds of the kind that contributed so largely to the expressiveness, for instance, of the language of Shakespeare. Dialect, too, in general surpasses literary language in its fullness of expression for individual, concrete things. Cultivation of English has tended almost as much toward contraction as toward expansion. It is well known that English of the earliest, the Anglo-Saxon, period, had for many things a richer variety of names than the highly cultivated modern English can offer. Moreover, uniformity of expression leads to triteness, to journalese. Language, says George Moore, "like a coin too long current, becomes defaced." Sharpness of impression demands fresh creation, and this is ever to be found in the living idiom of the folk. "No dialect is ugly," says W. B. Yeats. "The by-paths are all beautiful. It is the broad road of the journalist that is ugly.... It is only from them (peasants) one could learn to write, their speech being living speech, flowing out of the habits of their lives, struck out from life itself." [3]

Dialectal speech, with its homespun genuineness, and responding as it does, directly to the creative energies of life, has ever appealed to the literary artist. Mistral, one of the greatest of modern French poets, as already mentioned, used as his literary medium the Provençal dialect of the South of France. The Low German dialects have been used with effect by German poets such as Fritz Reuter and Wilhelm Müller, and one of the greatest of modern German plays, Hauptmann's *Die Weber* (The Weavers) appeared originally in the Silesian dialect with the title, *De Waber*. In Norway, it has already been remarked, a

---

[3] Quoted by G. Moore, *Hail and Farewell*, Vol. I, pp. 55, 56.

national literary language has of late been recreated out of material offered from the different native dialects.

In Great Britain the northern dialect of English has served as a literary medium for a distinguished series of Scotch writers from the fourteenth century to the present. William Barnes has made use of the Southern dialect in a series of *Poems of Wessex*. Australian dialect appears in a number of productions such as *The Sentimental Bloke*, by C. J. Dennis. In the most distinguished English literary movement of the last half century, the Irish Literary Renaissance, effective use has been made of the Anglo-Irish dialect, rich in idioms surviving from Elizabethan English or translated from the native Gaelic speech. In the middle of the nineteenth century, Lowell chose as the literary medium for his *Bigelow Papers*, the rural dialect of New England. Writers like Whitcomb Riley and Eugene Field have shown some of the artistic possibilities from the use of the dialectal speech of the Middle West. As remains to be seen, beginning with Walt Whitman, more and more use is being made in American literature of the native resources of American dialect.

In English literature, from the earliest period, dialect has been used for the sake of the local color afforded by it. In the language of Chaucer's Reeve the dialect of Norfolk is thus used. In the English drama of the sixteenth century the Southern dialect is associated with clownish humor. In his *Shepherd's Calendar*, Spenser gave a rustic tone by the use of words from Northern dialect. In American novels and short stories use is made of local peculiarities in speech in order to impart vividness and reality to scenes from provincial life.

But dialect words have a value not alone on account of the local color they afford. They form a most important contributory element in Standard English. From dialectal sources, mainly Scotch and Irish, have come such words as *fad, grouch, galore, croon, raid, glamour, outcome, greed, stingy, heckle, canny, uncanny, wee, hemlock, queer, rickets, shoddy, shucks, spree, shunt, sprint, swank, trolley, bogie, lorrie, tram.*

But particularly in the last three decades, in the reaction from the formal dignity of the Victorian period, there has been a tendency observable in practically all literary art, to freshen the language by importations from all sources. Kipling contributed freshness to his style by the free use of elements from the outskirts of legitimate speech, by the use of the technical terms of modern science, by the use of the unrefined elements of slang and dialect. Such words as *yanked* and *burl* and *fudge up* exemplify his use of dialect. H. H. Johnston, in *The Gay-Dombeys,* introduces *comey,* 'tribute,' and *chop,* 'food,' from the jargon of the African coast as well as British dialect words such as *pawky* and *slithery.* James Stephens, in *The Hill of Vision,* introduces *spalpeen, wambled, smithereens, limber,* 'lithe,' *cranky, shebeen,* and *bashing.* St. John Ervine uses *tomtoady, dreepy, moidhered, scragged* (schoolboy), *swizz, argle-bargle* 'talk,' 'gabble,' *dithers, frowsty, fusty.* Hugh Walpole speaks of the "water as it *slutched* up the sand." But the writer who more consciously than any other modern British writer has exploited the rich mines of dialectal speech, is John Masefield. His *Reynard the Fox,* which bristles with audacities of every kind, can hardly be read with complete understanding without the aid of a dialect dictionary. In this work is to be observed a return to the earlier freedom of speech, the freedom of the Elizabethans. Richness in expression is gained not only by daring turns in the use of standard words, and by an easy command of the technical terms of horsemanship and of the fox chase, but by the use of racy dialectal words and expressions which admirably convey the feeling of that red-blooded sport. Isolated words such as *dunched* and *grue* and *kye* and *lees* and *stooks* and *stuggy* and *strake* and *skutch* and *skutter* and *tup,* fail to convey an impression of the effect of these words in the glowing verse of the narrative.

"No language," says Lowell, "after it has faded into diction, none that cannot suck up the feeding juices secreted for it in the rich mother earth of common folk, can bring forth a sound and lusty book." "The folk," says Plato, "is in the matter of language an excellent master." In its living dialects, we may conclude, the English language has a constant source from which to renew its energies.

REFERENCES FOR FURTHER READING

JOSEPH WRIGHT, *The English Dialect Dictionary* (London and New York, 1898-1905).
W. W. SKEAT, *Our English Dialects* (Cambridge, 1911).
Dialect Notes (Published by the American Dialect Society, 1890).
Publications of the English Dialect Society (London, 1877-).

CHAPTER III

AMERICAN ENGLISH

Closely related to the subject of dialect is the special form of English used in America, which some prefer to call the American Language. A German schoolmaster once inquired of the present writer, "Have you always lived in America?" When answered in the affirmative, he continued, "Wo denn haben Sie englisch gelernt?" Where then did you learn English? That is to say, an educated German was surprised to learn that the national language of the United States is English. The American language is English, but English with a difference. The story is told that when the English actor, Cyril Maude, was playing in New Mexico, a group of cowboys who had been in the gallery, left the theater saying, "We can't understand a thing the guy says." In London, before the war, one saw on store fronts, not only the familiar signs, "Ici on parle français," and "Man spricht deutsch," but an occasional "American spoken here." In all this there is evidence that the language of America is not entirely identical with that of England, that there is a difference between the "King's English" and what has been called the "President's English.

The English language was brought to America by English colonists of the seventeenth century. The language brought to America at that time differed in many ways from the English of present-day England, and one of the sources of difference to-day between the languages of the two countries is the preservation in the new country of many features of language lost in the mother country.

Lowell, more than a half century ago, pointed out that most of the distinctive features of the New England dialect, which he used in his *Bigelow Papers,* are in reality survivals from the seventeenth century of forms of language abandoned by the English of England. The features of seventeenth-century English pronunciation represented by such groups of words as '*nater,*' '*critter,*' '*figger,*' '*sartin,*' '*varmint*'; '*ile,*' '*jine,*' '*pizen,*' '*spile*'; '*ketch,*' '*git,*' '*obleeged*'; '*hanted,*' '*jant,*' give a distinctive quality to the speech of the rural New Englander of the nineteenth century. Lowell also shows that many of the dialectal words of New England are survivals from earlier English. In this class he includes, *guess, sick* (for ill), *bug* (for insect), *afeard, fall* (autumn), *loan* (lend), *fleshy, chore, creek* (Engl. 'estuary of the sea'), *poor* (lean), *dry* (thirsty), *allow* (affirm). To this list of New England survivals of earlier English words may be added the following examples from other sources:[1] *flap-jack, molasses, cord-wood, home-spun, brag, ice-cream, julep, swingle-tree, and-iron, fore-handed, bay-window, clodhopper, greenhorns, loophole, foot-loose, ragamuffin, rigmarole, to interview, to hustle, homely* (plain-featured), *burly, deft, scant.*

In the formation of American English there were added to the seventeenth-century form of English many words derived from the languages of the different peoples with whom the English-speaking colonists were brought into contact. First in importance in this connection come the words derived from the speech of various Indian tribes. From the Indians were borrowed not only the many geographical names, names of rivers, mountains, and lakes, but names for objects of the plant and animal world indigenous to the new country and names of implements and food preparations of a new kind. Among words of this kind are *opossum, moose, skunk, raccoon, chipmunk,*

---

[1] Mencken, pp. 56, 57.

terrapin, woodchuck, hickory, chinkapin, catalpa, persimmon, squash, paw-paw, pemmican, hominy, pone, succotash, tapioca, canoe, toboggan, moccasin, tomahawk, wigwam, tepee, pow-wow, squaw, papoose.[2] By the translation of Indian terms were formed other new words such as *war-path, pale-face, pipe-of-peace,* and *fire-water.*[3]

From the French in America were derived a considerable number of words such as *prairie, portage, rapids, bayou, seep, chowder, picayune, levee, chute, caribou, crevasse, shanty.*[4] From Spanish came, in colonial days, *Creole, calaboose, palmetto, pewee, quadroon, octoroon, barbecue, pickaninny, stampede.*[5] Later, after the war with Mexico, contact with Spanish-speaking inhabitants of Texas and the Spanish West resulted in the acquisition of such words as *adobe, broncho, burro, calaboose, canyon, chapparal, chile* (con carne), *cinch, corral, coyote, fandango, lariat, loco* (grass or weed), *peon, ranch, sombrero, vamoose.*[6]

Another European language which contributed elements to American speech, was that of Holland which, through the Dutch settlers of New York, contributed such words as, *cruller, cold-slaw, sleigh, stoop, cookie, waffle, span* (of horses), *pit* (of peach or cherry), *scow, boss, dominie,* and *Santa Claus.*[7]

The nature of the German contribution to the American vocabulary suggests a possible explanation of the waning of Puritanic ideals in latter-day America. Blue laws and Scotch Sundays are not in harmony with the spirit suggested by such words as *pretzel, lager-beer, pinocle, wienerwurst, frankfurter, schnitzel, leberwurst, blutwurst, rathskeller, schweizer, delicatessen, hamburger,* and *katzenjammer.* Of German origin also are probably such words

---

[2] Mencken, p. 40.
[3] *Ibid.*, p. 41.
[4] *Ibid.*, pp. 43, 86.
[5] *Ibid.*, p. 43.
[6] *Dialect Notes*, Vol. I, p. 183ff.
[7] Mencken, p. 43.

as *dumb*, 'stupid' (German *dumm*); *fresh*, 'impertinent' (German *frech*); *loafer* (German *laufen*, colloq. 'to walk'?); *out of sight* (German *ausgezeichnet*); *mucker*; *bum* and *bummer* (German *bummeln*).[8]

The English-speaking settlers in the United States, one must not forget, did not all come from England. The Irish element in the American population has not been without its influence. The fact should not be lost sight of, that the English of Ireland, like the English of the United States, is a transplanted language, and the time of transplantation was not far apart in the two cases, since the settlement of English in Ireland took place in great part in the sixteenth and seventeenth centuries. Hence it is that the Irish English, in its construction, its vocabulary, and its pronunciation, retains many features of an earlier stage in the history of English, so that Irish English and American English have features in common. But the Irish also brought with them to America a goodly number of elements in their language that are of Irish creation. In a recent book on the subject of Irish English [9] there is a list of Irishisms, many of which are familiar in America. Some of these expressions, quite possibly, were carried from America to Ireland, but in the majority of instances an Irish origin must be assumed. Some of these words and expressions are *banshee; cadger; blarney; brogue*, 'shoe'; *chook chook* (call to hens, Irish *tiuc* 'come'); *give in*, 'yield'; *let on*, 'pretend'; *cowlick* (of hair); *drugget*, 'carpet; *didoes*, 'pranks'; *galore; gazebo*, 'tall, awkward person'; *grumpy*, 'surly'; *going on*, 'making fun'; (beat) *hollow; heard tell; handy*, 'convenient'; *jaw*, 'impudent talk'; *larrup*, 'wallup'; *kybosh; wipe*, 'a blow'; *slob*; (cast) *sheepseyes; shanty; quit*, 'cease'; *mad*, 'angry';

---

[8] Mencken, p. 88.
[9] P. W. Joyce, *English as We Speak it in Ireland*.

logey, 'heavy'; *wad; thick*, 'intimate'; *spuds; sold*, 'tricked'; *smithereens*.

The importance of the foreign influences to which the English language, in its American environment, was exposed, must not be overlooked. At the same time it is not to be assumed that the American pioneer was lacking in creative power. Removed to a great extent from the influence of book language, and thrown into new surroundings, he was called on to use his powers of invention in providing names for features of life that were new. The physical characteristics of the new country, particularly, in many respects different from those of the old, called for fresh names, and before the Revolution there came into use such names as: *run, branch, fork, bluff, neck, barrens, bottoms, underbrush, bottom-land, clearing, notch, divide, knob, riffle, gap*, and *rolling-country*, new applications of older English words.[10] English names for similar physical features, such as *downs, wold, fen, bog, fell, chase, combe, dell, heath* and *moor*, in most parts of America survive only as literary terms difficult to apply to American conditions. American flora and fauna, also, differing frequently from the English, called for a new nomenclature. Hence the creation of such new names as *basswood*, or *bee-tree*, for English *linden* or *lime; buttonwood* for English *plane-tree; cottonwood* for certain American varieties of the *poplar; butternut* for an American tree also called the *white walnut; buckeye* for *horse chestnut; locust* for *pseudo-acacia; bayberry* for the *wax myrtle; johnny-jump-up* for the *wild pansy; choke-cherry; snowball* for *guelder rose; egg-plant* and its variant names, *egg-apple, mad-apple; peanut* (English, *groundnut*) and its variants, *monkey-nut, ground pea, earthnut, Manila nut, jur-nut, goober,* and *pindar.* Other plant and tree names of American creation are:

---

[10] Mencken, p. 46.

box-elder, burr-oak, live-oak, pin-oak, blue grass, eel-grass, oyster plant.

In a number of instances an older English name was newly applied. The name *cranberry* is an example. The name in America applies to a different species from the one in England called the cranberry. The same is true of the name *wintergreen,* which in America is one of the several names of the plant variously called *deerberry, hillberry, groundberry, spiceberry, teaberry, mountain-tea,* and *Canada tea.*

Wake robin, in England a variant name for *cuckoo-pint,* in America is applied to various varieties of the *trillium,* also called *three-leafed nightshade, white bath, birthroot, wood-lily,* and *tuckahoe* (Indian). The purple variety of the trillium also is known as *Indian balm, Indian shamrock,* and *nose-bleed.*

The names for plants and trees exemplify not only the variation of American from English nomenclature but also the ever-present tendency for dialectal variation in the case of names of things in provinces of life loosely governed by literary standards. The same features are even more strikingly exemplified in the names for birds and beasts. Of American origin are:[11] *catbird, blue jay, bobolink, meadow lark, bobwhite, hen hawk, hangbird* (oriole), *mud hen, bullfrog, pollywog, copperhead, katydid, cutworm, gartersnake, ground-hog, muskrat* (Indian), *mud-turtle, potato bug, June bug, woodchuck* (Indian), *gopher,*[12] *chipmunk.*

Frequently, as in the case of plant names, the English bird or beast name is falsely, or at least newly, applied in America. The name of the English robin in America is applied to a species of thrush. The name *swallow,* in the

---

[11] Mencken, p. 45.
[12] "The word *gopher* is appended to a squirrel in Wisconsin, to a rat in Missouri, to a snake in Georgia, and to a turtle in Florida." H. Bender, Princeton Lectures.

case of the chimney swallow, is applied to a swift. The name *nighthawk* is applied to a bird that is not a hawk. The name of the English *rabbit* is applied in America to various kinds of hare. The name *oriole* applies to birds of entirely different families in the two countries. The name *blackbird,* which in England applies to a species of thrush, in America applies to a bird more nearly related to the English *starling.* The name *meadow lark* is a striking instance of the vagaries of popular nomenclature, since this American bird has little resemblance to the English *lark.*

The resourcefulness in finding names for the new features of natural history in a new world environment also appears in the language devised to suit the new conditions of existence into which American colonists were thrown. The new conditions, and the way the colonist adapted himself, are reflected in new word uses or creations such as *shingle* (for wooden tile), *clapboard* (for weather-board), *frame house, log house,* and later, *log cabin.* These words, along with others of their kind, such as *backwoods, landslide, cold snap, pine knot,* and *snowplow,* vividly suggest the stern realities of pioneer life.[13]

With the arrival of a more stabilized mode of life, the earlier need for new names became less imperative. The earlier incentive to word creation was lost. But the creative spirit has by no means become extinct. America, up to the present, has never been without the tonic influence of frontier life. Men on the American frontier, like the pioneers who settled near the Atlantic coast, have ever been in the presence of new features of life to be named, and breaking as they have been obliged to do, with the older traditions of a settled life, in speech as in other activities, they have broken through the restraints imposed

---

[13] Mencken, p. 46.

by established usage. The spirit of creative activity which brought under human control the natural resources of a new country, has served also to stimulate activity in the fresh creation of word and phrase.

In illustration of the nature of the thousands of Americanisms collected in the two volumes of Thornton's *An American Glossary* may be cited such words and phrases as *blaze* (a trail), *blizzard, back number, backbone* (courage), *barber shop, barroom* (English *taproom*), *beeline, belittle, bleachers, blinders* (English *blinkers*), *bloomers* (from Mrs. Bloomer, who died in 1894), *blue laws, bluff, bob-sled, bogus, boom* (verb), *boost, brainy, breadstuffs, brief* (lawyers'), *bully* (adj.), *campus, cave in, chink* (space in wall), *chipped beef, clear out, cloudburst, cocktail, cold snap, collateral* (security), *commuter, contraband, cooler* (jail), *corn-cob, crib, husk,* etc., *cowboy, cowcatcher, crawfish, cutter* (light sleigh), *deadbeat, -broke, -head,* etc., *derail, diggings, dipper* (ladle), *dipper* (constellation), *dive* (low resort), *dry up* (keep still), *doughnut, dovetail* (verb), *fizzle out, fish story, freeze to, grit* (courage), *half-breed, hayseed, played out, poppy-cock, pot pie, make good, joy-ride, maverick, shyster, scalawag, snarl* (tangle), *snake* (verb), *snap, splurge, spree, spry, wilt, whole-souled, yegg.*

What is to be done with this barbarian incursion of words? Is the policy to be one of rigid exclusion? The associations of many of them make them as fit for cultivated use as a cowboy or a bartender is for drawing-room society. Yet the crude vigor of most of these words is not to be denied. Out of keeping with the elements needed for the expression of the refinements of sophisticated life, these words, nevertheless, afford means that are often indispensable in the expression of plain realities. Such words as *dry up, diggings, pan out, pay dirt,* which are word by-products of the California 'forty-niners,' have a crude force which gives to them greater expressiveness than more highly refined words could offer.

An impression of the indispensable nature of many Americanisms may be gained by a consideration of the vocabulary of American political life. As early as 1828 Noah Webster in the preface to his dictionary, included *selectmen, senate, congress, court,* and *assembly,* in a list of words either "not belonging to the language of England" or "applied to things in this country which do not exist in that." *Presidential, congressional,* and *gubernatorial* also were comparatively early in origin, although they did not come into use without challenge. The history of later American political life is involved in the history of the words created in the course of its progress. Without such words as *banner-state, favorite-son, dark horse, straight-ticket, split-ticket, pork-barrel, log-rolling, wire-pulling, land-slide, stump-speech, precinct, platform, plank, machine, boss, henchman, heeler, slate, primary, floater, repeater, bolter, stalwart, regular, omnibus-bill, sleeper, joker, gerrymander, roorback, mugwump, lobby,*[14] it would be impossible to create the atmosphere of American political life. Evidently the stock of words offered by the language of England would be totally inadequate, as inadequate as the stock of words in standard British use would be in giving an account of an American baseball game.

What is to be the final outcome of this independent creation of words in America? Is American English to become an independent American language? Assertion of the independence of American language from English authority followed closely the assertion of political independence. As early as 1778 Benjamin Franklin, when sent as ambassador to France, was instructed to use "the language of the United States." Noah Webster, in 1789, in his *Disser-*

---

[14] Mencken, pp. 83, 84.

tations on the English Language, advocated the establishment of a national language at the same time with a national government. Later, in the Preface to his *American Dictionary of the English Language,* published in 1828, he points out the inevitability of divergence in the languages of America and England, since "if the people of one country cannot preserve an identity of ideas, they cannot retain an identity of language." In spite, however, of assertions of independence and the recognition on the part of Webster of American modes of spelling and pronunciation that differed from English, American writers have been remarkably timid in the adoption of Americanisms which are used with less hesitation in colloquial speech. Lowell, in his *Bigelow Papers,* exploited to an extent the literary potentialities of the rural New England speech. Whitman, more bold, asserted that "the new times, the new people, the new vistas need a new tongue" and proclaimed defiantly, "yes, and what is more, they will have such a new tongue." In his poems he introduced not only the American *mocking-bird* and *hermit-thrush,* but among the ruder elements in his vocabulary, appear occasional Americanisms, such as, *side-walk, truck, lager-beer, snow-plough, engine* (locomotive), *train, coon, boss, heft, coon-hunt, good feeder.* The number of words, however, of distinctively American words, even in his promiscuous vocabulary, is on the whole surprisingly small. In the literary productions of some of the later poets following the Whitman tradition, the American element, inclusive of slang, is more conspicuously present. In the poems of Carl Sandburg, appear such words as *gunman* and *husky,* and the vocabulary of Vachel Lindsay is distinguished by the use of such words as *rag-time, drug-fiend, bazoo, crap-shooters, guy* (verb), *hoodoo* (verb), *cake-walk, scalawags, low-down.* H. L. Mencken not only defends Americanism in language, but in the rich vocabulary of contempt in his critical essays, includes words such as *flub-dub, poppy-cock, guff, numskullery, sinhound.*

The greater number of the Americanisms cited, in their open defiance of conventional refinement, are classed with slang, and have for literary purposes practically the same value and lack of value as slang. In other instances, however, American modes of expression have become stabilized so as to have a claim to standard use, at least in America, as good as that of the equivalent English expressions. In names for features of physical geography and in the terms for fauna and flora, the English of England is to an American almost a foreign tongue. *Linden, rowan, starling, chough, bracken, moor,* are to most Americans merely literary names not associated with anything definite within their experience. In many other sets of words the English names are equally foreign to an American. An American woman in an English dry-goods store almost needs an interpreter. In the first place the name of the establishment is not *dry goods store* but *draper's shop.* American *calico* needs to be translated into English *print,* since English *calico* means a white fabric. *Cheese cloth* needs to be translated by *butter muslin, shoe strings* by *boot laces, ruching* by *frilling, shirt waist* by *blouse, spool of thread* by *reel of cotton, undershirt* by *vest, wash-rag* by *face-cloth, corset* by *stays.* At the dining-table the translation of words is again called for. American *napkin* is *serviette,* rare (meat) is *underdone,* tenderloin is called *undercut,* dessert is *sweets.* The American finds that the word *sauce* in English is applied exclusively to a condiment for meat; that American *cracker* is called *biscuit;* that *pie* in English applies to *veal-pie, pork-pie, pigeon-pie,* and the like for which the American name is *potpie;* that *beet* is called *beet-root;* that *oatmeal* is called *porridge;* that if he gets ice water at all, it is called *iced water.*

In no other set of words, however, is the difference between English and American as thoroughgoing as in the vocabulary of the railroad. Even if we leave out of consideration the extensive slang vocabulary of the American railroad, including such terms as *alligator jaw* for the 'connection at an interlocking switch,' *buggy, dog-house, hack* for 'freight-caboose,' *hog* for a type of engine, *wild cat* for 'locomotive without cars,' we still meet with a completely different set of terms in the railroad systems which have developed independently in the two countries. Beginning at the head of the train we find English *pilot* for American *cowcatcher, locomotive* for *engine, locomotive-driver* for *engineer, stoker* for *fireman, buffer* for *bumper, van* for *baggage car, luggage* for *baggage, goods* for *freight, carriage* for *car, saloon carriage* for *parlor car, guard* for *conductor, brakesman* for *brakeman.* Leaving the train, we find *line* for *track, sleeper* for *cross-tie* or *tie, crossing-plate* for *frog, shunt* for *switch, gradient* for *grade, permanent way* for *road-bed.*

The language of Americans has in many ways drawn away from that followed in British usage. The signs of independence in American speech, it has been shown, are everywhere at hand. But that by no means tells the whole story. American language, strange to say, is characterized by timidity almost as much as by boldness. In America, in the case of most people, cultivation in language has had to be sought, not from association with a definite cultured class of people, but from books and from the instruction imparted by schools. The result of such conditions has been an artificiality in language. Freedom of creation does not go with following a pattern. Originality has been hampered. The language too often has the mark of laborious acquirement rather than the natural ease characteristic of the speech of one to the manner born.

This lack of independence in all stages in the history of

American speech has manifested itself in a deference paid to British usage. In our own day the influence of an assumed superiority in an English standard, manifests itself in many ways, amounting in extreme cases to an Anglomania. Preference is often given to English *railway* over American *railroad*, to English *motor car* over *automobile* (of French derivation). This spirit leads to the substitution of English *braces* for American *suspenders*, of *waistcoat* for *vest*, *blouse* for *shirt waist*, *biscuit* for *cracker*, *shop* for *store*. American schools labor to establish the English distinction between *sick* and *ill* and, in many instances, to give to the word *been* the English pronunciation with long *e* (as in *seen*), and to words like *dictionary* and *necessary* and *literary* the English trisyllabic pronunciation with a single stress, that on the first syllable. In several of the instances cited, the English usage may be said to have definitely prevailed and to be now that of the best American use.

What is to be the outcome of the struggle in American usage between the forces of purism, on the one hand, supported by a deference for English usage, and, on the other hand, radical forces supported by the recently stimulated spirit of American nationalism? It would be hazardous to make a prediction. At the present time, however, there is everywhere conspicuously present the spirit of revolt from restraint. And it is interesting to observe that while the English influence on American linguistic usage is still apparent, evidence of a counter wave is at hand. Not only are American names being introduced into England along with the things they stand for, from cash registers to cocktails and chewing gum, but not infrequently in London appears the American sign *drug store* appealing to the American tourist, and in English *lifts* appears not infrequently the name of an American *elevator* company.

REFERENCES FOR FURTHER READING

H. L. MENCKEN, *The American Language* (New York, 1919).
G. M. TUCKER, *American English* (New York, 1920).
BRANDER MATTHEWS, *Parts of Speech* (New York, 1910); *Americanisms and Briticisms* (New York, 1892).
JAMES RUSSELL LOWELL, *Introduction to the Bigelow Papers* (Second series).
J. M. BARTLETT, *Dictionary of Americanisms* (New York, 1848).
R. H. THORNTON, *An American Glossary* (Philadelphia, 1912).
Dialect Notes (Published by the American Dialect Society, 1890-).
R. M. HUGHES, "Our Statish Language," *Harper's Magazine* (1920).

CHAPTER IV

SLANG

The preceding chapters have perhaps made sufficiently clear that the words included in Standard English, form only a part of the stock of words available for English speech. The value of the provincial dialects as a source of new and more concrete forms of expression, and the special indebtedness of the American language to forms of speech without the bounds of literary language, have been called to attention. In addition to the dialectal words, the country cousins of the words in literary use, there remains to be considered a set of words whose irregular habits and uncertain associations have served to exclude them from cultivated society. This flourishing set of outlaw terms is customarily grouped promiscuously under the name *slang*.

In the consideration of this much discussed class of words, much confusion has arisen from the vague way in which the name is applied. It may be doubted if an exact definition of slang is possible. It is important, however, to arrive at an understanding of its nature, and one may well begin with a consideration of the name. The ultimate origin of the name *slang* is not certainly known; the word is itself probably a slang creation. It makes its first appearance in the eighteenth century, and like its French equivalent, *argot*, applied earliest to a special vocabulary of the underworld of thieves, a use in which it is hard to distinguish the word *slang* from the rival words, *cant* and *flash*. Somewhat later, at the beginning of the nineteenth century, the name *slang* came to apply to the special vocabulary of a particular calling or profession, as in the phrase "lawyers' slang." From about the same time, the early nineteenth century, the word is first cited in its prevailing modern meaning expressed in the words of the Oxford Dictionary, "a language of a highly colloquial type considered below the level of standard speech."

The word *slang*, then, is not old. The class of words, however, that it designates, belongs to all stages in language. In the Latin of the time of Marcus Aurelius, we are told that, "while the learned dialect was yearly becoming more and more barbarously pedantic, the colloquial idiom, on the other hand, offered a thousand chance-tost gems of racy or picturesque expression, rejected or ungathered by what claimed to be classical Latin."[1] That classical Latin itself, at some stage in its history, had not failed to avail itself of this fund of racy expression, is clearly shown by the etymology of many of its dignified words. Among the dignified English words of Latin derivation are many, the etymological meaning of which in the original Latin can be rendered in English best by a word or phrase that would now be classed as slang. It has more than once been pointed out that *recalcitrant* in its origin was equivalent to modern 'kicker,' *apprehend* to 'catch on,' *assault* and *insult* to 'jump on,' *impose* to 'put over on,' *excoriate* to 'take the hide off.' In the same way *polite*, in its origin, was equivalent to 'smooth,' *inveigh* to 'sail into,' *diatribe* to 'rub in,' *fool* to 'wind bag' or 'blow hard,' *effrontery* to 'face' or 'cheek,' *interrupt* to 'break in on,' *perplexed* to 'balled up,' *precocious* (literally 'early ripe') to 'half-baked,' *delirious* (literally 'out of the furrow') to 'off one's trolley,' *supercilious* to 'high brow,' *depraved* to 'crooked.' Evidently many a word of classical Latin was elevated from a lower stratum of words which in modern English would be classed as slang.

---

[1] W. Pater, *Marius the Epicurean*, p. 84.

Elizabethan English, also, less exclusive than literary English of our day, is rich in words which would now be classed as slang. One in search of such words may find rich store in the plays of Shakespeare and Ben Jonson. The low comedy scenes, in particular, offer material of this kind in abundance. In Ben Jonson's plays are found such words as *carwhitchet* (perversion of catechism), 'pun'; *bale* (of dice), 'pair'; *bid-stand*, 'highwayman'; *bob*, 'jest' or 'taunt'; *buck*, 'wash'; *bullions*, 'trunk hose'; *burgullion*, 'braggadocio'; *buzzard*, 'simpleton'; *by-chop, by-blow*, 'bastard'; *catchpole*, 'sheriff's officer'; *circling boy*, 'sharper'; *city-wires*, 'women of fashion'; *clap*, 'clatter'; *clem*, 'starve'; *coffin*, 'raised crust of pie'; *cog*, 'cheat'; *conny catch*, 'cheat'; *crimp*, 'game of cards'; *hay in his horn*, 'ill tempered'; *huff*, 'play the braggart'; *kit*, 'fiddle'; *main*, 'main concern'; *provant*, 'soldiers' allowance'; *puckfist*, 'boasting fellow'; *ruffle*, 'swagger'; *shot-sharks*, 'drawers'; *smelt*, 'simpleton'; *spittle*, 'hospital'; *suck*, 'extract money from'; *swad*, 'clown,' 'boor'; *trig*, 'dandy.'

Two or three plays of Shakespeare afford such instances as: *board*, 'address'; *dry*, 'dull,' 'stupid'; *kickshaw (quelque chose)*; *sink-a-pace (cinque pas)*; *gaskins*, 'breeches'; *bawcock (beau coq)*; *praise* (appraise); *tend* (attend); *tester, testril*, 'sixpence'; *sneck up*, 'go hang'; *beagle* (term of praise) 'true bred'; *rascal*, 'lean deer' or, figuratively, with the modern meaning; *sheep-biter* (term of contempt); *scab* (term of contempt); *bum-baily; clodpole; gorbellied knaves; fat chuffs; clay-brained; knottypated.*

An idea of the earlier richness of the English language in words of this kind may be gained from a list of earlier synonyms for the modern miser such as *hunks, skinflint, chinch, clutchfist, gripe, huddle, kumbix, micher, nipcheese, nipfarthing, nipscreed, pennifather, pinchfist, pinchpenny, snudge.*[2] For richness and variety in words of this class it may be questioned if the regulated language of our day will stand comparison with the English of earlier centuries. It is also worthy of note that in the words quoted from Ben Jonson and Shakespeare will be found most of the features of modern slang; the thieves' jargon, the metaphorical turns, the clipped forms, the perversion of foreign words, the eloquence in contempt.

Coming down a hundred years, to the end of the seventeenth century, one meets with a new variety of these words. In Congreve's *The Way of the World* one meets: *rivetted,* 'married' (*Cf.* modern *spliced,* Scotch *buckled,* Australian *hitched*); *bum-bailiff; slap* (into a hackney coach); (let 'em) *trundle,* 'go away'; *snug's the word; fobbed; tatterdemalion; swimmingly; smoke him,* 'make fun of'; *rat me;* a *washy rogue;* and in Farquhar's *Beaux Stratagem,* one meets: *sure,* 'certainly'; *sauce box,* 'saucy one'; *smoke,* 'discover'; *pump him; upon the tapis; mercenary drabs; sponge upon; in that pickle,* 'drunk.'

The relation of such words to standard literary use shows some interesting reversals in propriety. Few of the cited expressions hold a place in the slang of our day. Such words as survive at all, are words such as *rascal,* which have shaken off their slangy associations and have found a use with fixed meaning in standard language. Slang has become legitimate English. In a number of interesting instances a change has taken place in the reverse direction. Legitimate forms of speech have taken on a slangy color. There have been pointed out as instances of the early appearance of modern slang, phrases and expressions such as, "thei skipten out" (Wycliffe), "come off" (Chaucer), "skin of the teeth" (Job), "I will fire thee out of my house" ("Ralph Roister Doister"), "not in it" ("Winter's Tale"), "let me tell the world"

---

[2] Trench, *English Past and Present,* p. 204.

("Twelfth Night".) In such cases the anticipation of modern slang is more apparent than real. The earlier meaning of the expressions quoted, did not offer the quality of suggestion that gives the slangy character to their modern equivalent. What was once legitimate has later become slang.

The examples offered of the slang of other days will suffice to dispel any illusion that slang is a creation peculiar to modern speech. Any one with remaining doubt on the subject will do well to consult the seven-volume collection by Farmer and Henley entitled *Slang and Its Analogues*. In the sixteenth century, as has been pointed out, native vigor was held less in check than in modern times by artificial considerations of propriety. The less critical attitude of that period, which recognized the pun as a legitimate figure of speech, tolerated other modes of expression which the more exacting standard of later times excludes as cheap wit. In profanity too, a form of speech akin in spirit to slang, the Elizabethan gallant was master of a variety richer than modern English can offer. The vigor of this form of speech was not confined to the cultivated speech of men, but was also a mark of caste among women, as we may infer from the admonition of Hotspur to his wife:

> "Swear me, Kate, like a lady, as thou art
> A good mouth-filling oath; and leave *in sooth*
> And such protests of pepper-gingerbread,
> To velvet-guards and Sunday citizens."
> —"Henry IV," Part I, iii, 2.

In considering the nature of slang one must not make the mistake of regarding it as identical with colloquial speech. Slang, while particularly prevalent in colloquial speech, has its origin in a striving for renewed concreteness and for novelty. These qualities are obviously by no means in themselves distinctive features of slang. The man of letters, no less than the man in the street, aspires to qualities so eminently desirable. The distinctive feature in the case of slang is the strained character of the effort, which leads to the adoption of figures too far-fetched or drawn from sources too vulgar to serve the purposes of serious art. But that is not all. The literary language during the last three centuries has been subjected, to an ever increasing extent, to the rule of propriety. So far is modern slang from being influenced by such considerations, that one of the chief sources of its novelty lies in its conscious defiance of propriety. Its figures are consciously far-fetched and are intentionally drawn from the most ignoble of sources. Closely akin to profanity in its spirit, its conscious aim is to shock. It bids defiance to the laws of decorum as profanity bids defiance to the third commandment. A quality revolted from in modern slang is that expressed by the word of modern creation, *high-brow*. The revolt from high-brow affectation in speech may be seen in the modern extended use of the word *bunch,* which is made to replace words offered by cultivated language such as *group* and *cluster*. Aversion to the high-brow style in language drives to the other extreme, to the language of the rough-neck.

But there is another aspect to be regarded. The name *slang* applies usually not to words and expressions of fresh creation, specially fitted to the single occasion, but to expressions stereotyped in character, adopted into the general stock in trade of the popular speech of a particular period. A conspicuous fault of slang is its unoriginality. The creative wit exhibited, even if not cheap wit to start with, is borrowed wit, or in borrowed slang phrase, 'canned wit.' Furthermore the very best of English words are unable to stand the wear that attends popular vogue. The experience of such a word as *strenuous* in the days just passed, shows how easily a good word may be worn out.

Obviously a word adopted for the sake of novelty, in popular vogue, cannot fail soon to become trite and stale.

If, then, slang is defined as a form of colloquial speech created in a spirit of defiance and aiming at freshness and novelty, but preserved in fixed phrases which have become the property of current popular speech, evidently it must be ephemeral in character. Like novel modes of dress adopted by current fashion, it has its fleeting day. Nevertheless as the form of speech most actively alive, slang exhibits some of the most interesting phenomena of language. In its daring figures of speech and its creation of new words or transformation of old ones, in its adaptation of foreign material, it exemplifies in active operation natural processes which enable one better to understand the processes which have served in the creation and shaping of language now accepted as standard.

The sources of slang are extremely varied. From the vaudeville stage and from the sporting pages of newspapers are started in circulation winged words, the products of sophisticated wits. From quite a different direction come the words and phrases that express the spirit of frontier life, of lumber camp and mining camp. From such sources come fresh figures that are created in part from the desire for gay ornamentation in speech, in part from lack of command of standard resources of expression. The word creations of the Argonauts of California, the rivermen of the Mississippi, and the ranchmen of Texas have afforded rich mines of expression for such literary exploiters as Bret Harte, Mark Twain, and O. Henry, and have offered patterns that have been followed by other later sophisticated creators of slang phraseology.

Similar in nature to the word creations of frontier life are the special, semitechnical vocabularies that grow up in the speech of men engaged in various special activities. Within a profession there comes into use a familiar set of expressions not sanctioned by the standard speech of general use, expressions which form a special semisecret code. To the vocabulary of railroad men belong such words as *car whacker* for 'repairer'; *hog* for 'locomotive'; and *hogger* or *hogshead* for 'engineer'; *gold buttons* or *brains* for 'conductor'; *brakee, hind-pin,* or *hind-shack* for 'trainman'; *hut, cottage,* or *dog-house* for 'caboose'; *highball* for 'full-speed signal'; *washout* for 'stop signal'; *pulled a lung* for 'pulled out coupling'; *cripple* for 'damaged car'; *go to the hammer treck* for 'go for repairs.'

The interurban railroad in turn has its own vocabulary such as: *dinkey* for 'city car'; *high ball* for 'limited'; *steel boy* for 'steel car'; *the baggage* for 'express car'; *heavy load,* when cars are close together; *pulling heavy,* when a number of big cars are on the same line.

The development of the motor car in its turn has resulted in the creation of terms almost countless such as, *flivver, skid, backfire, hitting on all four, go into high speed, step on it,* and their like. Humorous depreciation of the Ford has found expression in a long series of names with varying shades of contempt from *flivver, Henry* and its feminine *Henrietta, tin can, can opener,* and *sardine box,* to *sputter bus, tin Lizzie, road louse,* and *perpetual pest.*

The theater has its word contribution to offer: *fake* and *gag* and *guy* (verb), and *fiasco, business, properties, skyborders, bunch lights, traps, raking pieces, cut drop,* and *billboard ticket;* and the newer motion picture industry, with its traditions in the making, is responsible for *reel off, register, atmosphere, sob stuff, shot, panning, a wild piece, a full shot, a still, a close up, a set off, atmosphere, camera-hound, fade-out, on location, footage, camera lice, grip, ham, projection-room,* and for the vogue of *vampire,* and its clipped form *vamp.*

The political world is a fertile field, with its **bosses** and **henchmen** and **heelers**, its *pipe-laying* and *wire-pulling,* and *taking the stump,* and its long series of names for parties and factions: *Know Nothings, Half-breeds, Stalwarts, Swallow-tails, Mugwumps,* and *Bull Moose.*

The riddle language, by which orders are conveyed from the waiter to the kitchen in a restaurant, often involves a strain of the imaginative faculty as in *stack of bucks; Adam and Eve on a raft, wreck 'em; two, sunny side up; two with their eyes open; two on a slice of squeal; twelve alive on the shell; bossy in the bowl, boiled leaves on the side* (beef stew and a cup of tea); *slab of moo* (beef). One complete order in this lingo runs: *One splash of red noise* (tomato soup); *platter Saturday nights* (beans); *dough well done, cow to cover* (bread and butter); *Eve with the lid on* (apple pie); *chaser of Adam's ale* (glass of water).

The drug store contributes: *knock-out drops* for carbolic acid; *turps* for turpentine; *mud* for antiphlogistine; *Old Joe* for U. S. Dipsensary book of formulæ; *rollers* for pills; *plugs* for corks; *fakes* for patent medicines; *scoop* for ice cream dipper; *flapper* for ladle stirring the syrup; *tamper* or *ramrod* for implement to pound ice down; *tub* for ice cream receptacle; *scooters* for trucks in moving tubs; *slap* dishes for wash dishes; *swab* for mop; *scrub* for small boy.

Even the glass blower has his code of words, such as *gaffer* for man who finishes the neck of a bottle, *buck* for bottle rack, and *tempo* for time for whistle to blow.

In the language of the orchestra a complete set of new names has been created: *sliphorn* (trombone); *hambone* (do); *lantern* (baritone); *dog-house, dog-kennel* (bass violin); *gob stick, sliver sucker* (clarinet); *whistle* (flute); *hobo* (oboe); *pretzel* (French horn); *tin pan* (tympanum); *shiny back* (orchestra musician).

In the lists above it will be observed that the sources of slang words are to be found in pleasurable activities.

Slang is associated with the joy of life, with absence of restraint. Its spirit is that of reckless abandon. It may be called language on a picnic. Hence it is in the field of sport that one finds the spirit of slang most rampant.

The continually renewed vocabulary of baseball is too familiar to require illustration. To the student of language, however, it has a special interest because nowhere else is slang production in such full activity, and nowhere else can one better observe the rapidity of change in fashion, a rapidity which renders faded and obsolete to-morrow the highly colored expressions of to-day. The spirit of joyous abandon is particularly evident in the enticing game of craps or 'African golf.' The spirit of the game finds expression in such language as *come seven, come eleven bones* or *galloping horses* or *African golf balls* or *spotted cubes* or *galloping dominoes* for dice. *Snake eyes* for a pair of aces; *Little Joe* for a four; *Big Dick* for a ten; *box cars* for two sixes; *fade* for a bet against the thrower. Eloquent is the exultation in the phrase, *read 'em and weep*.

It will be observed that the spirit of slang is that of open hostility to the reputable. In consequence the sports most prolific in their yield of slang terms have been the sports lowest in the scale of respectability. From sports associated with nobility and dignity have come many English words of unimpeachable propriety, such as *check* from chess; *bias* from bowling; *thrust* and parry from fencing; *bandy* from battledore and shuttlecock; *pitfall* from hunting; *let slip, full cry, hark-back, get wind of, at fault, run counter, at a loss, lose track,* from hunting with the hounds; *pounce upon, cajole, decoy, reclaim, full pitch, trepan, allure, towering passion,* from the once fashionable pastime of falconry. Sports more questionable in their gentility have also made their contribution of words now in standard use. From cockfighting, once higher in esteem than at present, have come *high feather* and *show fight, fight shy* and *crestfallen*. From early dicing days have come *hazard* and *chance* and *the die is cast, play the deuce,* and *within an ace of*. From the one-time fashionable card game of primero have come *jeopardy* and *vie with*. From cribbage comes *left in the lurch*.[3] Of more recent origin are such terms as *bluff,* derived from the language of the card-table and now accredited in good use. *Lead up to* and *discard* are now well established in legitimate speech, and *backing,* though somewhat more questionable in tone, has now become interchangeable with 'financial support.' Less completely dissociated from the gaming atmosphere, but freely applied in colloquial use to general meanings, are such expressions as: *new deal, above board, cards on the table, force one's hand, show one's hand, something up one's sleeve*. Even *stand pat,* through persistent use in one political campaign, has lost its vivid sporting suggestion and become associated with the general idea of conservatism.

It is apparent that these terms of sport are not in fast colors since they so readily fade into reputability. The color of slang, however, is constantly renewed by words and expressions rich in variety, which when brought by figurative use into association with ideas of serious and dignified nature, produce the humorous incongruity which is a chief end of slang. The game of poker yields *ante up, cold feet, pass the buck*. Cockfighting yields *well heeled,* and, probably, *yellow streak*. The race track provides *dark horse, welsh* (verb), *also ran, touted;* also, it is said, *get his goat,* and *twenty-three for you;* and pugilism yields such expressions as: *take the count, on the ropes, side step, got the punch, down and out*. A remarkable instance of the union of humor and pathos is offered by the inscription said to be engraved on the tombstone of George Dixon, the

---

[3] *Cf.* E. Weekley, *Cornhill Magazine,* 1921.

once redoubtable negro lightweight. The simple inscription reads:

"1-2-3-4-5-6-7-8-9-10."

He had taken the count for the last time.

One of the most prominent features of slang, it has already been remarked, is the open revolt from propriety. This spirit of defiance of decorum manifests itself in the number of slang words recruited from the peculiar language of the underworld. The constantly renewed jargon of this class has continued to be a constant source of supply to the vocabulary of slang. Back in the sixteenth century there was a lively interest in this *peddlar's French* or *fustian* or *gibbridge,* as this form of language was variously called. Collections of words belonging to this interesting vocabulary, such as those appearing in Awdeley's *Fraternitye of Vacabondes,* Greene's *Connycatching Pamphlets,* and Harman's *Caueat or Warening,* enjoyed remarkable popularity, and a fashionable affectation led to the adoption of many of these words in the smart language of the time. From the lists of words collected in the works mentioned, may be cited such words as *booze, duds, filch, munch, prig, tipling-house, typ* (secret), *peach* (impeach), *foist, snap, drawers* (hose), a *staulinge ken* (a house that will receive stolen wares), *glymmar* (fire), *a gentry cofe's ken* (a gentleman's house), *to stall* (to make or ordain), *to myll a ken* (to rob a house), *fylche, betty* (picklock), *fencer* (receiver of stolen goods), *grub* (provender), *mill* (beat), *nap* (arrest), *snic* (cut), *tic* (trust), *tip* (give), *hook* (steal), *queer.* Many of these words are well known in modern English, and it is interesting to note that a number of them, such as *filch* and *munch* and *prig* and *queer* and *by hook or crook,* have quite outgrown their early associations and are now firmly established in standard English. Of similar extraction are many other standard

English words, such as *flog, flimsy, fop,* and *fun.*

It is obvious that the majority of these words, even if admitted into standard English, have outgrown their original usefulness as part of a secret code in the 'fraternity of vagabonds.' But the semisecrecy of this mode of speech, combined with a careless form of humor, is maintained by a constantly renewed supply of word coinages, so that the 'crook chatter' of the present day excites the same kind of interest and continues in the same way to provide words for an affectedly coarse manner of speech. *Pulled a leather up in Chi,* translated into legitimate English, means 'picked a pocket in Chicago.' Further specimens from this mode of speech still in use are: *dope* (facts), *pinch* (arrest), *gun* (policeman), *yegg* (safe blower), *nick* (steal), *can openers* (burglar's tools), *sweat* (third degree), *rocks, sparkles* (diamonds), *plant* (hiding), *covered* (shadowed), *skirt, Jane* (girl), *pipe* (see), *stir* (prison), *stretch in stir* (term in prison), *harness bull* (policeman in uniform), *dip* (pickpocket), *lamp* (see), *bracelets* (handcuffs), *box* (safe), *frisk* (search), *jimmy* (iron bar), *hardware* (tools), *kick in* (give up), *knock down* (steal), *get nailed* (get arrested), *pay dirt* (money), *peach* (inform).

The continued exploitation of this form of speech by literary artists[4] has made much of this modern lingo familiar enough. Expressions such as *hit the hay, hop a rattler, pound one's ear,* need no translation. Words of this origin, such as *graft,* not infrequently fit modern ideas so closely as to find a place in good colloquial language. The behavior of the words *pard* and *pal* has been interesting to observe. *Pard* has lost little, if any, of its objectionable associations, but *pal,* because of its sentimental association with the idea of an exceptional fidelity

---

[4] For example, O. Henry. *Cf.* also Henley's *Straight Tip to All Cross Coves.*

among thieves, seems on its way to a higher station in language.

To the realm of sport, then, particularly the sport of the least reputable sort, and to the underworld of the hobo and thief is to be traced much of the 'rough stuff' which forms an essential element in slang. The irreverent quality of slang, however, is arrived at in other ways. An element that enters into the explanation of the clipped words discussed elsewhere, is the playful familiarity with dignified elements in language. Economy of effort is not the sole cause of such words as *still* for distillery, *wig* for periwig, *brandy* for brandy wine, *Mespot* for Mesopotamia. Youthful irreverence is back of such words as *math* for mathematics, *ec* for economics, *prof* for professor, *prexy* for president; an irreverence tinged with affection like that shown by such names as *Johnny* and *Billie* for professors not only prominent but popular. The same spirit explains *bonner* for bonfire, *langers* for Auld Lang Syne, and *godders* for God Save the King, words recently cited from the vocabulary of the Cambridge University undergraduate.

The same spirit of playful irreverence serves to explain other words. It manifests itself in an affected provincialism exhibited in the use of such dialect words as *tote, nit, two bits, dowse the glim, blatherskite*. It is responsible also for the creation of a number of parody words which mock the dignity of formal language. In this class of words, created in the spirit of burlesque, may be included such words as *absquatulate, rumpus, gumption, rambunktious, bumptious, sockdologer, spondulix, rapscallion, curmudgeon, tatterdemalion, dingus, contraption*.

It must not be assumed that slang is a spontaneous growth. It is not to be regarded merely as a weed; it is often a hothouse product. Its relation to standard English is in many ways like that of jazz to normal music;

slang, like jazz, is cultivated, often by forced methods. From musical comedy and the vaudeville show and the popular weeklies have started many a word or phrase that have circled the globe. Names and expressions such as *Jim Crow* and *quicker than you can say Jack Robinson* are set in circulation by popular songs, in the case of these two phrases, street ballads of nearly a century ago. Literary artists, such as O. Henry and George Ade, are the ones through whom the artistic possibilities of slang have been realized. Baseball slang, at least the most vivid part of it, is a cultivated product, the creation of the sporting writer, with whom the constant renewal of this form of language has become a studied art. This highly artificial jargon of baseball is by no means as old as the game itself. In fact its cultivation, we are told by good authority,[5] goes back only to the decade between 1880 and 1890. Its creation is accredited to two Chicago sporting writers, Charlie Seymour and Lennie Washburn, whose linguistic tricks of fancy were offered to the public on the sporting pages of the Chicago *Inter-Ocean* and the Chicago *Herald*.

That slang is not a feature of language peculiar to the present day is clear enough. The older disposition also, both in this country and in England, to look on slang as a product of American vulgarity, no longer seriously prevails. Slang is not a phenomenon of any one period or of any one language. Present-day conditions, however, may be said to favor its propagation. It is not without significance that the only language with a slang vocabulary richer than that of English, is French, the language subjected more than any other to artificial regulation. Farmer and Henley, in their Dictionary, record more than forty English synonymous slang expressions for the impatient exclamation 'Go away'; but along with these, they record parallel expressions from other languages, from German

---

[5] Hugh Fullerton.

twelve, and from French more than fifty. It is worthy of record also that the names for slang in German, in Spanish, and in Italian, as well as in French, are words like the English word *slang,* connected with the world of thieves and hoboes.

The conditions of army life during the war helped to make familiar the slang of other nations. When the American soldier in France was brought into association with his Australian allies, he learned that "Aussie's" English often differed from his own. He learned *shickered* for drunk, *smoodging* for making love, *buckshee* for something issued free, and a number of synonyms for his own slang words, such as *bloke* for 'guy,' *skiting* for 'four flushing,' *nark* for 'crab.' Occasion for misunderstanding was ever at hand, since certain slang words unoffending in one language, in the other, have meanings distinctly offensive. For instance the word *grafter,* in American use, insulting in its force, in Australian means simply a 'hustler.' On the other hand *spieler,* conveying to an American a meaning innocent enough, to an Australian means 'crook' or 'jail bird.'

An examination of an Australian slang glossary reveals that there is shared by the two distant countries a remarkable amount of slang language, words and phrases such as *also ran; block,* 'head'; *bookie; boss; chump; cop,* 'secure'; *cove; dago; dope; duds; get wise; groggy; king pin; moniker; pal; peach,* 'pretty girl'; *rattled; sore-head; stunt; togs; yap.* Truly slang is winged language, even if in many instances the wings consist of leaves of popular weekly journals. But Australia, as the American soldier learned, has a set of expressive terms more peculiarly its own, such as: *sundowner* (hobo); *back chat* (back talk); *barmy,* 'silly'; *beak,* 'magistrate'; *beano,* 'a feast'; *boko,* 'nose'; *bonzer, boshter, bosker,* 'supremely good'; *brown,* 'copper coin'; *clobber,* 'clothes'; *cliner,* 'eligible girl'; *cob-*

ber, 'pal'; *derry*, 'an aversion'; *gizzard*, 'heart'; *guyver*, 'make believe'; *nark*, 'annoy'; *shook on*, 'struck on,' 'infatuated'; *squiz*, 'brief glance'; *tom*, 'girl'; *tug*, 'a hardy rogue'; *get wet*, 'lose temper.'[6]

When American troops began to arrive in Europe during the war, the impression made by their appearance was conveyed by a British army officer to an American correspondent with the words, "My word, old chap, they're top hole." This utterance was distinctively English in every phrase, and strikingly reveals that there is a British colloquial English distinct from American colloquial English. The early years of the war were remarkably productive in slang language among the British troops, much of which has become widely familiar. Shells were termed *souvenirs*, which in turn were classed as *Will-o'-the-wisps, humming birds, sighing Sarahs, crumps, duds, porridge pots, whizz bangs, woolly bears, woolly Marias*, etc. Bullets were *haricot beans*, wire entanglements were *fly traps* and *spider webs*. *Show* for 'battle,' *picture show* for 'big battle,' *scuttled* for 'captured,' *washed out* for 'wounded,' *put in a bag* for 'killed,' are further specimens of the well-known war slang in use among the British. Daring figures of speech, like those cited above, usually with ironical belittling of danger, were characteristic. Variety was gained by humorous perversions of French expressions, such as *napoo* (*il n' y en a plus*) 'all done,' and by words of Hindustani origin such as *blighty* for 'home,' *go west* for 'die,' *dekko* for 'look,' *pukka* for 'all right,' *char* for 'tea,' *chello* for 'get out of the way,' *jildi* for 'hurry,' *hickboo* for 'enemy airplane' and *cushy* for 'easy.' The Hindustani words were in part expressions borrowed from Indian troops in France, but more often were words already before the war assimilated in the vocabulary of Tommy Atkins, and now taken up,

---

[6] C. J. Dennis, *Doreen and the Sentimental Bloke.*

along with other elements in their military training, by the new recruits of Kitchener's army.

During the war, also, the commingling of social classes brought to the surface a rich variety of words belonging to the speech of submerged classes in Great Britain, words exhibiting the form of humor everywhere characteristic of slang. Words of this class which have been recently cited are: *daisy roots,* 'boots'; *almond rocks,* 'socks'; *artful dodger,* 'lodger'; *isabeller,* 'umbrella'; *field of wheat,* 'street'; *cherry ripe,* 'pipe'; *suppose,* 'nose,' etc. In this underworld speech a popular method of word formation is back slang, or *Kacab genals,* consisting of words with letters inverted from the normal, as in *elrig,* 'girl'; *Kennurd,* 'drunk'; *yennep,* 'penny.'

By the time the American Expeditionary Force reached France, the methods of trench warfare were well established, also to a great extent the form of language adapted to the new conditions. From English and French instructors American troops learned the new features of warfare, and although Americans in general do not enjoy the reputation of being apt at learning foreign languages, they absorbed with remarkable readiness the new forms of language established in use. They soon became familiar with such words as *carry on, waxy, fed up, funk hole,* and *cheeryo,* and adopted into their active vocabulary such words as *batman, bully beef, busted, cooties, hardtails,* and *slacker.*

The distinctively American contribution is not easy to determine in this jargon largely international. The words in most common use among American troops showed qualities like those in the slang of their British allies. Once more was offered an illustration of the close affinity between slang and profanity, for along with the luxuriant growth of slang there is reported from all sides an unparalleled prevalence of profanity. The satire on pretension, however, which appears in such names as *brass looie* for lieutenant, and *shave-tail* for second lieutenant, seems American in quality, as does the contempt for servility, in the name *dog-robber* for orderly. *Hard-boiled,* perhaps suggested by *half-baked,* is one of the most effective word creations. French speech amused the American soldier and provided him, as it had done the British soldier before, with a set of useful words such as *savvy; compray; napoofinee; sanniferan,* 'no matter'; *dupan,* 'bread'; and *deedonc,* 'Frenchman.' Admiration for the French does not appear in the old epithet, *Frogs,* newly applied to them, nor in *tea-kettle,* the American soldier's name for the French locomotive.

The rapid evolution in the meaning of words in this language in a fluid state is illustrated in the case of the word *dud.* An early onomatopoetic coinage for an unexploded shell, it soon became shifted to mean a threat from an officer, and eventually became generalized to mean an empty threat of any kind.

The vocabulary of names for men in different forms of service was fairly complete. The enemy was called *Hun,* or through French influence, *Boche. Doughboy* finally emerged from competition as the prevalent name for American soldier in the ranks. *Gobs* for men in the navy, *leathernecks,* for marines, *limeys* for English sailors, became firmly established. Probably most rich of all was the vocabulary of food terms, due in part to a humorous discontent, in part to the prevalent disposition and determination to make light of the serious, even of that important thing, food. Hence the rich variety of terms, ancient and modern: *slum* (gullion) ; *mess; chuck; grub; hash and chow* for 'food'; *bullets* or *artillery* for 'beans'; *jawbreakers* and *hard tack* for 'biscuit'; *native sons* for 'prunes'; *spuds* for 'potatoes'; *shrapnel* for 'grapenuts'; *bailed hay* for 'shredded wheat biscuits'; *gold fish* and *deep sea turkey* for 'salmon'; *red eye* for 'catsup'; *punk* for 'bread'; *gooey* for 'hash'; *sand and specks* for 'salt and pepper'; *corn wooly; hard oil* for 'butter'; *sea gull*, naval for 'chicken'; *sixteen to one* for 'milk'; *leather* for 'meat'; *strawberries* for 'prunes.'

Each department of the service developed its vocabulary. The sea has always had its special lingo, and naval service in the war was fertile soil for new words. *Gadget* is a word applied to any mechanical device lacking a more definite name; *doozy* is 'easy' or 'agreeable.' The range of possibilities with the metaphor is tested in the variety of names for such objects of importance as coins, called *washers, clackers, jack, liberty bait, gilt, armor plate, holy stones* and *joy berries;* and girls, designated as *calicoes, judies, dames, wax dolls, jelly beans, widders,* and *weazels.*

The Motor Transport Service, whatever its general speed, was not slow in word creation. Directions for starting a *Quad roadster,* in the parlance of the service, employed the following language: *give her plenty of juice, twist her tail, warm up, hook her into high, tramp on her tail, give her the gas.*

But no other branch of the service created as many new slang terms as the air service, due no doubt to the fact that aviation is itself of recent development. The airplane itself was called *can* or *bus,* or under French influence, *zinc* or *taxi* or *coucou.* The airmen were called *birds,* and the same metaphor underlies the names for different classes of airmen. A new airman was an *egg;* further advanced, he became a *vulture;* arrived in the first class, he was called a *goopher. Gimper* meant a bird that would faithfully stand by a comrade, a *cuckoo,* one who did his fighting with his mouth; a *keewee* (Australian bird that does not fly), a non-flying aviator; a *fish,* a man who could not fly. *Chippies* were the carpenters in the naval air service. *Tail* and *joystick* and *mill* (French *moulin*) were names for different parts of the airship. *Zoom, dive, vrille, pique, tailspin, flip, stunt* (loop the loop), *pancake,* and *stall,* were names for various movements. *Spike-bozzle* was a striking name for 'chase an enemy airship,' *crock up* meant 'crash,' and *crocked* meant 'disabled,' while *knocked off, bumped off, huffed,* were the careless sounding synonymous expressions for 'killed.' *Archie* or *Archibald,* for anti-aircraft guns, and *blimp* for small airship, are other striking creations. From the French came not only the names *zinc,* and *taxi* and *coucou,* names already cited for airplane, but *mill* (motor); *turn the mill* (start the motor); *sauce* (gasoline); *vrille, enpanne* (broken down); *coquard* (insignia); and *pique* (charge at enemy plane). Of East Indian origin was *hickboo* (from the Indian name for 'eagle') used as a signal that 'enemy aircraft were about,' or 'to be on the alert.'

Probably even more active than English or Americans in the creation of war slang were the French. There is hardly a type of word in the English slang of the war that cannot be paralleled in French. Clipped forms like *fortif* (fortification), *colo* or *colon* (colonel), and metaphors such as *abeilles* (bees) or *pruneaux* (prunes) or *marrons* (chestnuts) for 'bullets,' abound. There is everywhere in evidence the form of irony consisting of making light of the serious, either the terrible or the beloved, and the range of fancy, as indicated by variety in names, is probably greater than in English. The helmet was variously called *pot de fleurs,* 'flower pot'; *cloche,* 'bell'; *eteignoir,* 'extinguisher'; *blockhaus,* 'melon'; *bol,* 'bowl'; *panier à salade,* 'salad basket'; *marmite,* 'sauce pan'; and *casserole.* The bayonet was called *Rosalie* (proper name); *aiguille à tricoter,* 'knitting needle'; *tourne-broche,* 'roasting spit'; and *cure dent,* 'tooth pick.' The beloved "75" was called *l'aboyeur,* 'barker'; *le raleur,* 'groaner'; *le glorieux,* 'glorious'; *le petit français,* 'little Frenchman'; *le bébé,* 'baby,' and *Julot* (a diminutive of Jules).

Other interesting words are *babillarde,* 'prattler,' for 'letter'; *moulin à café,* 'coffee mill,' for 'machine gun'; *poule,* 'chicken,' for 'girl' (cf. Engl. *flapper,* Germ. *Backfisch*); *bûche,* 'log,' for 'match'; *la valse lente,* 'slow waltz,' for 'go over the top'; *singe,* 'monkey,' for 'bully beef'; *Josephine,* for a 'pipe'; *sèche,* 'dry,' for 'cigarette'; *saucisson,* 'sausage,' for 'finger' or for 'captive balloon.'[7]

The Germans, in their turn, were provided with verbal apparatus as well as with other forms of equipment for war. Their slang exhibited much the same characteristics as have been pointed out in the slang of French and English. Some specimens translated are *field-gray* for 'potato'; *gas bomb* for 'cigar'; *brothers of the chatter line* for 'telephonists'; *jaw-basket* for 'gas mask'; *Gewitter tulpe, storm tulip* for 'steel helmet'; *Kommiss Jesus* for 'chaplain'; *Lieber Gott* for 'lieutenant'; *England's terror* for 'Zeppelin'; *hawks* for 'enemy airmen'; *regular subscriber* for 'airman coming over regularly'; *Heldenkeller* (hero cellar) for 'dugout'; *Flying Dutchman* for 'cavalry'; *bull dog* for 'large Italian gun'; *coffee mill* and *mowing machine* for 'machine gun.'

In all languages an important source of slang has been the language of students. From the days of the wandering students of the Middle Ages to the present, the authority-defying spirit of student life has expressed itself in an outlaw form of speech. From the language of English schools and universities have come into standard English such words as *fag, snob, funk, mob, cad, tandem, chum,* and *crony.* In our own time it sometimes seems that the inventiveness of early days is exhausted, as if musical comedy and vaudeville and the popular weeklies had stifled all

---

[7] *Cf.* A. Dauzat, *L'Argot de la Guerre.* Paris, 1918. (This book contains a list of about 2000 words.)

originality. The language of students seems not only ungrammatical, but threadbare.

There is, however, another aspect to the subject. Student spirit is the spirit of youth, and one of the most significant features of the period in which we live is the revolt of the young. There has doubtless been undue commotion over the child of two and a half years who addressed his parent as "Old bean." Doubtless, too, the fears sometimes expressed of a "Soviet of youth" are exaggerated. But the fact remains that youth is in active revolt. One of the most active forces in the creation of slang is youthful irreverence. With modern youth freed from illusions, it is natural in student language to expect the active propagation of slang.

Youth is not the age of fastidious criticism. In the language of youth one is not surprised to find forms of slang either already far advanced in decay or at least beginning to show taint. No one with any critical development could use such stale wit as that in expressions still current in student language such as *Ain't it the truth? Every little thing; I don't have to; Can you feature that? I should worry; Hold 'er, Newt; Search me; Go way back and sit down; You're in the wrong pew; Get it in the neck.* Nor can there be seen any superiority in more recent expressions of the kind circulating in the year 1920 such as *Ain't you right? Sweet Papa! Oh, baby! How do you get that way? You don't know the half of it; Watch your step; Jazz baby; Believe me, baby; You know me, Al.*

But along with readiness to assimilate second-hand wit, student language still manifests, occasionally, some power of creation. In student use in the year 1920 were in circulation such new words as *razz* for 'heckle' (probably from the slang of aviators); *flusey* for 'girl'; *spuzzy* for 'snug,' 'comfortable'; *spuzzed up* for 'dressed up'; *Be shaggy* or *I'll knock you in a row* (when bumped in a dance); *having the impuck* for 'slightly indisposed.'

Occasionally a figure for daring creation is to be classed as poetic, as in *fire bugs* for 'electric lights,' *horn in* for 'butt in,' *neck and nothing* 'gowns,' *oozed out* for 'slipped out' of a room, *skulldragging* for study, and *a dish of shimmie* for 'jelly.'

Hearty enthusiasm in youth finds an expression such as *Yes, indeed,* a dead form of language. *I should say* soon proves inadequate, and the conditional future changes to the active future, *I'll say.* The process once started runs to the limit, *I'll tell the world.* Synonymous expressions follow in rapid succession, from *You bet* and *You betcha* and *You bet your neck, bottom dollar, etc.,* to *ask me* and the genuine heartiness of *Yea bo.*

The irreverence of youth manifests itself in the names applied to everything with which he is directly concerned. The thought of money in all ages has proved stimulative to the creative spirit of slang. Hence the almost countless terms new and old, finding use particularly in the language of the young. *Kale, iron, slippery stuff, soup-puddin', jack, Jewish flag* for paper dollar, *collateral, chink, cash, tin, dough, brass, ready coin, dibs, spondulix, shekels, oof,* are but a few names from a variety almost infinite. There are 120 words for money in Hotten's *Slang Dictionary,* 1869.

The range of slang expression is perhaps nowhere better illustrated in the names for parts of the human anatomy. *Dome, bealer, coco, crock, cranium, skull, knob, belfry, peak, brainbox, bean,* only begin the list of names for head. *Gub, trap, mug,* for mouth; *beak, conk, noodle, boho* for nose; *flappers* for ears; *lamps, orbs* for eyes; *ivories* for teeth; *map* for face; *fins, mitts,* for hands; *flippers* and *lunch hooks* for arms; *bay window* for 'front exposure'; *pins* for *legs; hoofs* and *trotters* for feet, do not begin to exhaust the list.

SLANG

Youthful impatience with anything or anybody that interferes with a good time is expressed by such names as *kill-joy, frost, wet-blanket, crab, frost, cramp, crêpe-hanger, calamity Jane.* Intolerance of dullness and slowness of wit appear in such synonyms as *goop, mutt, poor fish, crab, simp, duffer, dumb-bell, bad lot, nut, bonehead, nobody home, bats in belfry, muff, geezer, hoot-nannie, wall-eyed shrimp.* To these may be added, from the language of girls, *pessimistic pimple, seam squirrel, poor crumb, poor potato, gouppe, library lizard, poor prune, hambone, limping lump of brick dust, pineapple, mess, cuckoo, old priss, old Jane, pussy foot, dirty bum.*

In such terms of friendly abuse is to be observed a measuring of wits like the measuring of physical strength in the mock fights of earlier youth. The same form of word hazing appears in the variety of synonymous expressions for dissent such as *rave on; where did you get that stuff? how do you get that way? how can you just be so? run up a tack and sit on it until I call you; can the comedy; take it away; give it air; hang crêpe on your nose, your brains are dead; can you feature that? cut your kiddin'; come off your perch* (or horse); *stop spoofing me; amuse yourself, don't mind me; what's eating you?*

In the vocabulary of modern youth, chivalry is dead. The maiden is no longer placed on a pedestal or throne. She no longer is worshiped as a divinity. A girl is a *jane*, a *dame*, a *moll*, a *flapper*, a *worm*, a *skirt*, a *smelt*, a *squab*, a *chicken*, a *doll*, a *sardine*, a *flirt*, a *damsel*, a *frail*, a *hairpin*, a *piece of calico*, a *petting skirt.* If she is popular, she is a *darb*, a *peach*, a *bird*, a *belle*, a *live one*, a *baby vamp*, a *whizz*, a *pippin*, a *star*, a *sweet patootie*, a *baby*, a *choice bit of calico*, a *sweetums*, a *snappy piece of work*, a *pretty Genevieve*, a *thrill*, a *flesh and blood angel.* If she is unpopular, she is a *pill*, a *pickle*, a *lemon*, a *dead one*, a *priss*, a *tomato*, a *chunk of lead*, a *drag*, a *gloom*, a *rag*, an *oil can*, a *crumb*, a *nutcracker face*, a *flat tire*, a *mess*.

The girls' list of names for members of the other sex is nearly as rich. Noncommittal in general are: *dude, goof, john, jake, raspberry, yap, guy, kid*. The young man who does not take his girl about is a *chair-warmer*, a *tight wad*, a *porch warmer*, a *lounge lizard*, or *parlor leech*, a *flat wheeler*, a *ham*. The one in favor, however, is a *candy-leg*, a *gold mine*, a *Jack full of money*, a *nifty guy*, a *thriller*, the *regular guy* or the *full guy*.

The objections to the use of slang are too obvious and have been too often urged and too well expressed, to need detailed repetition here. The specimens used above in illustration, offer all the evidence needed for conviction and sentence. "There is," says Hazlitt, "nothing vulgar in the common English idiom," but "all slang phrases are for the same reason vulgar," on account of "ignorance and conceit." Its aim is wit, but the form of wit usually is immature and cheap.

The objections against slang are, however, less against its use than against its misuse. It usually originates, it has been pointed out, in a deliberate defiance of propriety, and like profanity, to which it is closely allied, by its discharge of inhibited feelings of disgust or anger, affords a grateful relief which is expressed by laughter. Language, however, is a social instrument. As such, its character should be determined by the character of the hearer nearly, if not quite, as much as by that of the speaker. Hence the intentional irreverence and impropriety of slang are out of place in language addressed to persons to whom respect is due. Slangy language is in many ways like shirt-sleeve dress, and both are out of place on formal occasions or in the presence of new acquaintances or of persons who from considerations of sex, rank, or age, are entitled to respect.

But slang is not only cheap wit; it is second-hand wit. As such, it is necessarily short lived. By way of illustration consider the richly developed language of pugilism of a century ago. In DeQuincey's account of a fight in his *Murder Considered as One of the Fine Arts* appear the following expressions: *squared at him; a turn up was the consequence; M— was floored; he managed his pins capitally, but the shine was now taken out of him; hit him repeatedly on the conk; tried the weaving system.* In *Dombey and Son*, Dickens makes use of *severely fibbed; heavily grassed; tapped; bunged; had received pepper; had been made groggy; had come up piping.* Of these expressions those that are not entirely obsolete, are intolerably stale. DeQuincey and Dickens evidently could not qualify as reporters of a modern prize fight. The fate of the pugilistic phrases quoted is destined as the fate of all language of their kind. What can be more revolting than phrases like *Whoa, Emma; Ah there! Get there, Eli; Go it, Susan, I'll hold your bonnet; Everybody's doing it; Good night, Irene; O you kid!,* in vogue not so long ago?

Originating as slang expressions often do, in an insensibility to the meaning of legitimate words, the use of slang checks the acquisition of a command over recognized modes of expression. An acquaintance of twenty years ago who had eloquent command of such expressions as *proper, fierce, throw one in, hand him one, cop out, ten bones, worst I ever seen, looks good to me, throw the harpoon, string of con, bulling around, stalling, grand poobah, bull con stall,* and many other like expressions, once fresh, but now stale or obsolete, on one occasion was brought into conversation with a man with whom it was desirable to use legitimate English. Usually a fluent talker, the man so eloquent in slang, was entirely at a loss for words, but finally, in despair, to use his own expression, "gave it to him in similes and let it go at that."

More insidiously dangerous than the forms of slang with sharply stamped meaning, are the meaningless words, or "counters," which in the "lazy man's dialect" take the place of real words. "They are," says the Autocrat of the Breakfast Table, "blank checks of intellectual bankruptcy." Newspaper humor provides illustrative examples:

> Two adjectives Susannah knows
> On these she takes her stand;
> No matter how this world goes,
> 'Tis either "fierce" or "grand."
> —*Birmingham Age-Herald.*

Strikingly limited, though at the same time strangely sufficing, is the language of the returned soldier, "Pink," in the following dialogue:

> "Did ye git clean over, Pink?"
> "Oh, boy, did I?"
> "Git sick on th' ocean?"
> "Oh, boy, did I?"
> "Didja go over the top, Pink?"
> "Oh, boy, did I?"
> "How'd it feel?"
> "Oh, boy, believe me."
> "Pink, didja kill any Germans?"
> "Oh, boy."
> —*Kansas City Star.*

Obviously addiction to the use of such convenient substitutes for expression must result in atrophy of the faculty of using language.

To the student of language, slang is a subject of unending interest. In these "gypsy phrases" may be observed in activity most of the creative forces of language. Every known figure of speech is brought in service: metaphor as in *pussyfoot;* metonymy as in *speak easy* and *bootlegger;*

onomatopœia as in *whizzbang* and *sputter-bus;* antonomasia in *Busy Bertha* and *Henrietta;* hyperbole in *sky-scraper* and *skin of the teeth;* understatement in *whistle* for 'flute' and *kiss the eye teeth* for 'hit in the mouth'; irony in *clear as mud.* The heavy artillery of the battlefield is brought into use in the description of a baseball game: a player makes for first base "like a big tank run wild"; Ruth "wields his shock bat" or "conducts a mopping up party"; and the pitcher "loses all liaison with the plate." The current of thought is not conducted by short circuit, but makes prodigious leaps by means of far-fetched figures. The leap of fancy is indeed bold in such expressions as *canned* for 'discharged,' *soup bone* for 'pitcher's arm' and *pull a boner* for 'make a misplay.'

The bold creation of slang to be sure soon fades into the commonplace, as in the case of creations once vivid, such as *sweater, bleacher, shin-plaster, razor-back, sky-scraper, crawfish, cracker* and *bell-hop.* The color, however, is constantly renewed by means of fresh creations: *stop crowing* becomes *come off the perch; in the face of* the wind becomes *in the teeth of* the wind; keep your eyes *open* becomes keep your eyes *peeled; numskull* becomes *bonehead; tell the world* becomes *inform the pleiades;* give a boy *the mitten* becomes *jipp* a boy; *hot air* becomes *baked wind; camel* cigarettes become *humps; bluffer* becomes *four flusher; take the cake* becomes *take the Huntley and Palmer.* In this way *pluck*, which originally meant the liver and lungs of a beast, during the Crimean War came to be used to express the meaning 'stamina,' and we are told, became a favorite term in Mayfair, even among the ladies. Thus faded into respectability, it has had to be superseded by a new strong word not yet admitted into drawing-room circles.

In a number of instances the freshening process has been repeated a number of times. *Interrupt* was more vividly expressed by *break in on,* which in turn has been succeeded by *butt in,* which in turn has yielded in part to *horn in.* The successive names applied to the 'man of fashion,' run in chronological sequence something as follows: *trig—blood—Marconi—buck—incroyable—dandy—dude—swell—toff.*

The exact boundary line between slang and legitimate speech it is not possible to draw. In a series of words such as *milksop, mollycoddle,* and *Willie boy,* one has been fixed in standard speech for more than five centuries, one is unmistakably slang, and the third is in the no-man's land between. *Blockhead* is admitted; *bonehead* is outside. The same distinction holds between *bustle* and *hustle, persiflage* and *camouflage.* One may say *up the chimney,* but *up the flue* is rated as slang. *Jarring note* is unimpeachable, but the same cannot be said of the expression, *Wouldn't that jar you? Lit up* for intoxicated is evidently slang, yet Stevenson in his expression "lit internally with wine" is clearly within the bounds of propriety. Obviously words and expressions have besides their central meaning, a fringe of associated meanings, and upon the character of the associations depends their eligibility for polite use.

It has been said that as a result of the Napoleonic wars the language of the bourgeoisie in France replaced that of the aristocracy. That the English literary language should be influenced by the social commingling during the war and the prolific creation of new forms of expression is what might be confidently predicted. The realization of the prediction is in fact already at hand. A recent article in *Blackwood's Magazine* may be made to illustrate the transformation that has taken place in the literary language. In the course of this short article appear such expressions as "the deal was *crabbed,*" "after all the *jiggery-pokery* about the sites," "*slithered* over muddy roads," "British supplies were *scrounged*," "Whom Tommy loves, he *chips*."[8]

The effect of the war, however, has been only to accelerate a movement already in progress. The general spirit of revolt of the present day has done much to relax the constricting bands of propriety. From the writings of Maurice Hewlett have been gathered such expressions as: "here he was then up against it"; "I went to London, I got busy;" "it's up to you"; "have no use whatever for." John Galsworthy indulges in, "If she gets swelled head, the world will get cold feet." Sir Philip Gibbs does not hesitate to make occasional use of terms such as *fuggy* (referring to the slow times of the past generation) and *dinky*. Sir Harry Johnston keeps his language close to the vernacular by the use not only of homely dialect words, but of colloquialisms new and old such as *pernickety, scallywag, stodging,* and *diddled*. Joseph Conrad imparts a racy quality to his colloquial language by means of such expressions as, *sat tight, nothing in it,* and *croak* (for 'die'). The increased informality of modern life, and the growing intimacy of modern literary style, and the consequent added freshness to expression are exemplified in a recent article in the *Atlantic Monthly* in which effective use is made of: *cavort, bull-fiddle* (for 'cello), *whizz-bang, blind pig, bang up, dig up* (for 'get') and *flivved* (verb).[9] A recent English writer who in her novels aims to set forth the spirit of modern youth,[10] creates a modern atmosphere by the use of words and expressions such as: *tosh, stunt, crabbed it, get pipped, butt in, such a gumph, diddle, swanking, caving in* (for 'giving up'), *talks through his hat*.

Of the new elements in the language the dictionaries

---

[8] *Living Age*, May 3, 1919.
[9] R. H. Schauffler.
[10] R. Macaulay, *Potterism*.

have not failed to take cognizance. In a recent edition of one of the standard American dictionaries, place has been found for *blimp, barleycorn, cootie, whizz-bang, gin-mill,* and *gippo.*

Oral speech is naturally more directly responsive than written to newer tendencies in language. The new 'punch' given by some of the newer creations, is not to be dispensed with. From the pulpit Dr. Hugh Black proclaims: "Nations can have *swelled heads* as well as men"; "Let the family *go to pot* if it likes"; "Louis XVI, the *best of the bunch.*" Ex-President Wilson in his public addresses did not hesitate to use expressions such as *butting in, the whole thing,* and *up to me.* Lloyd George in the course of the war, spoke of Russia as "still *on the ropes*" and of Germany's hope that the U-boats would "put England *out of business.*" Even Mr. Asquith was quoted as using the phrase "*deliver the goods.*" That slang is patronized by royalty in colloquial use we have evidence from the enthusiastic remark of an American girl concerning the Prince of Wales: "And, oh, he does use the most delightful slang in such a fascinating manner." Finally there is the authority of King George himself. "What the Americans have really done," he is quoted as having said, "is perhaps best expressed in their own idiom. They have 'put *pep* into us.'" Slang was thus made for one occasion, at least, literally a part of the "King's English."

References for Further Reading

FARMER and HENLEY, *Slang and its Analogues,* 7 vols. (London, 1890-   ). One volume edition published in 1921.
BARRÈRE and LELAND, *Dictionary of Slang, Jargon and Cant,* 2 vols. (1889–1890).
J. C. HOTTEN, *Slang Dictionary,* new ed. (London, 1874).
GREENOUGH AND KITTREDGE, *Words and Their Ways,* in *English Speech* (New York, 1901), Ch. v.
BRANDER MATTHEWS, *Parts of Speech* (New York, 1901).

H. Bradley, Article on "Slang." *Encyclopedia Britannica.*
A. Dauzat, *L'Argot de la Guerre* (Paris, 1918).
A. Niceforo, *Le Génie de l'Argot* (Paris, 1912).
H. L. Mencken, *The American Language,* 1st ed. (New York, 1919).
C. A. Smith, *New Words Self-Defined* (New York, 1919).
R. P. Utter, *Every-day Words and Their Uses* (New York, 1916).

From among the numerous articles on slang which have appeared in periodical literature may be cited:
Atlantic Monthly, 71, 424, 426; *Blackwood's Magazine,* 8, 177, and 143, 640-704; *The Dial,* 15, 86 and 108; *The Forum,* 51, 416; *Harper's Magazine,* 87, 304 and 30, 601; *The Nation,* 51, 288 and 53, 261 and 57, 155; *North American Review,* 141, 431-435; *The New Republic,* 2 articles, December, 1916.

CHAPTER V

TECHNICAL WORDS

The well-ordered precincts of standard speech, as has been indicated, are adjoined on different sides by speech districts less reduced to formal cultivation. In one direction cultivated speech merges almost imperceptibly into the fertile area of dialect richly productive of fresh native elements in speech. On another side its boundaries intersect those of the playground of language, the field of slang. In quite a different direction it spreads out almost interminably into an industrial district, the district formed by an ever expanding technical vocabulary. Like the industrial district of a great community, the technical vocabulary has absorbed foreign elements in enormous numbers. Like the industrial districts, also, its external appearance is marked by creations imposing in character, surrounded by vast stretches of the tawdry and the squalid. Less rich in appeal to feeling than the artless products of the native dialects, technical words, of varied source and often clumsy workmanship, form by far the largest element in the growth of the vocabulary, and in the history of the language have contributed most largely to the expansion in expressive power which distinguishes cultivated language from uncultivated modes of speech.

A casual inspection of a few pages of any large dictionary will suffice to convey an impression of the range and, at the same time, the minuteness of expression made possible by means of technical terms. It is also likely to leave a humiliating impression regarding the range of one's personal vocabulary. A recognition of the meaning of any large proportion of technical words and phrases belongs to an instructed few, and a ready command of such words can be aspired to only by one who has deepened his knowledge in the special subject concerned. One of the principal ends in fact served by educational processes is to fill with a content of meaning the special terms which are required for precision in the different special subjects. From the early days when, in studying the "three R's," one struggled with the definition of such terms as *multiplication* and *least common multiple*, to the days of preparation for a profession, when one has to learn of *felonies* and *misdemeanors*, of *certiorari* and *quo warranto* or of *exegesis* and *homiletics* or of *metabolism* and *anabolism* and *radiotherapy*, or *strains* and *stresses* and *ions* and *valences* and *anodes* and *kathodes*, a main concern of education is the acquisition of the specialized knowledge crystallized in technical terms.

For detailed discussion of special subjects the indispensable nature of a special technical vocabulary is apparent. One could not go far in the discussion of church architecture without the use of such names as *consol* and *corbel*, *quoin* and *crocket*, *entablature* and *embrasure*, *buttress* and *battlement*, *canopy* and *tabernacle*, *pinnacle* and *finial*, *vaulting* and *tracery*, *mullion* and *fretwork*; of domestic architecture, without such words as *jamb* and *lintel*, *panel* and *wainscot*, *surbase* and *molding*.

The enchanted atmosphere of sea life cannot be created by one who has not at his command the magic of such terms as *sheets* and *shrouds*, *bark* and *brigantine*, *jib* and *spinnaker*, *studding sail* and *staysail*, *scuppers* and *davits*, *gaff* and *boom*, *jibe* and *luff*, *sloop* and *yawl*, *dinghey* and *jolly-boat*, *ketch* and *junk*. It is questionable if any but the initiated can ever use with confidence such terms as *cope* and *chasuble* and *dalmatic*, *lauds* and *matins* and *nocturns*, *gradual* and *introit*, *asperges* and *tenebrae*, and equally questionable if persons of male sex can ever speak with precision of *rep* and *dimity*, of *chiffon* and *foulard*, *tulle* and *voile*, of *yoke* and *plait*, *gimp* and *gamp*, *tuck* and *gore*, *flounce* and *shirr*.

The indispensable nature of the technical words is readily apparent. Not only, as the boundaries of knowledge are extended, are new names needed for new things in the annexed provinces, but with the ordering and classifying processes which distinguish modern inductive science, names are needed which have, above all, the quality of precision. The effort after greater precision is evident in many technical words. The word *consumption,* used as the name for a wasting disease vaguely understood, goes back to the Middle English period. Effort after precision led to the adoption in the sixteenth century of the name *phthisis* taken from the Greek. A more clear understanding of the nature of the disease led to the modern name *tuberculosis* first cited as late as 1860. The same explanation applies to such a series of words as *germ, microbe, bacillus,* and *bacterium,* to the substitution of *hemorrhage* for bleeding, of *tetanus* for lockjaw, of *anemia* for deficiency of blood, of *aphasia* for loss of speech, of *amnesia* for loss of memory, of *hernia* for rupture or breach. Dangerously close to pedantry is the use of the technical name *phlebotomy* for bloodletting, of *myopia* for nearsighted, of *coryza* or *rhinitis* for common cold, of *fornunculosis* for boils. With the development of the modern dye industry based on coal tar products, the basic word resorted to, is not the word with popular associations, *indigo,* but the Arabic word for 'indigo,' *anil,* from which is formed the adjective *aniline*. Under the influence of the scientific desire for precision, older popular words are modified in meaning. *Fish,* for example, which in popular use applies to any animal that lives entirely in the water, is restricted by the zoölogist to mean "any branchiferous vertebrate with a complete cranium and a lyriform shoulder girdle."[1] The word *berry*, which is one of the two English fruit names of native English origin, and which in popular use appears as an element in such names as *huckleberry, strawberry, blackberry, mulberry, checkerberry*, in its technical meaning applies to only the first fruit in the series named, but on the other hand applies to other forms of fruit not popularly known as berries, such as the banana, tomato, grape, and currant.

The *fir* tree has suffered the same limitation of meaning as the *fish* and the *berry*. The spruce, the name of which is an abbreviation of *spruce fir*, is quite excluded by science from the fir family. The fir proper is referred to the genus *Abies*, and the spruce to quite another genus, *Picea*. Other trees popularly known as *firs*, but now excluded from the family, are the red, yellow, or Douglas *fir* of western America, now referred to the genus *Pseudolsuga*, and the Scotch *fir* now referred to the genus *Pinus*.

The inexactness in the popular names of plants has been referred to in another connection [p. 17]. The adoption of technical names has served to clear up much confusion. The plant variously known as *deadly nightshade, death's herb, banewort, divale*, and *poison black cherry*, is given the name, euphonious as well as precise, *belladonna*. The plant variously known as *henbane, hog's bean, insane root*, and *poison tobacco*, receives the dignified but foreign-appearing name, *hyoscamus*. Boneset, or *thoroughwort*, is called *eupatorium*. *Bloodelder* or *bloodwort* or *dwarf elder* is called *ebulus*. The *whortleberry*, also called *bilberry* and European *huckleberry*, is called *vaccinium*. Wormwood is somewhat disguised under the name *absinthium*. *Cayenne pepper*, also called *African pepper, chillies, bird pepper*, and *red pepper*, receives the name *capsicum*, which through familiar use as a domestic remedy, tends to gain a place in the popular vocabulary.

---

[1] *Century Dictionary.*

In many instances the competition between the precise technical names of plants and the popular names which are so often inaccurately applied and are so bewildering in variety, is like a contest between a well-organized military force and undisciplined peasantry. The technical plant names, arrayed in botanist's manual or in florist's catalogue, with the authority of science, quite overpower the simple names of popular origin. The resulting losses in popular words with their definite associations of homely lore or tender sentiment, are in many cases to be deplored. The issue of the conflict, however, has not in all cases been decided, and it is to be hoped that sentimental reinforcement from the modern public may give the popular words an even chance in the struggle. Among words involved in the struggle referred to may be mentioned: *aconite* against *monkshood* and *wolfsbane;* *digitalis* against *foxglove, foxfingers, ladies' fingers, deadmen's bells,* etc.; *delphinium* against *larkspur;* *genista* against *broom.* The generic term *spiræa* seems in fair way to overcome a small host of popular names applied to its various species and varieties, such as *dropwort, meadow-sweet, queen-of-the-meadows, steeplebush, hardhack, queen-of-the-prairies, goats'-beard, Italian may, St. Peter's wreath,* and *bridal wreath.* The special name *polyanthus* serves to dissociate this spring flower from its natural association with the *primrose,* and the lovely name *gillyflower,* because of its ambiguity, has yielded to the unlovely name *stock.* Even the old flower names, *daffodil* and *jonquil,* so rich in lovely associations as well as in euphony, are slowly yielding ground to the generic name *narcissus,* which, in addition to its natural charm, is supported by its greater scientific precision.

The subject of flower names has been dwelt on somewhat at length because nowhere is more clearly apparent the conflict between the popular words, rich in association, and the technical words with their sharper precision. There can be as little question of the value of the technical names as of that of the names of popular creation.

The dictionary may be said to be the geography of human knowledge. The marvelous extension, in recent years, of knowledge into regions hitherto uncharted, has required the addition of countless names to mark the new features discovered. The two supplemental volumes of the *Century Dictionary* which, in 1909, were added to the earlier six volumes issued in 1891, offer an indication of amazing activity in widening the bounds of knowledge. The two volumes offer a collection of about a hundred thousand words not included in the earlier volumes, and a large proportion of these added words are of new creation, technical in nature. These words reflect not only a revision of the contents of the older fundamental sciences, but the beginnings of new sciences, or branches of science, that have come to engage the attention of the learned world. In underlying theory and in application to practical use, remarkable progress is registered in electricity, in aëronautics, in radioactivity, in bacteriology and serumtherapy, in sociology and eugenics, in experimental psychology and psychoanalysis. An impression of the activity in the creation of technical scientific terms may be gained from the fact that a glossary recently prepared of medical terms alone included more than thirty thousand words.

The elements of which technical words are composed, are somewhat varied. In the technical words associated with the mechanic arts noticeable use is made of elements from popular speech, as in the names for varieties of nut, such as *thumb-nut, flange-nut, circular-nut, milled-nut, cap-nut, lock-nut;* or of heads of a nut, such as *square-head, cheese-head, T-head;* or in such miscellaneous names as *ball-and-socket joint, toothed-wheel, spur-gear-wheel, herring-bone-gear, rack and pinion, worm-wheel, spiral-gear, shoe brake, V-shaped brake, friction-clutch.* In electrical engineering the same popular quality is generally observable in the technical terms. There are, to be sure, *dynamo* and *armature, anode* and *kathode,* in which the learned vocabulary of pure science appears. But the electro-mechanical terms are in general made up of popular elements such as *coils, spools, brushes, levers, cells, fuse, switch, current, resistance, plug, coupling.* Among the new words recorded in the *Century Supplement,* the word *horse* appears as the first element in more than forty new compounds, *eye* in about the same number, and *dog,* faithful and serviceable as the animal of which it borrows the name, provides the first element in more than fifty new words. The character of the words cited reflects the character of the class of men at whose hands the mechanic arts get their development.

In the vocabulary of the pure sciences, however, there is a different story to tell. In the earlier stages of modern inductive science, in the sixteenth and seventeenth centuries, as is shown elsewhere in this volume [p. 118], the Greek language served as a linguistic godparent. In this earlier period was created a pattern of Greek design for scientific words. Certain Greek elements appeared so frequently in new English compounds as to acquire the value of English prefixes or suffixes available for new creations. Illustration of the assimilation of this Greek element in the English technical vocabulary is afforded by the words in the *Century Supplement.* For instance, the Greek *allo-* appears as a prefix in more than fifty new words, *amphi-* in nearly seventy, and *neuro-* (Greek *neuron,* 'nerve') appears as the first element in more than one hundred and twenty-five new compounds. The modern activity in the invention of machinery which saves human labor, is indicated by the appearance in the *Century Supplement* of more than one hundred and seventy new

TECHNICAL WORDS   77

words with the Greek prefix *auto-*, supplementing about one hundred and thirty such words in the original Dictionary.

The exploitation of the Greek language as a mine of material for scientific nomenclature, has continued uninterruptedly in modern science. The almost unlimited number of new products of modern organic chemistry is kept pace with by the chemical technical vocabulary, and the combination of elements in the names of the new chemical products corresponds in complexity with the combination of elements in the compounds themselves. Space obviously forbids the citation of many illustrative examples such as *benzoylvinyldiacetonealkamine, diethylsulforemethylethylmethane,* and *tetramethyldiaminobenzophenone.* The zoölogical sciences offer specimens, which, if not quite as long as the chemical words cited, nevertheless, for size and form, deserve a place in the language section of a zoölogical museum. In such a language zoo might be placed such words as *hematoporphyrinuria,* and *hypsibrachycephalous.* An interesting illustration of the gulf which separates such sesquipedalian monsters from the words of popular speech is offered by the *lopholatilus chamæleonticeps.* This fish, formerly rare, a few seasons ago appeared in quantities sufficient to be available for the food market. As a marketable commodity, however, its name had to be simplified, and one syllable was made to suffice, so that the fish in the market lists bore the simple popular name *tile fish.*

If the technical words created by modern science serve as monuments to scientific purposes, from earlier times, there are words which, less imposing in size perhaps, serve nevertheless as monuments to earlier stages in the development of modern science. The dates of the first appearance in English literature of different words serve well to mark the various stages in modern progress. Some of the stages in the development of chemistry are indicated by the following words with their dates attached: *analysis* (chemical) 1667, *acid* (substantive) 1696, *alkaline* 1677, *molecule* 1794 (French 1678), *atom* (chemistry) 1819, *ion* 1834, *electron* (as a name for the simplest element) not yet recorded in standard dictionaries. For the history of physics the following words and dates have their story to tell: *atom* (physical) 1650, *gravity* 1652, *electricity* 1646, *barometer* 1665, *thermometer* 1633, *actinic* 1844, *chromatic* (colors) 1835. In medical science landmarks are such words as *to disinfect*, 'destroy germs,' 1658, *antiseptic* 1751, *vaccinate* 1803, *anesthetic* 1837, *tuberculosis* 1860, *bacteriology* 1884. As examples of other words of similar importance may be cited: *adverb* 1530, *algebra* 1551, *aorist* 1591, *aorta* 1594, *agriculture* 1603, *addition* (arithmetical) 1542, *alcohol* (fluid) 1672, *aluminium* 1812, *anatomy* 1544, *anthracite* 1812, *aeronautics* 1753, *balloon* (aeronautic) 1783, *æsthetic* 1832, *agnostic* 1870, *athletics* 1727, *cryptogam* 1847, *atavism* 1883, *subconscious* 1832.

The lists of words cited above will serve not only to indicate important stages in modern culture history, but will illustrate the way in which words introduced with technical meanings, with the diffusion of knowledge, find their place in the vocabulary of popular speech. From technical sources as well as from dialect and from colloquial speech, the expressive power of the language is enlarged. The popularization of technical terms goes on most rapidly, no doubt, in the case of medical terms. Names of diseases and of remedies become, unfortunately, all too soon familiar. Hence the most learned of technical words, such as *tuberculosis, appendicitis, pyorrhea, tonsilitis*, and *adenoids*, all of recent origin, are already well established in popular use. For centuries the technical medical terms have been making their way into popular speech, and many of them through current use, have undergone popular modification in form so as to show little trace of their

TECHNICAL WORDS

learned origin. To this class of words belong *quinsy* (O. Fr. *quinancie*, Greek *kunagke*, 'dog throttling'), *palsy* (Greek *paralusis*), and *dropsy* (Greek *hudrops*).

From the technical vocabulary of law have entered popular speech such words as *purchase, size, convey, assets, improve, attach, distress, abate, claim, quit, privilege, culprit,* and *alibi,* through slang use, seems to stand a chance of making its way into standard speech with the meaning 'excuse.' From military language come such words as *harbor, arrange, alarm, alert, to park* (an automobile). From Christian appropriation to technical uses of older terms, is due the present popular meaning of such terms as *pastor, convert, salvation, worship,* and *doom*. From the special vocabulary of the sea have come such words as *veer, leeway, ahead, bulk, berth, average, mainstay, rummage, freight, aboard, to backwater, to stand by, aloof*. From the learned language of botany come, besides the words cited above, also such popular names as *chrysanthemum, magnolia, begonia, wistaria, bougainvillœa,* and *dahlia,* the last five learned formations based on the names of their botanist discoverers.

The pedantry which displays its wisdom by the exhibition of a command of technical words is familiar enough. It provides a fertile theme for satire. An engineer, in a recent newspaper anecdote, having become tired of the learned jargon about him, proceeded to describe the working of a marvelous machine he had seen. "By means of a pedal attachment," he said, "a fulcrumed lever converts a vertical reciprocating motion into a circular movement. The principal part of the machine is a huge disk that revolves in a vertical plane. Power is applied through the axis of the disk, and work is done on the periphery, and the hardest steel by mere impact may be reduced to any shape." The marvelous instrument thus described, is a grindstone.

The value, however, of the technical element in the English vocabulary must not be judged from an exhibition of its misuse. It is evident that any language that expresses the thought of a living people must be a growing language. In this growth the technical element is a most considerable one. The English language continually draws new life blood from the fresh stores of dialect and from the novel creations of slang. More important, however, than either of these sources of words, is the speech activity of men creating names for the new products of art and science and thought. To the expressive powers gained through such efforts the English language owes in great part its pretension to the rank of a cultivated language.

CHAPTER VI

THE NATIVE ELEMENT IN THE ENGLISH VOCABULARY

Having begun the story of English words *in medias res* by plunging into the very midst of the creative activity which is shaping a language to express the spirit of modern thought, it is now time to revert in the narrative, to consider the matter of ancestry and to distinguish the different elements that enter into the composition of this language of varied strains. The element that naturally should first engage the attention is the native element, the warp about which has been woven the complex modern fabric.

Any one that undertakes for the first time to read a passage of the English written before the Norman Conquest is bound to be impressed by the difference between the language of that time and the language of to-day. The Old English seems to be a foreign tongue. The difference from modern English, apparent everywhere, is especially conspicuous in the language of poetry. Such words as *eoh* for 'horse,' *līg* for 'flame,' *rīc* for 'warrior,' *tīr* for 'glory,' *folde* for 'earth,' *ēce* for 'eternal', have little or no relation to modern English; the variant names *metod, scyppend, frēa,* and *drihten* will hardly be recognized as English names of the Christian God.

If one is acquainted with modern German he will soon begin to recognize among the words so un-English in appearance, a number that resemble words in modern German. In such words as *niman,* 'take'; *wunian,* 'dwell'; *mid,* 'with'; *ēac,* 'also'; *lēof,* 'dear'; *sige,* 'victory'; *here,* 'army'; *weorthan,* 'become'; *weorpan* 'throw'; he will perceive a relationship to the familiar German words: *nehmen, wohnen, mid, auch, liebe, Sieg, Heer, werden, werfen.* Obviously early English resembles German more closely than does modern English.

It would be a mistake, however, to assume that English is derived from modern German. The fact is that modern English and modern German go back to a common source. The earliest English was brought to the island of Great Britain in the fifth century A. D. by Germanic, or Teutonic, invaders from what is now northern Germany, the base of the peninsula of Jutland and the adjacent coast territory. The island of Britain at that time was inhabited by partially Romanized Britons, a people of Celtic race akin to the modern Irish and Welsh and Bretons and Highland Scotch. To Britain was brought a new form of speech, of Teutonic origin. Bede, one of the earliest of English historians, refers to the three principal tribes of invaders as Angles, Saxons, and Jutes, and from the name of the Angles, the imported language took the name *Englisc,* which later has become *English.*

The affinity of this earliest form of English to the Teutonic languages of the continent was close. Any one that can read the early English, or Anglo-Saxon, poem *Genesis,* will be able to read with little difficulty the continental Saxon poem, *Heliand* of approximately the same period. The English language, therefore, in its origin belonged to the Germanic, or Teutonic, group of languages. To be more specific, it belonged to the Western division of the Germanic languages, the division from which have sprung on the continent, not only modern High German, the literary language of modern Germany, but various low German forms of speech, such as the Frisian, the Flemish of Belgium, and the closely related literary language of Holland. The relationship of English is particularly close to the Frisian dialect, which is sometimes spoken of as 'Continental English.'

One degree more distant was the relationship of early English to the other Teutonic languages, to the East Teutonic division including the Gothic, and to the North Teutonic, including the Danish, the Swedish, the Icelandic, and in addition, the Norwegian dialects from which in our own time has been formed anew a Norwegian national language.

Old English, or Anglo-Saxon, like its kindred Teutonic languages on the Continent, was an inflected form of speech. Much of the complexity of inflection that had belonged to earlier stages in the history of Teutonic languages, as for example, in the Gothic of the fourth century, had been simplified. The inflections in Old English were at about the same stage that is to be observed in the literary German of to-day. The later history of English has seen the loss of most of the earlier inflections. Their disappearance in modern English, however, has not been one without trace. Many of the irregular features of modern English are to be explained only by a knowledge of the earlier inflections of which the modern irregular features are exceptional survivals. Some knowledge, therefore, of Old English grammar is essential in order to understand features of modern English.

Let us take, for instance, the case of modern adverbs. In Old English, adverbs were formed by the addition of the ending *-līce* to adjectives, but also by the use of the oblique case forms of adjectives and nouns. In modern English the ending *-ly*, which represents the Old English *-līce*, has become the nearly universal sign of the adverb, but there are a few adverb forms which are to be explained as survivals of other early modes of adverb formation. The older genitive singular form ending in *-es*, for example, survives in modern adverbs such as, *needs, nights,* *once, whilst,* in such expressions as, 'must needs go', 'work nights.' The dative plural ending *-um* as applied to the noun *hwīl* meaning 'time,' survives in *whilom* and has been newly applied to form *seldom*. More interesting still is the case of the so-called 'flat adverbs' which have been the subject of so much debate. In Old English a class of adverbs was formed by the addition of the dative or instrumental singular ending, *-e*. Since this ending later was lost in English pronunciation, these adverbial forms became indistinguishable in form from the corresponding adjectives. Hence in such modern phrases as 'go slow,' 'work hard,' 'buy cheap,' we have what have been called 'fossil' survivals of an older mode of forming adverbs, a mode historically justified and not originating, as often supposed, from the omission of the usual modern ending *-ly*.

An interesting survival of the older inflection of the demonstrative pronoun appears in the use of the word *the* in such expressions as 'the more the better.' Here we have a survival of the old instrumental case form, rare even in Old English, but once common in earlier stages in the history of Indo-European languages. The older meaning of the word may be brought out by use of the paraphrase, 'by that much more, by that much better.'

Such adjective forms, as *sodden, molten, cloven,* appearing in comparatively rare phrases, such as 'molten lava,' 'cloven hoof,' and 'sodden mass,' represent survivals of older forms of the strong past participles, respectively of the verbs *seethe* (once meaning 'boil'), *melt,* and *cleave*.

In one exceptional instance a Latin word has found a place in an English inflectional series. The word in question is the ordinal numeral, *second* (Latin *secundus* 'following'). The older native form, *ōther,* 'second,' however, has not been entirely lost, but survives in the expression 'every *other* one' which obviously means 'every *second* one.'

Another interesting survival of an older inflectional form is the archaic form *twain* for 'two.' The numerals *one, two,* and *three* in Old English were inflected as adjectives with distinction for the three genders. The regular modern form *two* comes from the Old English feminine and neuter *twā*. The Old English masculine *twegen*, however, survives in *twain,* which was still in current use in the sixteenth century as shown by the language of the English Bible.

Distinctions in mood more or less regularly maintained in Old English have been to a great extent lost in modern speech. The subjunctive form in modern English is regularly preserved in only one construction, that of the condition contrary to fact exemplified by expressions such as 'If I were you, I should go.' There are, however, surviving relics elsewhere. An older optative construction survives in phrases such as *good bye* (for 'God be with you'), *fare well,* and *God bless you.*

One of the most interesting of fossil phrases is the archaic combination, *had liefer. Liefer* is a fossil survival of the comparative form of an adjective, frequent in Old English *lēof* meaning 'dear' and surviving elsewhere in the expression, 'I had as lief.' In the word *had* is to be seen the survival of an earlier meaning of *have* (still to be seen in such expressions as, 'as some will have it'), that of 'hold' or 'regard,' also a survival of the subjunctive mood. The expression *I had liefer,* therefore, means 'I should regard preferable.'

After the model of this phrase are supposed to have been patterned the more common expressions, *had rather* and *had better.* The word *rather,* at first meaning 'sooner,' at an early stage came to express the meaning 'preferably,' and the expression *had rather* thus naturally fell into the mold created by the earlier parallel phrase, *had liefer*.

The phrase *had rather*, thus originated, came into competition with the phrase *would rather* (preterit subjunctive of *will* meaning 'wish' or 'like,' and *rather* in its earlier meaning 'sooner') and although for a time yielding ground, in our own day still maintains an almost equal competition with the rival phrase.

The phrase 'had better' seems to have developed through the successive stages:

1. *Better him were* 'better for him would be';
2. *He were better, he had been better*, direct assertion in the subjunctive taking the place of the earlier reflexive form, just as *I like, I lack, I repent, I need*, take the place of *me lacks, me likes*.
3. *He had better*, in which the influence of the analogous *had liefer, had rather*, is in evidence, supported by a prevailing tendency in modern English for *had* to replace *were* as a tense auxiliary.

The earlier full inflection of English words thus serves to explain many anomalous forms of words and combinations of words surviving in modern English. But it is the words themselves that are of immediate concern. A mere glance at a passage of old English prose or verse is sufficient to reveal that a rich store of native English words has been lost beyond hope of recovery. Besides words already cited, may be mentioned such words as: *witodlīce*, 'truly'; *myrrelse*, 'injury'; *heolstor*, 'darkness'; *māthumgesteald*, 'treasure'; *holm*, 'sea'; *gūth*, 'battle'; *hlōth*, 'troop'; *hweorfan*, 'turn'; *ides*, 'woman'; and even such elemental particles as the prepositions: *ymb*, 'about'; *oth*, 'until'; *mid*, 'with'; and the simple conjunction, *ac*, 'but.'

A greater number of the native words, however, have maintained some place or other in later forms of the language. Of these a comparative few have survived to our

THE NATIVE ELEMENT   87

day practically without change in form or in meaning. Under this head may be included such simple words as: *God, oft, and, in, word, full, from, for, to.* Not infrequently in such simple words there has been a slight change in form with little if any change in sound or meaning, as in: *ofer,* 'over'; *thæt,* 'that'; *ǣr,* 'ere'; *æfter,* 'after.'

In a far greater number of instances, however, there has been change in sound, or meaning, or a restriction of use, so that in the modern word the older word is hardly recognizable. By way of illustration take the word *wanton.* In this word survives not only the old privative prefix *wan,* 'without,' but in disguised form, the past participle *togen* of the common Old English verb *tēon,* one of whose meanings was 'to train' or 'to rear.' This native English word, therefore, means etymologically 'without training,' and at first applied to children, has later come to have a general application. Other common Old English words not easy to recognize in their modern representatives are such words as *hlāford,* 'lord'; *hlæfdige,* 'lady'; *ætwitan,* 'twit.'

The changes in sound from Old English to modern usually follow definite rules. The Old English *k* sound, represented by the letter *c,* under certain conditions regularly becomes *ch,* as in *cēosan,* 'to choose'; *hwilc,* 'which'; *rīce,* 'rich'; *mycel,* 'much.' In the same way Old English *sc* regularly becomes *sh,* as in *sceolde,* 'should'; *sceamu,* 'shame'; *sceadu,* 'shadow.'

In the case of the long vowel sounds there has been a universal shift in pronunciation. Thus the Old English words, *āth, tācn, arās, stān, lār, swā, mār, gāst,* appear respectively as *oath, token, arose, stone, lore, so, more, ghost.* The Old English *clǣne, rǣran, strǣt, dǣl, hǣlan* (pronounced as in *ban, fair,* etc.) appear as *clean, rear, street, deal, heal.* The Old English *spēd* (pronounced 'spade'), *grēn, wēpan,* appear as *speed, green, weep.* The Old English *scīnan* (pronounced as in 'seen'), *hwīt, īdel, līf,* appear as *shine, while, idle, life.* The Old English *rōd, mōd, fōt, mōna, hrōf* appear as *rood, mood, foot, moon, roof,* the long *ō* sound having changed to the long *ū* sound. Finally the Old English *ūt, scūr, scrūd, hū, thūsend,* appear as *out, shower, shroud, how, thousand.*

The loss of inflections and the change in the pronunciation of native English words, a change reflected to a considerable extent in changed spelling, would be sufficient in themselves to make modern English words vastly different from the words brought to Britain by Teutonic invaders in the fifth and following centuries.

Less apparent than the external changes in native words, but even more profoundly affecting the nature of the language, is the all but universal change that has affected the meanings of words. Even words little changed in sound or appearance have undergone striking transformations in sense. An impression of the sweeping nature of this change in meaning may be gained from the following lists of words:

Old English	*Modern English*
wadan, to advance	wade, advance in water
stingan, to pierce	sting, pierce (by bee)
spillan, to destroy	spill, destroy liquid
rēcan, to smoke	reek, emit vapor
clǣne, pure	clean, physically pure
feo (h), cattle, property	fee, money paid for professional service
cræft, force	craft, force of cunning
sorh, anxiety, care	sorrow, grief for past
sellan, to give	sell, to give for money
eorl, nobleman	earl, special title of nobility
rǣdan, to interpret	read, to interpret written signs
hord, treasure	hoard, miser's treasure
mōd, courage	mood, state of feeling
wīf, woman	wife, married woman
dēor, beast	deer, a particular wild beast

THE NATIVE ELEMENT

Old English	*Modern English*
starian, to look	stare, to look in fixed manner
mete, food	meat, flesh food
tācn, sign	token, sign of love, etc.
tellan, to count	tell, to relate
murnan, to feel concern (for future as well as for past)	mourn, to grieve for loss
dysig, foolish	dizzy, unsteady on feet
swerian, to speak	swear, to speak under oath
scipu, boat	ship, large boat
gāst, spirit	ghost, spirit of dead
myrgth, joy	mirth, merriment
hǣlan, to cure	heal, to cure a wound
seothan, to boil	seethe, to stir in agitated manner (of liquids)
bealg, bag	belly, abdomen
drǣdan, to fear	dread, to fear in vague manner something in the future
gærs, herb	grass, particular form of herbage
hamm, back of leg	ham, leg of beast used for food
wagian, to shake, tremble	wag, to shake (tail or tongue or head)
fugol, bird	fowl, domestic bird
steorfan, to die	starve, to die from hunger
hund, dog	hound, variety of dog

The prevalence in English of these changes in meaning may be made more apparent by a comparison of some of these English words with the cognate words in modern German, many of which have undergone little change in meaning. The following lists will illustrate:

Old English	*Modern German*
rēcan, to smoke	*rauchen,* to smoke
feo (h), cattle	*Vieh,* cow
cræft, force	*Kraft,* force
sorh, anxiety, care	*Sorge,* anxiety, care
rædan, to interpret	*raten,* to advise
wīf, woman	*Weib,* woman
tācn, sign	*Zeichnen,* sign

Old English	Modern German
scipu, boat	Schiff, boat
gāst, spirit	Geist, spirit
dēor, beast	Tier, beast
hǣlan, to cure	heilen, to cure
steorfan, to die	sterben, to die
hund, dog	Hund, dog
fugol, bird	Vogel, bird

A number of causes have contributed toward the sweeping changes of meaning that have come about in the native English words. In the first place may be mentioned the contemptuous attitude of the conquering Normans toward native 'Saxon' ideals. The adjective *doughty* will serve to illustrate. This word which, before the Conquest, served to express a high conception of virtue or excellence, under the influence of Norman contempt, took on its present shade of meaning, its earlier meaning being conveyed by a French word, *courtois*, which, changed in form and narrowed in meaning, survives in the modern *courteous*. Another word similarly affected is *churl*. This word, which in its Old English form, *ceorl*, meant 'freeman,' affected by Norman contempt, has been degraded to its present meaning.

In other instances the narrowing of meaning is due to Christian appropriation of older words for special Christian meanings. This influence has affected words both of native and of classical derivation. Native words thus affected are: *fiend* (O. E. *fēond*, 'enemy,' *cf.* Germ. *Feind*), now referring to the arch foe of the Christian faith; *doom* (O. E. *dōm*, 'judgment'), now referring to the Christian conception of the last judgment; *worship* (O. E. *weorthscipu*, 'honor'), now referring to honor paid the Deity; *heaven* (O. E. *heofon*, 'sky,' the plural form of which, *heofenas* was appropriated as the name for the future home of the blessed); *bless* (O. E. *bletsian*, 'to consecrate by blood sacrifice'), now 'to consecrate' in Christian sense.

THE NATIVE ELEMENT 91

In the majority of cases, however, the cause of change is to be sought, not in external influences, but in tendencies inherent in language. It should be held in mind that in the period following the Norman Conquest the English language for two or more centuries survived only in the familiar use of uncultivated people. Words exclusively literary in character went permanently out of use. The native English words that have remained in the language, therefore, were the words in popular, colloquial use. In such use, not held fast in meaning by a fixed literary use, the native words were subject, with little restraining influence, to the shifts in meaning everywhere to be observed in popular speech. Shifts of the kind classed by the rhetorician as figures of speech under the names metonymy and synecdoche, are very much in evidence, shifts from one idea to another closely related idea, shifts between cause and effect, between a part and the whole, between material and product, and the like.

Illustrative examples are everywhere at hand. The word *swing* in early English meant 'to strike'; it was shifted so as to refer to the movement preceding the blow. The word *win* meant 'to fight' and came to apply to the result of successful fight. The word *knave* meant 'boy' (O. E. *cnafa, cf.* Germ. *Knabe*); through the intervening meaning of 'servant,' it has acquired its present meaning. In the same way *knight* (O. E. *cniht*, another O. E. word meaning 'boy'), has attained its present meaning, probably through the intervening stages of 'servant' and 'feudal servant.' The word *rich* meant 'powerful,' 'influential'; it now reflects modern ideals and refers to the source of power or influence resting in the possession of wealth. *Rime* from meaning 'number' has come to mean numbered language or verse. *Board* is now commonly applied to the food served at board or table. *Beam* and *tree* have for the most part changed places, the shift in the two words taking reverse directions. *Beam,* originally meaning 'tree' (*cf. the hornbeam,* an English tree, and Germ. *Baum*) has been shifted to mean a hewn product of the tree. On the other hand O. E. *trēo,* which once applied to wood cut for use, a meaning surviving in numerous phrases, such as *whiffle-tree, single-tree, cross-tree, roof-tree, rood-tree,* now in common use, applies to the source of the wood. *Bread* and *loaf* have made a similar exchange of meaning. Terms of measure get their names from the physical unit used or the act involved, in measuring. Thus *foot* originates in the use of the foot as a linear standard; the word *yard* is taken from the name of the stick used in measuring (O. E. *geard*), the older meaning surviving in *crossyards, steelyards. Yield,* originally meaning 'to pay' (*cf.* Germ. *Geld*), has been extended so as to mean 'to produce.' *Spell,* once meaning 'narrative' or 'recitation,' now refers to the magical effect of certain forms of recitation. The older meaning is discernible in such a phrase as 'under a spell.' *Show,* originally meaning 'to look on,' 'to observe' (*cf.* Germ. *schauen*), now means 'to cause some one else to observe.' *Hard,* originally meaning 'strong,' a meaning surviving in 'work hard,' 'fight hard,' etc., now refers to a physical quality of strong articles or substances. *Play,* once meaning 'movement,' 'motion,' (*cf. free play,* etc.), came to refer to motions for entertainment, and from that meaning has shifted to other less active forms of entertainment. A certain significance attaches to the fact that the word for 'play' used by athletic Anglo-Saxons should be rooted in the idea of motion (*cf.* French *jeu,* Lat. *jocus*). The word *sad* once meant 'sated' and then the weariness that comes from satiety. The moral is obvious. *To borrow* formerly meant 'to give pledge,' it now applies to the obtaining resulting from the pledge. The underlying idea of *wed* also is 'pledge'; the word now applies to the marital union associated with the pledge.

THE NATIVE ELEMENT

Keen (O. E. *cēne*), originally meant 'brave' (*cf.* Germ. *kühn*). In modern English it has been shifted so as to apply to a quality almost purely intellectual. In slang it has been still further shifted to express a vague meaning that does not admit precise definition. *Leer* (O. E. *hlēor*), formerly meant 'cheek'; it now applies to a form of expression in which the cheek is involved. *Cheap* (O. E. *cēap*), formerly meant 'barter' or 'price,' a meaning still apparent in such words as *chapman, cheapside,* and *Chepstow*. A clue to the origin of its present meaning is to be seen in the older phrase, *good cheap,* which meant 'good bargain.' The two words, *belly* and *bellows,* both go back to an O. E. word the original meaning of which was 'bag.' The older word for *belly* was O. E. *wamb* now applied to a single organ. A shift in a reverse direction has taken place in the case of *crop* (O. E. *cropp*), which originally applied to the 'head of a plant' (*cf.* Chaucer's "tendre croppes"). It has now come to apply collectively to the whole yield in agriculture.

There is practically no end of available instances. *Fathom* originally meant 'extended anus'; it now applies to a linear unit measured by the outstretched arms. *Acre* originally meant 'field'; it is now a unit in space measure. *Quick* meant originally 'alive,' a meaning surviving in phrases such as 'cut to the quick,' 'quick silver,' 'quick lime,' 'the quick and the dead'; it now applies to a quality of speed associated with being alive.

As further illustration of the extent to which change in meaning has affected the character of native words in English, there may be cited changes in some of the simplest elements in the language, adverbs of time, auxiliary verbs, and prepositions. In all languages human propensity to procrastination, combined with human reluctance to admit uncomfortable facts, has affected words intended to express the meaning 'at once.' Neither German *gleich,* nor French *toute de suite,* nor Dano-Norwegian *straks,* convey to the initiated any conviction of immediateness. Even the Italian double form *subito subito* fails longer to give assurance of early accomplishment. The Anglo-Saxon, therefore, is convicted of only a cosmopolitan weakness, a common human quality, when it is shown that terms now suggestive of deliberate leisure, such as *soon* and *anon,* once conveyed some impression of hurry, that these words in their earlier forms, respectively *sōna* and *on ān,* meant 'at once.'

Further evidence of human failings combined with evidence of human effort at being agreeable is afforded by some of the native auxiliary verbs. The O. E. *mæg,* from which modern *may* is derived, meant 'to be able,' a meaning still apparent in the preterit subjunctive form, *might,* as well as in the noun, *might.* On the other hand, the O. E. *can* (Mod. E. *can*), conveyed the idea of 'know how to.' This word in its later history has fully carried out the change of meaning, the beginnings of which may be seen in the corresponding French word, *savoir.* Modern *owe* comes from an O. E. *āgan,* meaning 'to own,' 'to possess,' suggesting that financial methods familiar to-day are not entirely modern in origin. Modern *ought,* which is past in tense but present in meaning, comes from *āhte,* the past tense of *āg.* The logical development of meaning is evident. Modern *should,* expressing present obligation, comes from the past tense of the O. E. *sceall* (Mod. *shall*), originally meaning 'owe.' The parallelism in the development of the later compound verb form, *have got,* meaning 'possess' or 'must,' is obvious. Modern *must,* on the other hand, is in origin a past tense form of a verb meaning 'may,' and originates in a softened manner of issuing commands.

Even words as elemental as the simple prepositions have undergone striking change in meaning. In the Old Eng-

THE NATIVE ELEMENT

lish period *on* had not only its present meaning but that of *in*, a meaning which appears in such modern phrases as *on hand, on time*. *Of*, in earlier English, meant 'from,' a meaning still apparent in phrases such as, 'ten minutes *of* ten,' 'out *of* prison. *But* was a preposition before it was a conjunction, and its old prepositional use still survives in 'all *but* one,' and the like. *With* in modern English has taken the meaning in earlier stages expressed by the lost preposition *mid*. The old meaning of *with*, 'against,' survives in such expressions as *withstand, withsay, withhold*.

In the changes of meaning that have affected native English words, one of the most conspicuous features has been the restriction in meaning, or specialization. Let us take for illustration two extreme instances. The words *sting* and *wag* have become so vividly associated in meaning respectively with the bee and with the tail of a beast that they can now hardly be dissociated. One can no longer speak in the manner of earlier English of spears that *sting* and leaves that *wag*. The restriction in meaning, in the case of *wag* reminds one of the last stage in the successive restrictions chanted in the old popular song "The Wild Man of Borneo."

This restriction of meaning due to acquired associations appears in the case of many native English words. *Hoard* (O. E. *hord*), which originally meant 'treasure' in a general sense, cannot now be separated in thought from the idea of a miser. *Writhe* (O. E. *wrīthan*), which originally meant 'to twist,' cannot now be dissociated from the idea of pain. *Ham* (O. E. *hamm*), originally meaning the back of the leg, is now inseparable in thought from a kind of edible flesh.

The special associations that have come to attach to words are in many instances to be explained by the fact that words become restricted in use to particular phrases, their earlier general place in language being usurped by other words,

This may be seen in the case of *fowl* (O. E. *fugol*). This word in Old English expressed the general meaning 'bird' as its German cognate, *Vogel*, continues to do. Later its place was filled by the word *bird* (O. E. *bridd*), which originally meant 'young bird,' 'chick,' just as in later times *rabbit*, meaning 'young rabbit,' replaced earlier *cony*, and as the pet names, *kitty* and *bunny*, sometimes now replace *cat* and *rabbit*, and in the West the word *pony* in great part supplants *horse*. The older name *fowl*, preserved only in such expressions as 'domestic fowl,' soon became inseparably associated with the barnyard.

To this form of restriction to use in special phrases native English words have been particularly subjected because of the exceptional number of foreign words that have been absorbed into English. From various sources, in the Middle English period there appeared such words as *dog* and *boy* and *girl* and *lad* and *lass*. The result has been that the older words *hound* (O. E. *hund*), *knave* (O. E. *cnapa*, 'boy'), *maid* (O. E. *mægth*), and *maiden* (O. E. *mægden*), limited in their use, have acquired new elements of meaning from their limited associations. Obviously the kind of words that were brought most into competition with the native words were the words of classical derivation. In many instances the native words have fairly held their own in the struggle for existence, as remains to be seen in a later chapter, but often they have had to give up the field to their classical rivals and have survived only in limited phrasal combinations and usually, in consequence, with restricted meaning. Examples are many. Through the French comes *joy* (Lat. *gaudium*), and the native word, *mirth*, retains only one phase of its original general meaning. In the same way *heal* yields before *cure*, *clean* before *pure*, *rue* before *repent* and *regret*, *spill* before *destroy*, *grass* before *herb*, *fiend* before *enemy*, *deal* before *part*.

THE NATIVE ELEMENT

An idea of the fatalities that have occurred among native English words may be gained from a consideration of their fossil remains which appear in isolated English phrases. The following expressions will serve to illustrate: *meat and drink, sweetmeats*, etc. (O. E. *mete*, 'food'); *Godspeed* (O. E. *spēdan*, 'to prosper'); *widow's weeds* (O. E. *wāede*, 'garment'); *for the sake of* (O. E. *sacu*, 'strife'); *sheriff* (O. E. *scir* and *gerēfa*, 'shire reeve'); *pay his shot* (O. E. *sceat*, 'tax'); *chill-blain* (O. E. *blegen*, 'swelling,' 'boil'); *read a riddle* (O. E. *rǣdan*, 'to interpret'); *stow away, bestow*, etc. (O. E. *stowe*, 'place'); *love token* (O. E. *tācn*, 'sign'); *rood tree, holy rood*, (O. E. *rōd*, 'cross'); *a good deal* (O. E. *dǣl*, 'part'); *litchgate, litchfield* (O. E. *līc*, 'body'); *every other one* (O. E. *ōther*, 'second'); *instead of, in his stead* (O. E. *stede*, 'place'); *Edinburgh* (O. E. *burh*, 'fortress'); *soothsayer, in sooth* (O. E. *sōth*, 'truth'); *all hallows, hallowe'en* (O. E. *halga*, 'saint'); *all told, teller* (O. E. *tellan*, 'to count'); *worth while* (O. E. *hwīl*, 'time'); *bide one's time* (O. E. *bīdan*, 'to wait'); *for the most part* (O. E. *mǣst*, 'greatest'); *moldboard* (O. E. *molde*, 'earth'); *frame rules* (O. E. *fremman*, 'to make'); *redstart* (O. E. *steort*, 'tail'); *mother wit* (O. E. *witt*, 'knowledge'); *mermaid* (O. E. *mere*, 'sea,' 'lake'); *old wives' tales* (O. E. *wīf*, 'woman'); *time and tide* (O. E. *tīd*, 'time'); *might and main* (O. E. *mǣgen*, 'strength'); *right angle, right away* (O. E. *riht*, 'straight').

Many of the native words are obsolete or obsolescent, surviving only in poetry or other forms of language in which an archaic quality is desirable. Examples of such words are: *ween*, 'to think,' 'to suppose'; *meed*, 'reward'; *fain*, 'gladly'; *leech*, 'physician'; *bower, blithe, rathe, lore, bale, dight, don, doff, ere, quean.*

Still other native words have found a prolonged existence in one or the other of the British dialects. *Nesh*, 'delicate' (O. E. *hnesce*) and *meare*, 'horse' (O. E. *mearh*), survive in the South of England. Scotch dialect, the Northern dialect of early English, preserves many other native words lost elsewhere, such as *dree,* 'to suffer' (O. E. *drēogan*); *weird,* 'fate' (O. E. *wyrd*); *bairn,* 'child' (O. E. *bearn*); *fey,* 'fated' (O. E. *fǣge*); *greet,* 'to weep' (O. E. *grēotan*); *speer,* 'to ask' (O. E. *spyrian*); *gang,* 'to go' (O. E. *gangan*); *ken,* 'to know' (O. E. *cennan*).

An appreciation of the meaning of many a phrase in earlier English literature will depend upon a knowledge of earlier meanings attached to words. The Authorized Version of the Bible, which is so imposing a monument to the effective literary qualities of the native element of the English vocabulary, also has served to preserve many an old word and old meaning. Its pages are thickly interlarded with older words and phrases kept from becoming entirely obsolete through the preservative properties of the sacred book. *Sore afraid, widow's weeds, fowls of the air, snare of the fowler, the quick and the dead, heal thine iniquities, wax old as doth a garment, these twain, clean and unclean beasts, cleave to the roof of the mouth, he will not forever chide, all to brake* ('broken to pieces'), will serve to illustrate how much the native words of English owe to the preservative power of biblical language.

CHAPTER VII

BORROWED TEUTONIC ELEMENTS

From our consideration thus far it is apparent that the history of the native element in the English language is sufficiently complex. Left entirely to its own resources the English language, by natural processes of word composition and extension of meaning, would have been able fairly well to keep pace in development with the expansion in the realm of ideas. But the English language was not left to isolated growth. More than any other of the important modern languages, it has been subjected to external influences, and more than any other modern language it has absorbed foreign elements in its vocabulary. The complexity of the subject is vastly increased by these new elements which, on the one hand, have added to the richness and variety of the language and, on the other hand, by the competition created have been responsible in some cases for the loss of native words, in other cases have contributed toward the narrowing of meaning in the native words, which, as has been shown, have in many cases survived only in restricted meaning or in isolated phrase.

First of all may well be considered the borrowings from the kindred Teutonic languages of the continent. Of these continental languages it is the Scandinavian group from which the earliest and the largest contribution was received. The Anglo-Saxons were hardly settled in their new home, had barely had time to begin the literary cultivation of their language, when they were brought anew into intimate contact with their continental kindred from the North. This new contact was brought about through the well-known

Danish Conquest of England beginning about 790 A. D. This Danish invasion, beginning with isolated raids on the English coast in the eighth century, in the ninth century resulted in the occupation of a great part of the territory of England by Scandinavian settlers. In the year 878 the English king, Alfred the Great, by the Treaty of Wedmore, was obliged to recognize Danish rule in the North over a territory covering two-thirds of modern England. Although in the tenth century, Alfred's valiant successors, Edward and Athelstan, reëstablished in the North the supremacy of the Southern English dynasty, in the eleventh century it was a Danish king, Canute, that conquered all of England, and brought the whole land to peaceful unity under his sway.

The effect of the Danish Conquest was a new infusion of Teutonic blood in the English race, a fresh contribution of Teutonic words to the English vocabulary. The amount of the new admixture in the English race it is not possible to estimate accurately, but an idea of the extent of the Danish occupation may be gained from the number of place-names in northern England with the Scandinavian suffixes, *-by, -thorp, -beck, -dale, -thwaite,* etc. The amount of the Scandinavian contribution to the vocabulary also is hard to estimate, and only of late has come to be fully appreciated. The language of the Scandinavian invaders was of common descent with the English, and many of its common words, names such as those for man, wife, house, life, winter; verbs such as those for see, hear, ride, sit, stand; and adjectives such as those for full, well, etc., if not identical with English words, differed only in shades of pronunciation or of meaning. Consequently it is difficult, in the case of many modern English words, to determine with certainty whether they are of native English or of Scandinavian origin.

The criterion of sound in many cases may be applied

in distinguishing the Scandinavian words. Since, as has been shown, in native English words the *sk* sound had regularly changed to *sh*, and since the *k* sound, before the vowels *e* and *i*, regularly changed to *ch*, the greater part of Teutonic words in modern English with the *sk* sound, such as *skill, skin, scare, sky,* and many words with the *k* sound before *e* or *i*, such as *keg, kettle, kirk,* are to be assigned to Scandinavian origin.

In cases where the Scandinavian form of a word differed from the native English form, sometimes both forms have survived with differentiation in meaning. The Old English word *hāl* survives in modern *whole;* the Scandinavian *heill* survives in *hale* (hale and hearty). Other word pairs of this kind are native English *rear, from, shirt, shriek* and the corresponding Scandinavian derivatives, *raise, fro* (to and fro), *skirt, screech*.[1]

In a greater number of cases, where the native form of a word and a Scandinavian came into conflict, there came into operation the principle of the survival of the fittest. In a number of cases the Scandinavian form once used in English, has gone out of use, as in the case of *gayte* (for goat), *gra* (for grey), *fisk* (for fish). In other cases the Scandinavian form survives only in Northern dialect, such as *kirk* (for church), *garth* (for yard), *laith* (for loath).

In other cases the competition between forms of words had a different outcome; the native English form gave place to a Scandinavian. The Scandinavian *kettle* replaced a native English *chetel, Thursday* succeeded native *Thunresdæi.* Other such pairs in which the native form has succumbed are: *swain—swon, sister—swuster, awe—eie, get—yete, eggs—eyren, give—yive.*[2]

In some cases where the English word and the Scandinavian agreed in form, the Scandinavian form has imparted

---

[1] Jespersen, *Growth and Structure of the English Language,* p. 67.
[2] *Ibid.,* p. 69.

a new meaning to the English. Thus the English word *dream*, originally meaning 'joy,' 'revelry,' acquired its present meaning. The same is true of *bread*, formerly meaning 'fragment' or 'loaf,' and *earl*, formerly meaning 'nobleman' in general and *plough* in Old English meaning 'measure of land.'

Regarding the nature of words derived from the Scandinavian, the most notable fact is their everyday character. They are words not borrowed by literary men nor from literary sources, but in general, words, of everyday speech derived from the intimate associations of everyday life, nouns such as *husband, fellow, skin, knife, wing, window, root, law, skill, anger, gate;* adjectives such as *meek, low, odd, wrong, ill, ugly, rotten;* verbs such as *thrive, die, cast, hit, take, call, want, scare, scowl;* even the pronoun forms, *they, their, them.*

The greater proportion of the Danish element in the population of the North is reflected in the greater amount of the Scandinavian element in the vocabulary of the Northern dialects of English. Many of the peculiarities of the Scotch dialect, in vocabulary and in pronunciation, one cannot be sure whether to explain as peculiarities of dialectal development or as due to foreign Scandinavian influence. Even certain peculiarities of provincial American speech, such as '*red up* a room,' 'ten minutes *till* ten,' are probably derived ultimately from the Scandinavian element in the population of Northern England or Scotland.

From no other foreign source has the English language derived words so elemental in character. Scandinavian elements combine with native elements in hybrid compounds such as *awkward* and *greyhound*. Since these Scandinavian words are so nearly related to the Anglo-Saxon, and since they were borrowed so early and have consequently undergone changes in form and in meaning along with the Anglo-

BORROWED TEUTONIC ELEMENTS

Saxon element, one may almost reckon them as belonging to the native stock of English words.

In later periods of English history the contact between English and Scandinavian-speaking peoples has never again been so close. From Scandinavian sources, however, have come a considerable number of later words, such as *geyser, saga, dahlia, flounder* (fish), *kink, slag, tungsten,* and *floe.*

In the case of words derived from the Low German dialects, one is also frequently upon uncertain ground. It must be remembered that the English language in its origin was a Low German form of speech. In consequence there are many English words nearly identical in form with Flemish, Dutch, or Frisian words, and one cannot be sure whether they are borrowed words or native words long in oral use but late in finding record in English written language. There are, however, a considerable number of sea terms usually explained as of Dutch origin, such words as *boom, cruise, sloop, yacht, ahoy, aloof, avast, belay, caboose, hoist, hold* (of ship), *companion-way, moor, reef, rover, skipper, smack, splice, strand, swab, yawl.*

In Elizabethan English many words of Dutch (or Low German) origin make their appearance. In the language of Shakespeare appear such words as *boor, burgomaster, deck, foist, frolic, fumble, geck* (fool), *gilder, glib, groat, heyday, hogshead, hoist, hold* (of ship), *holland, jeer, leaguer* (camp), *linstock, loiter, minx, mop, rant, ravel, ruffle, sloven, snaffle, snap, snip, snuff, switch, toy, trick, uproar, waggon, wainscot.* Many of these terms are evidently derived from military associations in the much fought over fields of Flanders. Other military terms of Dutch or Low German origin are: *freebooter, furlough, cashier, onslaught, domineer, forlorn, hope,* and *plunder.* From other occupations come *spool* and *stripe* and *scour,* said to have been brought to England by Flemish workmen in the reign of Edward III, and *tub* and *scum* and *hops,* terms of the brewing industry.[3]

In the assignment, however, of English words to Low German origin, for the reason already mentioned, extreme caution must be exercised. In the case of words such as *lazy* and *flabby,* which are late in making their appearance in written English, and which have been assigned to continental sources, there can be no certainty. Regarding words also such as *botch, bounce, boy, curl, girl, hawker, huckster, luck, mud, muddle, pamper, scoff, scold, shock* (of corn), *shudder, slender* and *slot,* which are taken from a longer list of words assigned by Skeat to Low German rather than to native English origin, possibility rather than certainty is in most instances the most that can be affirmed.

The Low German languages, however, have been a constant source of supply for new English words. From the Dutch of South Africa have come *trek, veldt, commando,* and *spoor,* 'footprint.' The Dutch have been the middlemen in the importation of words such as *monsoon* from the Arabic, *bamboo* and *cockatoo* from the Malayan. Directly connected with early American history, also, is a set of words which have survived in America from the speech of Dutch settlers in New York. The Low German speech of these colonial Dutch survives not only in proper names such as *Roosevelt* and *Schuyler* and *Gouverneur* and the numerous *Vans: Van Patten, Van Sanford, Van Sickle, Van Benschoten, Vanderlip, Vanderbilt,* but in a number of common words. Many of these words have been restricted in use to local dialect in New York state, such as *blummie, blummey,* 'flower'; *clip,* 'stony'; *grilly,* 'chill,' 'raw'; *mollykite,* 'foolishness.' Others have come into general use in the United States, such as *boss; cold-slaw; cooky,*

---

[3] For a more exhaustive list see Skeat, *op. cit.,* Ch. xxiv; also L. P. Smith, *The English Language,* pp. 191-193.

cookey, cookie; cruller; dominie, 'clergyman'; *dope,* 'thick liquid'; *hook* (Sandyhook), 'cape,' 'promontory'; *kill* (Schuylkill) 'creek,' 'stream'; *logy,* 'dull,' 'heavy'; *pit* (of cherry or plum); *patroon; scow; sleigh; snoop, snooper, snoopy; spook,* 'ghost'; *stoop,* 'porch'; *waffle.* At least one of these Dutch-American words, *Santa Claus,* has gained currency wherever the English language is spoken.

Some of the High German words that have found admission into American speech have already been mentioned. The contribution of High German words, on the whole, has not been great. Words such as *umlaut, ablaut, kindergarten, hinterland, landau, meerschaum, poodle, waltz, alpenstock, carouse* and *rucksack,* bear witness to the influence of modern German ideas. The influence of German science is appreciable in many ways. That the science of mineralogy found its earliest development with the Germans is plainly shown by the English words: *bismuth, blende, cobalt, gneiss, greywacke, quartz, shale* and *zinc,* all of them of High German origin.[4]

REFERENCES FOR FURTHER READING

W. W. SKEAT, *Principles of English Etymology,* Vol. I, Ch. xxiii (Oxford, 1887.)
O. JESPERSEN, *Growth and Structure of the English Language* (Leipzig, 1912).
L. P. SMITH, *The English Language* (New York, 1912).
W. H. CARPENTER, *Modern Philology,* Vol. VI, pp. 53-69.
H. L. MENCKEN, *The American Language* (New York, 1919).
E. BJÖRKMAN, *Scandinavian Loan Words in Middle English* (Halle, 1900, 1902).
GREENOUGH and KITTREDGE, *Words and their Ways in English Speech* (New York, 1901), Ch. x.

---
[4] H. Bradley, *The English Language,* p. 103.

CHAPTER VIII

CLASSICAL ELEMENT

"For vch gresse mot grow of graynes dede,
No whette were elles to wones wonne." [1]

This thought of the fourteenth-century poet of the *Pearl* applies with peculiar fitness to the case of modern European languages. What would have been the product of growth in the languages of northern Europe if they had each been entirely free from external influence, can never be certainly known. The fact is that one and all of them have been subjected to the influence of the earlier cultivated languages of southern Europe. Unlike plants which have found bare sustenance in an unimproved soil, they have, each and all of them, reached down into the cultivated and enriched soil of languages created by an earlier civilization. The earlier languages of Greece and Rome, languages in which the earlier culture finds expression, have provided an organized soil from which they have drawn.

The indebtedness to the classical languages is particularly great in the case of English. But the other cultivated languages have all drawn heavily from the same source. An examination of dictionaries of German or Dutch or Danish will discover few pages without words of classical derivation, and on many pages the number of classical derivatives will be found surprising. Long before the first English came to Britain, the various Teutonic peoples of northern Europe had come into contact with Roman civilization and had absorbed Roman words in their speech.

---

[1] For each herb must grow from grains that are dead; otherwise no wheat would be garnered for storage.

In fact the influence of Southern civilization may be traced to preclassical periods antedating the written records of history. In the archæological remains from prehistoric periods in northern Europe, may be traced the introduction, from the South, of the bronze which distinguishes the Bronze Age from the earlier Stone Ages. In the first centuries of the Christian era, the archæological remains bear witness to the extension of the influence of Roman civilization as far north as Denmark. "Many antiquities which have been identified as belonging to this epoch are of Roman manufacture, especially bronze vessels, articles of luxury and personal adornments of certain kinds. As a whole, the antiquities testify to the great influence upon general culture which had been brought to bear in Denmark by contact with the classic world."[2]

The evidence of language is in remarkable agreement with that of archæology, as to the penetration of Roman culture into the Teutonic North. Many Roman words which are common to most of the languages of the Teutonic group were absorbed at this early time and were later brought by the English to their new home in Great Britain. The nature of these words has been analyzed in an interesting manner by Professor Jespersen, who uses them to show the nature of this early Roman commercial penetration. To this period belongs the introduction of wine, the Latin name for which, *vinum,* survives not only in English *wine* but in German *wein* and Danish *vin.*

Derived from *caupones,* the Roman name for 'wine-dealers,' were a number of Teutonic words having to do with commerce, not only O. E. *cǣpian* (surviving in Mod. E. *cheap, cheapside, chapman,* etc.), but in the common German *kaufen,* 'to buy,' and *Kaufmann,* 'merchant.' Another Latin word of similar significance, *mango,* 're-

[2] *Guide for Visitors to the Danish Collection in the National Museum* (Copenhagen).

tailer,' yielded a number of earlier English words, and survives in the modern *monger, fishmonger, ironmonger, scandalmonger,* and their like. Other Latin terms introduced at this period and obviously associated with bargaining relations are *moneta* (O. E. *mynet,* 'coin.' Mod. E. *mint*); *pondere,* 'to weigh' (O. E. *pund,* Mod. E. *pound*), and *uncia* (O. E. *ynce,* Mod. E. *inch*). Many Latin names of receptacles were introduced at this time and bear similar testimony. Of these many survive in Modern English, often changed in meaning or in use, in such modern words as *dish, scuttle, kettle, mortar, ark.* The Roman influence on the Teutonic mode of living in this early period is indicated by the borrowing of such words as *coquus,* 'cook'; *coquina,* 'kitchen'; *motina,* 'mill,' and of fruit and vegetable names such as those for peach, plum, pea, cabbage (O. E. *cole,* Lat. *caulis, cf.* Scotch *kale,* German *Kohl*), *turnip* (O. E. *næp,* Lat. *napus*), *beet, mint, pepper,* and the names for *butter* (O. E. *butere,* Lat. *butyrum*), and *cheese* (O. E. *ciese,* Lat. *caseus*).

When the Teutonic Angles and Saxons and Jutes separated from their kindred on the continent and migrated to Great Britain, pagan though they were, and representing a relatively low stage of culture, they bore evidence of contact with Roman civilization, and in their language brought words of Roman origin. In Britain they came into hostile contact with a more highly civilized people, the Britons, who had been in part Romanized. Owing to causes which remain to be discussed later, the influence of the Celtic Britons on the language of the English newcomers was surprisingly small. In consequence not many Latin words were taken over by the English from the Romanized Britons. The Roman occupation of Britain, however, had left its impress. The Roman paved road, *strata via,* left its name in *street;* the Roman harbor, *porta,* left its name in *port;* and the Roman armed camp, *castra,*

CLASSICAL ELEMENT

left its name as the last element in the names of many English cities, such as *Winchester, Worcester,* and *Doncaster.*

Planted on the soil of Great Britain, the English language in its growth reflects the progress in culture of the new English people. The event which, more than anything else before the Norman Conquest, affected the character of the English people, was the introduction of Christianity. The influence of the new religion is apparent in the introduction of new Latin words, names for features of the Christian faith or the Christian mode of worship. To Christian influence is obviously due the appearance in English of words like *abbot, abbess, apostle, bishop, chalice, canon, canticle, chapter, choir, creed, cubit, deacon, angel, litany, monk, minster, pope, priest, psalter, saint, hymn.*

But Christianity exerted an influence wider than that indicated by the words cited. Early Roman missionaries, like missionaries of a later time, bore with them more than service and creed. Coming, most of them, from Rome, they brought the Roman language. But more than that, they brought Roman culture and Roman education. The Latin word *scola,* which appears in the English of this period as *scōl, scōlu,* 'school,' gives an indication of the newer culture. Through Irish missionaries was introduced an alphabet made up of an Irish form of Roman characters, which was supplemented by several characters from the Teutonic runic alphabet. Literature in its broad meaning, written language, had its beginning. Furthermore, use of the Latin language, the universal language of learning at this period, formed a link connecting England with the culture of other lands. Travel between Christian England and other Christian countries, particularly between England and Rome, resulted in a widening of the intellectual horizon. Schools and books led to a knowledge of things foreign to the experience of the Teutonic English. The extension of the field of knowledge is reflected in an extended range of the vocabulary. In the comparatively small body of English writings which have come down from this period, if the English glosses of Latin word lists are included, there appear about three hundred words of Latin origin. From an examination of these words one may learn concerning the influence of Roman culture, not only on religious faith and worship, but in names for divisions of time, for utensils, for articles of wearing apparel, and particularly in names of plants and trees and beasts, real and mythological.

From a complete list a few examples may be selected:[3]

Old English	Modern English	Latin
æstel	book-mark	h(astula)
ampelle	bottle	ampulla
aprotane	wormwood	abrotanum
armelu	wild rue	harmala
balsam	balsam	balsamum
berbene	verbena	verbena
bissext	leap year	bissextus
box	box tree	buxus
calend	month	calendae
cancer	cancer	cancer
candel	candle	candela
carcern	prison	carcer
carte	paper, document	charta
cealc	chalk	calcem
ceder	cedar	cedrus
comēta	comet	cometa
copor	copper	cuprum
cucler	spoon	cochlear
culter	coulter	culter
draca	dragon	draco
ele	oil	oleum
elpend	elephant	elephantus
Eotul	Italy	Italia
fefer	fever	febris
fenix	phenix	fenix

[3] T. N. Toller, *Outlines of the History of the English Language.*

CLASSICAL ELEMENT

Old English	Modern English	Latin
forca	fork	furca
gigant	giant	gigantem
gimm	gem	gemma
græf	style (for writing)	graphium
leo	lion	leo, leonem
lilie	lily	lilium
lopestre	lobster	locusta
marma, marmanstan	marble	marmor
mentel	mantle	mantellum
minte	mint	mentha
munt	mountain	montem
olfend	camel	elephantem
palm	palm-tree	palma
pistol	letter	epistola
plante	plant	planta
popig	poppy	papaver
porr	leek	porrum
pyle	pillow	pulvinus
rædic	radish	radicem
rose	rose	rosa
rūde	rue	ruta
Sæternes (dæg)	Saturday	Saturni dies
salfige	sage (plant)	salvia
sealtian	dance	saltare
sicol	sickle	secula
segne	drag-net	sagena
socc	sock	soccus
spadu	spade	spatha
sponge	sponge	spongia
tæfl	chess-board	tabula
temprian	to temper	temperare
tigele	tile	tegula
tiger	tiger	tigris
tunece	tunic	tunica

That the amount of borrowing from Latin was considerable, is apparent. More remarkable, however, than the borrowing, was the resistance offered to the use of foreign words. In this respect Old English showed a propensity like that in modern German, to create the equivalent of foreign words from native word material, to translate foreign words by means of native elements. Of these native compounds, most of which at later periods have succumbed in the competition with the Latin pattern words, the following are a few interesting examples:

Old English	Modern English	Latin
gōdspell (good message)	Gospel	evangelium (good message)
cnēores-bōc (generation book)	Genesis	Genesis
ūt-færeld (out-journey)	Exodus	Exodus
sēoæfteræ (the second law)	Deuteronomy	Deuteronomium
mildheortnisse (gentle heartedness)	mercy	misericordia
efnniht (equal night)	equinox	æquinoctium
Hælend (saver, healer)	Saviour	Salvator
dælnimend (part taking)	participle	participium
dægræd (day red)	dawn	aurora
æfēn-sang (even song)	vespers	vespestina
hundred man	centurion	centurio
wundor	miracle	miraculum
thrinnes	trinity	trinitas
wæcce (watch)	vigils	vigiliæ

The manner of representing Latin words by means of English elements is particularly interesting in the case of Latin *Discipulus,* 'disciple' (literally 'little learner'), which is translated *leorningcniht,* 'learning boy.' There is at least one instance where an Old English word comes from a mistranslation of a Latin compound. Old English *ymbsellan,* 'surround' (literally, 'give around'), originates in a mistranslation of Latin *circumdo,* wrongly supposed to be composed of *circum,* 'around,' and *do,* 'give.'

The reluctance to borrow Latin words, so apparent in the Old English period, does not survive in the period imme-

CLASSICAL ELEMENT 113

diately following the Conquest, and for centuries, the Latin vocabulary served as a mine, seemingly inexhaustible, from which were derived English words. In order fully to comprehend the influence of Latin on the English language, one needs to hold in mind the place held for centuries by Latin in the world of learning. Latin was a cosmopolitan language, more nearly a universal language than any modern language has been able to become, familiarly used not only in writing, but in speech and in song. The joyous spirit, for instance, of the medieval student finds expression in popular Latin songs. Traces of the former prominence of Latin in the world of learning survive in the use of Latin in school diplomas and in doctoral dissertations, a use which persisted down to our own time. In the University of Fribourg in Switzerland, certain lectures on history are still delivered in medieval Latin. Under such circumstances one will not find it difficult to understand how men, familiar with Latin not only in writing but in oral use, when desiring to express an idea for which there was no adequate English word, should introduce into English a familiar Latin word from Latin text-book or Latin liturgy or Latin Bible.

In the period following the Norman Conquest the need of new words in English was particularly obvious. The language was impoverished in its literary vocabulary on account of long disuse among the cultured classes, and when its use in literature was resumed, it was inevitable that the store of familiar words in Latin should be drawn on. This is, in fact, what took place, and from the thirteenth century on Latin words appear in increasing numbers. Wycliffe, in his Bible translation, makes frequent use of words such as *generation, persecution, sedition, tradition,* and *transmigration,* words which, one may be tolerably sure, a translation of the Old English period would have turned into native compounds. Concerning such words one cannot always be sure whether they were taken from the Latin directly or indirectly by way of the French language. Nor can one be sure whether words such as *attention, diffusion, fraction, duration,* and *position,* which appear in the writings of Chaucer, were imported by him or were adopted by him from the current speech into which they had already been imported.[4]

To the borrowing from Latin a new impetus was given by the revival of learning in the sixteenth century. Enthusiasm for the task of turning into English the new-found treasures in classical literature led to a kindred ambition to make the English language an instrument capable of expressing the new ideas. Words from Latin were now imported in wholesale fashion, in the conscious effort to enrich the English vocabulary. An extraordinary number of these newly imported terms found a permanent place in English use. From the long list of words beginning with the prefix *ab-,* the following selected specimens accompanied by the date of their earliest citation in the Oxford Dictionary, will serve to convey an impression of this classical tributary stream: *abbreviate* (1530), *abdicate* (1541), *abduce* (1537), *abduction* (1626), *abduct* (1834), *aberr* (1536-1658), *aberration* (1651), *abjure* (1501), *abnormal* (1836), *abnormity* (1731), *abolition* (1529), *aborigines* (1547), *absorb* (1490), *abstract* (*vs.* concrete) (1557), *abstruse* (1599), *absurd* (1557), *abuse,* noun (1538). Evidence of the same sort is afforded by the long list of English words beginning with *ante-,* the earliest of which is *antecedent* (1543).

By no means all of these Latin importations, however, found a permanent place in English use. Words such as *adminiculation, allect, annect, applicate,* and *assentation,* which were sponsored by the sixteenth-century writer, Sir Thomas Elyot, have been rejected and now seem pedantic

---

[4] *Cf.* L. P. Smith, *The English Language,* p. 67.

monstrosities. Even at the time when the importation of Latin words was most active, the extravagance of the movement was the subject of ridicule. Sir Thomas Wilson in his *Arte of Rhetorike*, published in 1553, satirizes the extravagant fashion in a fictitious letter supposed to be an application for a church benefice. The letter begins as follows:

   Ponderyng, expendyng, and reuolutyng with my self, youre ingent affabilitie, and ingenious capacitie for mundane affaires: I cannot but celebrate, and extoll your magnifical dexteritie aboue all other. For how could you haue adepted suche illustrate prerogatiue, and domesticall superioritie, if the fecunditie of your ingenie had not been so fertile and wonderfull pregnant. Now therefore beeyng accersited to suche splendente renoume, and dignitie splendidious: I doubte not but you will adiuuate suche poore adnichilate orphanes, as whilome ware condisciples with you, and of antique familiaritie in Lincolneshire.

The vogue for classical words led, in fact, not only to ridicule, but to a definite purist reaction. Sir John Cheke, first Regius Professor of Greek at Cambridge, not only advocated in theory the exclusive use of native English words, but put his purist theory into actual practice. He began a translation of the New Testament in which use was to be made exclusively of native words. The strange effect of this excessive purism may be judged from some of the words that appear in the Cheke translation, words like the substitutes for Latin used in the Old English period. Strange is the effect produced by words such as *moond* for *lunatyke* (Tyndale), *outpeopling* for captivity, *tollers* for publicans, *hunderder* for centurion, *frosent* for apostle, *biwordes* for parables, *crossed* for crucified, *freschman* for proselyte. A knowledge of the conflicting tendencies in the sixteenth century adds to one's appreciation of the remarkable diction in the Authorized Version of the Bible, the purity of which can be explained only as due to conscious art on the part of the sixteenth-century translators who obviously adhered to the purist party.

The conscious efforts at enriching the English language by words imported from the classical languages have not been repeated in later times. The sixteenth century was succeeded by a period of classic restraint. Many of the classical words already borrowed were sifted out in the course of the seventeenth century. The words retained were assimilated and fitted into idiomatic English.

At the same time the habit of borrowing has never entirely ceased. The development in science which has been so marked a feature of the last three centuries has been attended by the creation of technical words, and as already explained in an earlier chapter, the source to which the scientist has resorted most frequently for his new terms has been the classical tongues. Familiarity with different sciences brings familiarity with their technical terms, and in this way learned classical terms find their way into the popular vocabulary. From the technical vocabulary of law come into popular use such Latin terms as *alibi, subpœna, bona fide, proviso, alias,* and *affidavit.* From varied sources come such words as *post mortem, tandem, item, prospectus* (1777), *impetus, deficit, bonus, sinecure, excelsior* (1878), *millennium,* 'period of happiness' (1832), *delirium tremens* (1813), *terminus* (of railroad) (1836), *referendum* (1882), *libido* (20th century).

Borrowing from Latin, it has been seen, goes back to a period before the English language existed as a distinct language. The borrowing has never ceased. Various attempts have been made to estimate the total amount of the debt of the English language to Latin. The period in English literature when the classical element in the vocabulary was most freely used, was in the second half of the eighteenth century. In passages from the writings of Gibbon, it has been computed that thirty per cent of the words are of foreign derivation. In the writings of Gibbon's contemporary, Samuel Johnson, the percentage is nearly as high, twenty-eight per cent. Against these extreme figures may be set those for Tennyson's verse, twelve per cent, for Shakespeare, ten per cent, and for that monument of pure English, the King James version of the Bible, six per cent.[5]

One must not misinterpret these statistics. The statistics for the Bible are based on a count of all the words, repetitions included, in three of the gospels. Obviously the simple native elements are the ones most frequently used. In a concordance, or list of different words used, it has been estimated that only about forty per cent of the words in the Bible are native.[6]

Still another statistical method has recently been applied in the attempt to measure the amount of the debt of English to Latin. It has been shown that of the words beginning with A in Harper's *Latin Dictionary* about one in four or five have, directly or indirectly, found their way into English. That is to say, the English language has absorbed about a quarter of the whole Latin vocabulary.[7]

Along with the Latin element in English must in all propriety be considered the Greek, especially since with few exceptions the earliest Greek words to be introduced into English, as well as many at later periods, came through the medium of Latin, and since Greek derivatives in English are, many of them, more or less Latinized in form. Borrowing from Greek, like that from Latin, goes back to an early period. Among the words brought with them to Great Britain by the invading Angles and Saxons were at least two derived from the Greek. One of these, *devil*, seems to have found its way into the speech of northern

---

[5] Emerson, *Brief History of the English Language*, p. 119.
[6] Trench, *English Past and Present*, p. 31.
[7] Greenough and Kittredge, *Words and Their Ways in English Speech*, p. 106.

Teutonic peoples through the Goths, and the contact established by them with Greek Christianity.[8] The other word in question is *church*, which came through the Latin, but which, like most of the early Christian terms in Latin, is of Greek origin (*kuriakon*, 'Lord's house').

Of the Latin Christian terms, already cited, brought to England by the early Roman missionaries, a great many were of Greek origin. Such words as *abbot, monk, priest, clerk*, and *school* bear testimony to the early organization of the Christian church among Greek-speaking people. The early indebtedness to the Greeks in the science of medicine is indicated by such words as *dropsy, palsy, quinsy, tansy*, and *treacle*. These words adopted into popular use have become so modified that only the trained etymologist will recognize in them the Greek *hudrops* (from *hudr-* 'water'); *paralusis; kunagke,* 'dog throttle'; *athanasia,* 'deathlessness'; and *theriakon,* 'pertaining to a wild beast.'

But the importation of Greek words on a large scale did not begin until the time of the Revival of Learning. Since that time the influx of Greek words has been a continuous one. Modern science, stimulated by a knowledge of earlier Greek science, began by borrowing Greek names for Greek conceptions. In this way there became established a form of association between the Greek language and science, and the practice has become established of giving Greek names to conceptions arrived at by modern science.

It is not easy to convey an impression of the English debt to Greek in its technical nomenclature. Let us take by way of illustration a few particular sets of words. The terms of literature and rhetoric will serve the purpose. Of Greek origin are the following literary terms: *poetry, epic, lyric, drama, tragedy, comedy, bucolic, elegy, epigram,*

---

[8] Greenough and Kittredge, *op. cit.*, p. 156.

idyl, theater, scene, melodrama, prologue, episode, epilogue, rhythm, ode, threnody, epithalamium, strophe, antistrophe, dactyl, anapest, etc. To Greek, rhetoric owes the terms: *rhetoric, theme, thesis, topic, epitome, apothegm, emphasis, climax, apostrophe, metaphor, trope, phrase, paraphrase, paragraph, parenthesis, period, graphic, laconic, idiom, dialogue, apology, comma, colon, hyphen, synonym, anonymous, pseudonym, sarcasm,* etc.

Among the natural sciences let us take, for the sake of illustration, the science of botany. To Greek botany owes: *botany, ecology, taxonomy, protoplasm, cytoplasm, stigma, anther, petal, calyx, cryptogam, spore, endogen, exogen, angiosperm, gymnosperm, chlorophyl, perianth, parasite, epiphyte, geotropism, heliotropism,* etc.

In the field of sports Greek has yielded such words as *gymnastics, athlete, acrobat, trophy, stadium.*

In physiology and medicine the number of Greek words is almost countless, from the early names already cited, to modern *adenoids, osteopath,* and *pyorrhea.* Any attempt to count such words would be vain, since the immediate future is likely to bring into use a constant succession of new Greek derivatives, keeping pace with the progress in science.

A particularly interesting and valuable contribution of Greek to English is the series of personal names. Of Greek origin are such indispensable names as *Alexander, Bernice, Catharine, Christopher, Cora, Dorothea, Eugene, Eunice, George, Helen, Homer, Ida, Irene, Leon, Margaret, Myron, Nicholas, Peter, Phoebe, Philip, Phyllis, Sophia, Stephen,* and *Theodore.*[9]

The debt of English both to Greek and to Latin is particularly apparent in its stock of prefixes and suffixes. Detailed consideration of this subject must be reserved

---

[9] These lists of Greek words and names are from H. A. Hoffman, *Everyday Greek* (Chicago, 1919).

for another chapter.[10] Suffice it here to say that the value of these classical prefixes and suffixes to English is inestimable. These products of an ancient civilization serve to express some of the most striking features of modern life. The Latin *super* enters into word combinations to express the intense modern striving after progress in such words as *superman, supercircus,* and *superdreadnaught.* Another characteristic feature of modern life, the production of machinery that is superseding older methods of hand labor, finds expression in the hundreds of new names formed with the Greek prefix *auto-*.

The debt of the English language to the classical Greek and Latin is one hard to measure. In Rome and many other cities of modern Italy may be seen buildings constructed of material derived from structures of ancient times. In England the same is true. For instance, in the walls of the abbey church of St. Albans may be seen the narrow Roman type of brick derived from the ancient buildings of Roman Verulamium on whose site modern St. Albans stands; and in English towns along the Tyne may be discovered older buildings built from material that once composed the great Roman wall. The English language, in like manner, has pillaged antiquity. If the nature of thought is conditioned by the quality of the language which forms its supporting structure, then the debt of modern civilization is inestimable, since modern languages make use of words in which are concentrated the products of ancient thought.

REFERENCES FOR FURTHER READING

O. JESPERSEN, *Growth and Structure of the English Language* (Leipzig, 1912), §§ 28-32, 39-49, 114-151.
L. P. SMITH, *The English Language* (New York, 1912), pp. 40-48, 178-182.

---

[10] Ch. xviii.

T. N. TOLLER, *Outlines of the History of the English Language* (Cambridge, 1900), pp. 41-46, 78-101, 272-284.

H. BRADLEY, *The Making of English* (New York, 1904), pp. 80-82, 93-101.

GREENOUGH AND KITTREDGE, *Words and their Ways in English Speech* (New York, 1901), Ch. viii.

H. A. HOFFMAN, *Everyday Greek* (Chicago, 1919).

W. W. SKEAT, *Principles of English Etymology* (Oxford, 1887), Vol. I, Ch. xxi; Vol. II, Chs. x, xi, xiii.

CHAPTER IX

THE FRENCH ELEMENT

The English language has been said to be French badly pronounced. This remark, facetious in intent and exaggerated in character, nevertheless conveys a considerable element of truth. The English language has taken thousands of words from the French, and in consequence of the divergent development of words in the two languages, the English derivatives have come to differ greatly in form and in meaning from the corresponding words surviving in modern French.

The initial impetus toward extensive borrowing from French came as a consequence of the Norman Conquest of England. Even before the Conquest, to be sure, French words had begun to find their way into English. In the reign of Edward the Confessor, who in consequence of the Danish Conquest, had spent his early life in exile in France, the French atmosphere of the English court is responsible for the introduction of a few French words, about a dozen of which, including *purse, sot, castle, turn, trail, mantle, market, clerk,* and *false,* are recorded in English literature before the Conquest.[1]

In the few existing specimens of the written English of the twelfth century, the century immediately following the Conquest, there appear a small number of French words, consisting for the most part of terms such as *justice, war, peace, tower, treason, prison, court, crown, empress, sacrament, prior, chaplain, saint, grace, mercy, charity,* and

---

[1] F. Kluge, *Englische Studien,* Vol. XXI, pp. 334-335.

faith, which reflect the influence of French-speaking rulers and that of a church controlled by men trained in French schools. The great flood of French words, however, did not begin to come until more than two centuries after the Conquest and did not reach its height until the second half of the fourteenth century, under conditions which remain to be described.

The immediate result of the Conquest was that all the important places in church and in court, as well as in government, were filled by French-speaking adherents of the conquering Norman. In consequence French came to be the language of the law-courts, the language of the schools. Any Englishman, in order to defend his property rights or personal rights, needed to know French, the language of the law-courts. Any Englishman, in order to gain an education, needed to know French, the language of school instruction. The result may readily be imagined. French came to be the language of the higher social strata of whatever race; English was relegated to the use of the inferior classes. The native language continued to be used by the humble classes, but its position was much like that of the Welsh language in modern Wales.

The consequences to the English language are obvious. The language in which, during the period before the Conquest, had been composed a considerable body of literature, in verse and in prose, practically ceased to be used in literary composition. From the twelfth century, the century following the Conquest, have come down to us only a few specimens of written English. The language, confined in great part to use among the illiterate, suffered serious loss in its vocabulary. For instance, the remarkably rich special vocabulary of Old English poetry suddenly and completely disappeared, and in general the vocabulary became restricted to that in colloquial use among uncultivated people.

The growth in English national feeling, however, beginning in the second half of the thirteenth century and reaching remarkable intensity in the fourteenth century, is associated with a change in the position of the English language. English patriotism came to be associated with the use of the native English speech, and by the second half of the fourteenth century the English language was restored to use in law-courts, in school instruction, and even more important, in the productions of England's greatest literary artists. This half century is marked by a revival of literary composition in English, including such important works as the *Vision Concerning Piers Plowman, Sir Gawain and the Green Knight,* the works of Wycliffe, of Gower, and above all, of Chaucer.

The conditions for the importation of French words were remarkably favorable. There entered into the situation the impoverishment of the English vocabulary on account of centuries of disuse in literary composition, also the position of French in England, since the Conquest, not only an official language, but the language used by English literary artists and, in the time of Chaucer, hardly less familiar to them than their native English. That English under such circumstances should have absorbed French words almost to the saturation point, offers no occasion for surprise.

The transfusion of words from French to English, however, did not by any means cease at the close of this special period. The language having once formed the habit of borrowing, and having words French in form, was especially receptive to other words similar in form. Then, too, for centuries English culture, like that of the rest of Europe, leaned heavily on French. French literary works were translated into English and, more important still, literary products in Italian and Spanish, as well as in the classical Greek and Latin, reached English readers less

THE FRENCH ELEMENT 125

often through direct translation into English, than indirectly, by English translation of French translation. In consequence many words of Italian origin such as *caprice* and *alert,* and of Latin origin, such as *texture,* appear in English in a French form.

In another way the dominance of the French language in the period following the Conquest has permanently affected the English vocabulary. In certain departments of life words of French origin still continue to dominate. This is true, for instance, of the words for cookery and soldiering and dress. This French dominance is particularly manifest in the vocabulary of law. The prestige of the French language in legal affairs, established in the Norman period, has never been lost. In the year 1362, by royal decree, the English language was reëstablished as the language for pleading in the law-courts. But the established habit of using French persists in many cases. The phrase *le roi le veut* still is used as the sign of royal assent to acts of the British Parliament. The court crier's proclamation, *Oyez* (Lat. *auditis,* 'attention'), still marks the opening of American courts of law. It is, then, not surprising to find in legal French the origin of such ordinary English words as *mortgage, forfeit, bail, bailiff, jury, larceny, lease, perjury, assets, embezzle, disclaim, distress, seize, improve, culprit, attach, quit, matter of fact.*[2]

The stream of words from French to English has been a continuous one. In the time of Shakespeare, for instance, make their first appearance in English not only many an ephemeral word of the period, but a striking number of French derivatives that have since become permanently fixed in English. Some of these words, with the dates of their earliest citation in the Oxford Dictionary, are: *havoc* 1585; *budge* (verb) 1590; *buff* (animal

---

[2] *Cf.* L. P. Smith, *The English Language,* p. 35.

name) 1580; *plot* 1590; *march* (military) 1590; *lobby* 1553; *ninny* 1593; *mimic* 1602; *fallacy* (logical) 1562; *massacre* 1581; *sentinel* 1579; *officious* ('meddlesome') 1602; *attack* 1600; *ambuscade* 1582; *escalade* 1598; *barricade* 1590; *palisade* 1600; *cuirassier* 1551; *dragoon* 1622; *alexandrine* 1589; *quatrain* 1585; *gazette* 1605; *belvedere* 1596; *dessert* 1600; *fricasee* (noun) 1568.

The general influence of French culture appears in these words. In the second half of the seventeenth century the stream of imported words is swollen anew due to new conditions. In the oft-quoted words of Macaulay, "France united at that time almost every species of ascendancy. Her military glory was at its height. . . . Her authority was supreme in all matters of good breeding from a duel to a minuet. . . . In literature she gave law to the world." When one recalls the intimate relations at this time between the English court and the French, particularly the residence of Charles II in France in exile before the Restoration of 1660, one is not surprised to see signs of the influence of French culture, to be observed for instance in the extension of the Tudor English palace at Hampton Court, reflecting in its architecture and landscape gardening the Renaissance fashions prevalent in France. One finds it easy to understand the renewed readiness with which French words and expressions found adoption in English speech. The ascendancy of French culture is reflected in borrowed military terms such as *cannonade* 1655, *commandant* 1687, *campaign* 1656, *corps* 1711, *platoon* 1637; literary terms such as *lampoon* 1645, *memoir* 1673, *critique* 1702; art terms such as *contrast* (verb) 1695, *retouch* 1685, *group* (noun) 1686, *profile* 1656, *miniature* (noun) 1645, *flageolet* 1659, *recitative* 1645, *ritornelle* 1684, *serenade* 1656, *symphony* (mod. meaning) 1665; terms expressing varied aspects of elegant life such as *calash* 1666, *ombre* 1660, *piquet* 1646, *capot* 1651, *quint* (in cards)

1680, *caprice* 1667, *intrigue* (noun) 1656, *foible* (noun) 1673, *beau* (noun) 1687, *brunette* 1713; modes of dress and of cuisine: *ragout* 1664, *cravat* 1656, *pantaloons* 1661, *surtout* 1686, *gimp* 1664.[3]

A noteworthy feature of these words is not only their importance in English expression, but the permanency with which they have become established in English use. For they did not fail to feel the lash of satire from contemporary critics. Addison is in happy vein in the *Spectator* when he represents a young Englishman in the campaign in France writing to his father in terms which the old-fashioned English parent cannot understand without an interpreter. Swift, too, fiercely attacks the new words, including French importations, which, in his opinion, were corrupting the speech.

Another noteworthy feature of this later set of borrowed French words is the French mode of pronunciation which persists to some extent in most of them. The pronunciation of the *qu* in *coquette*, the *i* in *caprice*, *critique*, etc., the silent *t* in *piquet* and *ragout*, and silent *ps* in *corps*, above all, the final position of the accent in most of them, serve to distinguish these words from earlier importations such as *quit*, *nice*, *picket*, and *corpse*, which have been more thoroughly anglicized. A vacillation between the two modes of pronunciation is to be observed in such words as *trait*, where Americans pronounce the final *t* and English do not, and *croquet*, where the English accent the first syllable, Americans the last.

The habit of borrowing from the French, so early formed, has never been outgrown by the English language. From *persiflage* in the eighteenth century to *camouflage* in the twentieth, the stream of words, while thinner than in earlier periods, has been fairly constant. A comparatively recent introduction into English is indicated by

---

[3] Revision of list quoted by Skeat from Béljáme.

foreign features in the pronunciation or spelling of such words as *crêpe* 1825, *débris* 1708, *detour* 1738, *rôle* 1606, *régime* 1776, *prestige* (modern meaning) 1815, *mirage* 1803, *massage* 1876, *garage* 20th century, *naïveté* 1673, *morale* 1752, and *cuisine* 1786. Many of these newer arrivals have not been admitted to full citizenship but need to carry their passports in the form of italics. Occasionally a word such as *cortège* has been excluded as an undesirable. The Oxford Dictionary, which aims to cite the earliest record of words in English Literature, enables one to determine with some degree of accuracy the amount of borrowing at different periods. A recent statistical study by Jespersen of one thousand English words borrowed from the French (the first one hundred words recorded under the first nine letters and the first fifty under *j* and *l*), reveals not only the continuous borrowing from French during nine hundred years, but the periods when the borrowing was most active.[4]

Before 1050	2	1451-1500	76
1051-1100	2	1501-1550	84
1101-1150	1	1551-1600	91
1151-1200	15	1601-1650	69
1201-1250	64	1651-1700	34
1251-1300	127	1701-1750	24
1301-1350	120	1751-1800	16
1351-1400	180	1801-1850	23
1401-1450	70	1851-1900	2

If now we turn from the consideration of the conditions under which French words were borrowed, and the time when the borrowing took place, to a consideration of the sources from which the French words were themselves derived, we reach certain new and interesting facts about

---

[4] O. Jespersen, *Growth and Structure of the English Language*, p. 93.

THE FRENCH ELEMENT

the ultimate derivation of English words. In the first place it must be borne in mind that the name *French* itself is of Teutonic origin, derived from the name of the Frankish people who in the fifth century overthrew the Roman rule in Gaul and gave to the country its modern name, *France*. In the second place it must be held in mind that the original inhabitants of France were the Gauls, a Celtic people, who were never expelled or annihilated as the Britons of Great Britain seem to have been, but, remaining on their native soil, were Romanized in manners and in language, and form an element in the modern French people. Third, and most important, must be borne in mind the Roman element in the population of France, in consequence of the conquest of Gaul by Cæsar, and particularly the form of Roman speech which became the all but universal language of France, imposed on the Gauls by the conquering Romans and later adopted from the Romanized Gauls by the conquering Franks, Goths, and Burgundians. The French language, therefore, one will observe is not one of pure strain, but a composite speech based on the Latin introduced into Gaul but, like English, containing elements from a variety of foreign sources.

The Teutonic element in French is a considerable one, estimated at about four hundred and fifty words,[5] including Roman words borrowed from the Teutonic tribes, terms principally of war and feudalism introduced by the invading Burgundians, Goths, and Franks, and later terms derived from intercourse particularly with Scandinavians and with Low German neighboring people. Of these Teutonic words in French, the number that have entered English has been estimated at about three hundred,[6] and includes some of the most essential words of the English

---
[5] Brachet, quoted by Skeat, Vol. II, p. 244.
[6] Skeat, Vol. II, p. 244 and list in Appendix to *Etymological Dictionary*.

vocabulary, such as *blanch, blank, blue, booty, butcher, button, buttress, choice, coat, crush, dance, fee, flank, frank, freight.*

Regarding English words of Celtic French origin one is upon somewhat uncertain ground as in the case of English words derived from the Celtic of the British Isles. A list of words which may belong to this class is impressive, including such everyday words as *attach, attack, baggage, bar, basin, beak, branch, brave, bray, car, career, carol, carpenter, carry.*[7]

But of course by far the most important element in the French language is that derived from the Latin. The French language, along with the Italian, Spanish, Portuguese, Roumanian, and several dialectal forms of speech in Switzerland and elsewhere, is classed as a Romance language, that is to say, a language derived from one of the vulgar or popular forms of speech carried by the Romans with them to the various provinces. The form of popular speech carried by the Romans into Gaul differed in many ways from the classical form of Latin, which had become reduced to definite fixed rules and at an early time showed many of the marks of a dead language. For instance, in this form of Vulgar Latin the word for 'horse' was not the Classical Latin *equus,* but *caballus,* from which comes modern French *cheval* and the various related English words, such as *cavalry* and *chivalry.* The word for 'cat' was not Classical Latin *felo,* but *cattus,* from which come French *chat,* and through an earlier French form, the English *cat.* The Vulgar Latin in Gaul was also distinguished by concentration of stress on the accented syllable of the word and a consequent weakening or loss of the final syllables of Latin words, as well as modification of the syllable with the added stress. For instance, Latin *honorem* became French *honeur.* In the course of the

---

[7] Skeat, Vol. II, p. 242.

ninth, tenth, and eleventh centuries, the debased form of Latin was gradually introduced into use in writing and eventually came to be the cultivated form of speech, quite distinct from Latin, from which modern French has descended. From Latin, then, first debased in popular speech and then elevated anew to literary use, came one of the most important elements in the English vocabulary, an element to be reckoned with that derived directly from Latin in forming an estimate of the total contribution of Latin to the English vocabulary.

But the French language, although descended from a vulgar form of Latin, has never been free from the influence of cultivated Latin. Since its affinity to Latin is so obvious, and since Latin words, therefore, at all times have fitted naturally into the French vocabulary, French even more than English, has, throughout its history, borrowed words from the cultivated Latin, which under the influence of centuries of culture, had a more fully formed vocabulary, one better qualified to express intellectual attainment. In consequence, in the French vocabulary are to be distinguished different strata; on the one hand, popular words derived from Vulgar Latin but modified in form through popular use; on the other hand, words coming by learned channels from literary Latin. These learned words coming into French directly from Latin, coincide, therefore, with Latin borrowings in English. In consequence it is often impossible in the case of English words to determine whether they have been taken directly from Latin or, indirectly, through the learned vocabulary of French.

One interesting consequence of the double route followed by Latin words in entering French and in entering English is that frequently the one Latin word has been the source of two distinct words in French or in English; one a learned borrowing, the other descended directly through the popular language, with consequent modification in form and often in meaning. Such Latin doublets existed in English independent of French influence. The Latin word *monasterium*, for instance, of Greek creation, entered English at an early period and in popular use was changed in form to *minster* and in meaning so as to apply first to a church connected with a monastery and later, in loose popular use, to a large church indistinguishable from cathedral. Later the word was borrowed anew from the Latin in the form *monastery*, which has retained not only its early form but its original meaning. In the same way the Greek *presbuteros*, meaning 'elder,' entering English through Latin, has yielded two words different in form and meaning, the word *priest* modified by popular use, and the learned *presbyter* which gives its name to the Presbyterian church, the church governed by presbyters or elders.

If there are in English a number of instances of two or more words derived directly from one Latin word, in French the phenomenon is far more frequent. The greater number of French words, as has been remarked, are derived from Vulgar Latin, but have been modified in form and in meaning through centuries of popular use. These popular French words have in many instances been joined later by learned words direct from Classical Latin, which in turn have often found their way into popular use. Hence a conspicuous feature of the French vocabulary is the frequency of doublets such as: *fragile, frêle; blasphémer, blâmer; diacon, doyen; debit, dette; déposition, depôt; securité, sûreté.*

Frequently in the development of Latin words to their modern French form, several stages may be distinguished. Let us take, for example, the history of the Latin *fides,-em*. In Vulgar Latin the prevailing form of this word was the accusative form, *fidem*. In popular use this word lost its

THE FRENCH ELEMENT

ending, the vowel was modified to *ei*, and the *d* at the end of the root to the spirant *th*, so that about the year 1100, the word had the form *feith*, in which form it was borrowed into English. Later, in French, this word lost its consonantal ending, and it was again borrowed into English in the phrase *par ma fay*, which was in frequent use in the Middle English period. Later, the vowel sound was further modified so that the word appears in modern French as *foi*. Thus from one Latin word have come into English not only the learned form, *fidelity*, but the forms *faith* and *fay*, borrowed at different stages in the development of French. In this way is to be explained series of English words such as: *legal, leal, loyal; regal, royal; gentile, gentle, genteel, jaunty; annoy, ennui; feast, fête; corpse, corps; capital, chief, chef; feeble, foible.*

In still other instances different dialects of French contribute to English words which are variants of one original. Examples are: *warrant, guarantee; reward, regard; resin, rosin; ward, guard; warden, guardian.*

The result is that in the history of words there is a phenomenon analogous to that in the plant world, where a bulb splits into several parts, in this way forming the roots for several distinct plants. This phenomenon in the English vocabulary is a remarkably frequent one. Some interesting instances are: *abbreviate, abridge* (O. Fr. *abregier, abreger,* (Lat. *abbreviare* from *ad* and *brevis,* 'short'); *adamant, diamond; adjudicate, adjudge; adjutant, aid; advocate, avouch, advoke, avoke, avow; balsam, balm; camera, chamber; captain, chieftain; capital, cattle, chattel; collocate, couch; concept, conceit; deacon, dean; debit, debt, due; deposit, depot; diurnal, journal; dominion, dungeon; Egyptian, gypsy; exchequer, checker; fragile, frail; juniper, gin; Magdalen, maudlin; paralysis, palsy; potion, poison; pauper, poor; predicate, preach; radius, ray;*

recuperate, recover; reduplicate, redouble; revindicate, revenge; separate, sever; supervise, survey.[8]

In the case of the learned forms cited above, one cannot always be sure whether the English borrowing has been through the French or direct from the Latin, but most of such words have taken forms like those of learned words borrowed from the French. It should also be remarked in passing that the doublets here discussed are not the only ones in English, since, as remains to be shown later, within the English language a differentiation has taken place in a large number of instances, resulting in two or more words from one.

Closely related to the subject of doublets is another feature of the development of the borrowed French words in the English language. At the beginning of the chapter is quoted the remark that English is French badly pronounced. This statement has its foundation in the fact that many English words are closely similar to French words in appearance, but strikingly different in sound, and more subtly, but not the less really, different in meaning. The divergent development of words in the two languages offers interesting material for language study, affording, as it does, admirable illustration of the way in which a single word in different environments may come to express meanings radically different. The changes are by no means confined to one language, but in English the competition between native and borrowed words, which, it has been shown, led to change in the meaning of the native English words, had an effect hardly less striking on the borrowed words. The following parallel lists will illustrate the divergence in the use of words in the two languages. It must be remarked in advance by way of caution that

---

[8] For a far more extended list see E. A Allen, *Mod. Lang. Assoc. Publications*, Vol. XXIII, pp. 184-239.

THE FRENCH ELEMENT 135

the single meaning assigned to different French words is often only one of a variety of meanings.

English	French
abbot (Lat. origin)	abbé, priest
advice	avis, opinion
agreement	agrément, quality of pleasing
alter	alterer, to change from good to bad
amiable	aimable, kind
amuse	amuser, to entertain
ancient	ancien, old
annoy	ennuyer, to bore
appointment	appointements, salary
arrest	arrêter, stop
arrive	arriver à, to attain
assist	assister, to be present
assassinate	assassiner, to murder
assurance	assurance, insurance
bachelor	bachelier, graduate of a Lycée
bureau, chest of drawers	bureau, office
bounty	bonté, goodness
brave	brave, brave, honest, good
card	carte, ticket, bill, map, etc.
chair	chaire, pulpit
chamber, sleeping room	chambre, room
character	caractère, temper
command	commander, to order (at restaurant)
complexion	complexion, disposition
conscience	conscience, perception, consciousness
confectionery	confections, things to wear
constable	connétable, high dignitary
concurrence	concurrence, competition
content	content, satisfied, pleased
courtesan	courtisan, courtier
damage	(c'est) dommage, it is too bad
dame	dame, lady
defend	defendre, to forbid
demand	demander, to ask for
desire	desirer, to want to
dispute	disputer, to discuss, to argue
easy	(être bien) aise, to be glad
embrace	embrasser, to kiss

English	French
fierce	fier, proud
feast	fête, celebration, holiday
foil	feuille, leaf
figure	figure, face
gallantry	galanterie, politeness
gentle	gentil, nice
govern	gouverner, direct
grand	grand, large
grace	grâce, pardon, mercy
habit	habit, garment
harbor	auberge, inn
harness	harnais, trappings
herb	herbe, grass
honest	honnête, respectable, modest, polite, etc.
history	histoire, story
infant	enfant, child
intention	entente, understanding
jolly	joli, pretty
journey	journée, day, day's work
just	juste, exact, correct
large	large, broad
licence	licence, leave
liquor	liqueur
magnificent	magnifique, fine
march	marcher, to walk
mercy	merci, thanks
merchan	marchand, dealer
meddle	mêler, to mix
mistress	maîtresse, governess, landlady
money	monnaie, small change
noun	nom, name
nurse	nourrice, foster-mother
occasion	occasion, opportunity
parent	parent, relative
parley	parler, to speak
person	personne, no one
petty	petit, small
physician	physicien, physicist
plume	plume, pen

English	French
port	porte, gate, door
proper	propre, own
quart	quart, quarter
quit	quitter, to leave
reason	(vous avez) raison, right
reputation	reputation, character
rest	rester, to remain
robe	robe, gown, dress
sage	sage, good (in behavior)
siege	siège, seat
savage	sauvage, wild
spirit	esprit, wit, intellect
spiritual	spirituel, witty
sturdy	étourdi, giddy
tempt	tenter, to try
tense	temps, time, tense, weather
tableau	tableau, picture
tavern	taverne, restaurant
travel	travailler, to work
trivial	trivial, trite, vulgar
voyage	voyager, to travel
wicket	guichet, grating, door, shutter

CHAPTER X

VARIED SOURCES

Preceding chapters have shown something of the nucleus of Teutonic words that made up the earliest English language. They have shown how this vocabulary expanded under the influence of culture in the period before the Conquest, and how it shrank under disuse in the following period. They have shown how the impoverished language was enriched anew by words representing the products of classical culture, and how it has never ceased to derive words from its kindred Teutonic languages on the Continent.[1]

A wider field of influence remains to be considered, for the English language has laid under contribution the speech of almost every people on the globe. No other empire before the British, in the world's history, included within its bounds lands in all the five continents and islands in all the seas. The commerce of no other nation has ever been so wide in its range. British exploration and British commerce have reached every corner of the earth. Besides this, it must be held in mind that the most numerous single branch of the English-speaking peoples, is that occupying the United States of America, and that the English-speaking people of the United States includes in its numbers people from practically every quarter of the globe. Under such circumstances the English language has been brought into contact with practically every other form of speech and has not failed to absorb elements from them all.

---

[1] The word lists used in this chapter are based generally on those by Skeat, but with corrections and additions.

To begin with the race that came earliest into contact with the Teutonic English, we may well first consider the contributions to English from peoples of the Celtic race. Place-names and archæological remains bear witness to the earlier occupation by Celtic peoples of lands stretching across entire Europe, from Galicia in Asia Minor to the extreme western points of Europe, in Spain, in Brittany, and in Ireland. A few scattering elements of language, mainly place-names, survive to support the evidence of archæology concerning the earlier Celtic inhabitants of Europe. But the principal contact between English and Celtic speech was established by the English settlement of the British Isles. A good number of Celtic words have come into English through the French from the original Celtic inhabitants of France, one province of which, Brittany, is still occupied by a Celtic people speaking the Celtic Breton language. But it is from the Celtic inhabitants of the British Isles that Celtic elements have entered English speech most directly.

A point in English history much discussed and never finally disposed of, is the fate of the early Britons whom the Angles and Saxons dispossessed of their home in England. Had they generally, like their kinsmen in Gaul, adopted Latin culture and Latin speech, or were they annihilated, or completely expelled, or absorbed in a servile condition, in the new English race? It is a remarkable fact that the Celtic peoples of the British Isles to whom literary and culture historians are disposed to attribute some of the finest and noblest elements of the British spirit, should have left so little tangible evidence of their influence in the form of definite Celtic word contributions.

On the subject of words borrowed by the Anglo-Saxons from the dispossessed Britons, one needs to speak with caution. The number of such words that have been cited is remarkably small. Modern English words probably belonging to this class are *bin, brat, down* 'hill,' *mattock, crock.*

Later borrowings from Celtic inhabitants of the British Isles are somewhat more numerous, but are still, as compared with words from sources less close, remarkably few.[2] From the Welsh are derived *coracle, cromlech, crowder* 'fiddler', *eisteddfod, flannel, flummery, maggot.* From the Gaelic of Scotland come *cateran, clachan, clan, claymore, coronach, gillie, inch* 'island,' *loch, mackintosh, ptarmigan, reel* 'dance,' *slogan, whisky.* From the Erse of Ireland come: *brogue, bog, galore, pillion, colleen, culdee, gallow-glass, kerne, shamrock, lough, mavourneen, shillelagh, spalpeen, Tory, usquebaugh.* Surely this is an unimpressive list, or impressive on account of its very meagerness.

Apart from French the two modern languages to which English is most indebted, are the other Romance languages, Italian and Spanish. Italy, as the land from which spread the ideas of the Renaissance, was particularly influential in the sixteenth century. In the language of Shakespeare and his contemporaries words from the Italian appear frequently. To the sixteenth-century scholar, Roger Ascham, "English Italianate" was an object of special aversion. Many of these Italianate words have not survived, but a number of words, still in common use, had their introduction at this period, such as: *attitude, cicerone, fiasco, influenza, isolate, motto, stanza, umbrella.*[3] In later times the stream of Italian words, though slender, has continued practically without interruption down to the time of *macaroni, spaghetti,* and *wop.* The group of words: *aria, basso, cantabile, fantasia, finale, intermezzo, legato, maestoso, oboe, opera, piano, pizzicato, prima donna, staccato, tremolo,* bears eloquent testimony to Italian influence in English music. A similar group of terms: *bust, chiaroscuro, dado, fresco,*

---

[2] Skeat, Appendix VI, p. 3.
[3] Bradley, p. 105.

intaglio, cameo, mezzotint, colonnade, cornice, corridor, grotto, niche, pilaster, motto, replica, studio, terra cotta, indicates something of the indebtedness of English art to Italy.[4]

In the case of a great many words, French has been an intermediary. English has taken from French, words which French had taken from Italian. Indeed, such words exceed in number the words borrowed direct. A few examples are *alarm, alert, apartment, arcade, artisan, bulletin, cabriolet, cadence, caprice, caress, carnival, contrast.*[5]

A great many English words, derived from Latin, directly or through the French, resemble closely Italian words derived from the same Latin source. A comparison of these cognate words, English and Italian, and of certain English words borrowed from Italian, with the corresponding Italian words, offers further interesting illustration of the way in which one word in different languages may come to serve to express meanings far apart. In the following lists the meanings cited are not only the meanings of the Italian words, but meanings in which the contrast between Italian and English is particularly marked.

English	*Italian*
branch	branca, claw, clutch
fracas	fracasso, noise, wreck
disdain	disdegno, indignation
major	maggiori, ancestors
talent	talento, desire
principle	principio, beginning
caitiff	cattivo, bad
fastidious	fastidioso, tiresome, troublesome
voluble	volubile, variable
front	fronte, forehead, face
delicate	delicato, gentle
vague	vago, rambling, inconstant

[4] Bradley, p. 102; Jespersen, p. 152.
[5] Skeat, Appendix VI, p. 3.

English	Italian
robe	roba, goods, possessions
disgrace	disgrazia, accident, misfortune
insinuate	insinuare, indicate
fatigue	fatica, toil
suggestion	soggezione, constraint, awe
prejudice	pregiudizio, damage, harm
amorous	amorosa, affectionate
uniform	uniformare, to conform
proof	prova, experiment, trial

Borrowing from Spanish on a large scale began at about the same time as in the case of the Italian. In the sixteenth century Spain reached the height of her national power and glory, and at no other time have relations between England and Spain been so close in a political or in a literary way. The English language of the period reflects the influence by words, borrowed directly or through the French, such as: *armada, comrade, desperado, disembogue, dispatch, grandee, negro, peccadillo, punctilio, renegade.*[6]

In the succeeding centuries Spain contributed a number of words to the English language, including such words as *brocade, anchovy* (Basque), *armadillo, booby, capsize, caste, cigar, cork, guerilla, junta, embargo, mosquito, quadroon, cascara, sherry, tornado, vanilla.*

But in language as well as in history, some of the most interesting achievements of Spain are in connection with the discovery and settlement of America. This American activity on the part of Spain has left its record in language. From Mexico and the West Indies Spain introduced to Europe: *cacao, chocolate, cocoa* (nut), *tobacco, maize, hammock, barbecue,* and *potato,* and the Spanish form of the Indian names for these products found its way into English as well as into most other European languages. On the other hand, Spain left in record of her occupation of Florida not only the name of that state, but a Spanish name for

---

[6] Bradley, p. 103.

one of the most characteristic features of its waters, the *alligator* (Spanish *el lagarto* 'the lizard'). She introduced the Dutch (or Bohemian) coin, the dollar, with its Dutch name, to the Western hemisphere. She also left behind her in the western states acquired from her by the United States, not only inhabitants of Spanish blood, and proper names such as *Sierra* and *Colorado,* and interesting forms of architecture, but a set of words which have found their way into American English and are rapidly establishing themselves in universal English use. Among these contributions are numbered such interesting words as: *adobe, sombrero, canyon, lariat, bonanza, fandango, corral, vaquero, calaboose, lasso, ranch, loco'ed, broncho, cinch, bunco, vamoose, chapparal.*[7]

From Portuguese, the principal Romance language not yet considered, the amount of borrowing was somewhat less, corresponding to the relatively minor part of Portugal in the history of European culture and of American colonization. From Portuguese, however, directly or indirectly, come a number of important words, including *binnacle, caste, cobra, palaver, madeira, port* (wine), *molasses, pimento, tank, fetish.*

The European peoples most closely associated with the English-speaking peoples have been those belonging to the Teutonic and Romance groups. The progress of history, however, is marked by greater and greater intimacy between distant peoples; commerce in products and in ideas has been accompanied by commerce in words, so that there are few, if any, even of the more distant European peoples, from whom the English language has failed to import words. The world shattering events of the immediate past have made familiar to English-speaking peoples the Russian ideas expressed by the Russian words: *vodka, duma, pogrom, czar, mujik, bolsheviki, intelligentsia, soviet.* In

---

[7] Mencken, *The American Language,* p. 86.

earlier times, by various routes, English has received from various languages of the Balto-Slavic group to which Russian belongs, words such as *calash, cravat, siskin, mazurka, mammoth, polka, howitzer, slave, copeck, rouble, samovar, crash* (coarse linen), *verst, ukase, knout.*

From the Hungarian, a language quite outside the Indo-European family, have come words such as: *tokay, coach, shako, vampire.*

Leaving Europe and its languages, for the most part Indo-European, and passing over into Asia, one comes into contact with the Semitic group of languages, including Hebrew and Arabic. From Hebrew, the language associated with the origins of the Christian religion, the language once thought of as the original speech of first created man, the number of words borrowed is smaller than might be expected, due, as has been shown, to the part played by the Greek and Latin as mediums of transmission. A number of Hebrew terms, however, connected with Hebrew religion or custom or religious story, did find their way into English, though often over a circuitous route. Of Hebrew origin are such words as *alleluia, amen, bedlam, cherub, jubilee, manna, Jehovah, Messiah, Pharisee, Satan, rabbi, sabbath, lazar, maudlin, shibboleth.* Besides these terms more or less associated with religion, the Hebrew language contributed a share of the English words designating features of oriental life or products of oriental civilization, from which may be named: *camel, cider, ebony, elephant, hyssop, shekel, cassia, cinnamon, nitre, sapphire, simony, sodomy, damson, leviathan.*

From Arabic, likewise, have come a number of words, more even than from the Hebrew. These words coming into English, as they did most frequently, through other European languages, are most of them not peculiar to English, but belong to a stock of borrowed words common to many of the languages of Europe. Another feature of this set of Arabic derivatives that should be remembered, is that the Arabic-speaking peoples, through contact with the Christian nations of Europe, principally with Spain, not only conveyed ideas that were the products of Arabic culture, but purveyed to Western Europe many products of Greek culture in the period when direct contact between modern Europe and Greek civilization was broken. Among the Greek derivatives that reached Western Europe through Arabic channels may be mentioned: *elixir, talisman, alembic, alchemy, carat.* Among the words of Arabic origin may be named: *albatross, alkali, arrack, attar, azimuth, emir, fakir, fellah, harem, hegira, hookah, islam, koran, mohair, moslem, muezzin, mufti, sheik, sherbet, simoon, sofa,* all of which are classed by Skeat as direct derivatives. By more nomadic routes, through the medium of one or more other languages, routes often as circuitous as those followed by a caravan, have come: *naphtha, Saracen, jasper, myrrh, alcohol, algebra, artichoke, senna, sirocco, zero, arabesque, magazine, caraway, dragoman, crimson, carmine, minaret, alcove, amber, cipher, cotton, cubeb, garble, gazelle, giraffe, martingale, sash* (girdle), *mosque, nadir, ogive, sumach, syrup, talc, lime* (fruit), *mummy, tabor, tambour, tariff, zenith, admiral, assassin, bedouin, sugar, lute, mate* (chess), *mattress, rebeck, saffron, sultan, vizier, ghoul, houri.*

In this list occur a number of doublets, which serve to illustrate the various modifications undergone by the Arabic words on the various routes by which they have reached English. Thus the Arabic word for 'drink' has been imported into English directly in the double form *sherbet* and *shrub;* from Arabic to Spanish, thence to French and thence to English, the same word appears as *syrup.* In the same way the Arabic word *sifr,* 'cipher,' by the Spanish and French route, reaches English as *cipher;* through Low Latin and Italian it enters English as *zero.*

The list of words from the Arabic is an impressive one, revealing at the same time the extent of Arabic culture and the amount of the debt of modern civilization to the Orient. Similar evidence may be gathered from lists of words derived by routes more or less circuitous from the Persian, such as: *divan, mogul, pasha, azure, shah, pajamas, toddy, magic, caravan, satrap, tiger, rice, gherkin, scimitar, taffeta, julep, rook* (chess), *check, checkers, chess, chicanery, shawl, lemon, lilac, scarlet, van* (wagon), *borax, jasmine, lilac, calabash, spinach, kiosk, tulip, turban.*

From the Turkish the number of derivatives is conspicuously small, corresponding with the inferior rank of the Turkish race in culture and its dependence upon the culture of the other oriental races. The borrowed Turkish words refer almost exclusively to features of life distinctively Turkish. Among words of more universal application derived from the Turkish may be mentioned: *bosh, horde, turkey, turquoise, uhlan, coffee* (Arabic origin).

From India have come many words. First there are words which reached Europe at a comparatively early date, names for oriental contributions to European civilization. As examples of this kind of word, words that have reached English by various routes, may be mentioned *pepper, beryl, camphor, sandal* (wood), *indigo, china* (ware), *orange, aniline, candy, calico, cashmere, chintz, sandal, jungle, loot, rupee, punch* (beverage). More recent, and for the most part direct, borrowings from India are: *avatar, brahmin, juggernaut, pundit, rajah, sepoy, poobah, suttee, bandanna, bangle, bungalow, shampoo, thug, pariah, pucka, punkah, curry* (sauce), *kedgeree, cot* (bed), *dinghy, polo.*

In this connection a fact particularly worthy of remark is the small number of words derived either directly or indirectly from China or Japan. The aloofness of earlier European civilization from the Far East is perhaps a fair

VARIED SOURCES 147

inference. Possibly the word *silk* may be traced to Chinese origin. The Chinese, also, are thought to have had a hand in the creation of the word *typhoon*. From China come also *tea, serge, pongee, chowchow, cumquat, ginseng, mandarin, chop* (in chopstick) and perhaps *chop-suey*. It is not easy to extend the list. Even *china* as a name for chinaware seems to have originated in India (whence the pronunciation *chayney* which persisted well into the nineteenth century). From Japan comes *jinrickshaw*, often shortened to *rickshaw*. Recently introduced words such as *samurai, kimono, kudzu* (vine), *hara-kiri, jiu-jitsu, soy* (bean), and *satsuma*, seem to indicate that more words from the Far East may be expected in the near future.

From the languages of the less civilized peoples of Asia and the South Seas come a variety of words such as *bamboo, cheroot, teak, caddy, gong, guttapercha, junk, lory, amuck, orang-outang, sago, gingham, bantam, taboo, patchouli, tattoo, atoll, ukelele*. From various languages of uncivilized Africa come: *canary, chimpanzee, voodoo, hoqdoo, tango, guinea, gorilla, yam, zebra, gnu*.

The wide extension through colonization of the world's area occupied by English-speaking people has naturally exposed the language to new influences, through contact with new objects for which new names were needed, through contact with new peoples with new ways of seeing things. From Australia has come a contribution of new elements to the language, native Australian names such as *boomerang, wombat,* and *kangaroo,* but particularly English words in new combination or applied to new meanings, a feature of the language which remains to be discussed elsewhere.[8]

From America has come an even greater contribution of words, which bear eloquent testimony to the effects of the

---

[8] *Cf.* E. Morris, *Austral English.* J. Lake, *Australasian Supplement* to Webster's *International Dictionary.*

discovery of the New World not only in widening the range of observation in natural history, but in contribution to the material comforts of life long before American political ideals began to make their impress on European civilization. The words, *cacao, chocolate, potato, quinine, tomato, maize,* introduced to Europe by the Spaniards, have been mentioned. To these words may be added *mahogany, cassava, cayman, macaw, cannibal, canoe, chilli* (sauce), *guava, chile* (con carne), *hurricane, guano, papaw, buccaneer, caoutchouc, llama, pampas, puma, alpaca, condor, tapioca, tapir, ipecac, banana, jaguar, coyote, jalap, tolu,* brought to Europe by one or the other of the colonizing powers from the West Indies and South America.

From the North American Indians have been derived not only the place-names, euphonious and uneuphonious, but almost always felicitous, which give distinction to the geography of America, but an interesting set of names for animals and foods and distinctive features of life, some confined to use in the United States, but many of them established in universal English use. From words of this origin may be mentioned *caucus, powwow, hickory, hominy, moccasin, moose, opossum, pemmican, raccoon, skunk, calumet, squaw, toboggan, tomahawk, wampum, wigwam.*

From peoples with whom relations have been established in recent times come ever new additions to the vocabulary. From the Philippines is said to have come the useful word *hike.* The expressive word *husky* is said to be a perversion of the name *Eskimo,* first applied as a name for a dog. From the Eskimo language comes also the word *igloo.*

Throughout this discussion of the sources of the English vocabulary, it must be held in mind that the borrowing of words is by no means a unique peculiarity of the English language. English has drawn heavily from Latin, the language of the parent civilization, but so has German, so has Russian. The words *Kaiser* and *czar,* names of the

VARIED SOURCES

former rulers in Germany and in Russia respectively, are derived from the Latin *Cæsar*. A German dictionary opened entirely at random, reveals on the first page looked at, the classical derivatives borrowed directly or through French, such as: *Rotation, Rotator, Rotazismus, Rottmeister, Rotulieren, Rotunde, Roulade, Roué, Rouleau, Roulette, roulieren, Route, Routine, Routinier, routiniert*, and the page is typical rather than exceptional. The same page from the German dictionary shows *Rotang* 'ratan' (Malayan), *Rubber* (English), *Rubin* 'ruby' (French). The expansion of the English vocabulary by importation of foreign words from varied sources evidently is due in great part to an expansion in knowledge and culture by no means exclusively English. The same word which appears in English *pepper*, appears in French as *poivre*, in German as *Pfeffer*. The word corresponding to *potato* in French is *patate*, in German is *Patate* and *Potaske*, although both in French and in German the more usual word is one of native manufacture from native elements, French *pomme de terre*, commonly shortened to *pomme*, and German *Erdapfel* or *Kartoffel*. The following list of German words will show how even that protected language has not rigidly excluded the new words from various parts of the world: *Anschovis, Zigarre, Kork, Kängaruh, Kamel, Kannibale, Kanoe, Absinth, Azur, Gazelle, Iasmin, Iulap, Karawane, Guttapercha, Orang-utang, tättowieren* (tattoo), *Almanach, Barke, Quinin, Gummi, Basalt, Zebra, Kola, Kakao, Guano, Kautschuk, Tabak, Tamarinde, Tamtam* (tom tom). Such words have become part of a universal language.

The name used for potato may, however, be regarded as more or less typical, exemplifying a preference in French and particularly in German, for native word material. In languages other than English the feeling of nationality expresses itself in a preference for native words, in some countries, notably Germany, leading to organized opposition to the use of foreign words. In England this feeling is not unknown. From the sixteenth century on, opposition to foreign words has often been loudly voiced. The effect, however, has not been great, and the English language has been for centuries, if not the only importing language, at least the only language governed by a free-trade policy.

This propensity of the English has recently been explained by an acute foreign observer as due to "linguistic laziness."[9] The English weakness in foreign languages is notorious, and is shared by Americans. It is pointed out that English and Americans when importing foreign words, try, though often quite ineffectually, to give the word its foreign pronunciation. This disposition is in evidence, for example, in the case of Russian names, and is in marked contrast to French practice which gives French form and French pronunciation to foreign names, and in contrast to the earlier English practice which gave distinctively English form to the Italian cities of Florence (Firenze), Venice (Venezia), Leghorn (Livourno), Naples (Napoli), and to the German and Austrian cities of Munich (München), Nuremberg (Nürnberg), Leipsic (Leipzig), and Vienna (Wien).

The explanation advanced has some degree of plausibility. A more likely explanation, however, is to be found in the English disposition, shown in many ways, to absorb the products of other nations, to appropriate rather than to create. This disposition has been shown in the case of art. In the sixteenth century Holbein was brought over to paint the portraits of English notabilities. At the present time the great houses of England are filled with the art productions of all nations. The British Museum houses some of the principal art treasures of Greece and

---

[9] Jespersen, p. 156.

of Egypt. Eighteenth-century England brought Handel and Hayden to provide music. England of to-day, and America as well, more than other nations, listens to opera sung in foreign languages, in French or German or Italian, conducted and sung by foreign artists. The form of hospitality shown by England and America to products of foreign art and foreign industry, is shown also by the language spoken in the two countries.

CHAPTER XI

BLENDING OF THE VARIOUS ELEMENTS

Coming as they do from such varied sources, the words of the English vocabulary offer some curious phenomena. In connection with the French words of Latin origin, and in connection with words of Arabic origin, mention has been made of the doublets, that is to say, independent words springing from one word owing to different modifications undergone on different routes into English. The various routes that have led to the English language have produced some strange transformations. The word that coming through Anglo-Saxon English produces *shirt*, a garment for the upper part of the body, coming through Scandinavian channels produces the *skirt* for below the waist. In the same way the word that in native English becomes *wain*, comes through the Dutch as *wagon*. From the Persian word for 'turban,' *dulband*, have come not only English *turban*, but *tulip*. The native English *thatch* comes directly from a Teutonic word which through the Dutch yields *deck*. One Persian word for ruler, through its use as the name for the 'king' in the game of chess, and through the migrations of that game, has yielded the common English verb *check;* imported directly in more recent time, the same word appears as *shah*. What is nothing less than a linguistic freak is the pair of words, names for related musical instruments, coming from the Greek *pandoura*, one coming through Italian and French in the form *mandolin*, the other through the Italian, but with Negro modifications, as *banjo*.

The possibility of the multiplication of words is mani-

BLENDING OF THE VARIOUS ELEMENTS

fest. There is, however, a procedure, the reverse of this which has affected many words and which has had a tendency to reduce the number of words. In many cases a word of foreign origin is identical in form with another English word, or if not identical, so closely resembles the English word as to fall into the same sound mold. Hundreds of instances of homonyms, as such word phenomena are called, are to be found in the English vocabulary. Thus five distinct Latin words have entered English with the one form *bay*, and five distinct meanings are preserved: (1) color of a horse; (2) a kind of laurel; (3) an inlet of the sea; (4) a form of window; (5) a bark of a dog. Two words distinct in origin and distinct in meaning appear with the form *curry*, in the phrases 'curry favor' and 'curry sauce.' Three distinct meanings, (1) a mother of beasts, (2) a block to waters in a stream, (3) a form of imprecation, are expressed by three words with the one form, *dam*, yielding a kind of ambiguity grateful to certain people opposed to open profanity. There are two distinct words involved in 'ear of corn' and 'human ear.' The form *flag* represents words from three distinct sources. *Gin*, a form of drink obsolescent in America, coming from the Latin *juniperus*, is quite distinct in origin and in meaning from *gin* in 'cotton gin,' which comes from Latin *ingenium*. *Hue* meaning 'color,' of native derivation, is distinct from *hue* in the phrase 'hue and cry' which comes through the French. *Jet*, the name of a mineral, comes from the same Greek word from which comes *agate;* *jet*, the verb, meaning 'to throw out,' 'to spout,' comes through the French from the Latin. The spelling *lay* in English may represent a verb, 'cause to lie down,' a noun, 'song,' an adjective meaning the reverse of clerical, or an adjective used in the phrase, 'lay figure.' *Main* represents two distinct words in 'the main chance' and in 'might and main.' There is ambiguity in the expression 'it takes more than one swallow to make a summer' owing to the fact that two distinct words have an identical form.

The chief end of the homonym, in the minds of many, is the pun. Perhaps the explanation of the higher estimation of the pun in Shakespeare's time is due to the fact that people of that time were more alive to the incongruity of these words, one in form but diverse in origin. The punning possibilities in the homonyms represented by the forms *wood* and *saw* have been partially exploited in the permutations and combinations of these sounds under the heading "The Story of Esau Wood," the unlimited possibilities of which may be judged from the following passage:

All the wood Esau Wood saw, Esau Wood would saw. In other words, all the wood Esau saw to saw Esau sought to saw.—Finally, no man may ever know how much wood the wood-saw Wood saw would saw, if the wood-saw Wood saw would saw all the wood the wood-saw Wood saw would saw.

In most cases confusion of homonyms is consciously produced, the work of the punster. In a relatively small number of instances, however, the confusion passes from jest to earnest; the confusion becomes fixed in meaning as well as in form. Thus in modern English, distinction has been lost between *cinder* from O. E. *sindor,* 'slag of metals,' and *cinder* from O. Fr. *cendre,* 'ashes'; between *business* from O. E. *besignes,* 'busyness' and *business* from O. Fr. *besogne,* pl. *besognes,* 'care,' 'occupation'; between *nephew* from O. E. *nefa* and nephew from O. Fr. *neveu.* In fact, in such modern English words both form and meaning are composite in character.

The great number of homonyms bears eloquent witness to the great variety of elements that compose the English language, since obviously the number of instances where an imported form would coincide with a native form,

BLENDING OF THE VARIOUS ELEMENTS 155

would be comparatively rare, the exception rather than the rule. Imported words have usually undergone certain modification in form in the process of assimilation into English, but not sufficient to cause them to lose their distinction in form or in meaning.

What then has been the effect of the policy of free-trade followed in the English language? What is the relative value of some of the different elements that compose its vocabulary? Regarding the words derived from the more remote languages there can be little difference of opinion. Most of the words from the languages of other continents have been introduced as names for things the knowledge of which among English-speaking peoples is derived from commerce, intellectual as well as mercantile, with more distant parts of the world. Most of these imported commodities, with many of their imported names, English-speaking peoples use in common with other cultured peoples. In some cases, for instance in that of *caoutchouc*, there is an apparent advantage in the figurative substitution of the English word *rubber* for the awkward foreign word used in many European languages. Few English-speaking people, on the other hand, will contend that English, by adopting the imported word *potato*, has done less well than French with its clumsy *pomme de terre* and its ambiguous shortened form, *pomme*. Nor is any one likely to object to such words as *candle, church, priest, chalk, copper, sock, soap, lily,* and *tiger* which were imported into English before the Norman Conquest along with the first knowledge of the things they name. The practice of adopting foreign names for foreign commodities, from *cinnamon* to *quinine*, from *pepper* to *paprika* is hardly open to valid criticism.

In the case, however, of later words from classical sources, there exists greater division of opinion, or perhaps one may better say, opinion is more vaguely defined. Such words often come into competition with words of native origin, and there often arises an embarrassing question of choice. But in our day there will be few so radical as to deny the value of the classical contribution to the English vocabulary. There can be little question that the reawakening of the human spirit that came with the revival of classical studies was aided by the ready-formed classical words that served to form roads across new tracts of thought. The more abstract classical terms in many cases had, over the more concrete native terms, the advantage of algebraic over arithmetical symbols. By means of the abstract terms it was possible to attain heights in speculation and breadth in generalization unattainable by means of terms still attached to the soil of concrete meaning.

Let us take a few concrete instances. The word *conjugate* is more nicely fitted to use as a term of grammar than would be a newly created English word which should express the meaning 'yoke together' which underlies the Latin derivative. In the same way *conflict* has an advantage over 'strike together' which would be the English translation of the elements in the Latin word. *Connect* has the same advantage over 'tie together,' *construct* over 'heap together,' and *consternation* over 'strewing over' or 'throwing down.' There is evident value, for certain purposes, in detachment from meanings too vividly concrete.

In the development of modern science which followed in the wake of the revival of classical studies, it is not easy to see how the classical words could have been dispensed with, although the German language, to some extent, has done so. The desired precision which is so requisite, has been afforded by the classical words which are dissociated in great part from the distracting effect of concrete meanings. Consider, for instance, the value of such borrowed words as: *addition* (mathematical) 1542, *adverb* 1530, *algebra* 1551, *agriculture* 1603, *anatomy* 1544, *architect* 1563, or of such later ones as: *æsthetic* 1798, *anthracite* 1812, *antiseptic* 1751, *agnostic* 1870. The precision of expression reached by these borrowed terms to express conceptions reached by modern thought, finds its parallel in modern scientific language. The advantage to precision, for example, of such terms as *ventral* and *dorsal* and *caudal* over the native words *under* and *back* and *tail* in the discussion of the anatomy of lower forms of animal life can hardly be doubted. *Iron pyrites* is obviously superior to *fool's gold*. Even in simple language, words such as *difficult* offer less room for ambiguity than words such as *hard* with their variety of possible meanings.

Another familiar use of classical derivatives is as a means of softened or veiled expressive meaning. This mode of expression, although not favored by the literary fashions prevailing at the present time, nevertheless serves a real purpose. Conspicuous examples of words serving this purpose are *perspire, abdomen,* and *viscera,* which permit the avoidance of the vivid physical suggestion offered by the native English equivalents.

Furthermore the sonorous quality of the longer classical words serves to contribute euphony and majesty to expression. The effects attainable by their use may be observed in wonderful passages in the writings of Jeremy Taylor, Sir Thomas Browne, De Quincey, and Milton. The magnificent possibilities appear in a phrase such as *multitudinous seas incarnadine*.

On the other hand the misuse of the learned classical element in the vocabulary is familiar enough. The desire for precision which leads to the adoption of a technical term of classical derivation in place of a vague popular name is carried to pedantic excess when it leads to the popular use of *vertigo* for dizziness, of *coryza* for cold, of *urticaria* for hives. This pedantic form of language, so often attributed to the native of Boston, appears in burlesque in a sentence such as "Gastronomic satiety admonishes me that I have arrived at a state of deglutition consistent with dietetic satiety," obviously an uneconomic way of saying "I have plenty."

The fondness for the formal dignity gained by classical diction prevailing at the end of the eighteenth century, led Samuel Johnson to write in a style characterized by Macaulay as not English, but Johnsonese. Even worse, the high sounding phrases of this kind are echoed and re-echoed in the hollow phraseology so often stigmatized by the epithet 'journalese.'

But the misuse of the classical element in English, reinforced by national feeling, has led to opposition hardly less extravagant, and to the advocacy of the use of native words exclusively. From the time of Sir John Cheke and his kind in the sixteenth century, down to popular works on English composition in the nineteenth century, there has been often expressed the sentiment that 'the good old Anglo-Saxon words are best.'

Let us consider then the place of native words in the language. It has recently been pointed out that one-fourth of the task of expression in English is accomplished by nine words: *and, be, have, it, of, the, to, will,* and *you.* It will be observed that all nine of these words are of native origin. Further it is pointed out that these nine words with thirty-four others form half of the words actually used, and these additional thirty-four likewise are, without exception, of native origin: *about, all, as, at, but, can, come, day, dear, for, get, go, hear, her, if, in, me, much, not, on, one, say, she, so, that, these, they, this, though, time, we, with, write, your.*[1]

Furthermore, in pairs of synonymous words, one native, one classical in origin, such as *conflagration* and *fire, san-*

---

[1] The source of these statements is not known by the present writer, but their general truth may be tested by a count of the words on the present page.

BLENDING OF THE VARIOUS ELEMENTS 159

guinary and *bloody*, *rigid* and *stiff*, *corpulent* and *fat*, *perspire* and *sweat*, *abdomen* and *belly*, the greater directness, downrightness, in the native words is striking. "It has not wit enough to keep it sweet," said Samuel Johnson on one occasion, and then, after a pause, apparently not content with this homely wording, "It has not vitality enough to preserve it from putrefaction." The superior vividness of the expression with native words is obvious. The effect of the repetition is that of anti-climax.

To push too far, however, the distinction between the native and the foreign element in the English vocabulary is a common mistake. A better distinction to be made is that between bookish words on the one hand and, on the other hand, popular words alive with meaning from use in living speech.[2] In the language of everyday conversation, to be sure, the native words play a prominent part. The importance, however, of the imported element even here must not be lost sight of. Imported words such as *easy, large, sure, bet, boot, quiet, brave, peace, city, soldier, hour, move, turn, table, second, anxious, place, very, save, single, clear, plain*, enter most intimately into the life of everyday speech. In not a few instances the guest word has made the native word a comparative stranger among its own kin, living only in the more formal relations of literary language. Thus the native word *fair* applied to looks, has been supplanted in familiar use by *beautiful*, *speed* by *prosperity*, *dale* by *valley*, *cleave* by *divide*, *wold* by *forest*, *fastness* by *fort*, *quake* by *tremble*, *blithe* by *joyous*, *brimstone* by *sulphur*, *woodcraft* by *forestry*, *quicksilver* by *mercury*, *looking-glass* by *mirror*.

The nature of the place won for themselves in English speech by words of foreign derivation has recently been shown by means of a test. A class at Columbia University was asked to select fifty English words of basic impor-

---
[2] Greenough and Kittredge, Ch. iii.

tance in the expression of human life. From two lists prepared, seventy-eight words were finally selected, and these seventy-eight words included thirty-nine from French as compared with thirty-five of Anglo-Saxon derivation. A public-speaking club also prepared a list of the twenty-five most beautiful words in English as follows: *melody, splendor, adoration, grace, eloquence, virtue, innocence, modesty, faith, joy, honor, love, divine, hope, harmony, happiness, purity, justice, truth, liberty, peace, radiance, nobility, sympathy, heaven.* From this list were stricken out as lacking in beauty [3] one native word, *truth*, and three words imported through the French, leaving twenty-one words distributed by origin as follows, three Anglo-Saxon, one Scandinavian, three Latin, fourteen French.

In the light of such evidence no one can wisely urge the use of native words to the exclusion of classical derivatives. In fact, the test of derivation can hardly be said to have a practical importance in determining the use of words in English. In the melting-pot of English speech have entered elements from varied sources. Some of these elements have not entered into perfect fusion and are still distinguished on the printed page by the use of italic letters; a greater number have become so completely blended as to be indistinguishable except by the trained analyst of language, and, as has been seen, enter into the expression of the most essential facts of life.

The intimacy of the relation between the foreign and the native element in English vocabulary is shown by the union of classical prefixes and suffixes with native words as in: *co-worker, pro-German, re-birth, ante-room, superman, breakage, laughable, righteous, wreckage, yeomanry;* and of native prefixes and suffixes with classical derivatives as in *unruly, besiege, bashful, misplace, outrival, outcry, overcharge, outline, outmeasure, by-product, finest,*

---

[3] R. Weeks, *The Nation*, February 23, 1911.

BLENDING OF THE VARIOUS ELEMENTS 161

forceful, napkin, beautiful, painting, falsehood, priesthood, statecraft, uncivil, overturn, undermine, understudy, relentless, tireless; and of independent native words with independent classical derivatives as hybrid compounds such as: *window-pane, table-cloth, faint-hearted, simple-minded, Saturday, birthplace, bellflower, candlestick, staircase, grandstand, cocktail, fireplace, outrage.* Attempts, on the whole ineffectual, have been made to sharpen the distinction between the native prefix *un-* and its classical equivalent *in-,* and to have *in-* used only in combination with classical words and *un-* with native words. The native *un-*, however, is too intimately blended in such words as *unable, undiscovered, unpleasant, unclaimed, unjust,* ever to be replaced.

There has recently been cited a remarkable instance of hybrid compounding, of an English word made up of elements from five different languages. The word in question is *remacadamizing,* which may be analyzed into: *re* (Latin), *mac* (Celtic), *adam* (Hebrew), *ize* (Greek), and *ing* (native English), surely a remarkable demonstration of the capacity of the English language for assimilating foreign elements.

From this consideration of the elements that make up the English vocabulary, it appears that each has its place. Not the origin of the word, but its fitness for the occasion must determine its use. The language affords a wide range of expression. It offers, for instance, *homicide,* a learned term with sharply defined meaning; on the other hand, *murder,* which conveys the intellectual content of homicide along with a variety of vividly associated feelings. *Homicide* conveys a clear but thin note; *murder* conveys a rich variety of overtones. In fact, the English language in its command of expression is like a musical instrument with many pedals and stops. It affords remarkable means of shaded expression, now gentle and vague in such words as *imprecation, benediction, apprehension, venial, adroit, arid, provident, abdomen,* and *sanguinary;* now sharp and loud in the synonyms corresponding: *curse, blessing, dread, forgivable, handy, dry, foresighted, belly,* and *bloody.* Its range in tone is a wide one, from *gastralgia* to *stomach ache,* from *fornunculosis* to *boils,* from *pediculous* to *lousy.* One may choose between *asphyxiated, suffocated,* and *smothered;* between *corpulent, stout,* and *fat;* between *arrested in development, checked in progress,* and *stunted in growth.*

The choice of words afforded is ever before one. One may choose between: *emaciated* and *thin, rigid* and *stiff, mendacious* and *lying, acute* and *sharp, veracious* and *true, morbid* and *sickly, osseous* and *bony, cinema* and *movie, carrousel* and *merry-go-round, odor* and *smell* or *stink.* The longer words, sonorous in quality, formal in tone, vague in meaning, so much beloved by the great writers of the eighteenth century, have in later times much fallen into disfavor. Hazlitt says, "I hate to see a load of band boxes go along the street, and I hate to see a parcel of big words without anything in them." More recently Sir Arthur Quiller Couch has said that an "abstract word wraps a man's thought round like cotton wool." The learned form of language, says Macaulay, is "a language which nobody hears from his mother or his nurse, a language in which nobody ever quarrels or drives bargains, or makes love, a language in which nobody ever thinks." In general it may be said that mastery over the English language depends most of all upon effective command over the simple words, of whatever origin, those words which alone form the living elements of speech, by which instead of the muffled effects produced by pompous and high-sounding phrase, one may reach the sensitive chords of human feeling.

CHAPTER XII

NEW CREATIONS AND COMPOUNDS

The preceding chapters in this work have had to do with classes of words and the sources from which the material of the English vocabulary has been drawn. But language must grow in order to keep pace with the progress, material and spiritual, of the people that use it. It remains, then, to be seen how a language that served the purposes of an early period has been made to serve the purposes of a life that has become more and more complex. It remains to be seen how the language has expanded physically, through the formation of new words, how words have been modified in form in the process of adaptation, and how, by subtle shifts, a limited set of words has been made to express an illimitable variety of shades of meaning.

To begin with, there has been a certain amount of new word-creation. Of words newly created the most obvious kind is that produced by vocal imitation of sounds in nature. This kind of words, usually called onomatopoetic, but recently more happily named 'echoic,'[1] is known to all languages. Many of them have been inherited by English. Such words as *bomb, murmur, cuckoo,* go back through French and Latin, to an antiquity hard to determine. Words like *papa, mama, baby,* originating in baby speech, belong to practically all languages. Among 'echoic' words that originated independently in English may be cited: *buzz, fizz, purr, quack, hiss, boom, gibber, jabber, giggle, titter, whirr, ding-dong, hee-haw, tick-tack, hoot, chatter.*[2]

---

[1] J. A. H. Murray quoted by Bradley, *op. cit.*, p. 155.
[2] Bradley, *op. cit.*, p. 155.

The creation of words of this kind is never at an end. In the South African War the sounds of the machine-gun gave origin to *pom-pom*. In the World War in the same way originated words like *crumps, dud,* and *whizz-bang*.

Besides the class of words arising from direct vocal imitation of sounds in nature, there is a class of words which owe their origin to a form of association established between the meaning and a certain form of vocal effort. Quickness of movement, for example, is obviously associated with sharpness and brevity of sound. In other instances the nature of the association is less easy to indicate. The association may be not an essential one, but an artificial one created through analogical force. For example, the initial sound *bl-* becomes associated with the expression of disgust, less from physiological reaction, although that may be a contributory element in the explanation, than because of its repeated occurrence in *blasted, blamed, blooming, blowed, blessed, bloody, blithering.* An English-speaking person can hardly fail to feel a certain quality common to words ending in *-sh*, such as: *crush, bosh, slosh, squash, plush, hush, mush, flush, blush, tush,* and *cushy,* and a quality related but different in: *mash, crash, splash, hash, rash, smash, trash, quash, clash, dash, rash.* Again, there is a quality common to words beginning with *fl-,* as in *flame, flit, flutter, flare, flicker, flimmer, flash, flurry, fluster, flirt, flag.* This association between certain sounds and certain meanings comes to form a part of the 'Genius of the Language' and affords a basis on which new words may be created, a word creation which, therefore, is never at an end. Murray, in the first volume of the Oxford Dictionary, cites from among the words beginning with *b* the following words of more or less recent creation: *bamboozle, bang, bilk, blab, blabber, blare, blear, blight, blizzard, blob, blot, blotch, blubber, bluff, blunder, blunt, blur, blurt, bluster, bogus, boom, bore,*

NEW CREATIONS AND COMPOUNDS 165

bosh, bother, brash, brunt, bub, bum, bump, bunch, bungle, burr, bustle, buzz.

Words of this kind, it will be remarked, are prevailingly of a plain, direct type; the relation between sound and sense is immediate. They appear more frequently in the vulgar speech, which is more directly responsive to the genius of the language, and are more slowly adopted into the more artificial, cultivated speech. Originating in the cultivated language of nonsense, however, words such as *chortle* and *galumphing* have gained some currency in popular use. Gelett Burgess has made the attempt further to enlarge the resources of expression by the sheer creation of words "from instinctive inarticulate emotions, hot from the depths of necessity." It remains to be seen if plausible words such as *fuddy* for 'untidy,' *bimped* for 'jilted,' *snosh* for 'vain talk,' *oofle* for 'try to find a person's name without asking,' *jujasm* for 'an expansion of sudden joy,' eloquently expressive as they are of the spirit of nonsense, can possibly gain general adoption.

Closely related to words of this kind are a number of new creations which aptly express certain shades of meaning and which have been appropriately named 'blends.' In words of this type, as the name applied to them indicates, two words have been fused, only a part of each remaining, and the meaning, as well as the resulting form, is a blend of that in the two component words.[3] As examples of words of this type that have become well established in standard speech, may be mentioned: *lambast* (lam + baste), *grumble* (growl + rumble), *dumbfound* (dumb + confound), *gerrymander* (Gerry, name of Governor Gerry, of Massachusetts + salamander), *scurry* (skirr or scour + hurry), *flaunt* (fly or flout + vaunt), *squirm* (squir + swarm or worm), *dang* (damn + hang), *squawk* (squall + squeak), *lunch* (lump + hunch or

---

[3] L. Pound, *Blends.*

bunch), *luncheon* (lunch + nuncheon), *flurry* (fly or flaw + hurry), *boost* (boom + hoist), *squash* (squeeze + crash), *splatter* (splash + spatter), *foist* (fist + hoist), *blurt* (blow or blare + spurt), *chump* (chop + lump).

This method of word formation is one in frequent current use. A familiar instance is *humanzee* (human + chimpanzee) better known as "Snooky." The method is applied with serious intent in *travelogue* and in creating a name for a new horticultural cross-breed, the *plumcot* (plum + apricot, influenced, however, by *cumquat*). More often the process is used with humorous intent, as in the case of the creations of Lewis Carroll such as: *mimsy* (miserable + flimsy), *snark* (snake + shark), *galumphing* (gallop + triumphing), *chortle* (chuckle + snort). In such modern formations as *swellegant, fidgitated, Ulsteria* (in southern Ireland), *versiflage, girlevue, yellocution, futilitarian, flumonia, alcoholiday, kissletoe-vine, amorality,* the double entendre has satiric force but a cheapness of quality akin to that in a pun.

The natural processes at work creating new words may be discerned in the case of the words mentioned. There remains, however, to be mentioned a number of words of the most everyday type, which if not actually created 'out of the blue,' at least as yet have never had their origin otherwise satisfactorily explained. From these words without known etymology may be mentioned *dog*, and *curse*, which made their appearance before the Conquest; *girl, boy, lad, lass, big, bad, pig,* and *cut,* before Chaucer; *bet, jump,* and *dodge,* before 1600; *pun,* in the seventeenth century; *fun, bore, slang, fudge,* in the eighteenth; *rollicking* and *loaf* (verb), in the nineteenth,[4] not to speak of such word phenomena in modern slang as *stunt* and *hooch.* The very casual nature of the origin of these slang terms doubtless affords a clue to the origin of the

---

[4] Smith, *op. cit.*, pp. 99, 100.

NEW CREATIONS AND COMPOUNDS 167

other words which at an earlier period have found their way into standard speech.

As a minor source of increment to the vocabulary, also, should be mentioned here the doublets which have already been discussed. Words, like bulbs of certain plants, have the paradoxical property of multiplying by division. By this process in the history of English have originated the double forms: *of, off* (O. E. *of*); *through, thorough* (O. E. *thurh*); *cud, quid* (O. E. *cwidu, cudu*); *porridge, pottage* (M. E. *potage*); *shoal, shallow* (O. N. *skjalgr*); *shade, shed, shadow* (O. E. *sceaadu*); *mead, meadow* (O. E. *mæd, mædw-*); *grammar, glamour* (Fr. *grammaire*); *strap, strop* (O. E. *stropp*); *metal, mettle* (Fr. *metal*, Lat. *metallum*); *cloths, clothes* (O. E. *clāthas*); *dent, dint* (O. E. *dynt*); *dike, ditch* (O. E. *dīc*); *corps, corpse* (O. Fr. *cors*, Lat. *corpus*); *courtesy, curtsy* (O. Fr. *cortesie*); *fancy, phantasy* (O. Fr. *fantasie*); *Lombard, lumber* (Fr. from Ital. *Lombardo*); *mister, master* (O. Fr. *maistre*); *posy, poesy* (O. Fr. *poesie*); *preen, prune* (O. Fr. *poroindre*); *sexton, sacristan* (O. Fr. *secrestain*).

But far and away the most prolific source of new English words has been from the combination of older elements. The science of chemistry reveals how a limited number of elements, brought into varied combinations, yield a seemingly unlimited variety of substances. In the same way in language simple elements combine to form compounds responding to the infinite variety and complexity of thought.

The natural propensity of English of the earliest period toward the formation of compounds, has already been commented on. Many apparently simple words of modern English are in reality early English compounds disguised. To early stages in the history of the language go back such words as *barn* (O. E. *bere* + *ærn*, 'barley-place'); *lord* (*hlāf* + *weard*, 'bread keeper'); *lady* (*hlāf* + *dige*, 'bread kneader'); *gossip* (*gōd* + *sibbe*, 'good kinsman'); *Hussy* (*hūs* + *wīf*, 'house-wife'); *gospel* (*gōd* + *spell*) 'good narrative'); *world* (*wer* + *eld*, 'man age'); *steward* (*stig* + *weard*, 'sty keeper'); *sheriff* (*scīr* + *gerēfa*, 'shire reeve'); *worship* (*weorth* + *scipu*, 'honor'); *don* (*dōn* + *on*, 'put on'); *doff* (*dōn* + *off*, 'put off'); *daisy* (*dæges* + *ēage*, 'day's eye').

The spirit of the Elizabethan age, less curbed than that of later lines, frequently found expression in compound words, many of them rejected in later times, many, on the other hand, forming expressive elements in the language of to-day. In the writings of Thomas Nash, who vigorously defends the "boystrous compound words" for which he has been criticized, appear such useful words, new in his time, as: *huntsman, freshman, bookseller, keyhole, long-winded, shallow-brained, bookworm, potluck,* and *horseplay.* The language of Shakespeare offers such bold word formations as *wind-changing* Warwick, *furnace-burning* heart, *honey-heavy* dew, *pity-pleading* eyes, *peace-parted* souls, *carry-tale, find-faults,* and *mumble-news,* which have not held a permanent place in the language. Other similar creations of the period, however, which are used by Shakespeare have endured in the language. Of this class may be cited *short-lived, health-giving, well-knit, hollow-eyed, life-preserving, rawboned, bold-faced, ill-boding, tear-stained, crestfallen, untutored, well-proportioned, pepper-box, highborn, red-hot, care-crazed, snail-paced, wrynecked, green-eyed, mouth-filling, blood-stained, moss-grown, wild-goose-chase, tempest-tossed, heartache, heart-whole, lack-lustre, hairbreadth, ill-starred, even-handed, whey-faced, breakneck, wasp-headed, time-pleaser.*

Many of these products of an earlier time have fallen by the wayside. Among the losses may be registered such words as *hotspur, aleknight, malt-worm, hangby, carry-tale, crackhemp, crackhalter, crackrope, findfault, lack-*

NEW CREATIONS AND COMPOUNDS 169

brain, makepiece, tearsheet, ticklebrain, tosspot, wantwit. From this earlier age, however, has come down as a heritage, a rich variety of terms of contempt, such as: *killjoy, pickpocket, scarecrow, spitfire, daredevil, hangdog, lickspittle, makeshift, pinchbeck, skinflint, slipshod, turncoat, swashbuckler, breakneck, telltale,* with which may be compared modern *speak-easy* and *bootlegger* and such juvenile expressions as *tattletale* and *copycat.*

For an impression of the prevalence of word compounds in the seventeenth century one should recall the names given by Bunyan to the characters in *Pilgrim's Progress.* The synonyms for miser and for woodpecker quoted from Trench elsewhere in the present volume, afford further illustration.[5]

The faculty of word combination so much alive in the sixteenth century, manifested itself also in the formation of word groups not joined into compound words, but serving admirably for the expression of definite single conceptions. Many of these phrase combinations have been woven firmly into the texture of English speech. Some expressions of this kind which form living elements in the language of to-day are *try conclusions, full sail, a man of his word, setting jesting aside, out at the heels, turn over a new leaf, eye to the main chance, man about town* (all from the play *Sir Thomas More,* about 1590).[6] The plays of Shakespeare, the language of which so well reflects the speech of the time, afford instances of scores of these expressions, such as *honor at the stake, curd your blood, a pitched battle, take exceptions at, as good luck would have it, know the world, throw cold water on it, have the heart to do it, play on words, come fairly off, be better than my word, give him his due, bear your years well, lay odds, fall foul, well on your way, pink of courtesy, merry as the*

---
[5] *Cf.* Trench, *English Past and Present,* pp. 204, 205.
[6] Oliphant, p. 8.

day is long, too much of a good thing, lead by the nose.[7]

In the following centuries the English settlers in America were confronted with the task of devising names for the unfamiliar plants and trees and birds of a new country. Here again the native genius of the language for compounds asserted itself in the production of such names as *bullfrog, canvas-back, lightning-bug, mud-hen, cat-bird, razor-back, garter-snake, ground-hog, live-oak, potato-bug, turkey-gobbler, pokeweed, copper-head, eelgrass, reedbird, eggplant, bluegrass, peanut, Junebug, butter-nut.*[8]

Other interesting words of this kind have their origin in Australia, where the English colonists were confronted with the need of names for features of the flora and the fauna of a new country. Of Australian creation are names: for birds such as *friar-bird, frogsmouth, honey-eater, ground-lark, forty-spot, whip-bird, lyre-bird,* and *coach-whip;* for fishes such as *long-fin* and *trumpeter;* for plants such as *sugar-grass, hedge-laurel, ironheart,* and *thousand-jacket.*[9]

In some of these creations of the Australian colonist there appear signs of imagination. In most of them, however, and in all the creations of the American pioneer, there appears a naked directness of manner akin to that in older English compounds such as *turncoat, telltale, cut-throat, pickpocket, matchmaker,* and *jailbird.* Probably it is the shirt-sleeve quality of such words that bars their admission in great numbers into the polite circles of modern standard speech. The continued life, however, of the spirit that created them is conspicuously present in such creations of modern popular speech as *speak-easy, boot-legger, pussyfoot, skyscraper, bell-hop, hayseed, shin-plaster, bucket-shop, lounge-lizard, porch-lizard, bar-room-lizard,* and the various compounds with *-hound,* such

---

[7] Oliphant.
[8] Mencken, p. 45.
[9] Quoted by Jespersen from Morris, *Austral English.*

NEW CREATIONS AND COMPOUNDS 171

as *rumhound, thrillhound, camerahound, newshound, jazzhound, teahound, mealhound,* and the like.

But while the English language has by no means lost the ability which characterized its earlier periods, to make new word combinations, its most prolific method of creating new words is by means of prefixes and suffixes. In its supply of these elements the English language has ready at hand rich material for the manufacture of new words.

English prefixes and suffixes, like the words to which they are joined, are of varied origin. Among those available are the native prefixes: *mis-, un-, after-, be-, for-, wan-,* etc., and the native suffixes: *-ness, -less, -ly, -ish, -er, -y, -head, -hood.* Along with these may be listed the Latin: *pro-, post-, inter-, ante-, pre-, co-, sub-, super-,* and *-ation, -ative;* the French: *dis-, en-,* and *-age, -al, -ment, -able, -ous, -ose, -ese, -fy, -ate,* from the Latin; French from German: *-ard, -esque;* French from Spanish or Italian: *-ade;* Greek: *a-* ('without'), *hyper-, pseudo-, arche-, neo-,* and *-ize, -ist, -ism, -ite, -itis;* Scandinavian: *-ling;* Flemish: *-kin.*

The combination of elements, native and foreign, has been discussed in an earlier chapter under the head of hybrids. It would be the method of pedantry to insist on the absolute segregation of these elements, all of which have been assimilated into English. There are too many combinations of foreign words with English prefix or suffix such as *underestimate, because, faultless, beastly, useless, useful, relationship, self-interest, forecastle* and *gentleman;* or of native words with foreign prefix or suffix, such as *righteous, renew, rebuild, recall, intertwine, co-worker, anteroom, bondage, readable,* words that could not well be dispensed with. It is not possible to frame any definite rule to govern such combinations. One can only apply the general principle of congruity, of combining the simple with the simple, the learned with the learned.

Such combinations as *superclean,* or *hypoclean,* or *antetime,* or *hypersweet,* or *afternatal,* are inconceivable. On the other hand hybrid combinations such as *disband, dishearten, distrust, intermingle, intertwine, belabor, afternoon,* and *foreordain* cannot be subject to any criticism that is serious.

Purist effort to maintain a distinction between native *un-* and Latin *in-, im-,* perhaps has had some effect. *Unexperienced* (Shakespeare and Milton), *unfirm* (Shakespeare), *unmaterial* (Daniel), *unperfect* (Shakespeare and Sidney), *unpatient* (P. Plowman), *unpartial* (Sidney), have yielded to *inexperienced, infirm, immaterial, imperfect, impartial.* The preference, however, for the Latin prefix may be due to a distinction in meaning that has grown up. *Unmoral,* for example, expresses a different meaning from *immoral.* In any case the application of the principle will hardly be seriously urged against the use of such firmly established hybrids as *unpleasant, unable, unusual, uneasy, unpopular, unprofitable,* and their like.

The gala period for new derivative words in English, as for new compounds, was the sixteenth century. In the freedom with which words were borrowed and combined into new compounds and formed into new derivatives, the language for the time ran riot. The critical spirit which dominated the succeeding century led to a sifting of the elements in the vocabulary. Of the new word formations, we are told, "nearly all that survived 1688 are still in use."[10] The result of the sifting process was, in some instances, an abandonment of new forms, in other instances, due to the retention of the new forms, a loss of older English words. A consequence was the almost complete extinction of many native English elements, a loss which has been the subject of sentimental regret on the

---

[10] Murray, Article on "English Language" in the *Encyclopedia Britannica.*

NEW CREATIONS AND COMPOUNDS 173

part of some. For example, take the prefix *wan-*, which survives in the solitary word *wanton*. This prefix in earlier times entered into the composition of words such as *wanthrift*, 'extravagance'; *wanhap*, 'misfortune'; *wanlust*, 'languor'; *wanwit*, 'folly'; *wantrust*, 'lack of confidence'; *wantruth*, 'falsehood'; *wanchance*, 'ill-luck.'[11] In the same way the word *bishoprick* offers the only instance of the survival of the once active suffix *-rick*.

The casualty list among words was an appalling one. In one family of words, those ending in *-ful*, the losses include such expressive words as *blameful* (Shakespeare), *crimeful* (Shakespeare), *dareful, deathful, ruthful* (all from Shakespeare), *chanceful, dismayful, doomful, debateful* (from Spenser); *diseaseful* (Bacon), *causeful* (Sidney), and literally hundreds of others. The list of lost words in *-less*, such as *aidless, bragless, effectless, heirless* (all from Shakespeare), is nearly as long. *Gainsay* survives from a family that once included *gainscope, gainstand, gainstrive*, etc. *Blameworthy, trustworthy, noteworthy, praiseworthy, seaworthy*, are about the only survivors from a fairly numerous group of words in *-worthy*. *Laughingstock* is about the only survival from a class that once included *gazing-stock, jesting-stock, mocking-stock*, etc.[12]

Another cause for the decay in word-building power of the native prefixes and suffixes, apart from the competition of the classical elements, is the fact that they have in most cases entered into such entire fusion with the rest of the word as to lose their independence. This is evident in such a word as *wanton*. The *-th* in *warmth, health, growth, wealth*, is a noun-forming suffix once general. It appears also in *height*. Bacon also used *lowth*, Horace Walpole, *greenth*, and Ruskin, *illth*. None of these new scions have

---

[11] Trench, *English Past and Present*, p. 207.
[12] *Ibid.*, pp. 213, 214.

taken root, and the same may be predicted as the future for *coolth*, recently sponsored by H. G. Wells.

The prefixes of classical origin have been much more active, possibly due to the fact that they make a more homogeneous combination with the learned words adopted to record the progress in modern knowledge. Latin prefixes and suffixes abound. The inkhorn term in *osity* and *-ation* have from the first met with strenuous opposition, but on the whole have held their own, and the less ponderous endings in *-al*, *-ous*, and *-ary* are among the most widely used of endings. Such prefixes as *re-*, *pre-*, *ante-*, *post-*, *pro-*, *inter-*, *intra-*, and their kind, are very much alive especially in the learned word formations of modern times. *Pre-*, *ante-*, and *post-* are closely associated with conceptions growing out of modern historical interests and evolutionary theory. Latin *pro-* and Greek *anti-* are active in compounds expressing the redistribution of national sympathies in modern changing world politics.

But most active of all are the elements from the Greek. There are, for instance, recorded in the Oxford Dictionary more than five hundred words beginning with the Greek *anti-*. It should be held in mind that Greek has served as a kind of godmother to modern inductive science. The revival of Greek studies in the sixteenth century was accompanied by a revival of the scientific spirit, and the beginnings of many of the most important of modern sciences in the seventeenth century synchronizes with the dominance of classical taste and classical standards, and the habit then formed of going to Greek for the elements to be used in forming new names in medicine, physiology, physics, and chemistry has become firmly fixed. The very spirit of modern thought finds expression in suffixes like *-ize* and *-ic*, and *-ist* and *-ism*, and prefixes such as *hyper-*, *hypo-*, *neo-*, *auto-*, *tele-*.

Progress in the modern development of applied science

NEW CREATIONS AND COMPOUNDS 175

may be measured by the history of these word elements. For instance the prefix *tele-*, which appears in but two words in the dictionary of Samuel Johnson compiled in 1755, in the Oxford Dictionary, appears in 130 words. Progress in labor-saving devices is registered by words in the dictionary. In the Supplementary volumes to the *Century Dictionary*, published seventeen years after the appearance of the original six volumes, and recording the new word creations of that intervening period, there are 168 words beginning with *auto-*. The Latin suffix *super-*, also, has found new life in recent times, and expresses a modern spirit very much alive, particularly in America, that of effort to surpass all previous achievement. The evolutionary ideals of the period find expression in *superman*, made after a German model and set afloat by Bernard Shaw. *Superdreadnaught* and *supercircus* are more recent formations on this model.

But modern English recruits its forces not only from learned sources, but, as has been shown in earlier chapters, from the uncultivated dialects and from the actively alive popular language. In popular speech new prefixes and suffixes are brought into use, not only *-hound* and *-lizard* already mentioned, but *-fiend* in such words as *book-fiend*, *dope-fiend*, and *chess-fiend*. After the pattern of *fire-proof* are formed *bomb-proof*, *fool-proof*, etc. The almost attained is expressed by series of words beginning with *near-*, such as *near-great*, *near-champion*, *near-beer*.

One of the most actively alive of all elements in modern speech is the suffix *-ie* or *-y*. This ending has a variety of associated meanings. As a diminutive ending it appears in child names such as *Willie*, *Johnnie*, and their kind, and as a sign of affection, in pet names such as *birdie*, *bunny*, *kittie*. The suffix has Scotch associations through such words as *bailie* (for bailiff), *brownie*, *kiltie*, and the various names connected with the Scotch game of golf, such as *caddie, brassie, mashie, stymie, dormie,* and *birdie.* The group of words including *whisky, brandy,* and *toddy* contribute a certain popular quality to the ending. These mixed associations and a pleasing ambiguity that results, probably serve to explain the prevailing popularity of the ending in modern speech, appearing in such words as *movie, stogie (toby), bookie, newsie* (newsboy), *rooky, slavey, trusty, cootie, sweetie, jitney,* and the shortened forms, *taxi* (cab), *muni*(cipal), and *divvy* (divide).

The creative spirit in language is to be seen in most free activity in new countries. The luxuriant growth of new words in popular speech has recently been pointed out as an aspect of the spirit of California. The new words there in use include not only *cafeteria,* but *eateria, grocerteria, shoeitorium, suitorium, cleantorium, theatorium,* and *shinerium.*[13]

Popular speech has been active in another form of word making. In earlier periods it was responsible for such shortened forms of words as *van* (vanguard), *van* (caravan), *patter* (pater noster), *canter* (Canterbury gallop), *wig* (periwig), *curio* (for curiosity), *cheat* (escheat), *wag* (waghalter), *spend* (dispend), *sport* (disport), *rum* (rumbullion), *spite* (despite), *mend* (amend), *cab* (cabriolet), *grog* (grogram), *hobby* (hobby horse), *hock* (Hochheimer), *tend* (attend), *drawing-room* (withdrawing-room), *still* (distillery), *cute* (acute), *brandy* (brandewine), *it will be a cold day* (in June), *after all* (is said and done). The fashionable speech of the age of Queen Anne is responsible for: *mob* (mobile vulgus), *hypo* (hypochondria), *blues* (blue devils), *incog* (incognito), *plenipo* (plenipotentiary), etc. English university life of earlier times created *chum* (chamber fellow), *fag* (fatigue), etc. Of more recent origin are: *bonner* (bonfire), *langers* (Auld Lang Syne), and *godders* (God save the King) already

---

[13] H. Rhodes, *Harper's Magazine,* June, 1920.

NEW CREATIONS AND COMPOUNDS 177

cited. From various sources, more or less modern, come such shortened forms as: *defi* (defiance), *rhino* (rhinoceros), *info* (information), *pull* (leg pull), *chromo* (chromolithograph), *photo* (photograph), *memo* (memorandum), *Mespot* (Mesopotamia), American *cycle* and English *bike* (bicycle), *motor* (motor car), *gas* (gasoline), *pram* (perambulator), *prep* (preparatory), and the countless creations of modern slang.

Another type of word, for the creation of which popular use, in this case popular misunderstanding, is responsible, is the so-called back-formation.[14] The old word *pease* (surviving in *peascod*) which is really singular in form, is mistaken for a plural, and from it is made the new singular form *pea*. In the same way have been created: *skate* (earlier skates), *eave* (earlier eaves), *shay* (chaise), *Chinee* (Chinese), etc. *Swashbuckler* is interpreted as a noun of agent derived from a verb, and out of this misunderstanding springs *swashbuckle*. In this way have originated *edit, rove, hawk* (verb), *beg, asset* (O. Fr. *assets*), *cherry, sherry, bodice, quince, peeve* (verb), *vamp, burgle, jell, launder* (verb), *opine* (verb), *scavenge* (verb), *frivol* (verb), *gyre* (gyroscope), *gimble* (gimlet) (the last two from Lewis Carroll), *henpeck* (verb) and *sunburn* (verb).[15] *Grovelling*, an adjective meaning 'face down,' is taken for a present participle and thus gives rise to the verb *grovel*.

The creation of new words has obviously been constant from the earliest times down to the days of *sabotage* and *normalcy*. Modern inventive activity, which has been a main factor in physical progress, has been accompanied by an activity in word invention. *Anzac* is a useful collective name which seems to be permanently established. Some of

---

[14] The term is an invention of Sir J. A. H. Murray.
[15] *Cf.* E. Wittman, A Study of Back Formations, *Dialect Notes*, IV, Part II.

the modern trade names are worthy of admiration, not only sheer creations such as *kodak* appears to be, but condensed words such as *Nabisco* (National Biscuit Company) and *Socony* (Standard Oil Company of New York) and *En-ar-co* (National Refining Company), and words with thinly veiled meaning such as *Uneeda*, applied in England to a cigar, in America to a biscuit, and *Odorono*.[16]

In the creation of new words, however, the major share of the credit must be assigned to popular speech, the most living part of the language. Even felicitous combinations making their earliest recorded appearance in the writings of literary artists are often creations of the popular muse rather than of conscious art. As compared with the number of words created in modern times by popular speech, the number of words that may be assigned to the creation of definite individuals is relatively small. A recent study [17] of neologisms by living authors reveals on the one hand a prevailing desire among writers to get along with words in existence, on the other hand, among the word-creations set in circulation by individual writers, such as *dolorifuge* by Thomas Hardy, the small number that find a place in general use. There are, to be sure, in all periods instances of words whose creation may be connected with definite individuals, from the time of *eureka* attributed to Archimedes and *soliloquy* attributed to St. Augustine. As more modern examples may be cited such words as *raid* and *glamour* introduced into standard English from the Scotch dialect by Scott, and *outcome* by Carlyle, and such new creations as *altruism* (Comte), *agnostic* (Huxley), *atoll* (Darwin), *aniline* (Fritzsche), *dynamite* (Nobel), *superman* (G. B. Shaw), *sea-power* and *eventless* (Admiral Mahan), *osteopath* (Dr. A. T. Sill), *bloc* (Clemenceau), *nihilist* (Turgenev), *hypnotism, hypnotic*, etc., which super-

---

[16] *Cf.* L. Pound, *Word Coinage and Modern Trade Names, Dialect Notes*, January, 1914.

[17] L. Mead, *Word-Coinage* (New York, 1902).

seded earlier *mesmerism* (Dr. James Braid), *cyclone* (H. Piddington, 1848), *anæsthesia* (O. W. Holmes).

REFERENCES FOR FURTHER READING

The New English Dictionary, Introduction to the several sections.
H. Bradley, *The Making of English* (New York, 1904), pp. 111-159.
O. Jespersen, *Growth and Structure of the English Language* (Leipzig, 1912), pp. 157-177.
L. P. Smith, *The English Language* (New York, 1912), pp. 81-108.
H. Hirt, *Deutsche Etymologie* (Munich, 1909).
L. Bloomfield, *The Study of Language* (New York, 1914).
L. Mead, *Word-Coinage* (New York, 1902).
R. C. Trench, *English Past and Present,* 16th ed. (London, 1899), pp. 144-295.
R. C. Trench, *The Study of Words,* 22nd ed. (New York, 1891), Lecture v.
H. L. Mencken, *The American Language* (New York, 1919).
T. L. K. Oliphant, *The New English* (London and New York, 1866).
Gelett Burgess, *Burgess Unabridged* (New York, 1914).
C. F. Johnson, *English Words* (New York, 1891).
G. L. Kittredge, Harper's *Magazine,* CVI, 301.

CHAPTER XIII

FOLK-ETYMOLOGY

When British soldiers in India heard the Mohammedans in their religious procession of the Moharram beating their breasts with the accompanying cry, "Yā Hasan! Yā Hosain!" they translated the wailing sound into the more familiar English sounds, "Hobson Jobson." The phrase has been applied as the name for a familiar process in language history more usually known as "Folk-Etymology."

Foreign words when adopted into English need to be assimilated. Sounds in foreign speech that are strange to English speech need to be fitted into the English scheme of vocal sounds. Thus in words borrowed from French the peculiar French sound of *u* has usually been converted in English to the diphthong *iu* (as in *new*) or to the simple 'oo' sound. Thus French *vertu* is turned into English *virtue*. In the same way foreign words, when adopted into English, need to be fitted into the English word system. There is ever present the disposition to fit the strange elements into familiar word molds, involving, in many instances, strange distortions.

English-speaking troops on the Continent during the World War experienced language difficulties similar to those of the British troops in India, and they handled their difficulties in precisely the same way. French words and phrases recast in English form produced strange effects. *Vin blanc, bon jour, au revoir, très bien, toute de suite, camouflage,* were converted into *vinegar blink, barn door, olive oil, three beans, toot sweet,* and *camel flags.* The

American mode of thought leaves its imprint on *busher*, for the less familiar *boche*, and motor *Laura*, for motor *lorrie*.

The same spirit of careless humor played remarkable freaks in the transformation of French and Flemish place-names. Ypres was promptly converted into *Wipers*, a translation which, however, is said but to have repeated the practice of English soldiers in campaigns of other centuries. Martinpuich was converted into *Martinpush*, Fonquevillers into *Funky Villas*, Ploegsteert into *Plow Street*, Wyteschaete into *White Sheet*, Armentières into *Arm-in-tears*, Argonne into *Oregon*, Delville woods into *Devil's* woods. Quite idyllic in nature is the translation of Mouquet farm into *Moo cow farm*. Deliciously ironic was the name *ewe lambs* applied to the Prussian *Uhlans*. The spirit of humor back of these curiously distorted forms helps one to understand the earlier English place-names discussed in a later chapter, such as *Shotover, Beachy Head, Maidenhead, Bridgewater*, products of earlier folk activity in converting French into English. A modern word full of humor and at the same time suggestive force, is *cherrybangers*, the name given in England to the crowds of tourists seeing the sights from the char-à-banc, quite different in sound and spirit from the synonymous word in American popular speech.

The humor of the naval service has not been behind that of the land forces in playing pranks with words. The conversion of Bellerophon into *Bully Ruffian* has long afforded amusement. Similar naval perversions of romantic or grandiloquent names are Ariadne into *Hairy Annie*, Narcissus into *Nasty Sister*, Cressy into *Greaser*, Inconstant into *Inkstand*, Hecate into *He Cat* or *The Tom*, Miantonomoh into *My Aunt Don't Know You*.

Less self-conscious often are the attempts to connect unfamiliar words with known meanings. Dame Quickly converted homicidal into *honey-suckle* and, without any apparent logic, homicide into *honey-seed*. In twentieth-century speech frankfurter is converted into *frankfritter*, Armistice day into *armystich* day, and the housemaid converts the unfamiliar radiator into *red heater* and aristocracy into *richtocracy*.

Enough has been offered here to illustrate the ever present human tendency, sometimes unconscious, sometimes intentionally humorous, to convert unfamiliar words into familiar forms, to connect the unknown with the known, in order to make it an integral part of a system. In the earlier history of words evidence of this tendency is everywhere to be found. The classic illustrative example is the word *asparagus*. This word, so Latin in appearance, did not fit naturally into everyday language, and the effort to fit the word into simple, natural speech, led to the semi-plausible *sparrow-grass*. In at least one twentieth-century restaurant appears a rival form, *asparagras*. The similar perversion of artichoke into *hearty choke* did not win such general adoption, probably because the humorous intent is too conspicuous.

Owing to the incessant activity of this popular tendency in speech, one in search of the explanation of a word needs to proceed constantly with caution. The hunt for etymologies offers many pitfalls. *Ravenous*, for example, which seems obviously to be derived from the bird name *raven* (O. E. *hræfn*), is in reality derived, through the Old French *ravinos*, from the Latin *rapina*, from which we get by more direct route the word *rapine*. *Pantry* in its origin is not associated with pans but with bread (O. Fr. *paneterie*, Mod. Fr. *pain*). *Buttery* goes back to M. E. *botery*, a corruption of *botelrye* from O. Fr. *boteillerie*, a place for bottles or liquor, and hence in origin is associated with bottles rather than with butter.

The effort, strained in many instances, to connect

unfamiliar words with familiar ones, is everywhere to be detected. The influence of *buzz* is to be seen in the transformation of O. Fr. *busart* (Latin *buteo*, 'falcon' + *ard*) into *buzzard*. *Sovereign* (O. Fr. *soverain*, Lat. *super*), is influenced by *reign*. *Riband* (O. Fr. *riban*, origin uncertain), is influenced by *band*. *Wiseacre* (M. Dutch *wijsseg-ger*, 'wise speaker'), is brought into association with the unrelated word *acre*. *Acorn* (O. E. *æcern*), is falsely connected with *corn*. *Surround* goes back, through the French, to a late Latin *superondare* (*onda*, 'wave'), 'to overflow,' 'to deluge,' but is influenced in form by the word *round* of unrelated origin. *Curtail* is derived from the O. Fr. *cortald* (*court*, 'short' + Teut. *-ald*), but through use in the form *curtal*, to designate a horse with docked tail, has come to be associated with *tail*. *Hoe-down* is probably not connected with *hoe* but with *hay*, a name for the old ring dance. *Cutlet* in origin is not related to *cut*, but comes, through the French, from the Latin *costa* meaning 'rib' and, therefore, means literally 'little rib.' The French *gentil* has been borrowed into English four successive times, and has assumed in English four different forms with four different meanings as: *gentle, gentile, genteel,* and *jaunty*. In the last instance it has been influenced in form by English *jaunt* to produce *jaunty*, which is about as close as English spelling can come to representing the pronunciation of modern French *gentille*. *Cold-slaw*, of Dutch origin, is connected in origin not with *cold* but with *kool*, Dutch for 'cabbage.' *Blunderbuss*, also of Dutch origin, is derived from *donderbuss*, 'thunder gun.' *Isinglass*, influenced by English *glass*, goes back to Dutch *huysenblas*, literally 'sturgeon-bladder.' *Hiccough*, in origin an imitative word (*cf.* the more popular form *hickup*), has been mistakenly connected with *cough*. *Country-dance* is originally the *contre-dance* (*contre*, 'opposite'). The folk-etymology in this instance is more than usually plausible.

ENGLISH WORDS

Pediment, the name for the triangular part of the front of buildings in Greek style, goes back to an earlier *peremint* and is probably to be traced back to *pyramid. Causeway* comes from *causey,* which is from a French dialect word corresponding to modern standard French *chaussée. Pickax* is not by origin related to *ax,* but comes from the O. Fr. *piquois. Demijohn,* likewise, is an English version of French *dame-jeanne. Catsup* and *ketchup* represent a double attempt to give an English form to the Malayan *kĕchap* which, according to one account, comes from the Chinese *koe-chiap,* 'brine of pickled fish.' *Pearl,* in *pearl-stitch,* a word heard so frequently during the war, comes from an earlier *purl,* meaning 'to twist.'

Many names for plants and beasts represent attempts to read meanings into unfamiliar words. *Barberry* comes from a medieval Latin *berberis,* unrelated in meaning to berry. *Gillyflower* goes back to an O. Fr. *girofle,* derived ultimately from the Greek *karuophullon,* 'nutleaf.' *Hollyhock* and *holy oak,* rival names for a common plant, both show misdirected effort, since the word is connected neither with *holly* nor with *oak,* but comes from the compound *holy* + obsolete *hock* (O. E. *hocc,* 'mallow'). At least three words have been falsely associated with the rose. *Primrose* comes from an O. Fr. *primerole,* which in turn is derived from the first word in the Med. Latin flower name, *primula de ver,* 'first little flower of spring.' *Tuberose* goes back ultimately to a Latin *tuberosa,* feminine for *tuberosus,* 'tuberous.' *Rosemary* goes back, through the French, to the Latin *ros marinus,* 'sea dew.' *Mushroom* has nothing to do with *room* but comes from the O. Fr. *mouscheron,* which is derived from *mousse,* 'moss.' *Buckwheat* comes from the Dutch *boekweit,* 'beech-wheat,' a name the relation of which to this kind of grain is readily apparent.

Among names for beasts and birds one finds further phenomena of the same kind. The *cockroach* is the Spanish *cucaracha* cast in an English word mold. The *mongoose* is an animal native to India and the East. His native name is *mangus*. The *muskrat*, on the other hand, is an American animal, and his name represents the groping after an English meaning in the Algonquin *muskwessu*. The North American Indian *wuchak, ojeeg*, is adopted in English as *woodchuck*. The last part of the word *titmouse* is unrelated to *mouse*, but comes from the M. E. *mōse*, which comes from O. E. *māse*, a name for several kinds of birds. The same word appears in another bird name, *coalmouse*. The second element in *redstart* represents the O. E. *steort*, 'tail.' *Crayfish* and *crawfish* represent two stages in the process of folk-etymologizing. The word comes into English in the Middle English period in the form *crevice* from the O. Fr. *crevice*. The last element is first converted into *fish* and then the first element is changed to *craw* in order to associate the form with the familiar mode of locomotion of the animal. The O. Fr. *crevice* (Mod. Fr. *écrevisse*), is of Teutonic origin, O. H. G. *chrebiz*. The Teutonic word appears in modern German as *Krebs* and in English as *crab* (O. E. *crabba*).*

Names of cloths offer other instances of the same kind. *Lawn*, from the place-name, Laon, is associated wtih another English word *lawn* (from earlier *laund*). *Mohair* has no original connection with *hair*, but comes from the *Arabic mukhayyar*. *Tweed* is erroneously associated with the river name. It is a perversion of *tweel*, a dialect word connected in origin with *twill*.

In a number of words the popular misreading of the original name has led to the addition of a second element forming a tautological compound. The O. E. name for the reindeer, *hrān*, or its Norse cognate, *hreinn*, appears in the first element of the word, but from the habit of using the beast as a draught animal, this name is converted to *rein* and has had joined to it the word *deer*. The word *grey* in *greyhound* is itself the name for this kind of dog, but is erroneously interpreted as a color name, and *hound* is joined to it. In the same way *bed* is often joined to *cot*, which is itself an anglicized form of the Hindustani *khat*, 'bedstead.' *Salt* is a redundant element attached to *cellar* in *saltcellar*, since *cellar* in this case is falsely transformed from earlier *seler*, which goes back, through the French, to the Latin *saliaria*, feminine for *saliarius*, 'of salt,' and itself means a 'salt receptacle.' *Dove*, too, is redundant in *turtle-dove*, since *turtle* already means dove, derived by dissimilation from an earlier Latin *turtur*, probably of imitative origin from the cooing of the dove. The addition of *dove* was for the purpose of distinguishing the bird from the beast *turtle*, whose Spanish name, *tortuga*, in English was erroneously associated with *turtle*, the name of the dove. The Spanish word is derived from the Latin *tortus*, 'crooked,' whence O. Fr. *tortis* and English *tortoise*. The earlier use of *turtle* survives in biblical language, "The voice of the turtle is heard in the land."[1]

In some instances the misinterpretation involved in folk-etymology provides the basis for further word building. The word *lark*, in the sense 'frolic,' 'spree,' probably goes back to the O. E. *lāc*, meaning 'dance,' 'play.' The merriment plausibly becomes associated with the glee of the lark, and on the basis of this poetic reading of the word, a superlative form, *skylarking*, makes its appearance as a name for 'frolic.' The word *standard* is derived through the French *estendart* from the Latin *extendere*, 'to spread out' and, therefore, applied originally to the meaning 'flag' and is still applied as the name for the flag of a cavalry regiment. It became erroneously connected with the meaning 'stand,' involving change in meaning as well as in form. There appears to be a connection between this meaning mistakenly read into the word *standard*, and the use

---

[1] Greenough and Kittredge, p. 346.

FOLK-ETYMOLOGY 187

of the seemingly synonymous word *platform* in American politics as the name for the body of principles upon which a party stands. In the same way older *samblind* (O. E. *sam*, 'half,' cognate with Latin *semi*) becomes converted into *sandblind*. Popular reasoning is that if *sandblind* means half blind, complete blindness is expressed by the word *stoneblind*. The idea has been carried farther by Carlyle and other writers, who apply *gravelblind* as the name for an intermediate stage of blindness. In *by-law*, the first element is the Norse *by*, meaning 'city,' and the word, therefore, meant originally 'city law.' The first element has come to be associated with the more usual meaning of the English word *by*, and the word has come to apply to regulations supplementing the constitution of an organization. It seems not unreasonable to suppose that the prevalent use of this compound is at least partly responsible for the other modern *by*-compounds, such as *by-product*.

The word *rarebit*, in the phrase *Welsh rarebit*, results from the attempt to read meaning into the common phrase *Welsh rabbit*, the simple humor of which failed to reach. *Welsh rabbit* is in reality a product of popular humor having many parallels, such as *Digby chicken* for smoked herring; *Folkstone beef* for shark; *deep sea turkey* or *seagoing turkey* for salmon; *Cape Cod turkey* for codfish; *colonial goose*, Australian for leg of mutton; *Scotch woodcock* for poached eggs on toast; *Carnegie derbies* for steel helmets; *Alaskan sable* for skunk; *Hudson seal* for muskrat fur; *Marsh squirrel* or *Marsh rabbit* for muskrat; *Alabama wool* for cotton; *Missouri meerschaum* for corncob; *side-door Pullman* for box-car; *Irish confetti* for bricks; *bog orange* for potato; *pedlar's French*, a sixteenth-century name for slang; *African golf* for craps; *Jew piano* for cash register; *Jew Packard* for Ford.

Folk-etymologizing is a process associated, as the name itself indicates, with the unlettered class. Not unfrequently, however, learning itself has shown its ability to make mistakes. In the sixteenth century *abominable* was often written *abhominable,* from the erroneous idea that the word was composed of Latin *ab +homine,* 'from man.' The word *halcyon,* too, rests on a false etymology, which has provided the basis for a charming fable. In reality derived from the Greek *alkuon,* 'kingfisher,' which appeared in Latin as *alcyon,* it also appeared in Latin with an initial *h-* as *halcyon,* from the supposed derivation of the word from the Greek *hals,* 'the sea,' and *kuon,* present participle of *kuein,* 'to conceive.' The bird was, therefore, conceived of as 'breeding on the sea.' The fable goes that the kingfisher lays its eggs on the sea at the time of the winter solstice, in nests that charm the elements to a calm during the incubating period. Hence the phrase, 'halcyon days.' The form of the word *corporal* also rests on false learning. In reality derived from a Latin *caporalis* (Latin *caput,* 'head'), a form represented by the French *caporal,* it took its English form through the influence of the word *corporal* (Latin *corpus,* 'body'), or of the word *corps.*

In a similar way the forms of many common English words reflect a misdirected zeal on the part of sixteenth-century scholars in attempting to show the derivation of English words from Latin originals. For instance the words *debt* and *doubt* which had come into English through the French, and which in Chaucer's language had appeared respectively as *dette* and *doute,* were changed in spelling by the insertion of a *b* in order to show the relation to Latin *debitum* and *dubito,* respectively. Other words which were treated in a similar way were *subtle* (Chaucer, *sotil* or *subtle*), *Arctic* (Chaucer, *Artik*), *receipt* (Chaucer, *receit*). In some cases, such as *perfect, verdict, Arctic, subject,* the new spelling has influenced the pronunciation; in other cases, such as *debt, doubt, subtle,* the earlier pronunciation has persisted.

FOLK-ETYMOLOGY

The *l* in such words as *fault, assault, cauldron,* which does not appear in the earliest English forms of these words derived from the French, owes its insertion to the effort to make English words conform to supposed Latin originals. The same is true of the *d* in words such as *advice* and *adventure* (earlier, *avis, aventure*), the *qu* in *liquor* (earlier *licour, lykor*), the *-ure* in *leisure* and *pleasure* (earlier *layser, plesur*). The spelling *victuals* (Chaucer, *vitaille*), is another instance of the influence of Latin spelling, in this case without influence on the pronunciation.

Such mistaken zeal on the part of scholars has in many instances led to mistakes as glaring as those of more humble origin classed under the head of folk-etymology. For instance, in *island* (M. E. *iland*, meaning 'water land'), the *s* was inserted in order to show the supposed connection with *isle* (from Latin *insula*), and *rhyme* (Chaucer, *rime*), was re-spelled so as to show the imagined relation to *rhythm. Scissors* (M. E. *sisoures*, O. Fr. *cisoires*), gets its initial *sc-* from its supposed derivation from the Latin verb *scindere*, 'to cut.' *Could* owes its *l*, which though written has never been pronounced, to the influence of the parallel forms, *should* and *would* in which the *l* has an historical justification, even if it is not pronounced. The ending *-gue*, apparently of French origin and belonging appropriately, therefore, to words such as *vague, vogue, catalogue,* and their kind, was applied inappropriately to several English words. The ending has stuck in the case of *tongue* (M. E. *tonge*), and *rogue* (16th cent. *roge*), but fortunately the historical spellings *dog* and *king* have completely displaced the forms *dogue* and *kingue,* which appeared occasionally in sixteenth-century writings. Another written form which in the sixteenth century came into general use was the initial *wh-* for the *h-* sound. The influence of *who* and *whom,* where the spelling is historically justified, led to its extension not only to *whole*

(O. E. *hāl*), and *whore* (M. E. *hore*), where it has remained, but occasionally to *whome* (home) and *whot* (hot).

The process of folk-etymology is, then, only a popular form of a tendency, prevailing among the lettered as well as among the unlettered, to attempt to bring about uniformity and system into speech. One English word is modeled after another. *Donkey* is formed after the analogy of *monkey, parsnip* after the analogy of *turnip, benignant* after that of *malignant*. Strange appearing words, native as well as foreign are recast in familiar molds. Attempt is made, on the part of scholars, to restore distorted forms of classical derivatives to their original form.

REFERENCES FOR FURTHER READING

A. S. PALMER, *Folk-Etymology* (New York, 1883).
A. S. PALMER, *The Folk and their Word-Lore* (London and New York, 1909).
GREENOUGH AND KITTREDGE, *Words and Their Ways in English Speech* (New York, 1901), Ch. xxiii.
E. WEEKLEY, *The Romance of Words* (London, 1913), Ch. ix.
H. YULE and A. C. BURNELL, *Hobson-Jobson,* new ed. (London, 1903).
STRONG, LOGEMAN and WHEELER, *The History of Language* (London, 1891).

CHAPTER XIV

SOME FIGURES OF SYNTAX

The structure of a language, it has often been observed, expresses the character of its creators. Much has been heard recently of the British propensity to 'muddle through.' This national failing, because it has frequently been associated with eventual success, has come to be not only admitted with complacency, but even made the subject of boast. It is possibly not too fanciful to associate this quality with certain features of the English language. The flexibility of English, a quality to which it owes so much of its expressive power, has been gained at the cost of frequent deviation from the course of precision and logic. In other words, in the formation of the language felicitous results have frequently been reached by processes which might be called 'muddling through.'

Let us first consider the different functions that English words have been made to serve. One of the most striking features of the English language is the possibility of using a word without change of form as noun and as verb, as noun and as adjective, or as adjective and as verb. Thus the word *book* may be used as noun or as verb, the word *white* as noun or as adjective, the word *sour* as adjective, as noun, or as verb. In the Old English period, inflectional endings served not only to distinguish case and number and mood and tense, but also to distinguish from each other the inflected parts of speech, the noun, the verb, and the adjective. When in the Middle English period, the older definite inflectional endings were reduced to the indefinite ending -*e*, many of the old distinctions were obliterated, and by the year 1500, with the loss in pronunciation of the final -*e,* the older method of distinguishing between noun and verb and adjective had practically ceased to be. The Old English nouns *fisc* and *lufu* and *tācn* and the infinitives, *fiscian, lufian, tācnian,* had arrived at the common forms *fish, love,* and *token,* used interchangeably as nouns or as verbs. Since verbs from the French had followed the English modes of inflection, they, too, in English lost their original distinctive forms. With the habit of using verb and noun forms interchangeably, established in the case of a number of common words, it was natural to extend the practice widely. The practice thus established was made extravagant use of, particularly in the sixteenth century, and has continued with little restraint to our day. For instance, the name of almost any part of the human body may be turned to use as a verb. One may *head* a movement or *toe* the mark, may *eye* an opponent or *foot* a bill, may *unbosom* one's self or *stomach* an affront. In a good many instances a word may be used without change, as noun or adjective or verb, as in the case of *clear* or *sour.*

In some instances a noun or adjective form has in part replaced a distinctive verb form. Thus the verb *doom,* identical with the noun, has usurped part of the functions of *deem,* the original verb form connected with *doom.* The verb *clean* has in great part displaced the distinctively verbal form *cleanse.* The word *bath* as a verb sometimes replaces *bathe.* There is a particularly active tendency to use a verb as a noun expressing a slightly different phase of meaning from the distinctive noun form. Thus *meet* expresses a meaning differentiated from *meeting.* Other such verb forms used as nouns are: *show* (exhibition, or spectacle, or entertainment), *esteem* (estimation), a *catch,* (of fish), a *stand* (of grain), an *assist* (in baseball), or the spreading popular use of *eats* or *eat* for *food* or *restaurant.*

SOME FIGURES OF SYNTAX

A word which affords an interesting exhibition of the processes under consideration is the modern Americanism *hold up*. In its origin, a verb in the imperative mood, short for 'hold up your hands,' it comes to be used as a noun naming the action of a highwayman, and then the noun in turn is converted into a verb appearing in expressions such as 'hold up a train.'

In one particular instance, as has been pointed out in an earlier chapter, objection has been raised to the confusion of two distinct parts of speech. This objection is directed against the confusion in form of adjective and adverb. With the loss of the earlier word endings, adjective and adverb had arrived at an identical form. One set of adverbs, however, those originally ending in *-līce*, remain distinctively adverbial in form, with the ending *-ly*. In modern times there is a persistent tendency to recreate the earlier distinction in form by the uniform application of this ending *-ly* as the adverbial sign. The few remaining 'flat adverbs,' that is to say adverbs without the ending *-ly*, and therefore indistinguishable in form from adjective, are under critical fire from the grammarian.

This effort, however, at maintaining distinction in form, runs counter to the prevailing tendency. In general, at the present time the practice of interchange between parts of speech is very much alive. In fact this process affords one of the most widely used means of recruiting new words for new aspects of thought. The activity in interchange may be illustrated by the modern use of such words as *sense* and *glimpse* and *urge*. The noun *sense* is made to serve as a verb expressing a meaning more definite than 'feel' or 'perceive,' in fact 'to perceive through the organs of sense.' *Glimpse*, in like manner, is made to serve as a verb expressing the meaning 'to look at briefly.' On the other hand the verb *urge* is made to serve as a noun expressing an 'impelling feeling or force.'

The obliteration of older distinctions in form has doubtless at times caused a loss in logical precision; but in compensation the somewhat blundering method has contributed to the language a fluidity remarkably conducive to ease and flexibility in expression.

The double or triple function which words have been made to serve in the cases considered, has been paralleled elsewhere in language. In many instances ideas to be expressed have different aspects, and in many instances a word, unchanged in form, is made to express more than one of these aspects. Verbs, for instance, present one aspect toward the actor or subject, another aspect toward what is acted upon. Viewed from one side, the verb is active; viewed from the other it is passive (Lat. *passivus*, 'suffering'). In the classical languages, the active and passive aspects of the verb are systematically distinguished by difference in conjugation. In English in many instances the same word serves both purposes. For instance one may 'work a machine' or the 'machine may work well,' that is to say 'be worked well,' two different uses of the word *work*, in one of which it is active, in the other passive in function. The same two sides of a verbal idea appear without distinction in form in such parallel phrases as 'feel a stone,' 'stone feels hard'; 'wear clothes,' 'clothes wear well'; 'look at a person,' 'a person looks well'; 'smell a flower,' 'the flower smells sweet'; 'taste an apple,' 'apple tastes sour'; 'sound a bell,' 'bell sounds clear'; 'rent a house,' 'house to rent'; 'to do nothing,' 'nothing to do'; 'to blame nobody,' 'nobody to blame.'

In some instances this double use of a word has been challenged. Take for example the word *learn*. This word, down to the nineteenth century, and in uncultivated speech of our own day, expressed not only the meaning 'to acquire knowledge' but the active meaning 'to teach.' In the case of some words there has been a permanent shift from one aspect of an idea to the other. The Old English *fāeran* meant 'to cause fear'; a meaning appearing in the older phrase 'I fear me'; in modern English it means 'to suffer fear.' The Old English *scēawian* meant 'to look at'; its modern equivalent *show* expresses an active aspect of this meaning, 'to cause to look at.' In the same way Old English *warnian*, meaning 'to take heed,' appears in modern English as *warn*, meaning 'to cause to take heed.'

If now one turns to nouns, one finds similar differences of aspect, at times expressed by different words, at other times with no distinction in name. *Gaoler* and *prisoner*, for example, are words which, as far as form goes, seem practically synonymous, but which serve to express two distinct aspects of the idea; that of the active agent and that of the passive endurer. The noun *acquaintance* not only expresses an active knowledge, but is applied passively to a person who is known. A similar distinction appears in the two adjectives, *laborious* and *industrious*, the first applying to what is done, the other applying to the active agent. The simple word *clear* expresses different sides of an idea which may be differentiated by the two words, *perspicuous* and *perspicacious*. *Frugal* (Lat. *frugalis* from *frux*, plural *fruges*, 'fruits'), applies both to persons and things; *luxurious*, of similar formation (Lat. *luxuria*, from *luxus*, 'abundance'), applies usually to one aspect of the idea. The native word *freedom* now applies only to something enjoyed; in earlier English it expressed also an active quality practically equivalent to *generosity*. This earlier meaning of the word appears in "Trouthe and honour, fredom and curteisye," the list of admirable qualities ascribed by Chaucer to his Knight. An expressive ambiguity arises from the double meaning in such words as *self-made* and *self-starter*. *Self* may be regarded as the active agent or as the object. In order to express distinctly both sides of the meaning, one would need to say *self-made-self* and *self-*

start-self. In the same way arises a partial distinction between the words, *work* and *labor*. *Work* applies both to the active expenditure of energy and to something accomplished; *labor* applies usually only to one phase of the meaning, that of exertion.

In the case of adjectives the double aspect of meaning is particularly obvious. It appears, as already pointed out, in the cases of *laborious* and *industrious* and of *frugal*. It appears in somewhat different form in such words as *awful* and *fearful*. In earlier times these words applied to persons 'subject to awe,' or 'subject to fear'; at the present time the prevailing use of these words is to express the opposite or active aspect, a quality of things that cause awe or fear, while the other aspect is expressed by such words as *awe-struck* or *afraid*. In the case of *healthy* and *healthful* two aspects are distinguished, but there is a definite tendency, requiring strenuous effort on the part of the precisian to counteract, to make *healthy* apply to both aspects, to give to it not only the passive meaning of 'enjoying health' but the active one of 'health-giving.' The doublet words, *secure* and *sure*, both of which go back to Latin *securus*, 'free from care,' and, therefore, applied originally to a passive state of persons, in modern English usually apply to things which give no ground for care. The word *care* itself, it will be observed, expresses two aspects of a meaning, a passive one expressed by the synonym *anxiety*, and an active one practically equivalent to *painstaking*.

Shifts in meaning of this kind, sometimes extremely subtle in character, are encountered on all sides. The word *horror* comes from the Latin *horror*, meaning 'shuddering, 'shaking from cold or fear.' The English derivative, besides this meaning, conveys the active meaning of that which arouses, 'trembling' or 'shaking.' The Latin *horridus* means 'rough,' 'bristly,' 'shaggy,' and *hispidus* is nearly synonymous. In the English derivatives *horrid* and *hideous,* there has been a shift in meaning to that which has the physiological effect of making a person rough and bristly, causing what is called goose-flesh or making the hair stand on end.

The fact that the same word offers different aspects of meaning, gives rise to varied combinations with other words. In the case of compound words and derivatives, the elements are at times brought into relations which often are almost inexplicable. Such combinations as *looking-glass, funny-bone, wish-bone, ice-water, working-clothes, best wishes, sick-bed, glad tidings, sweet tooth,* afford illustrations of the varied relations into which words may be brought with each other. The slang phrases, *glad-hand, glad-eye, glad-rags,* illustrate once more how slang but carries to extravagant lengths tendencies generally existent in language.

An interesting group of adjectives in which a shift from an active to a passive quality has permanently affected the meaning, is that including *elegant, nice, superb, curious* and *quaint.*[1] *Elegant* derived from the active present participle of the Latin *eligere,* 'to pick out,' or 'select,' has come to be applied to that which is 'picked out' or 'selected,' a meaning nearly that of the Latin passive participle appearing in English as *elect. Nice, f*rom the Latin *nescius,* 'ignorant,' through the French, where it was transformed to *nice,* comes into English about Chaucer's time with the meaning 'foolish.' This meaning was later narrowed to that of 'foolishly particular,' and still later, losing its link of connection with its original meaning, it came to mean 'fastidious,' 'precise,' nearly equivalent to the original meaning of *elegant.* Then came the shift, as in the case of *elegant,* from an active to a passive quality, in such phrases as 'a nice distinction.' Its later colloquial general-

---

[1] Greenough and Kittredge, p. 277.

ization in meaning is based on the last mentioned use. *Superb*, once expressing the active quality of 'proud,' as in the Latin proper name, *Tarquinius Superbus*, now applies to the passive counterpart. *Curious* originally expressed the active quality of painstaking. Then transferred to a passive quality, it referred to things with which pains had been taken, that is, to things 'highly wrought.' Highly wrought things of one generation, one's grandmother's wedding dress, for instance, seem odd or curious to a generation governed by changed fashions. *Quaint* has shifted in the same way. It comes from the Latin *cognitus* 'known,' through the French, where it took its present form. The earlier meaning survives in the English derivative, *acquainted*. As in the case of *curious*, there has been a shift in meaning from an active quality, appearing as one of the meanings of *acquaintance*, to a quality of the thing in judging which this skill was used, and only later, as in the case of *curious*, does the word arrive at the meaning 'odd.'

Shifts take place in both directions. In expressions such as *sweet expression* and *grim determination*, the adjective is shifted from the active subject to the passive object. The shift is in the reverse direction in such expressions as *a deep thinker, a solid reasoner* and *a fluent speaker*.

The double aspect in verbs and the ability to shift from one to another, is illustrated in the case of a great many verbs originally impersonal. Among verbs of this kind the older construction survives in the archaic, *methinks*, 'it seems to me,' and the everyday "*What ails you?* Much more frequently the older impersonal construction has yielded to a modern personal construction in which the object of the earlier phrase becomes the subject. Thus *me likes, me list, loth hem is* ('loth to them is'), shift to *I like, I list, they are loath*. In this same way the verbs *hap, rue, long, hunger, thirst, need, lack, want, repent,* and *grieve* have shifted in use from impersonal constructions to personal ones. This development from impersonal to personal constructions was furthered by the fact that the dative form, *you,* of the personal pronouns came to be used in the nominative case in place of the older nominative form, *ye.* In this way a construction such as *ou greue* (for 'you grieve') might mean either 'you grieve' or 'it grieves you,' an ambiguity surviving in modern *if you please.*

In a number of phrases, such as 'sow a field with corn' for 'sow corn in a field'; 'blame war on Germany' for 'blame Germany for the war'; 'wrap clothes about a person' for 'wrap a person in clothes'; 'beg a favor of one' for 'beg one for a favor'; 'threaten death to him' for 'threaten him with death'; 'clean the spot from the floor' for 'clean the floor of the spot'; one has to do with a word-metathesis. The metathesis, or shifting of the relative position of the sounds in a word, is a familiar phenomenon in language. In this way O. E. *fersce* has become modern *fresh,* O. E. *gœrs* has become *grass,* and in illiterate modern speech, *Auburn* is transformed to *Orbin.* In the case of word metatheses, the explanation is not quite so simple as in the case of sounds. What seems to have taken place in the case of the word *sow,* for example, is that this verb, which is always accompanied by some form of seed as object, has absorbed that element into its connotation and has become practically synonymous with the verb 'to seed,' and is therefore qualified to take 'field' as a direct object, leaving the phrase 'with corn' as a qualifying phrase. The meaning of the word is changed because the object has become implied with it.

One is thus led to the explanation of the loss of many of the reflexive verbs once frequent in English. There are still surviving reflexive phrases such as *enjoy oneself, exert oneself,* but in a majority of instances the reflexive object has been absorbed within the verb. In the case of the Scandinavian derivatives, *busk* (Icel. *buask, bua,* 'prepare' + *sik,* self) and *bask* (for *batha sik,* 'bathe oneself') the absorption has been a physical one. More often, however, the reflexive object has left almost no physical trace, as in the words: *hide* (oneself), *repent, sport* (oneself), *boast, vaunt, rest, dress, behave* (oneself), *indulge, make* (myself) *bold with you, put* (oneself) *to sea.* In all of these words and phrases the reflexive object is superfluous because already implied in the verb form.

The suppression of the superfluous reflexive object is but one instance of the suppression of a redundant element in language. The English language is filled with words, relics of phrases in which some of the elements have become superfluous. A few specimens of words of this kind are: *bridge* (for bridge whist), *auction* (auction bridge), *poise* (mental poise), *rifle* (rifle gun), *fob* (fob chain), *match* (sulphur match), *conceit* (self conceit), *cheap* (good cheap), *corn* (Indian corn), *rubber* (India rubber), *livery* (livery gown). Other examples are: *correspondence* (of letters), *camera* (obscura), *piano* (forte), *cardinal* (red), (stage) *play,* (telegraph) *dispatch,* (hunger) *starved, fall* (of leaf), (price of) *fare, concert* (of music), (price of) *admission, attic* (front), *curate* (curate's delight), *doctor* (of medicine), *double* (fault), (military) *effectives,* (high) *temperature, commit* (to memory), *act on one's own* (initiative), *concentrate* (one's mind), (doleful) *dumps, gate* (money), a *considerable* (amount of), *calico* (cloth).

From the facts presented in this chapter it will be seen that the language owes much of its flexibility to the varied syntactical relations into which its words may enter. It will also be seen that many words undergo permanent change in meaning through the influence of syntactical combinations. So far from systematic, however, are many of these changes, that they seem due less to logical method than to caprice, or what might be called 'muddling through.'

References for Further Reading

Greenough and Kittredge, *Words and Their Ways in English Speech,* Ch. xix.
Strong, Logeman and Wheeler, *The History of Language,* Ch. vii.
Jespersen, *Growth and Structure of the English Language,* pp. 163ff.

CHAPTER XV

TROPES

The preceding three chapters have offered an account of the physical expansion of the vocabulary and of some of the physical changes it has undergone. They have shown how words are increased in numbers by new creation and by varied combinations. They have shown how words are modified in form so as to fit in with the existing order and how they are brought into varied relations with each other. But these physical modifications go only a short way in the explanation of how language has been able to accomplish its function, the task little short of the miraculous, of making the limited variety of sounds producible by the organs of the human voice serve to express the almost infinite variety and complexity of human thought. The achievement of this function has been possible only through an inner or psychical expansion, a true evolution of the powers of expression. In this evolution much has been accomplished by a variety of shifts in meaning, by which a single word has been made to express not one meaning alone, but a remarkable variety of meanings. "It is thanks to the metaphor," according to the remark of Quintilian (VIII, 6), "that each thing seems to have its name in language."[1] In order to avoid the ambiguity connected with the name metaphor, in the present discussion the shifts in meaning will be referred to collectively as tropes.

In the development of language it is well established that the things first to receive names were the definite, tangible things coming most close in everyday experience.

---

[1] M. Bréal, *Essai de Sémantique*, p. 135.

The less tangible elements in life were named by means of figurative shifts of earlier names. Thus the concrete names of space relations, which were appreciable by sight and touch, were made to serve in expressing the relations of time, matters outside the direct range of the five senses. Thus *long* and *short* applied to time, are words originally expressing spatial dimension. The adjective *brief*, now associated with time, comes from the Latin *brevis* originally applied to space, a word surviving with its spatial meaning in the compounds *abbreviate* and *abridge*. Most of the names for divisions of time may be traced back to words expressing physical facts: *minute* (Lat. *minutus*, 'small'); *second* (Med. Lat. *secunda minuta*, 'second minute,' *i. e.*, further subdivision); *week* (underlying meaning probably, 'change'); *month* (moon); *year* (underlying meaning, 'spring'); *season* (Lat. *satio*, *sationem*, 'sowing'); *period* (Gk. *periodos*, 'circuit'). The verb *last*, 'to endure,' in earlier English applied to spatial continuance. *Endure* goes back to a physical meaning 'to become hard.' *Fast* in the sense of 'rapid,' is derived from an earlier meaning, 'firmly fixed.' *Rapid*, in turn, goes back to an earlier physical meaning, 'snatching'; it is related in origin to such words as *rapacious* and *rapine*. *Quick*, a native English word, had an original meaning, 'living,' a meaning surviving in such combinations as *quicksilver, quicklime, cut to the quick, the quick and the dead.*

What is true of the origin of terms of time is true of psychical terms in general. The word *psychic*, itself, is derived through the Latin from the Greek word *psyche* for 'soul,' which, however, is derived from *psychein*, 'to blow.' *Intellect* comes from Latin *inter + legere*, 'choose between.' *Perceive* and *comprehend* come from Latin words the literal meanings of which are 'to seize' or 'to grasp.' The figurative shift is repeated in the case of such English words as *grasp* and *catch*, in such expressions as *mental grasp* and the slang, *catch on*. *Ruminate*, it is well known, referred originally to the cud-chewing of the cow. *Brood*, 'to meditate,' goes back to the earlier meaning, 'to sit on eggs.' *Cogitate*, from the Latin *coagitare*, originally referred to a physical 'mixing together.' The more modern word *wool-gathering* expresses in a strikingly figurative way an inconclusive mode of thinking. Further instances are: *ponder* (Lat. *ponderare*, 'to weigh'); *deliberate* (Lat. *libra*, 'scales'); *reflect* (Lat. *reflectere*, 'to bend back), *examine* (Lat. *examinare*, 'to weigh carefully,' from *examen*, 'the needle or tongue in a balance,' *cf. exact*); *calculate* (Lat. *calculus*, 'pebble,' diminutive of *calx*, 'lime'); *investigate* (Lat. *vestigium*, 'foot-print'); *delusion* (Lat. *ludere*, 'to play, *deludere*, 'to play false'); *blunder* (*cf.* M. E. *blonden*, 'to mix'). The list might be prolonged indefinitely.[2]

In like manner moral conceptions have had to appropriate names from the physical world. Even the fundamental words, *right* and *wrong*, originally meant physically 'straight' and 'crooked,' respectively (*cf. right angle, right away*, etc., and O. E. *wringan*, 'to twist'), and it will be noted that in modern colloquial language the shift in meaning has been repeated in the case of the words, *straight* and *crooked*. The fundamental meaning of *good* is supposed to be 'fitting' or 'suitable'; that of *evil* is supposed to be 'excessive.' The word *bad*, which somewhat mysteriously makes its first appearance in the Middle English period, it is supposed, applied originally to a form of physical abnormality. *Moral* and *ethical* go back respectively to Latin *mos*, 'custom' and Greek *ethos*, 'custom,' 'manner.' *True*, as is pointed out elsewhere, in its remote origin, probably applied to the oak tree. *Integrity* originally meant 'wholeness,' literally 'untouched' (Lat.

---

[2] *Cf.* S. Kroesch, *Semasiological Development of Words for "Perceive,"* etc., *Mod. Philology*, viii, 461-510.

in, 'not' + *tangere*, 'to touch'). *Holy* comes from the O. E. *hālig* (from *hāl*, 'whole'). *Wicked* appears in Middle English as *wikke*, 'wicked' or 'feeble' (cognate with *weak*). *Virtue*, on the other hand, meant originally 'manly strength' (Lat. *vir*, 'man'). *Character* is derived from the Greek *charakter*, 'a tool for stamping or marking.' In English it has both its original meaning of 'mark' or 'kind' and, among other later meanings, that of 'moral strength.'

The way in which a simple set of words may be made to express a complex variety of meanings is illustrated further by the use made of names of such elemental conceptions as the parts of the body, the names of which are shifted to express a remarkably varied set of meanings in the inanimate world or in the world of thought. The name *head* appears in 'bridgehead,' 'head of a pin,' 'head of an institution,' 'head of a class,' 'fountain head,' 'head of a coin,' 'head of cattle', 'headland.' The Latin *caput*, 'head,' and its French derivative, *chief*, appear in a series of meanings equally varied, in such words as *captain, capital* (city), *capital* (property), *chief* (noun and adjective) and *chef* (of kitchen). The word *front* (Latin *frontem*, 'forehead') may apply to the whole face, as in *frontispiece*, literally 'appearance of the face,' to 'confidence expressed by the face,' as in *bold front*, etc., or to 'brazen impudence,' as in *effontery*, or to the 'foremost part of anything,' as in *battle front, water front*, or *front* of a building or figure. In the same way *foot* is applied as name for a part of a bed, of a grave, of a monument, of a stocking, of a table, of a page, of a street, or of a slope. It is the name of a unit of measure and of an element in versification. *Hand* is applied to a remarkable variety of meanings related to some feature of the hand, either to the member itself, to its action, to its position, or to its symbolic use, as exemplified in such expressions as *in strong hands, have a hand in, on the other hand, ask for lady's hand, hands* (in a factory), *an old hand, write a good hand, set our hand and seal, hand of a clock, six hands high, a hand at cards, play a hand, hand* 'applause at theater.'

In the same way the names of familiar animals are turned to a variety of uses. The name *dog* may apply to types of men, contemptible or merely sportive, to a constellation, or to a varied list of mechanical implements, such as an andiron, a clamp, a tooth-extractor, a tooth for a catch or click, a drag for a wheel, a lever used by blacksmiths, an appliance for toasting bread, etc. *Horse* is applied as a name to a body of mounted troops, to a supporting frame, as in 'saw horse' or 'clothes horse,' to a mass of rock within a vein of metal, to a dishonest aid used by school boys, and, like dog, to a variety of implements used in machine shop or in sea-craft. It appears also as an essential element in a variety of expressive phrases, such as 'Barbary horse,' 'dark horse,' 'Flemish horse,' 'green horse,' 'high horse,' not to mention the scores of compound words such as 'horse-chestnut,' 'horse-flower,' 'horse-laugh,' 'horse-power,' 'horse-sense,' 'horse-radish.'

Most of the instances of shifts in meaning here offered have been relatively modern. The process, however, must have played an important part in early stages in the development of speech. In fact, these tropes, or shifts in meaning, are in evidence at all stages in the history of language. They serve to explain the length of the lists of meanings recorded for simple words in the various large dictionaries. In the *Century Dictionary,* for instance, twenty-five different meanings are recorded for the verb *run* and twenty-three for the corresponding noun. In the Oxford Dictionary, the word *take* (originally meaning to 'touch with the hand') with its list of meanings and illustrative citations, occupies fourteen pages, forty columns.

In the case of a majority of the instances cited above, the

original meaning of the word is not lost sight of. In the phrase, 'on the other hand,' the word *hand* is used for side, the position of the hand. In 'hands of a clock,' the name is applied because of similarity, in the function of pointing out, in the case of the human hand and of the member of the clock. In a 'good hand of cards' the name *hand* is applied to the cards held in the hand. In 'six hands high' the word *hand* is applied to a linear unit measured by the breadth of the hand. In 'factory hands' the name is applied to the workmen who serve the factory as the hand serves the body. In each instance there is evident a relation to a central idea, and the process by which the different meanings have been reached is called *radiation*. The relation of the derived meanings may be indicated by a figure with a series of lines radiating out from a central point.

Let us take by way of illustration the various meanings of the word *pipe*. This word goes back for its origin to the Latin *pipare*, a verb of imitative origin from the peeping of a bird. From this verb was formed the noun *pipa*, applied originally to an instrument that made the sound named by the verb, usually a tubular wooden instrument. From this last meaning radiate out the meanings: (1) pipe of an organ; (2) gas-pipe, stove-pipe, etc.; (3) the cell in a bee-hive used by the queen bee; (4) a tube of clay used in smoking, and, by metonymy, *pipe* for *pipeful;* (5) a wine measure; (6) *pipe* colloquial for *windpipe;* (7) plural, *pipes* for *bagpipes;* (8) a spool (as of thread), obsolete; (9) various special meanings in hairdressing, in dressmaking, in engineering, and in metallurgy.

In the case of many words, however, the shift in meaning is not simple but multiple. The meaning reached by the first shift may in turn be shifted a second time, and so on indefinitely, so that the original meaning of the word may be quite lost to view. In the physical changes which words undergo, often a form is reached which shows little relationship to the original form. Thus in spelling there is little apparent relation between the word *key* and the O. E. *cæg* from which it is derived, between *chain* and *challenge* and the Latin originals, *catena* and *calumniari*. In the same way through multiple shifts in meaning a final meaning may be reached very different from, possibly the reverse of, the original one. *Nice*, as already pointed out, was brought into English in the French form, *nice* meaning 'foolish.' Its present proper meaning is the reverse of foolish, as in the phrase 'a nice distinction.' The color name *auburn* comes from the Latin *alburnus*, meaning 'whitish.' Its modification in form was received from French use, where it appeared as *alborne* or *auborne*, still meaning 'whitish.' In English, in the sixteenth and seventeenth centuries, the word was variously written, *abron, abrune* and *abroun*. Hence a confusion with the word *brown* and, consequently, its later meaning. In *Webster's Dictionary* the word *wold* is given two meanings: "1. A wood; a forest. 2. A plain, or low hill; a country without wood, whether hilly or not." The word comes from the O. E. *weald*, 'forest,' but persists as the name for places from which the forests have been removed. The word *fast* may mean 'firmly fixed' or the reverse of this, 'in rapid motion.' Obviously there are two different meanings of *fast* in the expressions *stand fast* and *run fast*. *Forfeit*, which originally meant 'wrong' or 'crime' (Fr. *forfait*), now usually refers to a penalty for wrongdoing. *Alto*, which means in Italian 'high,' has come through clipping of the full form *contralto*, to apply paradoxically to a female voice of lower range. *Desire* comes from French *desirer*, Latin *desiderare*, the original meaning of which was 'regret.'[3] *Daub*, which now means 'to smear,' comes from the Latin *dealbare* 'to plaster,' which is formed from

---

[3] Weekley, *Etymological Dictionary*.

the adjective *albus,* 'white.' *Virtue,* which, it has been pointed out, is formed from the Latin *vir,* 'man,' has taken as one of its modern meanings a quality belonging to women. The word *cease,* which now means 'to stop,' is derived from the Latin *cedere,* which meant 'to go.' A *fine* boy is a large boy; a *fine* needle is the reverse of large. The word *dress,* which comes from a conjectured Latin *directiare,* meaning 'to set straight,' expresses meanings quite different in the two expressions 'dress a child' and 'dress a fowl for the oven.' *Nervous* to the British means 'strong,' 'vigorous'; to an American it means a form of weakness. The word *flag,* which as a noun is associated with active emotion, as a verb means also 'to hang loosely and laxly'; 'to droop from weariness,' a meaning apparent in the adjective *unflagging.* In the seventeenth century *tumbler* meant a drinking cup with rounded or pointed bottom. In modern use the name has lost its original appropriateness.

As a result of these changes in meaning, there are produced frequent expressions of paradoxical character. A university course *ends* with a *commencement.* A steamer *sails.* An airplane *lands* on the sea. A German ship during the war was reported as *manned* with women. We have weekly *journals* (literally 'weekly dailies,' *cf.* Fr. *jour,* 'day'), in which appears *old news.* We have *golf greens* of sand. Blackberries are red when they are *green.* Things may be said to grow smaller; people are said to *enjoy* ill health. A *manuscript* (literally 'hand written'), may be *typewritten.* The older *kerchief* (literally 'head cover') appears in combinations the elements of which, if taken literally, are contradictory, such as *handkerchief, neck-handkerchief,* and *pocket-handkerchief.* A word, in fact, may come to be practically synonymous with its negation, as in the cases of *passive* and *impassive, ravel* and *unravel, valuable* and *invaluable.*

This paradoxical quality in words is particularly obvious in the case of proper names. Mr. *Black* is possibly white; Mr. *White* is not necessarily so. Mr. *Smith* may do clerical work; Mr. *Clark* may be a blacksmith. Mr. *French* may be an Englishman; Mr. *English* or Mr. *Scott* may be an American. *New College* is one of the older colleges of Oxford; *New York* has little to do with *new* or with *York*. American cities situated on the plain bear the name *Mount Vernon*.

Varied influences have been involved in the remarkable reversals of meaning just considered. In most instances there has been, not one, but a series of shifts. In the word *cardinal*, for instance, several distinct stages may be recognized. The history of the word begins with: (1) the Latin *cardo*, 'hinge,' from which was formed (2) the adjective *cardinalis*, 'hinging' or 'essential,' a meaning seen in the expressions, '*cardinal* points' and '*cardinal* virtues.' In the twelfth century the word was used (3) as a noun, the name of a church dignitary, *cardinal* bishop, *cardinal* priest or *cardinal* deacon, connected with one of the *cardinal* churches of Rome. From the color of the hat and robe of the church cardinal the word came to be used as (4) an adjective of color, as in *cardinal bird, cardinal cloak*, etc., and eventually (5) as a noun, the name of a color, first cited in this use as late as 1879. In all, five stages are represented in the history of this word. In the development of *nice*, already considered, six stages may be recognized: (1) Latin *nescius*, 'ignorant'; (2) French *nice*, 'foolish'; (3) English *nice*, 'foolishly fastidious'; (4) 'fastidious,' a personal quality; (5) 'precise,' a quality of things, expressing the quality of the judgment of a nice person; (6) the modern loose colloquial meaning. To this multiple change may be applied the expressive name *concatenation*, 'linking together' (Lat. *catena*, 'chain'), an adaptation of *enchaînement*, the word employed by French scholars. The successive changes are like links in a chain. Each meaning links with an earlier meaning, but the final meaning reached is quite removed from the original meaning, as the last link in a chain is removed from the first.

Let us take for further illustration the word *lozenge.* The Old French word, variously spelled *losange, losenge, lozenge,* meant first 'flattery' and then 'praise.' It then came to be applied to epitaphs and to monuments on which praise was expressed, and then to a diamond-shaped figure like that used in the monumental inscription, a meaning frequent in architectural use. It next has come to be applied to various things in this form, particularly to small cakes of sugar, usually medicated. In common use, the word is now applied to medicated confections of various forms, a meaning far removed from the original meaning, 'flattery.'

The word, *board,* is another interesting example. This word, of native English origin, started with the meaning still in use, 'a piece of timber.' The theatrical phrase, *on the boards,* exhibits a first stage in change of meaning. The word shifts further to mean 'an extended surface of wood,' as in *chess board, backgammon board,* and through this use, comes to mean 'a surface,' not necessarily of wood and, perhaps, as in the case of *backgammon board,* the interior of a frame or box rather than a simple flat surface. Separated from the idea of wood, it comes to refer to 'a flat fabric' of other material, as in *pasteboard, cardboard,* and *board* as a form of bookbinding. In its first stage of meaning, 'an extended surface of wood,' it becomes associated with a particular use, that of a table in serving food, and the meaning becomes shifted from the table or board, to the food served, as in *bed and board, a week's board,* etc. Used as the name for a table, the meaning becomes shifted to the council or committee that meets about the table, as in *board of health,* etc. The name for the flat surface of wood is applied to a variety of other uses, and the word becomes shifted so as to apply as the name of a shield, or of the side of a ship. From 'side of a ship' the meaning shifts to the ship itself, a meaning which survives in *aboard* (on board). The last word becomes further shifted in American use so as to apply to a railroad train as well as to a ship. The variety of meanings in this word is interesting since most of the different meanings survive in modern use. It should be noted that both radiation and concatenation are involved in the history of the word.

In the word *style* one may distinguish several stages: beginning with (1) Latin *stilus*, a pointed instrument used for various purposes; (2) this instrument used in writing on waxen tablets; (3) the manner of writing; (4) manner of expressing thought; (5) manner in general; (6) manner dictated by prevailing fashion. A similar series of meanings may be seen in the history of the word *knight*, which comes from the O. E. *cniht*, 'boy.' The second stage in meaning is 'servant.' A third stage is 'feudal servant,' which leads to the use of the term as a special title of honor, the fourth stage. In *squire* one may recognize: (1) Latin *scutarius*, 'shield bearer'; (2) shield bearer to a knight; (3) attendant on a knight; (4) a landed proprietor; (5) justice of the peace (American). In *canvass* the following stages may be recognized: (1) Latin *cannabis*, 'hemp'; (2) hempen fabric; (3) (as a verb) to scrutinize by tossing on canvass; (4) to investigate or sift by inquiry; (5) to seek orders or subscriptions. *Porcelain* has the following history: (1) Latin *porcus*, 'pig,' Italian *porcella*, 'little pig'; (2) the name of a shell so named because of its resemblance to a pig in shape; (3) the pottery product, so named because of the resemblance of its polished surface to that of the shell.

Salute (Latin *salus*, 'health') meant: (1) health; (2) greeting, consisting of the expression of a wish for good health; (3) greeting in a general sense. The native English *hail* has gone through the same stages in development. *Clumsy* (Scand. *klumsa*, 'numb') came to mean (1) awkward, a consequence of numbness, and then (2) awkward in general. *Awkward* in turn meant (1) backhanded, then (2) the reverse of graceful. *Baluster* has developed through the stages: (1) pomegranate flower (Greek *balaustrion*); (2) an architectural support used in Renaissance style with representation of the pomegranate flower; (3) one of the series of supports to a railing. *Trammel* (Latin *tres + macula*, 'triple mesh') meant (1) a net, a meaning that survives in use; (2) a form of shamble used in regulating the step of a horse; (3) that which confines or hampers, as in *untrammeled*. The verb *pester* (Latin *in + pastorium*, 'a clog for horses at pasture') develops through the stages: (1) to shackle or clog a horse; (2) to encumber, or clog in general; (3) to annoy. *Tease* (O. E. *tæsan*, 'to pull' or 'to pluck') applied (1) to the pulling apart of fibers, as in carding flax or wool; (2) to the pulling of hair; (3) to the general meaning 'annoy.' *Pocket-book* meant (1) a small book carried in the pocket, but came also to mean (2) a small book for carrying money, and finally (3) any money holder for the pocket, and sometimes (4) the pecuniary resources of a person. *Purse* has had a similar development through the stages: (1) Greek *bursa*, 'hide' or 'skin'; (2) a bag or pouch; (3) a money pouch; (4) any pocket receptacle for money. *Pen* goes through the stages: (1) Latin *penna*, 'feather'; (2) the quill used for writing; (3) a writing implement. *Pencil* appears in the stages: (1) Latin *peniculus*, 'little tail'; (2) *penicillus*, a painter's brush of hair; (3) an implement for marking. *Buckle* may be traced from (1) Latin *bucca*, 'cheek,' through (2) the Latin diminutive *buccula*, to (3) Old French *bocle, bucle*, 'the boss of a shield,' to (4) the modern meaning. In *scene* may be traced the stages: (1) Greek *skene*, 'tent'; (2) a stage; (3) the place of action in a play; (4) the place where any action takes place; (5) a variety of radiating meanings, among them, 'a view,' or 'landscape.'[4] The noun *stamp* goes back to the O. E. verb *stempan,* 'to stamp,' 'tread on.' From the verb apparently comes (2) the name for an instrument used to make impressions. The meaning shifts to (3) the impression left, and finally to (4) that upon which the impression is left, as in *postage stamp,* or 'a variety or brand indicated by the impression left,' and (5) 'kind' or 'variety' in general. *Chevron* goes back to (1) Latin *capra,* 'goat,' from which was derived (2) French *chevron,* 'kid,' which came to mean (3) a rafter, and the saddle peak formed by two rafters, which in turn came to name (4) the figure used for decorative purpose or in military designation. In the history of *bureau* one may start with (1) O. French *burel,* 'a coarse woolen stuff.' A second stage is (2) *bureau,* the desk or writing table, so named because covered with a coarse woolen stuff. From this meaning radiate a variety of meanings, as in the case of *board,* and the name *bureau* may apply to a place where business is transacted, or to the body of men who transact the business, for example, *a government bureau.* The word *Roman* became applied to the vernacular form of Latin from which developed the Old French language. It came later to apply to the metrical narratives which were characteristic literary products in Old French, and to imaginative narratives of adventure, a meaning conveyed by *romance,* the English form of the French word *roman.* In modern times the word *romance* conveys various meanings, associated qualities which were distinctive features of the medieval *romance.*

The variety of meanings which may find expression by means of words from one common original, may be illustrated by the words *molar, molest,* and *emolument,* all of

---

[4] Greenough and Kittredge, p. 246.

which, according to Skeat, go back to the Latin *molere,* 'to grind.' If one will go back to more remote origins, and will give one's vision a wider sweep, one will find far more extreme instances of meanings widely divergent from a common original. For instance let us take the Sanskrit *vanam,* which meant variously 'tree,' 'wood,' 'forest,' and 'piece of wood,' the original meaning probably having been 'tree.' From 'piece of wood' is reached the meaning 'piece of wood used for a plow.' From 'plow' comes the broader meaning 'cultivate land,' and from 'cultivate land' is reached the meaning 'dwell,' a meaning which appears in the German *wohnen.* From 'cultivate land' also, is reached the general meaning 'labor,' which appears in O. Norse *vinna* and O. H. G. *winnan.* From 'labor' is also reached the meaning 'fight,' which appears in O. E. *winnan.* This word in later English appears as *win,* meaning 'to gain' or 'to be victorious,' natural results of fighting. By still other shifts is reached the meaning, 'love,' which appears in the name of the goddess of love, *Venus,* and in the O. H. G. *wini,* 'lover,' 'friend' and the O. E. *wine,* 'friend.' Surely this is a varied set of meanings all going back to an early name for 'tree.'

The instances cited, which might be added to indefinitely, will suffice to show that in general there is usually no essential relation existing between the sound of a word and its modern meaning. In the case of certain onomatopoetic, or imitative words, unquestionably a direct relation exists. But in the great majority of cases the relation is no essential one, since one word may serve equally well to express meanings one of which is directly the opposite of the other. The ways by which meanings are arrived at are so devious and the processes are so complex that, although unquestionably governed by natural laws, they appear to be governed only by chance. Hence in many instances the failure of etymology as a practical guide, the futility of attempting to determine the present meaning by that with which a word started.

In the courses followed by words in their shifts of meaning, two processes have been named, that of radiation and that of concatenation. Both these processes are frequently involved in the history of a single word. A more graphic method, however, of illustrating the courses followed by words is offered by an analogy in physical nature in the case of a vine such as the strawberry vine. A single strawberry plant sends out a number of runners, each of which takes root and is ready in turn to send out runners in different directions. If one undertakes to represent by means of diagrams the way in which a small number of words have availed to cover the field of thought, the more regular figures suggested by the words radiation and concatenation will not convey an impression of the facts as precisely as will irregular lines like those made by the strawberry plant in covering an area of ground.

CHAPTER XVI

FIGURES OF SIMILARITY

"They that dally nicely with words may quickly make them wanton" is the opinion of Viola as expressed to the Clown in "Twelfth Night." Certainly the shifts in meaning undergone by words in popular use exhibit a bewildering variety which makes it appear that words are the playthings of chance. Is it possible to discover anything like law and order in the midst of this seeming wantonness?

Any search for governing principles in language must be guided by the consideration that speech is the external body of which the soul is thought. "A thought," says a recent Irish writer, "is a real thing, and words are only its raiment, but a thought is as shy as a virgin; unless it is fittingly appareled, we may not look on its shadowy nakedness; it will fly from us and only return again in the darkness, crying in a thin, childish voice which we may not comprehend until, with aching minds listening and divining, we at last fashion for it those symbols which are its protection and its banner."[1] The idea expressed here in such poetic manner, finds more literal expression in the words of the psychologist, Wundt. "Human speech and human thought are everywhere coincident. . . . The development of human consciousness includes in itself the development of modes of expression. Language is an essential element of the function of thinking." Whether, then, we follow the poet or the scientist, we must conclude that the laws of language are to be sought in the laws of mind.

---

[1] James Stephens, *The Crock of Gold*, p. 49.

Among the links of association that hold together the elements in human thought, none are stronger than those of likeness. Hence it is that in language no figures are more striking than the figures of similarity, the simile and the metaphor. The formative power of the metaphor in the shaping of language has often been called to notice. "Language," says Jean Paul, "is a dictionary of faded metaphors." "Examine language," says Carlyle, "what is it all but Metaphors, recognized as such, or no longer recognized; still fluid and florid, or now solid-grown and colourless?" "When I feel inclined to read poetry," says the Autocrat of the Breakfast Table, "I take down my dictionary. . . . Bring me the finest simile from the whole range of imaginative writing, and I will show you a single word which conveys a more profound, a more accurate and a more eloquent analogy." Practically the same idea has been expressed more recently. "Now the poet, since he is constantly seeing new resemblances, and uncovering new objects of ideas, which because they are new, lack words to express them, is constantly forced to make such extensions. By using figures he gains greatly in power of expression; indeed he is enabled to express ideas which would otherwise remain inexpressible. The poets, therefore, are the great builders of language."[2]

Our indebtedness to our ancestors for the expressive power of language springing from their earlier perception of the resemblance between things has likewise often been proclaimed. "Language," says Emerson, "is fossil poetry." "In common speech," says Mr. Santayana, "we find such ancient bits of wisdom embedded. . . . Words are at best the tombs of ideas, and the most conventional formulas of poets or theologians are still good subjects for the archæologist of passion."

---

[2] F. C. Prescott, *The Poetic Mind*, 1922, p. 225.

FIGURES OF SIMILARITY 219

A prevailing opinion, then, seems to be that the language we have inherited is the product of a conscious activity on the part of succeeding generations of our ancestors and that by their conscious poetic art, has been created the instrument of expression, wondrous in range and at the same day wondrous in delicacy, of which we make everyday use. Running counter to this view of language as the product of conscious effort, in the formation of which countless minds during many centuries have been active, is a deterministic theory which explains changes as usually the product of natural unconscious growth. Let us hear once more the words of the psychologist. "We regard it as a justifiable logical assumption," says Wundt, "that there is no phenomenon which was not in the entire series of its conditions definitely determined. . . . Change of meaning, like sound change, is everywhere subject to definite laws."[3]

The idea expressed by Wundt is echoed by a later writer.[4] "By far the most semantic changes are unconscious shiftings of meanings. . . . It is only the observer looking back over history who sees that a change has taken place. . . . The picturesque saying that 'language is a book of faded metaphors' is exactly the reverse of reality, where poetry is rather a blazoned book of language."

Here is conflict of opinion most sharply defined. On which side does the truth lie? Certainly much evidence may be brought to support the more poetic explanation of language as a coöperative product of conscious art. Far and away the greater number of metaphorical shifts that one meets with seem due to definite intention. There are, to be sure, instances of metaphors produced unconsciously. When a child calls a bird's nest *a house*, he is making use of the only word in his vocabulary for 'a place to live.'

---

[3] W. Wundt, *Völkerpsychologie*, II, pp. 437, 567.
[4] L. Bloomfield, *The Study of Language*, pp. 238, 247.

In the same way when he learns the name *burn* for a painful sensation in the finger, he quite naturally applies the same word to a painful sensation in the stomach. In the same way he applies the name *pepper*, which he knows, to another hot spice such as *cinnamon*, or applies to a factory with smoking chimney the name of something familiar to him that produces smoke in like manner, a *steamer*,[5] or, by a curious reversal of ideas, calls a soaring bird an "ayoplane." In all these examples there probably exists no conscious figurative purpose. The shift in the use of the word is due to the inadequacy of the child's vocabulary who seeks to make a known word fit new cases. The adult may find himself in a similar situation, particularly in trying to speak in a foreign language. The present writer remembers when he was driven to say *Eisenbahn Haus* 'railroad house' when he ould not think of the German word, *Bahnhof*, for 'station.' The frequency of figurative turns of expression in the speech of uncultivated people finds its explanation in part in the inadequate range of the speaker's vocabulary as in the case of the child or of the adult using a foreign language. When the California miner began the use of *pan out* in other than a literal meaning, it was possibly in part due to the fact that such words as *yield* and *produce* were not natural to his vocabulary. In the same way, when the Indian makes one word serve to express meanings as diverse as 'mystery,' 'spirit,' 'God,' 'fire,' and 'whisky,' the shifts in meaning are probably to be attributed as much to the poverty of his vocabulary as to his poetic sense of relations. On the other hand the native African, who is said to have described the toothache as "a lion roaring in the mouth," was using a true metaphor, a product of feeling at a heightened stage.

In many instances where a metaphorical shift of meaning seems to have taken place, the change lies not in the

---

[5] O. Jespersen, *Nutidsprog* (Copenhagen, 1916), p. 84.

FIGURES OF SIMILARITY 221

application of a new name, but in a change in the substance or article devoted to some use while the name remains fixed. Thus the name *pen* persists although the implement named has changed from quill to steel. The word *roost*, originally meaning 'roof' or 'ceiling,' persists as the name for a 'perch' even when the position of the perch has been shifted to out-of-doors. The name *perch* (Lat. *pertica*, 'rod,' 'bar') as the name for a bird's resting place, persists even when the resting place is a niche in a wall of stone. The word *match* (Fr. *mèche*, 'wick') which in earlier years applied to something easily ignited and used for "retaining, conveying, and communicating fire," applies since about 1830 to a source of fire in the form of a stick ignited by friction.

If in these instances shifts have taken place quite independent of any volition, on the part of the speaker, to indicate similarity between two things, on the other hand in an abundant number of instances the existence of a conscious purpose is plainly evident. Even in the language of children, there appears a naïve delight in calling attention to the likeness between things. The spirit of make-believe leads to metaphors, as when a child calls the letter O the moon, or calling attention to cinders falling from a chimney, exclaims, "It is snowing!" or observing a moist stone, cries out, "See how the stone sweats!"[6] The child who sees pansies, and then butterflies and says of the latter, "The pansies are flying," is doing the same thing as the poet when he feels the likeness between a thought and a bird and says,

> There flutters up a happy thought
> Self-balanced on a joyous wing.[7]

The process involved is that of bringing within the sweep

---
[6] O. Jespersen, *op. cit.*, pp. 84, 85.
[7] F. C. Prescott, *op. cit.*, p. 218.

of one mental glance like objects from different spheres, so vividly that the name of one may be applied to another. The imagination involved in this process is to be observed at all stages in the history of languages. Its effects may be seen in the far-fetched figures or 'kennings' which are so conspicuous a feature in the language of the early poets of the Teutonic and Celtic races, as when the *leek* is spoken of as "a tear of a fair woman" and the *hawthorn* as "the barking of hounds." It appears also in the worn out terms of modern journalese, as when an athletic coach is called a *mentor* or a legislator a *solon*.

The process is most active in the case of people in whom the imagination is less held in curb by reason, in the language, therefore, of children and of unsophisticated folk. Its effects, however, are omnipresent. Many a hackneyed word or phrase is in its origin a creation of vivid imagination. The word *spurn* in such expressions as 'spurn a suggestion' was vivid in its expressive-power when *spurn* still had its original meaning 'to kick.' To *spurn* a suggestion was then 'to kick it out of the way.' In the same way 'a flourishing enterprise,' with its full original force, conveyed the meaning, 'an enterprise in full flower.'

Vivid mental pictures, varied in kind, ranging from the fine and beautiful to the coarse and ugly, underlie the meanings given to many colorless words of everyday use. A *seminary*, an institution of learning, is literally a 'seed-plot' (Lat. *seminarium*, 'seed-garden'); a figurative shift in the reverse direction appears in speaking of a *nursery* for plants. Underlying the use of *scallop* as the name for the ornamental curve in an edge, is the picture of the graceful lines in the edge of the scallop shell. To *charge* is literally 'to load a car' (Lat. *carricare*, from *carrus*, 'chariot,' 'car'). Notice the variety of uses in which the earlier meaning is discernible, such as 'to charge with a duty,' 'to charge with a crime,' 'to charge a jury,' 'to charge for goods received.' To *stagnate* is literally 'to lie still like a pool' (Lat. *stagnum,* 'pool'). To *stimulate* is literally 'to goad on' (Lat. *stimulus,* 'goad'). The alcoholic associations of the related word, *stimulant,* do not begin until the nineteenth century. *Halo* comes through the Latin from the Greek, where it meant 'threshing floor.' Its astronomical meaning begins in the sixteenth century. *Iris* was originally the Greek name for 'rainbow' and for the goddess who personified the rainbow. The *trend* of events is literally the 'roll' of events (O. E. *trendan,* 'to roll,' 'to revolve'). *Scrofula* comes from the diminutive of the Latin *scrofa* meaning 'sow' which was supposed to be subject to this disease. *Hybrid* goes back to the Latin *hybrida,* a name applied to the offspring of a tame sow and a wild boar. *Sop,* with its variety of modern uses, goes back to the Old English *sopp,* meaning 'bread,' evidently used for dipping into liquids. *Urchin* meant originally (1) 'hedgehog.' Its present meaning is reached through the stages: (2) 'elf,' (3) 'mischievous boy.' *Magazine* originally meant 'storehouse' (through the French from the Arabic *makhasia,* plural of *makhazan,* 'storehouse'). Its use as the name of a publication, a storehouse of literature, begins in the seventeenth century. *Mediocre* is said to come from Latin *medius,* 'middle,' and dialectal Latin *ocris,* 'hill.' The underlying meaning, therefore, is 'half-way.'[8] The underlying meaning of *please, pleasure,* etc., which come through the French from the Latin *placere,* 'to please,' it has been suggested, is 'to smooth down' (*Cf.* the Greek cognate *plax,* 'flatness'). This explanation is supported by the analogy of *flatter* which comes from the French *flatter,* originally 'to smoothe.'

Metaphorical turns of expression of the kind illustrated are to be met with on all sides. The earlier English meaning of *musket* was 'sparrow-hawk.' That of *cloak* was

---

[8] Weekley.

'bell' (Late Lat. *cloca*, 'bell,' 'horseman's cloak'). The shift in meaning was based on resemblance in shape. The same Latin word by another shift yields the name *clock*. *Palliate* in the sense 'excuse' goes back to the Latin *pallium*, 'cloak.' A *ruche* takes its name from its resemblance in form to a bee-hive to which the Old French word *rusche* originally applied.[9] The history of the word *hearse* is somewhat more complicated. The word comes from the French *herse*, one of whose meanings was 'harrow.' The word in the Middle English period came to be applied to the framework for supporting candles over a bier, doubtless due to a resemblance in structure to a harrow. From similarity to this structure, in appearance or in use, the funeral car has taken the name.

The conscious intent in the shifts of meaning discussed above, while evident enough, in other instances is even more conspicuous. In the case of flower names, for instance, one meets with many names obviously created in the conscious attempt to express the sentiment associated with flowers. The native English word *daisy* means literally 'eye of day,' a poetic meaning less veiled in earlier forms of the word, such as Chaucer's *dayesye*. The *columbine* (Lat. *columba*, 'dove') takes its name from the fancied resemblance of the shape of the flower to five pigeons clustered together. The *tansy* is derived from the Greek *athanasia*, '*immortality*,' a meaning originally associated with this plant. The sentiment which cannot be dissociated from the *pansy* explains the nature of the name, from French *pensée*, 'thought' or 'remembrance.' The *aster* has borrowed the name of a 'star' (Greek *aster*, 'star'). *Rosemary* comes from an earlier *rosmarin*, meaning originally 'sea spray.' Its altered modern form is due to its sentimental association with the meaning 'rose of Mary.' *Anemone* comes from the Greek and meant origi-

---

[9] Weekley.

nally 'daughter of the wind.' *Geranium*, from the same source, meant originally 'crane's bill,' a name based on the shape of the seed pod. *Tulip* goes back ultimately to the Persian word which has come into English later as *turban*. The application of the name to a flower is evidently due to a similarity in shape. Associations sentimental in character are apparent in such later English creations as *lady-slipper, bleeding-heart, maiden-hair, heartsease, star of Bethlehem*.

Humorous intent is back of many metaphorical shifts in meaning. There can be no question of this in the case of such products of modern slang as *bleacher*, for the open stand for spectators at a baseball game, *shinplaster*, or *Jewish flag*, for paper money, *pussyfoot* for stealthy movement. Neither can there be any question in the case of such faded metaphors as: *cocoanut*, in which the Portuguese name *coco*, 'bugbear,' is applied on account of the monkey-like face at the base of the nut; *easel*, meaning originally 'ass,' applied to the artist's implement because of its duty, like that of an ass, of bearing a burden; *cab*, clipped form from *cabriolet*, which means literally 'little she-goat'; *patter* for 'mumbling sound' supposed to come from *pater noster* in the Latin Lord's Prayer; *phaeton*, the name of the driver of the sun's chariot, applied to a vehicle; *derrick*, the name of a famous hangman, applied to a scaffold for hanging, and later to a scaffoldlike structure; *gallowses*, 'braces,' a name surviving in American dialect, originally applied to a hanging apparatus different in kind; *roster*, a word of Dutch creation meaning originally 'gridiron,' 'roaster'; *potboiler*, a literary product intended to serve a utilitarian but necessary use; *salary*, from Latin *salarium*, 'salt money.'

More serious in nature is the conscious intent which explains such words as *contrite* and *tribulation*. *Contrite* comes from the Latin *conterere*, which means 'to rub together' and hence 'to bruise' or 'crush.' In the well-known biblical phrase, 'a broken and a contrite heart,' the earlier meaning appears and *contrite* is practically synonymous with *broken*, the word with which it is paired, but the transition to the meaning 'penitent' follows naturally. In the case of *tribulation* the original meaning was 'threshing' (Lat. *tribulum*, 'flail'). Under the influence of the Christian conception of purification through affliction, as wheat is cleaned by threshing, the word *tribulation* has come to mean 'affliction.' The Christian doctrine implicit in this word is developed in detail as the theme of a pleasing seventeenth-century poem by George Wither.[10]

In the case of *tribulation* the old saying that 'language is poetry' is literally substantiated. Poetic quality, however, is everywhere at hand in the case of words. The word *govern*, for 'to rule,' is evidently a conscious appropriation to a new use of the Greek nautical term for 'to steer.' The underlying metaphor is brought out more distinctly in the expression 'ship of state.' *Career* (Fr. *carrière*, 'race course') likewise owes its English meaning to a consciously metaphorical shift in meaning. In the case of the colorless word *course*, the same underlying metaphor is to be discovered, since the original meaning of the word was 'running' (Lat. *currere*, 'to run'). There is poetry in the metaphorical use of the word *flour* (for 'flower of the wheat') and even in *muscle* (Lat. *musculum*, 'little mouse'). Less poetic, but unquestionably creations of conscious speech activity, are such expressions as *ferret out* and *dog his path*.

There are countless other instances in which the conscious metaphorical intent, while not so freshly evident, nevertheless certainly underlies the present meaning of words. *Crystal* is in origin a metaphor (Greek *krustallos*, 'clear ice'). *Crater*, applied to a volcano, is a metaphorical

---

[10] Trench, *The Study of Words*, p. 50.

FIGURES OF SIMILARITY

use of the familiar classical word for 'bowl' (Lat. *crater*, Greek *krater*). More striking still is the figurative use of *grenade*, the old name for *pomegranate* (Fr. *grenade* from Span. *granada*) as the name for an explosive shell, and the use of *agony*, from the classical name *agonia*, 'athletic meet,' to express the idea of intense pain.

The way in which the names of tangible things of the physical world have been metaphorically applied as names for elements in psychical experience has already been pointed out. It is pleasant to think that the terms by means of which we bring within our intellectual grasp the elements of spiritual life are a heritage created by the conscious creative activity in language on the part of our ancestors. Homely but nevertheless poetic is the underlying meaning of *brood*, literally 'to hatch,' an activity, like that in ruminating, admirably suggestive of contemplation. Striking are the physical pictures reached through a realization of the original meaning of some of these words. *Perplexed* brings up a picture of being tangled in yarn, *concoct* a picture of boiling, *concrete* that of something grown together in one mass. To *eliminate* is literally to thrust out-of-doors (Lat. *limen*, 'threshold').

A casual study of the words in English will bring to light the way in which the limits of expression have everywhere been extended by metaphorical shifts in meaning and will at the same time bring to one's realization a perhaps hitherto unsuspected freshness in the original meaning of many words now faded into abstract symbols. *Intended* meant originally 'stretched' and referred to stretching the string of a bow in aiming. The word *bend* is a causative form of *bind* and applied originally to the bending of a bow when stringing it. *Irritate* referred originally to the 'snarling' of a dog. The original meaning of *frill* brings up associations none too pleasant, since the word, according to one explanation, applied originally to an animal's mesentery. *Exaggerate* meant originally "to heap up' (Lat. *agger*, 'heap'); compare the expression 'make a mountain out of a mole hill.' *Disparage* meant originally 'to marry unequally.' *Distinguish* comes through the French from the Latin *distinguere*, literally 'to prick off.' *Embarrass* comes through the French from the Italian *imbarazzare* or the Spanish *embarazar*, meaning 'to put within bars.' *Result* meant a physical 'rebound' or 'leap back.' *Exult* meant 'to leap or bound (for joy).' *Scrutiny* meant a careful search among broken pieces, from Latin *scruta*, pl., 'broken pieces.' *Scruple* meant 'a little stone' (in a shoe, for example). To feel scruples once had more definite sensation than conveyed by the modern use of the phrase. *Instigate* meant 'to prick' (as a signal). *Scandal* meant originally that part of a trap on which the bait was placed and which sprang up when the trap closed. *Abate* meant 'to beat down.' *Abound* meant 'to overflow.' *Maintain* meant 'to hold in hand.' *Rehearse* meant 'to harrow again,' originating in the same stage of agricultural life from which came *pecuniary* referring originally to property in the form of flocks, and *emolument*, cited above. *Error* meant simply 'wandering' or 'straying.' *Check* was originally the name of king in the game of chess. *Broach* meant originally 'to pierce with a spit' (O. Fr. *broche*, 'spit'). *Ardent* meant 'burning.' *Stunned* meant 'thunderstruck.' *Dilapidated* referred originally to crumbling stone work from Latin *dis* 'apart,' and *lapis* 'stone.' *Recalcitrant* meant 'kicking' (Lat. *calx*, 'heel').

Rich in suggestive power are such words as *pester* and *trammel*, which have already been mentioned. *Pester* goes back in its origin to the Latin *pascere*, 'to feed.' Through several intervening stages in meaning it reached the late Latin *pastorium*, 'a clog for a horse at pasture,' which modified in form in the French language and shifted metaphorically to the general meaning 'annoy,' appears as the English *pester*. *Trammel*, which goes back in meaning to the Latin *tres* + *macula*, 'triple mesh,' becomes the name for 'net.' This net, with the name *trammel*, is used as a shackle for horses in training them to amble (*Cf*. "manage in silken trammels"— G. Meredith). This word in turn is metaphorically shifted to mean 'encumbrance' in general, as in the adjective *untrammeled*. The words *hamper, impede* and, possibly, *embarrass*, will be found to be rooted in similar conceptions.

The metaphorical turns of meaning which have served in the production of the modern English vocabulary by no means belong exclusively to the past. As already pointed out, they are distinctive features of modern slang. In standard language, also, in our own time there is everywhere manifest the search for freshness of meaning by means of constantly renewed metaphors. *Cherish* a grievance becomes *nurse* a grievance; *fix* one's gaze becomes *rivet* one's gaze; *pass* time becomes *kill* time; *break* a record becomes *smash* a record, to *raise* prices becomes, in journalistic phrase, to *skyrocket* prices. There is manifest also the disposition to give liveliness to style by the metaphorical use of verbs of physical action in naming forms of activity of all kinds, in this way restoring to language some of the sharpness of meaning lost through the fading of earlier expressions. Cumulative illustration of this tendency and of the now fading energy in meaning that results is offered by the following list of phrases recently assembled:[11] *run* into debt, *rush* into print, *step* into a practice, *fly* into a passion, *spring* into notice, *jump* into a fight, *dive* into a book, *wade* into an adversary, *sink* into slumber, *leap* into notoriety, *break* into society, *stumble* into acquaintance, *glide* into intimacy, *fall* in love, *precipitate* oneself into wedlock.

Particularly evident is the presence of conscious intent

---

[11] G. B. Morewood, *Life*, Oct. 9, 1913.

in the case of words formed by the process of antonomasia, that is to say, by the use of proper names used as common nouns or adjectives for verbs. *Nimrods* and *Ishmaelites, Jonahs* and *Jehus* and *Jezebels, babel* and *maudlin* and *bedlam, pyrrhic* and *panic, mentor* and *solon, boniface* and *benedick, pander* and *meander, attic* and *Bœotian, Spartan* and *Gothic, vandal* and *hun, assassin* and *thug, slaves* and *gypsies,*—all originate as proper names, and adoption into use for common nouns or verbs or adjectives can be explained by no other motive than that of definite and conscious purpose to heighten effectiveness of expression by means of the indicated similarity to proper names vividly associated with certain qualities.

Figures of similarity concentrated in single words are usually in the form of metaphor or of antonomasia. The simile, consisting of a formal expression of likeness, ordinarily requires a group of words. There are, however, many instances, particularly among adjectives, of similes condensed to single words. Take for instance the names for colors. Of the seven names for the colors of the spectrum, obviously *violet, indigo* and *orange* originate as similes. The word *green* is closely associated in earlier stages of language with the idea of growing and is probably in origin a simile. *Blue, yellow* and *red* may have a similar origin, but go back so far in the history of language that one cannot be sure about their derivation. Shades of red, however, such as *scarlet* and *cardinal* originate as similes, the first from the name of a cloth, the second from the name of a church dignitary, itself in origin a simile from *cardo,* 'hinge.' Like *violet*, the color names, *mauve* and *pink* and *lavender* are similes borrowed from the names of flowers. *Drab* comes from the color of undyed cloth. *Purple* comes from the name of a fish. Thus it goes through the list of color names from *maroon,* derived from the name for chestnut, and *cerise* from cherry, to *taupe*

FIGURES OF SIMILARITY

(French *taupe*, Latin *talpa*, 'mole') and *henna* (Arabic *henna*) the name of the Egyptian privet from the leaves of which the dye is made.

Names of beasts yield numerous adjectives which are condensed similes. From Latin names come *leonine, canine, bovine, feline,* etc.; from English names come *foxy* and *horsy* and *dogged* and *goatee.* Suffixes such as, *-ous, -ive, -y, -ish* and *-like* serve in the formation of numerous adjectives of this kind, words in which the original simile is still living, such as *stony, icy, hearty, monstrous, titanic, gigantic, colossal, quixotic, adamantine,* and many others in which the obscuration of the meaning of the noun leaves the simile faded and obscure, such as *furtive,* 'thieflike;' *stubborn,* 'stumplike'; *trivial,* 'crossroads'; *saucy,* 'salty'; *savage* (Latin *silva,* 'woods'); *cordial,* 'hearty'; *urbane* Latin *urbs,* 'city'); *civil* (Latin *civis,* 'citizen'); *humble* (Lat. *humilis* from *humus,* 'earth'). Occasionally the simile takes the form of a compound word, as in the case of *cocksure, pigeon-toed, swallow-tail.*

The discussion in the present chapter has made clear the contribution of the simile and the metaphor to the expressive powers of language. Not only are these figures of similarity available as means of renewing the vitality in living speech, but their fossil forms enter largely into the composition of the formed strata of the language. By means of symbols derived from the material world of sense, it has been made possible to traverse the immaterial world of thought. Language, it may be repeated, is fossil poetry. To the humble creators of language may be applied the words originally applied to the poet:

..... As imagination bodies forth
The forms of things unknown, the poet's pen
Turns them to shapes and gives to airy nothing
A local habitation and a name.

CHAPTER XVII

FIGURES OF CONTIGUITY

Different in kind from the simile and the metaphor are the tropes classed as figures under the names, synecdoche and metonymy. In the case of figures of similarity the shift of names is between things of different classes but associated on account of likeness. In the case of synecdoche and metonymy the shift of names is between things associated by actual contiguity, either physical contact, or contact in various thought relations.

The simplest case is that of synecdoche, where the name of the part is applied to the whole, or that of the species to the genus, or that of an individual to a general class, or, less frequently, one of these shifts is reversed. Instances are familiar enough in common use, in such expressions as: 'all *hands* aboard,' 'a fleet of fifty *sail*,' and uses of words such as *wheel* for bicycle, *Nimrod* for hunter, *motor* for motor car, or the slang *hard tails* for mules. The shift in the reverse direction appears in *engine* for locomotive, *corn* for maize (Indian corn), *provisions* for food, *disease* for malady, *revolution* for change in government, *cattle* for cows, *currency* for money, etc. This latter kind of shift will receive more detailed discussion in the following chapter, under the head of specialization.

Under the head of metonymy are included a number of shifts of wide variety, due to association in a wide variety of relations: that of cause and effect, in *tongue* for language; that of material and product, in *copper* or *nickel* for small coins, *cold steel* for bayonet; that of sign and thing signified, in *gray hairs* for age, *bloodshed* for destruction of

FIGURES OF CONTIGUITY 233

life, *reds* for anarchists, *cross* for Christianity, *crescent* for Mohammedanism, *bench* for judge, *pulpit* for clergy, *cockcrow* for dawn; container for contained, in *kettle boils* for water boils, *head* for brains; instrument for agent, in *pen* for writer, *sword* for soldier, *mailed fist* and *shining armor* for fighting army; attribute for subject, in *youth* for young people, *salt* and *deep* for ocean; author for his works, as in 'read Shakespeare' for read the works of Shakespeare.

In the instances cited, the figurative shift is evident enough. But, as in the case of the metaphor, the wealth of instances of faded or disguised figures of this kind is something little realized. Embodied in everyday speech are countless examples of fossil metonymy and synecdoche of every kind. The word *front* originally meant 'forehead' (Latin *frons, frontem*), but came to apply by synecdoche to the whole face, before the metaphorical shift by which it came to apply to the forepart of a building, of a stage, or to the scene of war. In the same way the word *leer* originally meaning 'cheek' (O. E. *hlēor*) has come to apply to a form of facial expression in which the cheek is a conspicuous feature. The Latin *lingua*, meaning 'tongue,' has yielded the name *language*, a shift repeated in English, where the name *tongue* is figuratively applied to the speech in which the tongue plays an important part. The word *coin* (Fr. *coin* 'wedge,' 'die for stamping,' Lat. *cuneus*, 'wedge') has been shifted from the stamping instrument to that which is stamped. The word *desire* (Fr. *desirer*, Lat. *desiderare*) which originally meant 'to regret the absence of' now expresses the closely associated meaning, 'to wish for.' The development of meaning is paralleled in the case of *want* which originally meant 'to be lacking' (O. N. *wanta*). The word *chafe*, which originally meant 'to warm' (French *chauffeur*), is applied to the friction which accompanies one method of warning. The word *calm*, which originally referred to warmth, has come to apply to the atmospheric quiet which usually accompanies warmth. The word *yard*, which originally meant 'piece of wood,' as it does still in such words as *crossyards*, becomes applied to the unit of measure indicated by the wood.

The nature of the contiguity involved in these fossil figures is greatly varied. In the case of *book* the name of the material (O. E. *bōc*, 'beech-tree') is applied to the product. The development of meaning is similar in the case of *code* (Lat. *codex*, earlier *caudex*, 'tree-trunk'), *Bible* (Greek *biblion*, diminutive of *biblos*, 'inner bark of the papyrus') and *library* (Lat. *liber*, 'book,' originally 'bark of a tree'). In the case of *bounce* the word for 'thump' (M. E. *bunsen*) is applied to the accompanying rebound. The word *jerk*, which first appears in the sixteenth century, meant at first 'to strike' or 'beat.' In the case of *quick*, the name for 'alive' (O. E. *cwic*) is applied to the quality of speed which results from life. In the case of *fare*, a word meaning 'journey' (O. E. *faran*, 'to go'), is applied to the price of a journey, a development of meaning paralleled in the case of *admission*, often used for 'price of admission.' The word *fob*, which originally meant 'pocket,' in American use has shifted first to mean 'a pocket chain' and then, by a second shift, a 'pendant for the chain.' The name *manure*, which meant originally 'to work with the hand' (Fr. *manœuvrer*), has become applied to a substance used in hand cultivation of the soil. In the same way *plant*, which originally meant 'sole of the foot' (Lat. *planta*), has come to be applied to an action in which in earlier times the sole of the foot played an important part. *Hard*, which originally meant 'strong,' as in *hard cider, work hard*, etc., has come to apply to a physical property of things that are strong. *Buxom*, which originally meant 'obedient' (O. E. *būgan*, 'to bow,' 'to bend'), has come to apply to a kind of physique associated with the earlier meaning.

The dictionary has many interesting stories to tell from

FIGURES OF CONTIGUITY

word history. *Crop* originally meant 'the top of a plant' (O. E. *cropp*). One should notice the relation of the modern verb, 'to crop,' to the original meaning. The reader of Chaucer's Prologue will recall the "tendre croppes" inspired by Zephyrus in April. *Win* offers a fine suggestion regarding the means of success. The O. E. *winnan* meant 'to fight'; the word has later been shifted so as to apply to the success following fighting. *Bureau* gets its name from the coarse woolen stuff of russet color (French *bureau*, O. Fr. *burel*) that was used as a cover for desks and writing tables. While *book* takes its name from the older wood, *beech*, on which writing was done among the early Teutonic peoples, *volume* gets its name by metonymy from the form (Lat. *volumen*, 'roll') in which Roman written records were kept. The noun *miniature*, which, by way of simile, has yielded the adjective *miniature*, 'small,' is itself derived by metonymy from an earlier Latin *minium*, 'red lead,' a coloring substance used in making this kind of picture. The name *sycamore* has an involved history. It is derived ultimately from the Greek *sukomoros*, meaning 'mulberry,' but came to be applied as the name of a variety of fig tree. In England, in the presentation of the sacred dramas of the Middle Ages, the plane tree was chosen to represent the sycamore fig of the scriptural story associated with Zaccheus, and from this association the plane tree permanently acquired the name *sycamore*. In America the name has been applied to an American species of the plane, called also *buttonwood*, and in Australia the name *white sycamore* has been applied to one of the Australian nutmegs.[1]

Let us enumerate further instances of these shifts in meaning, many of which throw interesting light on phases of culture history. *Taste* (Mid. Engl. *tasten*, O. Fr. *taster* 'to handle,' 'to feel') has been shifted to the related sense

---

[1] *Century Dictionary.*

of the tongue. *Danger* comes through the French from the Latin *dominarium,* 'rule,' which is obviously to be associated with the idea of 'peril.' *Clumsy* goes back to an earlier meaning, 'numb,' of which the present meaning is a natural consequence. *Awkward,* in the same way, goes back to an earlier meaning, 'backhanded,' from which the present meaning is derived, likewise through the association between effect and cause. *Pay* meant originally to 'pacify,' 'please' (Lat. *pacare*), a meaning easy to associate with the present one. *Hurt* goes back to an O. Fr. *hurter,* 'to strike' or 'to dash against'; it now applies to an effect of which the earlier meaning was the cause, as in the case of *bounce.* The original meaning of *fast,* and one which it still retains in certain expressions, was 'firmly fixed.' Its present prevalent meaning is derived by a shift like that in *quick,* already mentioned. *Borrow* (O. E. *borgian,* 'to give a pledge') has shifted to mean 'obtain for temporary use,' with or without giving a definite pledge. *Table* is sometimes applied by metonymy to the food which a table bears, in this way duplicating the shift in meaning made in the case of *board.* The various stages by which metonymy has shifted the meaning of *nice* are discussed elsewhere.

In the case of *deer* the generic term (O. E. *dēor*), meaning 'wild beast,' has come to apply to a special kind of beast. The same is true in the history of the word *hound,* originally a generic term for 'dog.' In the case of *rabbit* the name for the young of the species has come to apply to the species as a whole. The same is true in case of the words *bird* and *pig,* a process which in the speech of to-day is being repeated in the case of the word *chicken.*

And so the story goes. *Climate* goes back to an earlier meaning, 'region,' a meaning surviving in the poetic word *clime. Ambition* meant originally 'going about' (for votes), from Latin *ambitio.* And this suggests another political term, *candidate,* which meant originally 'white robed'

(Lat. *candidatus*, from *candidus*, 'white,' 'shining') bringing to mind the Roman custom by which candidates for office wore white. *Bead* comes from the Old English *gebed*, meaning 'prayer,' a meaning in Catholic use not yet entirely dissociated from the word. *Barter* goes back to an earlier meaning, 'cheat' (O. Fr. *barater*, 'to cheat,' 'to beguile'), an etymology throwing interesting light on human infirmity, but perhaps affording some ground for optimism, since the word has nearly outgrown its earlier associations. *Story* (of a house) goes back to the Anglo-French *estorie* (Lat. *historia*). This use of the word originates in the earlier custom of embellishing the exterior of buildings "with scenes or sayings from history and legend."[2] *Worry* and *anguish* have parallel histories. *Worry* comes from the Old English *wyrgian*, 'to choke' or 'to strangle'; *anguish* goes back to the Old English *anguisse*, 'choking' (Lat. *angustus* 'narrow'). *Emblem* comes through the French from the Greek *emblema*, 'inlaid work,' a form of work characteristic of emblems. *Medal* comes through the French from Italian *medaglia*, the underlying meaning of which is 'metal.' *Explore* goes back through the French to the Latin *explorare*, the meaning of which was 'to cry out' or 'to shout,' actions characteristic of the exploration of dark places.[3] *Vegetable* goes back to the Latin *vegetabilis*, 'full of life' and is related by origin to *vigor*. *Schedule* comes ultimately from the Latin *schedula*, the diminutive of *scheda*, 'a papyrus strip.' *Sedulous* comes from the Latin *sedulus* (older *sedolo*, 'without guile,' 'honest'). *Sincere* comes from the Latin *sincerus*, 'pure.' *Franchise* comes from the French *franchise*, meaning 'freedom,' a meaning which persists in a few English phrases. *Fabric* goes back to the Latin *faber*, 'smith.' The modern application of the word to textiles goes back only to the eighteenth

---

[2] Weekley.
[3] *Ibid.*

century. *Family* goes back to an earlier collective meaning, 'servants of a household,' Latin *familia*, which comes from *famulus*, 'servant.' *Soothe* goes back to the Old English *sōthian*, 'to show to be true.' Its present meaning is derived from the soothing practice of assenting in conversation.[4] *Socket* comes from the Anglo-French *socket*, 'spear-head of the shape of a small ploughshare' (Fr. *soc*, 'ploughshare'[5]). Notice the interesting shift in meaning from the thing contained to the container. *Ferment* goes back to an earlier meaning, 'to boil' (Lat. *fervere*). *Fastidious* goes back to an earlier meaning, 'loathing' (Lat. *fastidiosus*). *Flavor* earlier had the meaning, 'smell' (O. Fr. *flaur, fraor*, probably from Lat. *fragrare*, 'to be fragrant'). *Orchestra* goes back, through several intervening stages, to the Greek verb for 'dance.' *Posy* is a contracted form for *poesy*. The association between flowers and poetry is probably through the language of flowers. *Sentence* once meant 'opinion,' 'thought' (Lat. *sententia*). Notice the meaning of the adjective *sententious*. *Period* goes back through French and Latin to the Greek *periodos*, meaning 'circuit.' In English an earlier meaning was 'complete sentence.' In the modern use of *sentence* the form of language is given the name of the thought content; in the case of *period* the name of the sentence is given to the mark that indicates its close. *Test* goes back to Latin *testum*, an earthen pot, used for trying metals. The verb *to test* is of American creation and is earliest recorded from the language of George Washington. *Fathom* (O. E. *fœthm*, 'outstretched arms,' 'embrace') has a history like that of *foot;* it is now applied to the unit of measure in length equaling that of the outstretched arms.

The words here cited offer an insight, not only into old customs, but into universal processes of thought. The

---

[4] Weekley.
[5] *Ibid.*

FIGURES OF CONTIGUITY

shifts to be observed are amazing in variety and varying in their direction. Interesting shifts in quite reverse directions have taken place in case of the two words, *tree* and *beam,* and in the case of *bread* and *loaf.* *Tree* had an earlier meaning, 'piece of wood,' which survives in such expressions as *roof-tree, cross-tree, whiffle-tree.* *Beam,* on the other hand, earlier meant 'tree,' as it continues to do in the name of one tree, the *hornbeam.* *Loaf* (O. E. *hlāf*) originally meant 'bread,' while the word *bread* in early English meant 'fragment' or 'piece.'

In the case of the shifts in meaning just cited, it is usually not a matter of great difficulty to discover the link of association connecting the later meaning with the earlier one. In many instances, however, the case is not so simple, as any one may discover if he will try to explain to himself the various meanings cited in any large dictionary for simple words such as *swing* and *smite* and *strike.* The clue to the origin of these variant meanings must be sought in the spider-web net of associations by which ideas in the human mind are linked.

As in the case of figures of similarity, also, it is not always easy to determine the share taken by conscious intent and that taken by natural processes not governed by the human will. In the case of figures of contiguity one cannot fail to recognize many changes which are unconsciously brought about. One must not lose sight of the fact that words, unlike mathematical symbols, are not absolute and unvarying in their meaning. Not only are different meanings frequently applied to the same thing, but the same name is not infrequently applied independently to a variety of meanings. Take for instance the popular flower name, *bachelor's button.* This name, according to the *Century Dictionary,* is applied to the red campion, to knapweed, to the ragged robin, to the globe amaranth, and to several other American plants. The relation between word and meaning is obviously a more or less arbitrary one.

In the consideration of this matter some clarity may perhaps be reached by making a distinction between the meaning attached to a word by the speaker and that gained from it by the listener. Shifts in meaning arise in part from the choice of words by the speaker, in part from the way they are interpreted by the person spoken to.

To the choice of the speaker must be assigned such a trope as the use of *hand* for workman. In the consciousness of a factory operator the feature of a workman most vividly present is the hand by which his work is to be accomplished. It is natural, therefore, for him to use the name of the feature most vividly before him. This tendency is even more evident in the use of *head* for cattle. To the drover thinking of the number of animals in a herd, the only part of the animal vividly present in consciousness is the head, which he looks at in making a count. In the same way a person about to punish a child, in the heat of his emotion may see vividly the details of the beating, and instead of using the literal expression *beat*, may say *warm* or *dust your jacket,* which are for the moment the dominant elements in his consciousness. In exactly the same way in speaking of morning, a person, instead of using the direct name, may make use of some feature of the morning which for the moment is in the foreground of consciousness. He may say *sunrise,* or perhaps it is the note of the cock that protrudes in his imagination, and he says *cockcrow*. In thinking of a quail it is perhaps the bird's musical call that comes to the foreground, and one, therefore, names him *bob white*. More extreme is the name sometimes given by children to a man's stiff hat. In the consciousness of a lively child, the feature of the stiff hat that dominates may be an interesting use to which the hat may be put; in this way originates the name *pea-bouncer*. In the same way a vivid consciousness of one

FIGURES OF CONTIGUITY 241

feature of the uncovered benches for spectators explains the origin of such a name as *bleachers*. Such slang uses as *copper* for a small coin, of *greenback* or *long green* for money in larger denominations, are to be explained in the same way. In all these instances the speaker gives to something as a whole the feature that is most prominent in his consciousness.

Probably more active still in the creation of the form of trope under consideration, is the part of the listener. The meaning of words is determined not more by the will of the speaker than by the interpretation put upon them by the listener. Even specific names, such as those of parts of the body, are not associated with meanings as definite and absolute as is sometimes supposed. The ideas evoked in different minds by such words as *thigh* and *loin* will show a surprising amount of variation. "Change in meaning is linguistic misunderstanding," is the contention of an eminent Austrian scholar.[6] Through different interpretations of a name, arise the various meanings attached to a word as it appears in various cognate languages. In different Indo-European languages, for instance, one word appears not only in varied forms, but with meanings as varied as 'head,' 'temple,' 'brain,' and 'horn.' To take another specific instance, the Indo-European word which appears in Latin as *coxa*, meaning 'hip,' in Sanskrit means 'armpit,' in Avestan, 'shoulder,' in Old High German, 'curve in the back of the leg,' in Bavarian, 'leg,' in Old Irish, 'foot,' in French (*cuisse*), 'thigh.'

To come nearer home, let us take the word *stomach*. This word comes from the Greek *stomachos*, which meant originally 'throat' or 'gullet.' Taken into Latin, the word at first applied to the œsophagus, only later shifting to the meaning that the word now conveys. How words may be shifted in meaning through misinterpretation, may be ob-

---

[6] R. Meringer, *Wörter und Sachen*, iii, 54.

served in the language of children. A two-year-old boy, having a pain in his foot, came out with the surprising assertion, "My torns is hurting." Evidently he was inaccurately appropriating to his own needs an expression overheard, which meant nearly, but not precisely, what he had in mind.

It is extremely important not to lose sight of the fact that few words have simple meanings. Practically all words have, besides their central meaning, a fringe of associated meanings. In fact, language owes much of its expressive power to the ideas and emotions associated with words. Brander Matthews offers admirable illustration of this quality of words in the case of the word *forest*. He tells [7] of a discussion of the different images called up by the word *forest* in the minds of a group of men including Thomas Hardy, George Du Maurier, William Black, Edmund Gosse, W. D. Howells, and himself. "To Hardy," he tells us, "forest suggested the sturdy oaks to be assaulted by the woodlanders of Wessex; and to Du Maurier it evoked the trim and tidy avenues of the national domain of France. To Black the word naturally brought up the low scrub of the so-called deer-forests of Scotland; and to Gosse it summoned up a view of the green-clad mountains that towered up from the Scandinavian fjords. To Howells forest recalled the thick woods that in his youth fringed the rivers of Ohio; and to me there came back swiftly the memory of the wild growths, bristling up unrestrained by man in the Chippewa Reservation which I had crossed fourteen years before in my canoe trip from Lake Superior to the Mississippi."

The example of *forest* may be taken as widely representative of words in general. Besides a central meaning in words there is usually a variety of associated meanings which appear in varying degrees of prominence determined by the

---

[7] *Scribner's Magazine*, November, 1916.

FIGURES OF CONTIGUITY 243

context or by the person. Take the word *dog* for example. The worthless or contemptible side of the animal is prominent when his name is applied metaphorically to a contemptible person. In the phrase, 'a gay dog,' his sportive qualities are prominent. In 'a dog's life,' the monotony of his existence is in the foreground. In the adjective, *dogged*, his faithful perseverance is for the nonce in mind.

The relation between the elements of sound and meaning that make up a word may, perhaps, be made more evident by following the example of the psychologist Wundt and using symbols. If we use s for the sound element, d for the dominating element in the meaning, c for elements of meaning constantly associated, and v for variable associated elements, and then set off the associated meanings from the dominating element in the meaning by including the associated meanings in parentheses, then the whole word would be represented as $s\ d\ (c,\ v)$.

In the tropes that we have had under consideration a prevailing tendency has been for one of the elements c or v to take the place of d. How this comes about may be illustrated by an expression from the fifteenth century "Boke of La Tour Landry" as follows,—"that it might be beter and more pleinly to be vnderstond." In this expression the word *pleinly* still retains its earlier meaning 'fully' (Latin *plenus*, French *plein*). But the associated meaning 'clearly' is already present, and later in the history of English, has quite overshadowed the earlier meaning.

Since the meaning of words is learned by repeatedly meeting them in use, their meaning is influenced by the context in which they appear. Among the many amusing features of the juvenile romance, "The Little Visiters," is the misinterpretation of many words by the nine-year-old writer. The word *mere* is one instance. This word comes from the Latin *merus* meaning 'pure,' and its early meaning is still discernible in many expressions. But from frequent use in such phrases as 'mere trifle,' 'mere nothing,' 'mere chance,' it comes to be associated with the meaning 'insignificant' or something the reverse of noble, and this meaning is evidently the dominating one in the mind of the youthful Daisy Ashford, as is evident in her use of the word in such expressions as: "Bernard gave a frown of jellously at her rarther *mere* words" (p. 79); "Personally I am a bit parshial to *mere* people" (p. 56); " . . . who have got something funny in the family and want to be less *mere* if you can comprehend" (p. 56). In the expression "pork with apple sauce," the associated meaning 'conserve' has overshadowed the earlier dominant meaning 'condiment,' so that in American popular use the word *sauce* has come to apply to stewed fruit used as an independent article of food. In such phrases as 'the enormity of the crime', the meaning of evil, gained from phrasal associations, has overshadowed the original dominating meaning of 'greatness,' and the meaning of the word *enormity* has become permanently affected, so that it cannot now be used in the sense 'enormousness.' By similar conditions of phrasal use, the word *unspeakable* has become dominated by the meaning 'evil,' while its original equivalent, *ineffable* (literally 'unspeakable'), has become dominated by the meaning of 'grand' or 'glorious.' Through precisely similar processes the two words, *inappreciable* and *innumerable,* in their origin similar in meaning, have come to stand for meanings nearly directly opposed, the one "too small to be worthy of consideration," the other "too many to be counted."

Examples of this kind of change in meaning are everywhere at hand. *Tremendous,* which means literally the 'quality that makes one tremble,' has come to stand for the associated meaning of great size. *Countenance,* which originally meant 'bearing' or 'manner of holding oneself'

FIGURES OF CONTIGUITY

(Latin *con+tenere*, 'to hold'), came to apply to the manner of holding one's features, a meaning surviving in expressions such as 'to change countenance.' In its latest stage the word has shifted to the naturally associated meaning, 'the face.' *Feature*, in a parallel manner, has shifted from an earlier meaning of 'shape' or 'build,' seen in the O. Fr. *faiture* (Lat. *factura* from *facere*, 'to make'). Something similar takes place in the case of *dress*. This word is supposed to be derived through the French *dresser* from a conjectured Vulgar Latin *directiare* meaning 'to set straight' (Lat. *rectus*, 'straight'). This earlier meaning still appears in such military commands as 'dress to the right.' Through continued use, however, in such phrases as 'dress oneself,' the word has come to be interpreted as 'clothe oneself.'

In a number of instances in recent times new uses of words like those cited have met with challenge. *Aggravating*, which comes from the Latin *aggravare*, 'to make heavy,' is popularly used with the meaning 'irritating.' But this use, which originates in a misinterpretation of phrases such as 'aggravating circumstances,' meets with opposition from those alive to the precise meaning of the word. In the same way *transpire*, in journalistic use, has arrived at the meaning 'to happen' or 'to occur.' This use meets with strenuous opposition from those alive to its earlier meaning, 'to become known.' *Implicit*, in like manner, through misinterpretation of phrases such as 'implicit confidence,' has come in popular use to mean 'unlimited' or 'absolute,' a use of the word vigorously objected to by people more sensitive to precise values.

It appears, then, that in many instances the shifts of meaning which in the present chapter are grouped under the heading, figures of contiguity, are due to the variety of elements in the meaning of a single word. One of these elements comes to overshadow the others, and the meaning comes to be concentrated on what was, to start with, but one phase of the meaning.

The element in the meaning that prevails is often determined by phrasal associations, as appears in the case of such words as *enormity, mere* and *aggravating* cited above. In this way is to be explained remarkable shifts of meaning that take place in words that form parts of fixed combinations. In the American use of the word *corn* there has taken place a shift from the general meaning 'grain' to the specific meaning 'maize.' The shift appears to be a case of synecdoche, the name of a class given to a member of the class. What has really taken place is not this direct substitution, but the word *corn* in the combination *Indian corn* has absorbed in itself the meaning of both elements in the combination. In this way are to be explained many remarkable changes in meaning. In this way *rubber* (for India rubber) becomes a name for the Indian *caoutchouc; crescent,* literally 'growing' (from crescent moon), comes to mean a figure like the new moon; a *strike* (for strike work) comes to mean an organized discontinuance of work. Scores of other instances, such as *conceit* (for self-conceit), *match* (for sulphur match), *play* (for stage play), *attic* (for attic front), *concentrate* (for concentrate one's mind), *coal* (for digged-, earth-, sea-, stone-, or pit-coal), *wag* (for waghalter), have already been cited in an earlier chapter. In such cases we have to do with an interesting reversal of a process described above. Instead of one element in the meaning content taking possession of an entire word, one sound element in a word combination takes possession of the whole meaning content.

Truly marvelous are the juggling processes by which words are transformed in meaning. Conscious volition on the part of the speaker has had some share. Much larger, however, in the case of the words considered in the present chapter, is the share due to unconscious tendency.

The subject is indeed a complex one. "Product of a myriad various minds and contending tongues, compact of obscure and minute associations," says Walter Pater, "a language has its own abundant and recondite laws, in the recognition of which scholarship consists."

CHAPTER XVIII

GENERALIZATION AND SPECIALIZATION

Springing from the changes which have affected the meaning of words are some results which have profoundly affected the character of language. In order to understand the nature of these results, let us turn to a useful distinction offered by the study of logic. The logician distinguishes between two aspects of the meaning of words. He uses the term *denotation* to mean the object or objects to which a name applies, and the term *connotation* for the specific qualities that make up the meaning content of a word. The wider the denotation of a word, he points out, the narrower the connotation; the fuller the connotation, the more restricted the denotation.

The extreme type of words of limited denotation is the proper name, as indeed the word *proper* indicates. In the phrase 'proper name' the word *proper* retains an earlier meaning still surviving in the French *propre,* meaning 'own.' The English 'proper name,' therefore, is the exact equivalent in meaning of the German *Eigenname* which means 'own name.' The denotation of a proper name is limited to an individual person or place. Its connotation, on the other hand, includes the countless special attributes or qualities belonging to a definite individual. The other extreme may be illustrated by such words as *person* or *place* or *thing,* three words the denotation of which covers practically the whole of existence, but the connotation of which is almost zero.

In the history of language it has already been pointed out that the concrete names with large connotation ante-

GENERALIZATION AND SPECIALIZATION 249

date the abstract terms. The aborigines of Tasmania according to an eminent authority, had no words for abstract ideas.[1] They had names for each species of *gum-tree, wattle-tree*, etc., but no class name for *tree*. They also had no names for general conceptions such as *hard, soft, warm, cold, long, short*, etc. The Society Islanders, in like manner, can talk of *dog's tail, sheep's tail*, etc., but have no general name for *tail*.

Modern cultivated languages, on the other hand, reflect the classifying habits of modern thought by their wealth of class names. Even in modern languages, however, there survive many examples of words representing earlier habits of thought. Names associated with animals, for instance, go back usually to early stages in language history, and among these animals there is often conspicuously absent the classifying tendency elsewhere prevalent. This lack of generalization appears in the words used for groups of animals. The English language speaks of a *flock* of birds or sheep, a *drove* of cattle or swine, a *herd* of cattle, a *bevy* of quail, a *covey* of partridge, a *swarm* of bees, a *school* of fish, and (in slang) a *bunch* of men. A similar variety, a lack of generalization, appears in the names applied to the domicile for different domesticated beasts, such as cow-*byre*, horse-*stable*, dog-*kennel*, pig-*sty*, dove-*cote*, falcon-*mews*, rabbit-*hutch*. Similar uneconomical methods appear in the independent names for different types of the same beast, such as *horse, mare, stallion, foal, colt;* and *cow, calf, heifer, bull, steer, ox*. This lack of generalization recurs in the names for the young of animals, such as *calf, colt, lamb, puppy, fawn, kid, cub, shoat, cygnet, eyas, parr* and *smolt* (for salmon), and in the female names, *cow, mare, ewe, doe, bitch, heifer, sow*. Color terms are specialized when applied to beasts, as in *bay* horse, *dun* cow, *fallow* deer. The absence of generic terms

---

[1] O. Jespersen, *Progress in Language*, p. 35 ff.

is at times a source of embarrassment, for instance in the case of the *hen* and the *cow*, for which the English language affords no convenient class name. In a number of instances the name for the young of the species has come to serve as the generic term, for instance *rabbit* (for older *coney*), *pig* (for *swine*), *bird* (for *fowl*) and, to an increasing extent, *chicken* (for *poultry*).

This absence of the classifying habit which is so conspicuous in words associated with animal life, appears also in the language of the sea, as illustrated by the varied and unrelated names for different forms of sea craft such as *ship, boat, brig, sloop, schooner, wherry, shallop, dinghy*. Such groups of words are characteristic of earlier types of language, contrasting with the larger and larger generalization which in general characterize cultivated language.

The development of language parallels in many ways that in mathematics. Man in his infancy is concerned only with the individual objects immediately about him. He counts with his fingers. Later, by the science of numbers, he forms a conception of groups of ten, based on the number of the fingers, and then of groups of groups of ten, etc., until he is able to bring within his mental grasp numbers far beyond the reach of the senses alone. Algebraic symbols, in turn, enable him to go still farther and to bring within his comprehension conceptions reaching the infinite or the infinitesimal. Similar stages of progress appear in cultivated speech. Beginning with special names for individual things, proper names, it next gave names to groups or classes of things, common nouns, eventually reaching names almost completely dissociated from objects apprehended by the senses, abstract words, which provide a form of symbolism by which it is possible to bring before the mind the elements in the immaterial world of thought.

In the creation of the general terms so necessary in the

GENERALIZATION AND SPECIALIZATION 251

expression of comprehensive thought, the figurative shifts discussed in the preceding two chapters have had a large share. Through association of likeness or of contiguity, names are turned to new uses of such wide variety that eventually the word acquires a generic meaning, often losing all connection with its original meaning. The word *tree* appears originally to have served as the name for a specific kind of tree as indicated by the meaning of the Greek cognate *drus*, 'oak,' and the Welsh cognate, '*derwen*, 'oak.' In the same way the generic word *oil* is derived from the Latin *oleum*, which at first applied to the specific oil of the olive. In modern American colloquial use may be seen the same generalizing process not yet completed, in the use of *honey* in such expressions as *quince honey* and *pear honey*, and of *butter* in such expressions as *apple butter* and *peach butter*. The origin of the generic color names, already discussed, illustrates the same tendency. Such words as *orange* and *violet* are general names, although not completely dissociated from their original specific meanings. In the case of *drab* (French *drap*, 'cloth') and *maroon* (French *marron*, 'chestnut') the dissociation in English is complete. Even a word as general in its meaning as *green* goes back to an earlier specific meaning of 'growing.' In origin it is to be explained as a figure of speech based, as in the case of the other words cited, on similarity, in this case, to the color of growing things.

Thought, even of the most abstract kind, is inevitably accompanied by concrete images. There constantly exists, therefore, the tendency to sharpen the meaning by the use of the names of the accompanying concrete images. Thus the general idea of great size brought before the mind the image of the enormous extinct type of animal, the *mammoth*, and the animal name has come to be associated with the general meaning of immensity. Thus a Russian animal name invented as late as 1696,[2] has come to serve as an English general name for size. The famous *Colossus* of Rhodes, in similar manner, has yielded the word of general meaning, *colossal*. In the same way are to be explained the synonymous terms, *gigantic* and *titanic*, and such terms for diminutive size as *puny* (O. Fr. *puisne*, Lat. *post natus*, 'younger,' 'junior') and *miniature* from the name of paintings of small size, which in turn took their name from Latin *minium*, 'red lead.'

Such instances of specific names turned to general meanings are to be met with on all sides. The *butcher*, the slayer of animals, gets his name from one animal, the original type of victim, the goat (Fr. *bouc*). The earlier specific meaning of the generic term *feel* is indicated by the O. E. *folm*, 'palm of the hand' with which *feel* is related. *Front*, which originally meant 'forehead' (Lat. *frons, frontis*) first came to mean 'face,' and then became generalized to its present general meaning of 'forepart.' From *tornus*, the Latin name for 'lathe,' has come the word of general service, *turn*. The native English word for 'turn' (O. E. *thrāwan*) came to be associated with the turning movement, either of the body or of the missile involved, in the act of throwing, but finally shifted to the general meaning 'throw,' replacing entirely the older English *weorpan* and in great part the borrowed Norse word, *cast*. The effort in living colloquial speech to vivify language by words with concrete associations is admirably illustrated by the multitude of synonyms, such as *peg, heave, chuck, burn, fire, sling, steam*, etc., which the language of sport has provided. From the sparkle of the beryl has come the generalized term *brilliant*. From the misery of the exile (O. E. *wreca*, 'exile') comes the application of the word *wretch* to the unfortunate as a class. *Arrive* (Lat. *ripa*, 'shore') which applied to the end of a voyage, has

---

[2] *Century Dictionary*.

GENERALIZATION AND SPECIALIZATION 253

become generalized so as to apply to the end of any journey. *Plunge,* which is derived from the Latin *plumbum,* 'lead,' has become generalized to mean 'violent entrance into a liquid' on the part of any object. *Hazard,* a name for a dicing game, has come to mean 'risk' in general. *Chance* is generalized from the meaning 'fall of the dice.' *Hustle* also is generalized from a seventeenth-century meaning of 'shake up coins in a hat in gambling.' *Course* comes from the Latin *cursus,* an earlier meaning of which was 'running track.' *Tyro* originally meant 'raw recruit' in military service. *Zest* meant originally a 'piece of lemon-peel.' Observe the phrase, 'to add zest to.' The same kind of generalization has taken place in the words *pester* and *trammel,* already cited. *Tease,* originally a term of weaving, through generalization, has quite drawn away from its earlier meaning. From the specific terms of the same occupation has come in more recent times the word *heckle,* turned metaphorically to a new meaning and apparently on the way to a wider generalization. Even a word as abstract in quality as *try* goes back to an earlier specific meaning, probably to that of threshing. Starting from this meaning the word is supposed to have developed the general meaning 'separate the good from the bad,' a meaning surviving in the phrase *try out* (fat or blubber). From this meaning the transition was easy to the meaning 'test' or 'prove' and eventually to the present sense.[3] From the theater comes *scene.* This word, which in the earlier stages of its history in Greek, expressed successively the meanings 'tent,' then 'booth' (on a stage), then 'stage,' has become generalized in meaning so as to fit the broader world's stage.[4] Another general term provided by the theater is *person,* a word which has become so generalized as to be almost equivalent to a pronoun of the common

---
[3] Weekley, *Etymological Dictionary of Modern English.*
[4] Greenough and Kittredge, p. 246.

gender. *Person* in its origin was sharply concrete in meaning. It comes from the Latin *persona,* 'an actor in a play,' so named from the characteristic mask with large mouth for the sound to pass through (Lat. *per* + *sonare*,[5] 'to sound through'). The ever living tendency in language to renew the concrete quality in words is illustrated by the succession of words which in modern colloquial speech have been used to fill the place of *person* and sharing with it the same experience of generalization. *Chap* is short for *chapman,* 'merchant.' *Fellow,* of Norse origin, meant originally 'partner.' *Guy* comes from the proper name, Guy Fawkes. It was applied as a name first to the ridiculous image of Guy Fawkes borne in procession, then to any ridiculous figure, then derisively to persons, and eventually, in the speech of American youth, to persons in general, with no intended disrespect. Other synonymous general terms from the creations of slang are: *stiff*, boldly figurative in its origin, and the later words, *gink* and *bloke,* creeping into American use from the slang of Great Britain and her colonies. Corresponding to *person* in the common gender, is the neuter *thing,* available as the substitute for any name when definiteness of connotation is not required. This word is supposed to have originated as a legal term, in this respect paralleling its German equivalent, *Sache.*[6] An earlier concreteness of meaning appears in *storthing* (*stor,* 'great' + *thing,* 'assembly') the name of the Norwegian parliament. Here again the disposition to renew the connection of general terms with a concrete meaning appears in such equivalents of *thing* as *business* (in 'the whole business'), *concern, affair.* In present-day American colloquial use the word *proposition* is paralleling in a striking way the earlier history of *thing,* and from the actively creative life of technical slang, comes *gadget.*

---

[5] Greenough and Kittredge, p. 268.
[6] Hirt, p. 256, Meillet, pp. 307-308.

GENERALIZATION AND SPECIALIZATION 255

Almost as broad as the word *thing* in its sweep of meaning is *paraphernalia,* the generalized meaning of which in English goes back only to the eighteenth century. This word in its history carries one back to an atmosphere of romance, to the wedding arrangements among the Greeks, with whom the word *parapherna* meant the articles belonging to a wife in addition to her dowry.

The effect of the generalizing process, and the resulting fading of concrete meaning, is shown in a remarkable manner in the series of words which in the history of English have served as intensive adverbs, the equivalents of modern English *very.* In earliest English, *swīthe,* which goes back to an early meaning of 'strongly,' was used with the general meaning 'very.' This word in the Middle English period was quite supplanted by the words *full* and *well,* which in turn were later superseded by *passing* and *sore,* two words familiar in the language of the sixteenth century in such expressions as 'passing strange' and 'sore afraid.' These words, now obsolete in this use, were in turn replaced by *very,* which to begin with, had the specific meaning 'truly' (Latin *verus,* 'true,' *cf.* Chaucer's "verray parfit gentil knight"). This word, in turn, in modern English, has almost ceased to lend intensive force to an adjective, and in the literary language, which affords only such substitutes as *exceedingly,* there is a palpable want of an effective, not profane, intensifying adverb. Living colloquial and dialectal speech, not so hampered, produces a variety of such words. *Mighty* and *powerful,* used in this way, repeat the sense-development met with in Old English *swīthe. Awfully* illustrates the popular resort to hyperbole and the consequent weakening in meaning from generalization.

To the process of generalization modern languages are indebted for most of the simple, seemingly protozoic but essential elements which serve the purpose of indicating grammatical relations. The conjugation of the verb *to be* is a composite one, made up of three elements independent in origin. The element which appears in the forms, *am, is, are*, goes back to an earlier specific meaning, probably that of 'breathe'; the element in *was* and *were* goes back to the meaning 'dwell'; and that in *be, being, been*, goes back to an earlier meaning 'grow.' The Greek cognate of *be* is *phuo*, which enters into such English derivatives as *physical, physiology*, etc.[7]

The English future auxiliaries, *shall* and *will*, are likewise products of generalization. *Shall* goes back to an earlier meaning 'owe.' Its Latin cognate, *scelus*, means 'guilt.' One of its earlier meanings may be seen in the use of *shalt* in prohibitions, as in the Ten Commandments. *Will*, on the other hand, goes back to an earlier specific meaning, 'wish,' 'choose,' and then 'intend.' Its earlier meaning appears in the Latin cognate, *volo*, which enters into such English words as *voluntary*. Even the word *do*, which has become so far generalized as to stand in the relation to verbs that pronouns occupy toward nouns and, therefore, may well be called a pro-verb, goes back to an earlier physical meaning of 'put' or 'place,' a meaning which survives in *don* (*do* + *on*) and *doff* (*do* + *off*). The earlier meanings of the prepositions, it is in general impossible to determine with certainty, but the development of some of those of later origin, such as *around* and *among*, offers suggestion regarding the origin of the more simple forms. The second element in *around*, for instance, is derived through the French from the Latin *rotundus*, which in turn is derived from *rota*, 'wheel,' and *among* goes back to an Old English *ongemang*, meaning 'in the crowd,' the second element of which is derived from the verb *gemengan*, 'to mingle.'

The activity of the generalizing process as exemplified

---

[7] Greenough and Kittredge, p. 238.

GENERALIZATION AND SPECIALIZATION 257

by the instances cited, might serve to create the impression that development in language is all in the one direction, that from concrete to abstract, from specific to general. Such is far from being the case. The tendency toward specialization is, if possible, even more active than that of generalization.

The most natural and obvious way to specialize the meaning of a word is to add a qualifying word. For example, by the addition of the adjective *Indian* to the word *corn*, which had the general meaning 'grain,' was produced the name *Indian corn* as the name for the new American grain, the Indian name for which was *maize*. In the same way from the general name *engine*, meaning 'mechanical device' or 'contrivance,' was formed the name *steam engine* for a special form of mechanical device.

In the preceding chapter it was pointed out how one word in a combination may absorb the meaning of associated words to such an extent that the associated words may be omitted as redundant. In this way the single word *corn* has come in American to express the special meaning 'Indian corn,' or 'maize.' In the same way in the nineteenth century the single word *engine* has become specialized to the meaning 'steam engine.' In this way scores of words have become specialized: *pipe* to the meaning of 'tobacco pipe,' *conceit* to that of 'self conceit,' *poise* to that of 'mental poise,' *palpitation* to that of 'heart-palpitation,' *execute* to that of 'execute a capital sentence,' *corpse* to that of 'dead corpse,' *snuff* (from the Dutch *snuif* for *snuiftabak*), *sale* to that of 'cut-price sale.'

More frequently, perhaps, the specialization is brought about, not by the actual addition of a qualifying word which is later omitted, but by the absorption of a qualifying element from external associations. It has more than once been pointed out that special classes of men tend to specialize the meanings of words connected with their special activities. The noun *run*, for instance, has quite different meanings to a trainman, to a theatrical manager, and to a baseball player. *Play* means one thing to a child and quite different things to actor, to gambler, and to tennis or golf player. The word *engine* conveys meanings quite specialized to a sawmill operator, to a locomotive engineer and to the driver of a motor car. The nature of the specialization is like that in the cases cited above, where one word has absorbed qualifying elements from the context. To a surgeon, for instance, the word *surgical* in *surgical operation* is as redundant as *tobacco* in *tobacco-pipe* would be to a smoker or *Indian* in *Indian corn* would be to an American farmer.

Let us take, for example, one particular set of words. The appropriation of words to their own special uses on the part of the early Christians is responsible for a large group of specialized words. The process began among the primitive Christians in the East. The Syriac word *abba*, 'father,' provided the name for a church dignitary. The common Greek word *presbuteros*, meaning 'elder,' provided the name for the church leader. The word coming through the Latin into English at an earlier period, has in English popular use undergone modification in sound, and has become modern English *priest*. Borrowed through literary channels, it retains its classical form in *presbyter*. The old meaning of 'elder' is still alive in the name *Presbyterian* which applies to a church ruled by 'elders.' In the same way the common Greek word *episkopos*, 'overseer,' was appropriated as a name for a superior officer and persists in English not only in the popular form, *bishop*, but in the learned borrowing, *episcopal*, which means 'governed by bishops.'

At a later period, within the history of the English language, the same kind of specialization under Christian influence continued. *Salvation* (Latin *salvare*, 'to save'),

GENERALIZATION AND SPECIALIZATION

became limited to the 'saving of the soul,' and was thus sharply differentiated from *salvage*, derived from the same Latin word. For the reverse of *salvation*, another word from the Latin was appropriated in the same way, the word *damnation* specialized from an earlier meaning of 'condemnation' in general. The native English *doom*, meaning 'judgment,' was narrowed to mean 'divine judgment.' *Convert*, meaning 'to turn,' came to mean 'to turn to the Christian faith.' The plural of the Old English word *heaven* (O. E. *heofon*, 'sky'), was applied as a name for 'the home of the blessed.' The pagan English *hell*, meaning 'house of the dead,' was specialized to mean 'the future home of the damned.'

Words become specialized in meaning not only through the character of the persons using them, but through the nature of the context in which they habitually occur. It must be borne in mind that the real unit in natural language is not the word, but the sentence. The meaning of words is learned by meeting them in varied combinations with other words. If a word becomes limited in use to a restricted number of expressions, its meaning will be affected by the limited kind of context with which it becomes associated. Let us take once more, by way of illustration, the word *room*. This word originally had the broad meaning, 'space,' a meaning which survives in such expressions as 'make room,' 'no room for,' and 'roomy.' From frequent use in combinations such as *sleeping room, eating room*, etc., the word, beginning with the fifteenth century, comes to have its modern specialized meaning, 'section of space in a building.' The meaning of a word obviously may become specialized through special phrasal associations. To the specialization due to phrasal associations is to be attributed the remarkable differentiation in meaning of such words as *unspeakable* and *ineffable* already referred to. Take once more the word, *enormity*. *Enormous* is derived from the Latin *ex,* 'from,' 'out of' + *norma,* 'rule' + the suffix *-ous.* Its etymological meaning, therefore, is equivalent to that of *extraordinary.* In ordinary use, however, the meaning of the word has become limited to extraordinary size, a meaning which appears in *enormousness.* The word *enormity,* however, which in form is equivalent to *enormousness,* has become limited on account of the regular association of the word with crime and offense. In consequence one may not speak, for instance, of the '*enormity* of Mammoth cave.' *Enormity* has absorbed qualifying elements of meaning from associated words, and now may be defined as 'monstrous wickedness.' In the same way *bray,* a word of Celtic origin, borrowed through the French, in earlier English referred to a loud harsh sound made by beasts of various kinds, such as bull or deer, or by human beings or even by the inanimate tempest. The word, however, has become specialized because it has absorbed new elements in its meaning content through vivid association wtih one kind of beast. In like manner *wag,* which at one time had the general meaning 'tremble,' and might be applied even to the motion of leaves of trees, has lost its general meaning, because it cannot divest itself of acquired associations. The native word *sting,* in like manner, yields its original general meaning to the borrowed word, *pierce,* because of its acquired connotation from vivid association. Even in such phrases as 'stinging sensations,' where perhaps the earlier general meaning 'piercing' may be intended, the vividly associated bee is almost unavoidably brought to mind.

The context that influences meanings is not always a context of words. In many instances a silent context in the form of irony or innuendo serves to cause a form of specialization which remains to be discussed in another chapter under the head of Degeneration of Words.

Specialization in the meaning of words is by no means

GENERALIZATION AND SPECIALIZATION

peculiar to English. The tendencies discussed have been tendencies of universal character and active in all languages. Yet an inspection of the parallel lists of words, English and German, English and French, and English and Italian, to be found in earlier chapters, will serve to convince that words in the English language have been more subject to this tendency than have words in other languages. The explanation is to be found in the extensive borrowing of words which has been one of the most striking features in the history of English. A consequence of this extensive borrowing has been that in many instances native word and borrowed word have come into competition with each other. The result has been that in many instances native words, if they survive at all, survive in only a small number of phrases. The narrowing of variety in phrasal associations in which a word is used, inevitably leads to a narrowed conception of its meaning. The history of the native word, *token*, will serve to illustrate. Originally having the broad meaning 'sign,' when brought into competition with the borrowed word, *sign*, it became restricted in use to a small number of phrases, such as 'love token,' 'token of respect,' and became correspondingly specialized in meaning. In this way *ghost*, which originally had the broad meaning 'spirit,' a meaning which survives in the name *Holy Ghost*, in competition with the borrowed word, *spirit*, became restricted to its present meaning, 'the returning spirit of one that is dead.' In the same way *fowl*, which once had the general meaning 'bird,' retains its full meaning in such biblical expressions as 'fowls of the air,' 'snare of the fowler,' but in living modern speech is limited to the meaning 'domestic fowls.' In fact, native English words that have escaped the prevailing tendency toward specialization, are exceptional.

Many illustrative examples of specialization will be

found in the chapter devoted to the native element in the vocabulary. Let us single out here a few interesting cases. The verb *last*, originally meant 'to extend continuously in space or in time'; it is now limited to continuance in time. *Stare*, which meant 'to look,' now means 'to look with fixed gaze.' *Reek*, which meant 'to smoke,' has become specialized so as to refer to an exhalation usually of an unpleasant nature. *Seethe*, which meant 'to boil,' has become specialized so as to mean the physical movement in a boiling liquid. *Hoard*, from the general meaning 'treasure,' has come to mean the 'treasure of a miser.' *Meat*, which used to mean 'food' in general, is now restricted in meaning to the flesh of animals. *Spill*, which meant 'to destroy' in general, now refers to the destruction of liquids. *Fiend*, which meant 'enemy,' now refers to the arch enemy of the Christian. *Bereaved*, the earlier meaning of which was 'robbed,' is now so specialized as to refer exclusively to losses through death.

But specialization has been by no means confined to the native English words. The imported words have been subjected to much the same influence resulting from competition. As shown in an earlier chapter, French words borrowed into English, have often been strikingly specialized in meaning as compared with the same words remaining in the French language. *Ancient*, for example, is much restricted in meaning compared with the French *ancien*. The same is true of such words as *dame, grand, arrest, march,* and *herb*, compared with the corresponding words surviving in modern French.

In fact, words of all classes are affected. *Apparition* (Lat. *apparitionem*), which once meant 'appearance,' has been so narrowed as to be practically synonymous with *ghost*. *Liquor*, once meaning 'liquid,' now means alcoholic liquor, and is still farther specialized in its French form

GENERALIZATION AND SPECIALIZATION 263

liqueur. *Carol,* once meaning 'dance,' came first to mean 'dance songs,' and then became specialized to its present meaning, 'a type of Christmas song.' *Idiot* goes back to a Greek word with the general meaning 'private person.' *Paradise* comes from the Greek name for 'garden.' *Execute,* through phrasal associations, came to its present specialized grim meaning. *Persecute,* which goes back to an earlier general meaning, 'to follow' or 'to pursue,' became specialized as a name for the special procedure against the early Christians. *Cannon* is derived through the French and Italian from a word meaning 'tube.' *Revolution* is for the most part specialized to the meaning 'revolution of government.' *Provisions* is limited to the meaning of 'food.' *Cattle* (Latin *capitale,* 'stock,' 'capital,' from *caput,* 'head') was narrowed to mean 'movable property' and finally specialized to its present meaning. *Fund* goes back to an earlier general meaning, 'bottom,' 'foundation.' *Cash* goes back to an original meaning, 'money box.' *Currency* goes back to a Latin word meaning literally 'a running.' The idea underlying its modern specialized meaning is the liquid element of a nation's wealth.

The subjects of generalization and specialization, though opposing tendencies, are here considered together because they are in large measure produced by the same kind of tropes, or shifts in meaning, and because they are so often associated in the history of the same word. In many instances a modern meaning has been reached only after successive generalization and specialization or the reverse. Let us take two instances. *Pipe* is supposed to have been an onomatopoetic creation made in imitation of the sound of a young bird. The word was applied to a musical instrument that made this sound. It then became generalized to mean 'a thing of tubular form,' such as a 'lead pipe.' In later times the word has become specialized in turn to the meaning 'tobacco pipe.' *Fee*, a native English word, goes back to an early meaning, 'cattle.' It then was generalized to mean 'property' in general, and later on, 'money.' In its last stage it has become specialized to mean 'money paid for professional service.'

CHAPTER XIX

EUPHEMISM AND HYPERBOLE

There remain for consideration a number of other features of language that have been productive of change of meaning. Two of these speech tendencies, unlike in themselves, have been remarkably alike in their effect on the meaning of words. The two tendencies in question are euphemism and hyperbole.

In order to appreciate the force of the euphemistic tendency one will do well to recall the source of the word *etymology*. The first part of the word is the Greek *etumon*, which meant 'true meaning.' The Greeks, as the word *etumon* shows, believed that there was a direct and essential relation between a word and its meaning. In other words, there was a direct relation between a thing and its name. This idea of the Greeks was widely prevalent elsewhere. Many are the stories in the world's literature in which magic power is attributed to certain words. Every one will recall the *open sesame* of "Ali Baba and the Forty Thieves." Several English words bear evidence to the belief in the magic potency of words. The word *spell* in Old English meant a 'saying' or 'narrative,' a meaning surviving in *gospel* (O. E. *gōd*, 'good' + *spell*, 'message'). The word, however, meant also a set of words with magic powers, a meaning surviving in such modern phrases as *under a spell, spellbound,* etc. The word *charm*, also (Latin *carmen*), bears evidence to the belief in the magic potency of words when sung. The same belief in the quality of sung words is attested by *enchantment* (Lat. *cantus*, 'song').

If one goes back to earlier stages in the development of civilization, one will find still more in evidence the belief in the magic power in words. This close relation supposed to exist between an object and its name serves to explain the verbal taboos or interdictions so characteristic of the speech of primitive peoples. It has been pointed out, for example, that the bear has no name of his own in Balto-Slavic or Teutonic languages. Direct naming of the bear was avoided by the use of such conventional names as *the eater of honey, the noise maker, the brown,* or *the licker*. In like manner the Lapps and Finns and Esthonians avoid direct naming of the bear through such substitute names as *glory of the forest, the old one, the hairy one, proud honey-foot, big foot,* etc.[1] The avoidance also of direct names for various forms of disease is indicated by the absence among kindred Indo-European languages of common names for the most usual of human infirmities, such as lameness, blindness and deafness. The influence of similar verbal interdiction is apparent in the avoidance among modern Irish peasantry of direct naming of the fairies, or *shee*. Such terms as *the gentry* and *the good people,* are the names substituted.

Among primitive folk immense power is attributed to sacred beings and objects, which are on that account taboo and not to be directly named. The same motives lead to the interdiction of direct names for the tribal chief or anything connected with him. The same interdiction, for similar reasons, applies to things associated with death. Among the natives of Madagascar and among American Indians there prevails a custom of changing name when some one of the name has just died.[2] Similar motives explain the avoidance of certain terms connected with sex and the distinction in language between the feminine and the

---

[1] Niceforo, p. 218.
[2] *Ibid.,* pp. 246-247.

masculine. Among the natives of the Caribbean Islands, we are told, there formerly existed a double language, one for men, the other for women.[3]

Contrary to the prevalent impression, then, it is often to the survival in modern life of features of primitive superstition, rather than to an increase of delicacy attending civilization, that is to be attributed the euphemistic elements in modern speech. In fact, one of the most distinctive features of sophisticated speech, as distinguished from unsophisticated speech in our time, is the absence of squeamishness and the ready courage to name things directly, to realize the ideal associated with the name of Swift, of calling a spade a spade. The old superstitions, however, are by no means entirely extinct. A taboo in our day attends the practice of boasting of personal escape from some prevalent ill. Effort to avoid the evil consequences of breaking this taboo are made, in a spirit by no means entirely playful, by the crossing of fingers and touching of wood. Every child has been warned of the dangerous consequences when swinging, of using the interdicted expression, 'Let the old cat die.' The primitive fear of using direct names for divinity survives not only in the ideas connected with the words, *profane, blasphemous,* etc., but in the delicate substitution of such names as *the Almighty, the Creator, the Lord, the Saviour, the Redeemer, Our Lady, Madonna,* etc. The earlier superstitious avoidance of direct names for a tribal chief survives not only in such practices as the use of phrases like *your Majesty, your excellency,* etc., but in the attitude of modern inferior to superior. A servant is addressed by the first name, but the taboo of the savages is not stronger than is that which prevents a servant or employee from addressing master or mistress by the first name. In European countries the distinctions prevalent in the use of

---

[3] Niceforo, p. 255.

the pronoun of address, undoubtedly are rooted in the same primitive superstition.

The name *euphemism* itself, it has been pointed out,[4] in its origin is associated with religious practice. It comes from the Greek word made up of the two elements: *eu,* 'fair,' and *phemi,* 'speak.' The imperative of the verb was addressed to worshipers in warning not to disturb a ceremony by the use of words of ill omen.

The influence of euphemism in modern speech is most apparent in the words associated wtih death. The grim reaper excites hardly less terror in man, the product of modern civilization, than he did in the savage in his most primitive stage. Hence the persistent life of the earlier euphemistic practices. If one goes back to the earliest stage in the history of English, one will find the avoidance of the direct name for 'die.' In the death notices of the Anglo-Saxon kings, the verbs used are not the comparatively infrequent English words, *steorfan* or *sweltan,* meaning literally, 'to die,' but such substitutes as *forthferan,* 'to go forth,' and *gewitan,* 'to depart.' In early English poetry the heroes did not literally *die,* but euphemistically *lay* or *fell.* The same feature of language is familiar in modern English. For the direct verb *die* are substituted such expressions as *passed away, departed, breathed his last, expired, was taken, went on his last journey,* etc. The same reluctance to use names directly associated with the dread theme appears in such substitutions as: *casket* for coffin, *funeral car* for hearse, *mortuary* or *funeral parlors* or *funeral home* for undertaker's establishment, and *funeral director* for undertaker, the last word itself a creation of the euphemism of an earlier period. The muffled quality of English adjectives derived from the Latin, as compared with the sharpness in meaning of native words, leads to the euphemistic substitution of *obituary* for death notice. Was

---

[4] Greenough and Kittredge, p. 301.

it sentiment or was it latent supersition that led the early Christians to adopt, as a name for the burial place in the catacombs, the Greek word *koimeterion,* which meant 'dormitory,' or 'sleeping place'?

Probably to be connected with primitive superstition is the squeamish reluctance to use direct names for different parts of the body, for certain physiological phenomena, and for various forms of disease. The Victorian fear of the use of the word *leg* has been largely overcome along with the Victorian fear of exhibiting that limb. There is also a reaction from the squeamishness that made the terms *ankle* and *neck* cover the greater part of the intervening anatomy. But a veil of propriety in language, as in dress, continues to cover a great part of the human body. Popular words, too vivid in their suggestive power, are replaced in polite use by such words as *abdomen* and *viscera.* The names of most of the garments under the outer layer of coat and trousers, or dress and blouse and skirt, are classed among the unmentionables. Even the word, *naked,* yields in part to the less staringly bold word, *nude.* Under euphemistic influence *sweat* yields to *perspiration, spit* to *expectorate,* and *sick,* because of vivid associations with nausea, yields to *ill. Gastralgia* succeeds the popular name associated with infantile pains. *Hernia* succeeds the Latin derivative, *rupture,* and the native English *breach.* The extremist in prudery is said to substitute *nose spasm* for *sneeze.*

It must be recalled that the word *disease* itself, literally meaning 'discomfort,' is a product of euphemism. Of similar origin is the name for mental disease, *insanity* (Lat. *in,* 'not' $+$ *sanus,* 'well,' 'healthy'), which in the sixteenth century came to succeed earlier *crazy* and *mad.* The synonym, *deranged,* is a product of the same tendency, and even the word *crazy,* so vividly associated with the frightful, had an origin somewhat euphemistic in nature.

The verb *craze* means 'to break' or 'crack,' and appears in *crazed* as applied to the cracks in the surface of certain forms of pottery. The modern substitution of *state hospital* for insane asylum, like that of *county infirmary* for poorhouse, is obviously euphemistic in origin.

In most of the instances of euphemism thus far cited, the influence of inherited superstition is more or less apparent. If the use of the euphemistic word does not spring directly from the inherited feeling, it is probably patterned after words thus created. The refinements of civilization, however, undoubtedly enter somewhat into the explanation of euphemism. It is shown elsewhere how a word depends for its effect not only on its central meaning but upon the meanings that have become associated with it. The following chapter discusses the way in which a word degenerates in meaning when it has absorbed disagreeable associated elements or when a disagreeable element of the meaning becomes too baldly prominent. The recourse of cultivated use in such cases is to find a euphemistic substitute. Thus the Old English *stink* with the general meaning 'smell,' comes to be too vividly associated with 'ill smell.' In consequence in Middle English *smell* takes its place, only in turn to undergo the same experience and be replaced by *odor*, which in its turn degenerating, has to be succeeded by such words as *fragrance, perfume,* or *bouquet.* The history of *cheap* is a parallel one. The word originated as an abbreviation of the phrase *good cheap,* meaning 'good bargain,' but inevitably an associated meaning of 'poor in quality' gained prominence, so that for the original meaning the euphemistic word *inexpensive* has had to be substituted. This form of euphemism appears in the case of many words in which a disagreeable meaning has become too sharply prominent. Thus we have the euphemistic substitution of *fresh* for *clean, soiled* for *dirty*, in the language of the laundry. In many instances the sub-

EUPHEMISM AND HYPERBOLE 271

stitution of a classical derivative for a native word has the desired euphemistic effect, like that of the soft pedal on harsh sounds. When Stevenson, for instance, speaks of a "pediculous malady," the effect is quite other from what would be produced by the synonymous *lousy disease.* The story is told of an Italian sign, "Pedicure," and below it the unnecessary English synonym, quite divested of euphemism, "corn-cutter." From such instances it is clear enough that the euphemistic element in the English vocabulary is not without its practical use.

Still another use of euphemism in polite use is the avoidance of a tone of harsh intolerance. This use of the euphemistic is illustrated by the scores of synonyms for *drunk* already referred to in an earlier chapter. To call a man a *liar* is forbidden by parliamentary usage, but the same meaning is conveyed by innumerable euphemistic methods. The harshness of censure that has become attached to the older words, *infidel* and *atheist,* is avoided by the softened expression, *freethinker.* A number of common English words originate in euphemism which has faded from view. Thus *immoral* etymologically is equivalent to *ill-mannered* (Lat. *mores,* 'manners'). *Immodest* is derived from the Latin *modus,* 'measure,' and therefore in its origin was a euphemism with the meaning 'extreme' or 'immoderate.' In the same way *decency* goes back to an earlier meaning, 'what is fitting' (Lat. *decus, cf.* English decorate). *Impertinent* had originally the moderate meaning of 'not pertaining'; *indolent* goes back to an earlier meaning, 'not grieving,' therefore 'taking no pains.' Even *indignant* and *indignation* go back to the mild meaning of 'not worthy.' Evidently euphemism has been a moderating influence checking intemperate expression in cultivated speech.

Still another phase of euphemism is that of serving a prevalent taste for the grandiloquent. The American dispenser of alcoholic beverages adopted as the name of his place of business, *saloon,* a word most aristocratic in its former associations. The barber has long been ridiculed for his pretensions to *tonsorial art* and *hair-dressing parlor.* The tailor adopts the high-sounding title *maker of men's garments.* The undertaker, under the name *funeral director,* attempts to escape the unpleasant associations attaching to his occupation, and the piano teacher assumes the dignity of *teacher of pianistic art.* Ironical use of this form of euphemism is to be seen in such names as *city hotel* for jail and *knight of the road* for highwayman.

By this grandiloquent use of euphemism we are led to another speech tendency different in origin, but affecting the meaning of words in much the same way as euphemism. It remains to discuss this other tendency well-known under the name hyperbole.

The terms euphemism and hyperbole are not mutually exclusive. If one defines euphemism as 'fair speech' and hyperbole as 'exaggerated speech,' it is apparent that the meanings may overlap. The fairness of speech may be gained by means of exaggerated forms of expression. The grandiloquent forms of euphemism cited above might almost equally well be classed under the head of exaggeration or of hyperbole. The same is true of the American use of some of the finer sounding street names. *Avenue,* for instance, which properly means 'an approach' (O. Fr. *avenir*), a meaning exemplified in the Parisian street name, *Avenue de l'Opera,* applied to the street leading to the opera house, in England, and particularly in America, is applied to streets in general. The English use of *avenue* as the name for a street bordered by trees is probably due to Evelyn.[5] The word *boulevard* has had a similar history. Its original meaning was 'rampart' or 'bulwark.' Later, when in Europe the older ramparts were razed, the site of the ramparts, now far within the city limits, was used for

---

[5] Weekley, *Etymological Dictionary.*

EUPHEMISM AND HYPERBOLE

a broad street. This original use of the word *boulevard* is also exemplified in Paris, where a series of boulevards forms a ring about the older part of the city. In English-speaking countries, however, the grandiloquent quality of the name has led to its application, with little discrimination, to pretentious streets, varied in kind. In the same way the associations that have formed about English names, such as *Banbury Road, Maiden Lane, Chancery Lane, Portland Place,* etc., has led to the indiscriminate application of these names, *road* and *place* and *lane,* so that in modern additions to American cities the older name *street* has become almost obsolete.

If in the words just cited there appear the qualities both of euphemism and of hyperbole, this is by no means universally the case. The two features of language are quite different in their origin. Euphemism is rooted in superstition, which leads to the avoidance of unpleasant words because of a supposed essential connection between a name and the thing named. Hyperbole, on the other hand, is rooted in enthusiasm, and owes its origin to the desire to give added vividness or intensity to expression.

Both euphemism and hyperbole have met with opposition. To euphemism are opposed those who believe in 'calling a spade a spade.' To hyperbole are opposed those who believe in precise statement of fact. But it has been made clear, it is hoped, that euphemism has its value. Hyperbole also has its use. It has long since been pointed out that the object of art is the presentation not of fact, but of sense of fact. Let us now take under consideration the classic instance of hyperbole, that of the 'wave mountain-high.' It is well enough known that the highest wave never reaches the height of the lowest mountain. The fact of the case might be more precisely stated by the phrase 'a wave forty feet high.' But such a statement would entirely fail to convey the *sense* of fact. For one on a vessel diving into a monstrous wave, the sense of fact would be truthfully conveyed only by some such phrase as 'mountain-high.' For the 'literature of power,' at any rate, as distinguished from the 'literature of knowledge,' hyperbole has a definite value.

Hyperbole serves to convey intensity of feeling. If one is fond of a person, one may express the feeling with differing degrees of intensity by the words, *like, love, adore*, or in colloquial speech, *be crazy about*. Similar variation of intensity mounting to hyperbole, appear in the series of adjectives for a good time, such as *good, fine, lovely, delightful, lark, circus*, etc. Pleasure may be expressed with rising degrees of intensity by *pleased, happy, delighted, charmed, enchanted*. Degrees of fright may similarly be expressed by *alarmed, frightened, paralyzed, petrified, scared stiff*. Anger may be expressed by the adjectives *angry, enraged* (Lat. *rabies*, 'madness'), *furious* (like a Fury), or colloquially, *hot* or *boiling*, or *mad* (literally 'insane').

The necessity of heightened modes of expression for intensity of emotion is evident. In this gradation of emotion it will be observed that the exaggerated mode of expression is more characteristic of the vocabulary of women than that of men. It will be noted also that the French language is more given to exaggerated expression of feeling than is the English. In fact many of the English words of greater intensity, such as *adore* and *enchanted*, are to be explained as Gallicisms. There is to be observed, also, the greater propensity toward exaggeration in colloquial speech than in regulated standard usage. The riot of hyperbole in colloquial speech may be illustrated by the language of a young lady from Nevada who, according to her statements, recorded in a newspaper report, "simply died from the heat," "was tickled to death by movie comedians," was "driven crazy by telephone pests," and was "frozen just stiff" while auto riding, and all in the course of a single week. The general tendency, which in this instance appears in such exaggerated form, may be traced throughout all living speech. Extreme exaggeration is reached in the slang of baseball, by an expression such as "behemoth of biff," applied to a record-breaking (or shall we say *smashing*) home run hitter; but the exaggeration is not greater than that offered in legitimate speech by the phrase *volcanic* applause, in which the mundane limit seems to be reached.

By the use of extreme forms of speech the capacities of language become exhausted. The frequency of the phrase, *roar of laughter,* is such that in the speech of many the word *roar,* separated from the phrase, has become synonymous with *laugh.* So great is the fading tendency in the language resulting from the use of exaggeration, that one needs to have one's attention called to the extreme hyperbole in casually used words of superlative force such as *daredevil, skinflint, lickspittle, numskull, bleacher,* and *skyscraper.* In many instances the original exaggeration has almost faded from view, as in the words, *enraged* and *furious* already cited, and in *inflamed* (literally 'set on fire'), and *astonish* and its doublet *stun* (literally 'thunderstruck').

Renewed intensity of expression is accomplished by vivid forms of expression much cherished by writers of the modern school. *Freeze on to* (for 'hold on') is, perhaps unfortunately, confined to slang use, but *ooze out* (for 'slip out') of a room, has of late gained literary recognition, and *rivet* (for 'fix') the gaze has found particular favor in Presidential use of language (1921).

The constant necessity of renewal of intense forms of expression may be illustrated by many series of words. *In the teeth of* the wind supersedes the earlier *in the face of;* he had *spotted* the man succeeds he had *noticed,* or he had *marked*. The series of words that have served to express the meaning 'very' has already been cited. The succession of terms for affectionate male comradeship, *crony, chum, pal, bunkie,* and *buddy,* affords further illustration. Another such series of words is: the Old English *scēne*, 'beautiful' (*Cf.* Germ. *schön*); *fair,* which survives only in phrases like 'fair maid' and 'fair lady'; *pretty,* which in the fifteenth century was shifted by a playful irony from its original meaning of 'sly,' 'roguish,' to its present meaning; *beautiful* (from the sixteenth century); and *adorable,* the word prevailing in twentieth-century feminine use.

Older titles of honor have faded in dignity through general use in an environment of democracy. On all sides, may be observed evidence of faded dignity in words. *Dame* and *madame,* from Latin *dominus,* 'master' (of slaves); *Mister* and *Miss* and *Mrs.,* from Latin *magister,* 'master' (in school and in craft); and *Sir, sire* from Latin *senior,* 'elder,' are survivals in English of titles once associated with high honor. The words *lady* and *gentleman* exhibit a similar faded respectability, although the latter word has of late taken on a dignity new in character. The word *gentleman* is an English hybrid, the first part of which is derived from the Latin *gentilis,* which meant a person of good family or birth (Lat. *gens,* 'race'). *Lady* is a native English title of honor (O. E. *hlæfdige*). Its loss in dignity through democratic use is exemplified by such phrases as 'lady friend,' 'ladies and gents,' 'chorus lady,' and 'wash lady.' In dignity the word *lady* has in recent years changed places with the plain word *woman.* This reversal in dignity is illustrated by the language of a colored woman who inquired, "Who is the colored lady working for the woman over there?"

The same tendency toward renewed intensity of expres-

EUPHEMISM AND HYPERBOLE 277

sion is illustrated by the history of the words: *yes* and *not*.[6] *Yes* is an intensive form for *yea*. It goes back to Anglo-Saxon *gese*, which stands for *gēa swā*, equivalent to 'yes indeed.' *Yes* does not appear in the King James Bible, and in Shakespeare its special use is in reply to a negative question.[7] In *not* have been absorbed successively two independent intensifying elements. The simple negative particle in early English was *ne*. To this was added the adverb *ā* meaning 'ever,' which fused with *ne* to make early English *nā*, modern English *no*. To this in turn was added the word *wiht* meaning 'thing,' surviving in modern English in two words, *whit* and *wight*. *Nā + wiht* yielded modern English *naught* in stressed positions, in unstressed positions, *not*. Modern English *not*, therefore, if its constituent elements are considered, means literally 'not ever a bit.' It finds a parallel in the French *ne—rien*, 'not a thing' and *ne—point*, 'not an iota.'

Running counter to the spirit of exaggeration is that of understatement. Understatement in its most usual form is a kind of irony reversed. Belittling terms are applied to what is most highly prized, to the tremendous, and to the terrible. It appears conspicuously in living colloquial speech. The ocean is referred to as the *pond*, the *big drink* or the *puddle*. In thieves' jargon to run away from prison is to be *absent without leave*. Money, a chief of human ends, is referred to with feigned indifference as *dough* or *kale* or *jack* or *brass*. The spirit of army life found expression by forms of assumed contempt such as *slum* or *hash* or *chow* for food, *punk* for bread, *hard oil* for butter, *leather* for meat. The serious was made light of by such expressions as *go West, click it, push up the daisies* for 'die' and *bumped off, knocked off* for 'killed.' Everywhere the same spirit is to be detected. A bachelor's quar-

---

[6] Greenough and Kittredge, p. 310.
[7] Weekley, *Etymological Dictionary*.

ters, elegantly fitted, it may be, are referred to as *diggings*. Ordinary cheese is called *rat-trap* cheese.

It would be the most dense of blunders to take these expressions literally. The use of semi-contemptuous terms such as *skirt* and *frail* and *jane* for 'girl,' does not mean that the young man has not a serious interest in the girls any more than the use of *flivver* and *tin Lizzie* proves that the Ford is not the pride of a man's heart, or than the use of the terms *rascal* and *rogue* and *villain* and *goose* proves that a mother does not love her child. In fact it has been said [8] that the greater intensity of feeling associated with terms of contempt makes them effective when turned ironically to expressions of affection. The word *pretty*, which originally meant 'sly,' is an instance of a word in which the ironical twist has permanently changed the meaning.

It has been said that, while American humor is based on exaggeration, English humor rests on understatement. Certain it is that understatement is a dominant quality of British speech. Sir Philip Gibbs in one of his dispatches from the scene of war cited some good instances of understatement from the language of British siege gunners. The devastated town of Albert was characterized by the statement, "Albert isn't the town it was." The Germans under fire were alluded to by saying, "Fritz must be having a *thin time* there." The Albert-Bapaume road "was not a pleasant place for Germans on a sunny afternoon." Among the British understatement is not only a native tendency, but a cultivated art. "In the British language," [9] says a recent American writer, " 'Rather' is a super superlative, but it sounds like a snub. When they mean superb, they say 'Rather'; when they mean 'You amaze me,' they say 'Really.' "

---

[8] Wundt.
[9] Simeon Strunsky, *Atlantic*, March, 1919.

EUPHEMISM AND HYPERBOLE

This tendency, however, is not a modern one with the British. In *Beowulf*, the Anglo-Saxon epic, understatement is a conspicuous feature. In the *Anglo-Saxon Chronicle*, of more than a thousand years ago, a king Cynewulf is fighting single-handed against many, and we are told that he fought *unhēanlice*, which may be translated 'not ignobly.' Coming down more than a thousand years, one finds an account by Mr. Kipling of a vessel lying at anchor in the St. Lawrence and two Englishmen looking up at the magnificent citadel of Quebec. "Not so bad?" remarked the first Englishman; from his companion came the characteristically British reply, "Not at all so bad!"

The contrast between the unchecked enthusiasm taking the form of hyperbole in American speech and the natural reserve expressed in the cultivated habit of understatement on the part of an Englishman, is illustrated by a recent incident. An American girl, who tells the story, is making a steep climb in Switzerland, and on her way up, meets an English girl coming down. "It is a bit exhausting, isn't it?" called the English girl from above. "I think it's terrific," I replied.[10]

---

[10] *Scribner's Magazine*, November, 1916.

CHAPTER XX

DEGENERATION AND ELEVATION

Sir James Barrie in "When a Man's Single," published about 1900, records a price scale announced by a London grocer as follows: "Eggs, new-laid 1s. 3d.; eggs, fresh, 1s. 2d.; eggs warranted, 1s.; eggs, 10d." About fourteen years later in May, 1914, the present writer observed in a London grocer's stall the following price scale: New-laid eggs, 10d.; Selected, 12d.; Warranted, 16d. In the period preceding the war the value of eggs had not greatly changed, but the value of words had. The superlative *new-laid* of 1900 had become degraded to the bottom of the scale.

The experience of the adjective *new-laid* serves to illustrate a kind of change prevalent among words. Words, like eggs, may degenerate. In fact degeneration of meaning is a conspicuous phenomenon in the science of semantics which deals with development in word meanings. Many of the illustrative words cited in the preceding chapter afford striking illustration of this feature of language. The figurative force of euphemism and hyperbole, like that of the figures based on association, such as the metaphor and metonymy, fades with continued use, and faded euphemism and faded hyperbole result in degeneration of meaning. Such words as *indolent, insolent, impertinent, immoral, indignant, misconduct,* and *misdemeanor,* already cited, will serve for illustration. The word *insane* is obviously no longer euphemistic, but the effect of its euphemistic use has been to lower the word from an earlier meaning of 'not well' (Lat. *in + sanus*) to its present terribly direct meaning. *Vulgar,* an adjective originally meaning 'belonging to the throng' (Lat. *vulgus*), has permanently taken the meaning of 'low,' 'debased.' The words *common* and *ordinary*, from use with euphemistic attempt to avoid the harshness of *vulgar*, are themselves well started on the same downward course. The word *homely*, from persistent euphemistic attempt to apply a pleasant term to one not possessed of good looks, has degenerated to the meaning 'ugly,' and the word *plain* is rapidly following the same course. *Base* and *low*, originally terms expressing physical position, when applied, as it seems euphemistically, to moral conceptions, have become permanently associated with the idea of 'evil.' *Degraded,* literally 'reduced in grade or rank' (Lat. *gradus,* 'rank') has been affected in the same way. The determined optimism which led to the use of *fair* and *pretty well*, rather than direct expression of discontent, has had the effect of permanently lowering the meaning of these expressions. The same euphemistic avoidance of the tone of complaint has caused the lowering of the word *mean* (Lat. *medianus*, from *medius* 'middle') to its present meaning. The word *middling* shows a bent in the same direction. The word *questionable,* applied to conduct, has in the same way come to apply to what is unquestionably bad, and in university life, the word *condition,* which is short for *conditionally passed,* and which was originally euphemistic in character, has now reached the stage where it is a direct name for a form of failure.

An effect quite similar to that produced by faded euphemism is often brought about through ironical use or through persistent innuendo. A *but* following a word or phrase, whether directly expressed or only implied, may quite change the effect of an innocent appearing expression. Because of this form of innuendo, in earlier times classed as a form of backbiting, a term complimentary in form may be the reverse of complimentary in the meaning it conveys. What less complimentary may be said of one than that he is *good-hearted* or *means well?* The word *worthy* has been affected in this way. This word in early English, in Chaucer for instance, meant 'entitled to honor,' 'noble.' From the same root was formed the noun *worship* (O. E. *weorthscipu*) which has come to be applied to the honor paid the Deity. But on account of the persistent note of contempt by which it has been accompanied, the word has been reduced to its present humble meaning. *Silly*, which originally meant 'happy,' has experienced the same change, and *simple* has in part been affected in the same way. In the same way *dame* has been lowered in dignity by an added suggestion of contempt.

The effect of hyperbole is the same in kind. In the history of the adjective *new-laid* may be seen how faded hyperbole results in degeneration of meaning. In the same way the exaggerated expression of promised promptitude has led to the degeneration of a whole series of words such as *soon, anon, presently,* and *by and by,* all of which originally meant 'at once.' The human frailty that leads to procrastination is reflected in the history of these words. The same kind of degeneration may be seen in the series: *swithe, full, well, passing,* and *very,* cited in the preceding chapter. The use of such expressions as *doubtless, in fact,* and *as a matter of fact,* as a means of strengthening assertions, has led to similar degeneration. In the opinion of Sir James Barrie, the phrase, 'the fact is' "is usually the beginning of a lie."

Closely related is the effect of pretentiousness. This quality always lends itself to ridicule and contempt. Hence the word *grandiloquent* rapidly takes on the meaning of 'pompous,' or 'bombastic.' *Grandiose* in standard use of the present day, expresses two different meanings registered in the *Century Dictionary* as (1) 'grand in effect,' 'imposing,' (2) 'vulgarly showy or flaunting.' *Smug*, which in the sixteenth century meant 'trim' or 'neat,' has sunk so as now to mean a contemptible form of self-complacency. *Specious*, which once meant 'beautiful,' 'fair,' now conveys the idea of 'ungenuine.' *Tinsel*, which is derived through the French, from the Latin *scintilla*, 'spark,' at one time applied to glittering metallic substances, but under the influence of hinted contempt for the garish and gaudy, has sunk to its present station. In this connection may be introduced the interesting history of the word *phaeton* as the name of a vehicle. The name was a grandiose one borrowed from the name of the son of Helios who tried unsuccessfully to drive his father's chariot, and applied in the early nineteenth century to a high, light vehicle. The word has now arrived at the place where it serves as a name for a low vehicle associated with ease and comfort rather than with resplendence and speed and not easily associated in thought with the car of the Sun God.

But it is for moral pretense that scorn is most heartfelt. Hence it is that *sanctimonious* (Lat. *sanctimonia*, 'holiness') has been colored by the contempt felt for the pharisaical. Even *charity* which goes back to the original meaning 'love,' and which is rated as the greatest of the virtues, in present-day use is coming too strongly to suggest a patronizing attitude and is yielding its earlier meaning to *benevolence*. In the same way *prude* derived from the feminine form of the French *preux*, a word related to *proud* and *prowess* and once summarizing most of what in the Age of Chivalry was regarded as human excellence, through ironical use, has come to apply to a person of affected modesty.

Minion, once a name applied without disparagement to a favorite, has degenerated under the influence of suspicion surrounding those who cultivate the good will of the great. The meaning of *scurrilous* is the result of a similar degeneration, which, however, came about before the word was brought into English. The Latin adjective *scurrilis* is derived from the noun *scurra,* which first meant 'fine gentleman,' 'gallant,' but later was lowered so as to mean 'jester,' 'buffoon,' a meaning which appears in the derived adjective.

In many instances change of fashion brings about a change in the attitude toward the meaning expressed by a word. A classic instance is the adjective *doughty.* This word is derived from the Old English noun *duguth,* the native English equivalent of the later French derivative *court.* The word expressed the courtly ideals of the early English. The present meaning reflects the Norman English contempt for Anglo-Saxon ideals. *Churl,* also, which in the English before the Conquest, was a term of respect (O. E. *ceorl,* 'freeman'), under the influence of Norman contempt for Anglo-Saxon manners, acquired its present meaning. *Dapper,* which once meant 'brave,' 'sprightly' (*cf.* German *tapfer,* 'brave') has been similarly affected by an attitude of contempt. In more recent times the same lowering of meaning may be observed in the word *elocution,* which has been so much affected by a changed attitude toward affected manners of speech, that it has been superseded by the name *public speaking.*

There are certain occupations and certain conditions in life the associations of which are the reverse of noble or distinguished. Rural life, for example, until recent times has been associated with ignorance and dullness. Hence the names associated with agriculture have in general declined in dignity. *Peasant,* from a French word meaning 'countryman,' conveys the idea of lower social class. The English *boor,* which once meant 'farmer,' is now associated with bad manners. *Rustic,* as a noun, suggests lack of social graces, and the word *farmer* itself, in the colloquial speech of the city (youth), stands for slowness of wit.

Villain, which began with the meaning 'peasant' or 'serf,' perhaps influenced by the unrelated word *vile*, has reached the lowest moral stage in meaning. The teacher shares, to an extent, the contempt felt for the farmer, since his earlier name, *pedant*, is now associated with contempt, and its derivative, *pedantry*, has come to stand for misapplied learning.

The immaturity of childhood is responsible for the degradation of such words as *childish* and *puerile*. Even words indirectly related to childhood are affected. *Naughty* (literally 'good for naught'), once in dignified use, has been limited in use through its intimate associations with childish conduct. *Fret* and *peevish* have been somewhat affected in the same way, and *bashful*, an adjective which Shakespeare could apply to a king and Clarendon to an army, is not now usually applied to adults. The weakness of old age is likewise responsible for the degeneration of words, as in the case of *senile* and *senility*.

But particularly influential in this way have been associations with the servant station. The quality of these associations appears in such adjectives as *slavish* and *servile*. To the same class belongs *menial*, originally an adjective expressing the quality of belonging to a household (Anglo-Fr. *meinie*, 'household'). Its contemptuous use does not begin until the eighteenth century. There are a number of words which share its fate through association with the idea of service. *Wench* in earlier English was a reputable name for girl or child. The word *maid* in poetical phrase still retains its old nobility, but in common use it has sunk to the level of 'servant.' *Knave* (O. E. *cnafa*, 'boy') has gone even farther. Not stopping at the first stage in the downward course, with the meaning 'servant,' it has descended to the meaning 'rascal.' In more recent times the spirit of democracy, which leads to the euphemistic avoidance of such terms of inferiority as *servant,* has led to the euphemistic use and consequent degeneration of words like *domestic* and *help.*

The degeneration in many of the words cited, apart from those representing faded euphemism or faded hyperbole, it will be observed, is due to a form of specialization. A new element is joined to the connotation of the word, and this colors the original meaning, in some cases quite overshadowing it. This new element may be added by means of innuendo, as in the case of *sanctimonious, specious,* or *good-hearted,* already cited. To this class of words may be added *adulterate* (literally 'alter,' Lat. *ad alterum convertere*) and its later parallel, *counterfeit* (literally 'imitate'). Degeneration of this kind appears in many words. *Curiosity* (literally 'caring for,' Lat. *cura,* 'care') and *inquisitiveness* (literally 'inquiring') have come to be names of objectionable qualities because the original meaning of interest has been expanded to an interest in things with which one has no concern. *Cheat* (from *escheat,* 'property lapsing to the crown when the owner dies intestate') comes to mean 'confiscate,' then 'defraud.' In *cheap* the idea of poor quality has come in great part to overshadow the original meaning 'inexpensive.' In this downward course the word follows in the wake of *vile* which comes from the Latin *vilis,* 'cheap.' *Daub,* which originally meant 'to whiten,' has come to mean 'to smear.' *Scavenger,* once the name of a customs inspector also entrusted with the care of the streets, has come to be the name for one entrusted with only an ignoble part of his original duties. *Stupid,* which once meant 'amazed,' 'dazed,' has come to apply to one with whom the dazed state is a permanent one. *Sullen* is a variant form of *solemn,* of which it expresses only the secondary meaning 'morose.' *Garble,* which once meant 'to sift' or 'bolt' (spices), has come to apply to a sorting for the purpose of creating a false im-

DEGENERATION AND ELEVATION 287

pression, as in such expressions as 'garbled account' and 'garbled text.' *Daft* once meant merely 'gentle.' Two words which in our own time are undergoing degeneration are *lengthy*, which has taken on the meaning 'tedious,' and *visitation*, now associated with affliction. In the language of the present day, also, the term *socialist* is degenerating under the influence of an imagined relation with anarchy, and as noble a word as *radical* is being subjected to the influence of the same kind of innuendo.

In some instances a word has degenerated through contamination from other words. *Villain*, it has already been pointed out, is probably influenced from a supposed connection with *vile*. In the same way the noun *fiddle*, a word of eminent dignity in earlier English and in French, has degenerated through the influence of the word *fiddle-faddle*, a reduplicated form of the obsolete *faddle*, to 'trifle.'[1]

In other cases the element joined to the original meaning is absorbed from the context. A clear case of this is the word *enormity* already cited. *Asylum* is another instance. Derived from the Greek *asulos*, meaning 'inviolable,' 'free from the right of seizure,' the word, through constant association with *insane* and *orphan*, has come in popular speech to mean a place of confinement rather than a place of refuge. One can no longer speak of a 'braying wind' or of 'wagging leaves' because the words *bray* and *wag* are now too vividly associated with beasts lacking in dignity. *Victuals*, a dignified word in its origin and in its earlier English uses, is now vividly associated with inelegant use. Similar degeneration has been experienced by such words as *rind*, *ditty*, *fry* and *pate*. There appears a striking incongruity in the use of these words in dignified associations by earlier writers. The serious intent of the sixteenth-century writers is defeated by the ludicrous effect on the

---
[1] Weekley.

modern reader produced by these words in such lines as those of Spenser:

> She fell away in her first ages spring
> Whilst yet her leafe was green, and fresh her rinde,

or those by Gabriel Harvey:

> The dapper ditties that I wont devise
> To feed youth's fancy and the flocking fry.

Holy Writ almost loses its sanctity when one reads "his violent dealing shall come upon his own *pate*" (Psalms 7, 16) or finds Paul referred to as "a *ringleader* of the sect of the Nazarenes." In earlier English the appearance of incongruity arising from words that have since lost in dignity, is, if possible, even more striking, as when in the Wycliffe Bible one reads, "Lo He shall not *nappe*, nether slepe that kepeth Israel,"[2] and how "Barnabas and Paul rent their clothes and *skipped out* among the people" Acts 14, 14).[3]

The phenomenon of degeneration of meaning is a striking feature in language history and has long occupied the attention of the student of language. A corresponding elevation of meaning has attracted less attention, but has played in the development of language a part hardly less important. If the association with such occupations as agriculture and teaching has led to a degeneration of meaning, on the other hand words of humble origin have been elevated through association with the more aristocratic things in life. The word *regal* suggests a splendor greater even than that surrounding an actual king. The word *court*, which goes back to a Latin word, *cohors, cohort-*, which meant 'inclosure' or 'poultry-yard,' through royal associations, aided by the influence of another word, Latin

---

[2] Psalms cxxi, 4. Quoted from Trench, *English Past and Present*.
[3] *Ibid.*, p. 223.

DEGENERATION AND ELEVATION 289

curia, has risen to its present dignity. The word *knight* (O. E. *cniht*), which, like the word *knave* (O. E. *cnafa*), once meant 'boy,' has developed in an opposite direction. Like *knave* it came to mean servant; but unlike *knave,* it came through military and feudal associations to its later use as a title of rank. *Squire,* which originally meant 'shield bearer,' through association with knighthood, was elevated in station. There is a group of names of dignity which were originally applied to servants of humble station but which were elevated through associations with royalty. *Marshal* is of German origin derived through the French, and once meant 'horse servant' (O. E. *mearh,* 'horse,' *scealc,* 'servant'). *Seneschal,* from the same source, originally meant 'senior servant.' *Constable* comes from the late Latin *comes stabuli,* which meant 'count of the stable,' and was equivalent to the Teutonic *marshal. Chamberlain,* derived from the same Teutonic source as *marshal* and *seneschal,* originally applied to one in charge of rooms. *Steward* (O. E. *stigweard*) meant literally 'sty-ward' at a time when *sty* had not degenerated to its present narrow signification. From it comes the Scotch and English royal family name, *Stuart,* which thus offers an instance of a reversal in dignity that is complete.[4] Associations with courtly life and manners serve to explain the elevation of such words as *chivalrous* (*cf.* Fr. *cheval,* 'horse') and *gallant* (O. Fr. *galer,* 'to make merry') and *majesty,* which goes back to a Latin root with the simple meaning 'greater.' If country associations have lowered the dignity of certain words, on the other hand associations with the city have led to elevation in the meaning of such words as *civil, civilize* (Lat. *civis,* 'citizen') and *urbane* (Lat. *urbs,* 'city').

If change in fashion has served to cause degeneration in meaning, it has also at times had the opposite effect. The name *Gothic,* applied contemptuously, in the days when

---
[4] Greenough and Kittredge, p. 296.

the taste for the classic prevailed, to a form of architecture that had its origin in the late Middle Ages, with change of fashion has come to designate something highly admired. *Quaker* and *Shaker,* applied contemptuously to the sect of Friends, have now come to be terms of honor. *Methodist,* a name applied in ridicule by Oxford students to the followers of John Wesley, now applies to a sect which glories in its name. *Yankee,* once a term of ridicule, is now accepted without offense. Names of political parties such as *Whig* and *Tory* and *Mugwump,* applied in ridicule, have been proudly adopted and elevated to the rank of cherished names. Most dramatic in character of all has been the reversal of meaning in the name *Contemptibles.* Applied in scorn by the German Kaiser to the small English expeditionary force, it has come to be the most distinguished of epithets.

It is highly interesting to observe the divergent directions taken by words in their sense development. There are few instances of words which have degenerated in meaning which cannot be matched by words that have been elevated in a corresponding way. If *rind* has been lowered in dignity by too intimate relation with the flesh of a beast not associated with elegance, *bristle* (originally belonging to pigs exclusively) and *sward* (O. E. *sweard,* 'skin,' 'bacon-rind') have risen through dissociation from their homely origin. If *childish* and *puerile* have been lowered to the expression of an unattractive aspect of early life, *boyish* and *youthful* have been correspondingly elevated. If *cheap* and *vile* have been turned to the expression of related ideas of one kind, *costly* and *precious* have turned in the opposite direction. If *rash,* which originally meant 'quick,' 'swift,' has been turned to the meaning 'foolhardy,' *sturdy* (O. Fr., *estordi,* 'reckless') and *stout* (which probably goes back to the Latin *stultus,* 'foolish') have counterbalanced the change. While the names of many parts of the human anatomy have descended to the class of unmentionables, *pluck,* originally a butcher's term, has come to express one of the most admirable elements in human nature, and *frill,* originally belonging to the mesentery, has come to apply to one of the ornamental features of dress. If *servile* has come to express a quality the reverse of admirable, on the other hand *service* has come to express what, according to prevailing modern ideals, is the noblest thing in life.

Many of the instances of elevation in meaning have their special interest. *Prestige* comes from a French word meaning 'magic,' which in turn is descended from the Latin *præstringere,* 'to bind before,' 'blindfold.' *Barter,* goes back to the French *barater,* 'to deceive.' *Blouse,* which first appears in English in the nineteenth century, is borrowed from the French, where it meant workman's or peasant's 'smock.' *Boudoir* also comes from the French, where its literal meaning was 'sulking room,' probably in origin like American slang *gab room* for 'girls' rest room.' *Ambition,* a highly rated quality in modern life, gets its name from the Latin *ambitio,* which meant 'going about' (for votes).

In fact, the names for the highest and the noblest elements in human life, in their origin often applied to things of comparatively slight, even trivial importance. *Splendid* goes back to the simple meaning 'bright.' *Magnificent* is made up from the two simple Latin words, *magnus,* 'large' and *facere,* 'to do' or 'to make.' *Distinction* goes back to a Latin verb, *distinguere,* which meant literally 'to prick off.' The word *virtue* is built on an insecure foundation, since it goes back to the meaning 'manliness' (Latin *vir,* 'man'), expressing only a nobler aspect of frail human nature. *Fame,* a prize much striven for, goes back to the Latin *fama* (from *fari,* 'to speak') and meant originally only 'report,' 'common talk.'

In human life, interest is drawn more strongly to instances of fall from fortune or power than to the more commonplace, or at any rate less distinguished, rise to eminence. It is the tragic side of life that most attracts attention. The same holds true in the history of words. Degeneration in meaning has always attracted attention and interest. The less dramatic elevation in meaning, perhaps because of its very obviousness, has been less noticed. It should be held in mind, however, that the two reverse processes balance each other. By degeneration, on the one hand, and elevation on the other, language attains the expression, not only of the depths of contempt, but of the ideal heights which are the goal of human endeavor.

REFERENCES FOR FURTHER READING IN CONNECTION WITH CHAPTERS XV—XX

J. B. GREENOUGH and G. L. KITTREDGE, *Words and Their Ways in English Speech* (New York, 1901).
E. WEEKLEY, *The Romance of Words* (New York, 1913); *Etymological Dictionary of Modern English* (London, 1921).
M. BRÉAL, *Essai de Sémantique* (Paris, 1899).
A. DARMSTETTER, *La Vie des Mots* (Paris, 1895).
STRONG, LOGEMAN and WHEELER, *The History of Language* (London and New York, 1891).
R. C. TRENCH, *The Study of Words* (London and New York, 1851); *English Past and Present* (London and New York, 1855).
A. DAUZAT, *La Philosophie du Langage* (Paris, 1917); *La Vie du Langage* (Paris, 1918).
L. BLOOMFIELD, *The Study of Language* (New York, 1914).
E. H. STURTEVANT, *Linguistic Change* (Chicago, 1917).
W. WUNDT, *Völkerpsychologie* (Leipsic, 1900-1909).
G. STERN, *Swift, Swiftly and their Synonyms, A Contribution to Semantic Analysis and Theory* (Göteberg, 1921). Reviewed in *Modern Language Notes* (April, 1922).
H. FALK, *Betydningslære (Semasiologi)* (Christiania, 1920). Reviewed in *Journ. of Engl. & Germ. Phil.* (January, 1922).
J. STÖCKLEIN, *Bedeutungswandel der Wörter* (Munich, 1898).
K. NYROP, *Das Leben der Wörter* (Germ. transl.) (Leipsic, 1903).

CHAPTER XXI

WORDS AND ARCHÆOLOGY

Words may be turned to a remarkable variety of uses. Not only may they be made to serve a practical purpose in the communication of thought and feeling, but as has been seen, they may be made to serve in exhibiting interesting processes of thought. In still another way they may be used. If their meanings are traced back to the customs and modes of thought in which they had their origin, words may be made to exhibit stages in the history of human culture.

Many a word of recent introduction into English, if its origin is sought, will conduct one on a long journey and may introduce one to a scene of romantic interest. The word *taboo*, for instance, transports one to the islands of the South Seas and brings before one a picture of a magic circle about some person or thing marked as sacred or accursed, a circle the circumference of which it is fatal to cross. Such a modern word affords a glimpse at the life of distant peoples of our own times. Many of the older words may be made to serve a similar purpose in bringing up scenes from lives of our own ancestors in the distant past. The word *read*, for example, in its history carries one far back in the life of the Teutonic race. It introduces one to a scene of magic among Teutonic peoples, where the priest, or head of the family, picks up from the white cloth on which they have been scattered bits of wood on which certain marks have been *written*, that is to say 'scratched.' He then proceeds to *read*, that is to say, 'to interpret' the marks on the wood, in this way forecasting events. Such words not only serve to corroborate evidence afforded by other historical sources, but in many instances serve as lights by which one is enabled to penetrate the darkness of a past not illumined by historical record. Let us see how words have been turned to use in this way.

Toward the end of the eighteenth century, when the Western world first became acquainted with Sanskrit, the ancient language of India, it was discovered that Sanskrit shares many features with the principal languages of Europe. Further study revealed that there is a considerable body of words common to the ancient languages of India and Persia and the languages of Europe, a body of words to be explained not as due to borrowing, but as a heritage common to these languages. A consequence of this new knowledge was a fresh enthusiasm for the study of words. It was felt that a study of these cognate words (*co + gnatus*, 'born together,' 'having a common ancestry') afforded a clue by which might be reached a knowledge of the elements in life common to the ancestors of the Indo-European peoples that used the related languages. Much was said about 'linguistic paleontology.' It was felt that just as the fossil remains in rock strata afford evidence of earlier stages in the world's existence, so the words common to languages of Europe and of Asia afforded evidence of a stage in human existence earlier than any for which there is any literary record, of a period when the various peoples of the Indo-European family had not dispersed from their common home. A key seemed to be provided for the mysteries of earlier stages in human history.

Earlier enthusiasm had later to yield somewhat to disappointment. Sources of error came to be recognized. In some instances words common to different languages came to be recognized as due to borrowing from one people to another, as reflecting, therefore, not a common original mode of speech, but the influence of the civilization of one people over that of another.[1] In other instances it came to be recognized that the use of an old name for a thing was not certain indication of the antiquity of the thing itself. The source of possible error in this latter respect may be illustrated by examples of words from our own times. For instance people in coming centuries would form a quite erroneous notion of professional baseball as played in 1922 from the name *pitcher* applied to one of the most important players. An earlier mode of *pitching* the ball to the batsman has been quite superseded in the course of the game's development, but the earlier word, *pitcher*, has continued in use. In the same way quite false inferences might be drawn from the word *camel's-hair*, now often applied to things made of material quite unrelated to the camel, or from the word *rubber* now applied to many uses besides the original one of rubbing out marks, or from the word *ballot* (Ital. *ballota*, diminutive of *balla*, 'ball') now applied to a printed sheet of paper. Obviously words are subject to changes in meaning which make them uncertain guides in tracing the history of things.

In consequence of the recognized dangers of error from the evidence of words alone, in the twentieth century the study of the history of names has come to be more and more associated with the history of the things named. Archæology has been brought to the support of etymology. The modern trend in this kind of study is shown in a twentieth-century German periodical devoted to the study of words in connection with that of the objects or ideas named by words, a program which is indicated by the title of the new periodical, *Wörter und Sachen*, 'Words and Things.'

Making due allowance, however, for possible sources of error, many a word offers in itself a flickering light, often dim to be sure, but enabling one to peer into the blackness of the past. Let us take by way of illustration certain

---

[1] Schrader, p. 51; V. Helm, p. 37.

English words derived from the Latin. For example, the English word *pecuniary* comes from the Latin *pecunia* meaning 'money.' But *pecunia* is an abstract term derived from the concrete *pecus,* meaning 'cattle.' By following the history of this word we are led back to a bartering period when property consisted not in coins but in herds of cattle. The etymologist ventures still farther back and traces the meanings of the word through 'cattle' to 'sheep,' and from this in turn to 'wool,' and from this finally to the fundamental idea of 'pull' or 'pluck.' This single word lights one back to a period when property consisted mainly in cattle and then to a still earlier stage when sheep formed the principal property of a nomadic or semi-nomadic people.

The history of the English word *fee,* like that of its Latin cognate, *pecus,* carries one back over the same route, from its present meaning, 'money for special service,' through the meaning 'money' in general, to an original meaning, 'cattle,' a meaning surviving to our day in the cognate German word, of similar sound but different spelling, *Vieh.* In the same way the history of the word *court* conducts one back from king to peasant. One may follow the modern word with its royal associations back through the military *cohort* to the early meaning of 'inclosure' or 'cattle pen.' *Emolument,* suggestive of quality and dignity, goes back to the humble and laborious grinding with a hand mill.

In the same way certain words serve to light up the course of development of human relations in modern society. The meaning in the words *civil* and *city* may be traced through successive stages back to a fundamental meaning of 'dear,' 'beloved.' The original word from which modern *city* and *civic* are derived expressed the love springing from relationship in family or tribe, and later has been turned to the new use of expressing the broader human ties of fellow citizenship and, in the case of *civil*, has been made to express politeness originating in city life. In like manner the word *free*, of which the underlying meaning is 'love,' conducts one back to a tribal social organization when the word in its earlier meaning of 'beloved' applied to members of the family or tribe as distinguished from the enslaved that served.

The study of the series of words, cognates, common to the different Indo-European languages, has its obvious fascination. By the study of words combined with the evidence afforded by anthropology and archæology has been reached a fair degree of certainty that the original home of the Indo-European race was in the great plain of central and southeastern Europe.[2] By means of word study we may get glimpses not only of the mode of life of the parent Indo-European people, but of some of the stages by which a more complex civilization has been reached.

The names of beasts and birds, for instance, afford indication of the animal environment of early Indo-European life, of the acquaintance formed with new species from foreign sources and of the gradual subjection of animals to domestic uses. Cognate words in various Indo-European languages indicate that the Indo-European people, before the separation of the various nations, were acquainted with many of the animals known to-day, including most of the well-known domestic animals. Various forms of the name *wolf*, for example, appear not only in German *Wolf* and Gothic *wulfs* but in Latin *lupus* and Greek *lukos* and, in a feminine form, in Old High German *wulpa*, Old Norse *ylgr*, Sanskrit *vrkīs*, and, perhaps, Latin *vulpes*. The series is by no means so complete in the case of every name, but is sufficient to indicate a common knowledge of certain animals among Indo-European peoples. For instance, cognates of the English *bear* appear in German

---

[2] H. H. Bender, *The Home of the Indo-Europeans*, p. 50.

bär, and Lithuanian *beras* (meaning 'brown'). In other languages another name is used for what was unmistakably the same animal, as in Latin *ursus,* Greek *arktos,* Sanskrit *ṛkṣas.* The two series of words serve to indicate a common acquaintance with the bear. From similar evidence may be inferred early familiarity with such animals as the elk and the hare.

Series of cognate words in various Indo-European languages for hound, ox, cow, ewe, goat, sow, swine, pork, and for *eoh,* an early English name for 'horse,' indicate that acquaintance with at least six types of domestic animals goes back to a time before the separation of the Indo-European peoples. Some of the modern names for these domestic animals are of later origin. The word *dog,* for example, seems to have been first used in Britain, although the word has spread from English into the languages of most West European countries. The word *horse,* too, which appears in German as *Ross,* is of uncertain origin, but apparently relatively modern, possibly related in meaning to the Latin *currere,* 'to run.' But series of cognate words indicate to a certainty the acquaintance with the six named domestic animals in the earliest stage of the history of Indo-European peoples.

That these animals, however, played their modern part in domestic economy in primitive times, is not so evident. The existence of cognate series of words for milk and for wool indicates the early subjection of the sheep and cow to domestic use.[3] The case of the horse, however, is different. The oldest English name for horse, *eoh,* a form long obsolete, has many cognates; Sanskrit *açva,* Greek *hippos,* Latin *equus,* Irish *ech,* Lithuanian *aszwa,* Old Saxon *ehu.* But the evidence of words supported by earliest literary records indicates that the horse was not a draught animal in earliest times. To our day, particularly among

---

[3] Schrader, p. 158.

primitive folk, the ox performs the humble work of the draught animal. The vehicle to which the horse was earlier attached seems to have been the racing chariot. The development in later Latin of the new names, *caballus* (French *cheval*, English *chivalry*, etc.) and *paraveredus* (Germ. *Pferd*), seem to indicate that the horse had been turned to new kinds of employment.

In the case of some of the other domestic animals there is a different story to tell. There is no series of cognate names to show that the ass and the mule belonged to primitive Indo-European life, and the evidence of words in this respect is corroborated by the negative evidence of archæological remains. Of the two, the mule seems to have come earliest into use. In Homeric times the mule was the beast of burden, and the ass is mentioned only once in the Homeric poems.[4] The English word *ass* comes from the Latin *asinus*, which, in turn, is probably of Semitic origin. The word *donkey* is supposed to be derived from the color name *dun* with the addition of a double diminutive ending. This word, of late origin (first cited in English in 1785), expresses a feeling of affectionate regard for the faithful 'little dun-colored beast.' The *camel* also seems to have come late into the service of Indo-European peoples. His name, like that of the ass, of Semitic origin, indicates his probable earlier home. Æschylus is the earliest European writer to mention him.

The most conspicuous absent member among the domestic animals of the Indo-European household is the cat. The animal in earlier times associated with the pursuit of the mouse was the weasel or the marten, as is indicated by the Latin word, *mustela*, for weasel. The Latin word *cattus* first made its appearance about 500 A. D.[5] and was first definitely applied to the domesticated animal about

---

[4] Schrader, p. 159.
[5] Hirt, *Etymologie*, p. 133.

600 A. D. in an account of Gregory the Great who is described as fondling a cat in his lap.⁶ The cat as a domestic animal goes back to a high antiquity in Egypt; but she is not mentioned in Holy Writ. There was no cat in the Garden of Eden, and she was not among the animals that entered Noah's Ark. Late legend has it that Noah, threatened by increase in mice, passed his hand three times over the head of the lioness and she sneezed forth the cat.⁷ The origin of *cattus* is obscure, but it has spread through the languages of most of Europe almost entirely displacing the classical Latin *felo*. The spread throughout Europe of the use of the cat as a domestic animal is relatively modern. The lack of authentic knowledge concerning the introduction of the cat into English domestic life is agreeably supplied by the immortal story of Dick Whittington whose fortunes were founded on the importation of the cat.

In the case of bird names there is such lack of uniformity, even in modern times, that they afford somewhat uncertain evidence. From the names of domestic fowls, however, one may derive interesting hints applicable toward culture history. The names for the duck, the goose, and the hen appear in cognate series that indicate general acquaintance with these birds among the primitive Indo-European people. But the duck and the goose and the hen seem to have been known as wild rather than as domestic birds.

In the Indian Rig Veda, for example, the goose is classed with birds of the hawk type, and in the Iliad the *chen*, 'goose' is mentioned in a series with the wild swans and the cranes, though in the Odyssey it is represented as domesticated.⁸ Among the Britons in England Cæsar records (Book V) that cock and goose were cultivated not as

---

[6] Schrader, p. 163.
[7] A. Repplier, *The Fireside Sphinx*, p. 2.
[8] Od., xix, 536, 548.

WORDS AND ARCHÆOLOGY

sources of food but as ornamental birds, evidently playing a part comparable to that played by the modern swan and peacock. Attempt has been made to show that the cock and hen entered domestic use under religious auspices.

A frequent source of obscurity in the history of the names of the domestic animals is the multiplicity of names, unrelated in origin, corresponding to difference in sex, in age, and in domestic use. Thus we have *cow, calf, bull, heifer, ox, steer,* etc., and *sheep, lamb, ram, ewe, buck, wedder,* etc., *cock, hen, chicken, pullet, rooster,* etc. It is a recognized fact in language history, as already pointed out, that these specific names originate earlier than class names, and in some cases even in modern English, embarrassment arises from lack of a convenient class name. What, for instance, shall one use as a class name for hen or for cow? Much the same is true in the history of names for trees and for metals. The names of trees have often been cited in evidence regarding the geographical location of the original common home of the Indo-European peoples. The number of names of trees common to the Indo-European languages indicates an original home and a mode of life closely associated with forest trees. Further, the names common to the different languages are names of trees like the birch, the fir, the willow and the beech, which belong to the flora of northern Europe, an argument supporting the idea of Europe as the original Indo-European home.

A striking feature of the series of cognate names for trees is the varied application of names in different languages. Thus the English word *beech* has as cognates the German *Buch* and Latin *fagus* meaning 'beech,' but also the Greek *phegos* meaning 'oak,' the Curdish *būz* meaning 'elm,' the Old Bulgarian *buzu* meaning 'elder.' The English class word *fir* appears in German *Föhre* with the same meaning; but the cognate Latin word *quercus* means 'oak.' The English *tree* appears in Gothic *triu*, 'tree'; in Sanskrit *dāru, dru-,* 'wood,' *drumas* 'tree,' *druṇam,* 'bow'; Avestan *dārav-,* 'wood'; Albanian *dru,* 'wood,' 'tree'; Old Bulgarian *drevo,* 'tree,' *'wood'*; Russian *derevo,* 'tree'; Lithuanian *derva,* 'resinous wood'; Lettish *dair,* 'oak'; Cornish *dar,* 'oak'; Greek *doru,* 'spear,' *drus,* 'oak,' etc.[9] The original meaning is believed to have been 'oak,' and the history of this word, as elsewhere pointed out, illustrates a principle, familiar in language history, by which class names have been derived from names of specific things. In these cognate words may also be seen exemplified the shift in meaning by metonymy from material to thing made from material, as in the varied uses of this word in different languages as name for 'wood' or 'bow' or 'spear,' a shift in meaning further exemplified in the English compounds *roof-tree, shoe-tree, cross-tree, rood-tree,* etc. Another word of quite different kind connected with the word *tree* is our English word *true,* an interesting illustration of the way in which names for moral qualities are derived from the names for things of the physical world. The modern poetic conception of 'hearts of oak' as expressing strength and truth was anticipated many centuries ago by the anonymous poet creators of language.

From the names of forest trees one may get many an interesting suggestion regarding the floral environment of the primitive Indo-Europeans. The names of cultivated trees have another kind of story to tell and one not less interesting. By means of them one is enabled to trace the spread of the knowledge of horticulture from the East, through the civilizations of Greece and Rome, to the countries of northern Europe. The English language has for fruit trees and for other trees of cultivated types a series of names which are paralleled by cognates in most of the

---

[9] Hirt, *Etymologie,* pp. 147-148.

other Teutonic languages. Thus English *apple* is German *Apfel;* English *peach* is German *Pfirsich;* English *cherry* is German *Kirsche;* English *plum* is German *Pflaume.* But these common Teutonic names, with the exception of *apple* and *berry,* are not of Teutonic origin. That ideas on arboriculture were gained by early Teutonic peoples from their Roman neighbors is indicated by such names as: *almond, box* (wood), *ebony, fig, chestnut, cherry, cypress, larch, laurel, peach, pear, plum, poplar, quince,* all derived from the Latin. The earlier Eastern origin of the cultivated varieties of these trees is indicated by the fact that the Latin names, in turn, are in great part derived from the Greek. The earlier Greek derivation of these trees from Oriental sources is to be supposed, although the exact course followed in their introduction from the East can not always be clearly traced. The word *peach,* however, comes from Old French *pesche,* which in turn comes from Latin *persicum,* from growing on the *Persica arbor,* 'Persian tree.' The name *quince* comes, through French and Latin, from the Greek name meaning 'Cydonian apple' from the name of *Cydonia,* a city in Crete. *Currants* is derived from the name of the Greek city, *Corinth. Damson* is derived from Latin *prunum Damascenum,* 'plum of Damascus.' The name *cherry,* which comes the usual route through French and Latin from the Greek, possibly was derived from *Cerasos,* the name of a city in Pontus.

The comparative study of names of trees and beasts and birds leads one back to primitive conditions of Indo-European life and, combined with the study of primitive survivals in various places, and with archæological remains, enables one to form a fairly detailed conception of certain features of early life. We are led to conceive of our ancestors as living in a country well provided with the forest trees of northern Europe, acquainted with dog, horse, cow, sheep, hog, and goat, and with domestic fowls, but with no certainty that these members of the animal kingdom were reduced to human service, except in the case of cow and sheep. Animal husbandry of an elementary stage, however, is indicated.

The history of words indicates also the beginnings of the cultivation of the field in a primitive Indo-European period. Many of the common agricultural plants, such as barley, rye and flax, have cognate names in various Indo-European languages, which indicate a knowledge of these plants common to the various peoples. From cognate names for *field* and *mow* and *furrow*, common to various Indo-European languages, one must also infer modes of cultivation common to Indo-European peoples.[10] Again, however, in the case of cultivated plants, as in the case of cultivated trees, a striking feature is the influence of Roman civilization as exemplified by borrowed Latin names. In English most of these names for cultivated plants have come from the Latin. Many of them, such as *mustard, cauliflower, cabbage, peas,* come through the French at a comparatively late period; but a considerable number of others were derived from the Latin at an early period of contact between Teutonic peoples and Romans, including *beet, fennel, mint, anis, rose, lily, thyme, pepper, plant,* and *senep,* the Old English word for mustard, Greco-Latin *sinapi.*[11] Even more striking is the number of agricultural products and implements the names of which indicate the influence of Roman modes of agriculture. Such words are *wine, flask, pluck, press, flail, sickle.*[12]

If in the case of animal husbandry and agriculture the evidence of words shows that beginnings had been made in the primitive Indo-European period, in the case of the metal names the reverse is true. Indeed a study of the Indo-European names for the various metals throws much

---

[10] Hirt, *Etymologie,* 151-152.
[11] *Cf.* Toller.
[12] *Ibid.*

light on the stages of civilization. Human progress is well indicated by the gradually acquired mastery of the mineral world.

There is no generic name for *metal* common to Indo-European peoples. The word *metal* itself makes its earliest appearance in the writings of Herodotus, where it appears as *metallon* and means not 'metal' but the 'mine' from which the metal is derived. The word borrowed into Latin in the form *metallum* also means 'mine.' For the individual metals, also, there is lacking the complete set of cognate words in any one case to show that the particular metal was known to the Indo-European people before their separation. The word *hammer*, of which cognates appear in many Indo-European languages, and of which the original meaning seems to have been 'stone,' carries one back to the period before the use of the metals, to the 'Stone Age.'

But even in the late Stone Age one metal seems to have been known to the Indo-European peoples, that is to say, copper, used in ornaments and in various weapons made of copper cast in stone molds. Copper later became combined with tin to form bronze, which seems to have been introduced by commercial routes to northern Europe, where it formed a distinctive element which gave its name to the Bronze Age which succeeded the Stone Age. The earliest name of this metal was that in Latin *aes*, Gothic *aiz*, Sanskrit *ayas*, Avestan *ayah*, a series of cognates which attests the general knowledge of the metal. Distinction in name between the simple metal and the alloy was relatively late. The name *copper* itself is relatively modern and comes from the name of the island, Cyprus, once rich in the metal. *Bronze* is a modern word transmitted through French to other European languages and originally associated with the city of Brindisi in the Latin phrase *aes Brundusinum*.

In the case of other metals there is no such set of cognate words to indicate widespread knowledge in the primitive period. For gold different Indo-European peoples had different names. The Greek *chrusos* is supposed to be of Semitic origin. The Latin *aurum* seems to have originated in Latin from a word meaning 'shining' or 'yellow.'[13] From Latin this word was transmitted to various Celtic languages and to Albanian and Lithuanian. Still another name is one appearing in English *gold*, cognate forms of which appear not only in other Teutonic languages but in various Slavic languages. Its original meaning is unknown, but the name may have been derived, as was that of copper, from a geographical name.[14]

The inference to be drawn is that gold was not known to Indo-European peoples before their separation. The same is to be inferred in the case of silver, for which there is no common Indo-European name. Acquaintance with silver was gained independently by the different Indo-European peoples through commercial relations and folk communication, direct or indirect, with the region of the Black Sea. From the Pontic City *Salube* the metal silver gets its name.[15]

For iron also there was no Indo-European name common to Indo-European peoples. This metal, one must infer, became known to the various Indo-European peoples later than copper, after they had settled in their historic homes. The Greeks became acquainted with iron, in the post-Mycenæan and pre-Homeric times, from Pontus and Asia Minor. The Teutonic people made the acquaintance of iron in the fourth century B. C. from the Celts, and the name, of Celtic origin, appears in the various early Teutonic dialects as Gothic *eisarn*, Old Saxon *isarn*, Old English *isern*, Old Norse *isarn*, Old High German *isarn*. The

---
[13] Schrader.
[14] Hirt.
[15] Schrader, p. 120.

name *steel* was relatively late. At the same time evidence that the art of hardening iron was early known is offered by the appearance of the word in the early Teutonic dialects as Old High German *stahal,* Old Norse *stal,* Old English *stēle.*

In line with the evidence of the word *iron* is the word *lead* which, like *iron,* was adopted into the Teutonic languages from Celtic, offering proof of the early importance of the Celtic peoples at a time when they occupied a great part of central Europe from Asia Minor to Spain.

Definite milestones in more recent human progress are offered by names of metals such as *nickel, cobalt, platinum, aluminum,* and *tungsten.* The etymologies of these words afford interesting information concerning the currents of influence that affect modern culture. The name *cobalt* originates in the jocose or slangy language of German miners, from the name of a mountain spirit. The name *nickel* was first applied by Cronstedt, a Swedish mineralogist, in 1754. It is an abbreviated form of the German *Kupfernickel.* The name *nickel,* like *cobalt,* is derived from the name of a demoniac being, *nickel,* a pet form of *Niklaus. Tungsten,* of still more recent application to practical use, also has a Swedish name made up of the elements, *tung,* 'heavy' and *sten,* 'stone.' The name *platinum* suggests Spanish origin. The name seems to be due to the silvery appearance of the metal and is derived from the Spanish *plata,* 'silver.' *Aluminum* is so recent in its adoption that it has not as yet become standardized in form, the English using the form *aluminium,* Americans preferring the simpler form *aluminum.* The metal was discovered by Davy in 1812, and the name is based on the word *alum.*

The study of words affords indication, then, of the way in which man has become master of many of the elements of nature and has brought under his control, as sources of raw material, the animal, the vegetable and the mineral kingdoms. In a similar way the study of names of things affords, at least in outline, a map of human progress in adapting these things to human needs.

In the matter of food, full lists of cognates make it clear that the art of cooking food goes back to the earliest stages of Indo-European life. Later improvements in culinary art may be traced by means of words.[16] The Old English *hlāf*, meaning 'bread,' which survives with change in meaning, as well as in form, in the modern word *loaf*, appears in cognate forms in various languages and seems to have meant a flat, unleavened, bread, presumably like that still used in Norway and Sweden. The word *bread* itself, which has come to take its place, is associated in its origin with the meaning 'yeast' and possibly marks the introduction into use of more modern leavened forms of bread. In like manner *cheese*, among early Teutonic peoples, seems to have been a sort of curded milk, and the introduction of a newer kind of cheese-making is indicated when the native Teutonic name, which still survives in Dano-Norwegian *ost*, is replaced by the Latin *caseus*, which becomes German *Käse*, English *cheese*.[17]

In the matter of clothing, the history of the words used as names offers similar interesting information. Series of cognate words, not only for clothing but for nakedness, afford convincing evidence of the use of clothing in the primitive stage of Indo-European life, and names associated with animal skins, with weaving, and with spinning, afford information regarding stages in the development of clothing and of the textile arts. The evidence afforded indicates that the primitive Indo-European garments consisted of mantle and hose or breeches.[18] Among the Teutonic

---

[16] Schrader, p. 245.
[17] *Ibid.*, p. 251.
[18] *Ibid.*, p. 268.

peoples the earlier name for hose was the one appearing in Old High German *bruoh,* Old Norse *brōk,* Old English *brōc,* and it is interesting to note that this word was borrowed into Celtic in the form *braca* and into Slavic in the Russian *brjuki,* indicating the spread among the neighboring peoples of Teutonic modes of clothing the lower part of the body.

From words used as names for dwelling may be drawn many interesting inferences concerning primitive life. A number of these words are associated with an earlier meaning of 'cave,' suggesting cave dwelling customs of earlier times. For instance, the Old English word, *cofa,* 'room,' lost in modern English, is cognate not only with the Old Norse *kofi,* 'hut,' Middle High German *kobe,* 'stall,' and Old High German *chubisi,* 'hut,' but with Greek *gupe,* meaning 'underground dwelling.'[19] Other similar words have been cited by scholars from older languages. In spite of these words linking back with more primitive forms of cave dwelling, there is plentiful evidence in the history of words to show that Indo-European peoples in the stage before separation already lived in houses with doors, posts, and roofs. The materials of construction indicated are wood, wattle, and clay, and the oldest form was circular. That stone structures were not used by early Teutonic peoples, is shown by the fact that nearly all names associated with stone structure, such as those appearing in English as *wall, tile,* and *mortar,* are derived from Latin.

The oldest names for the contents of a dwelling carry one back to decidedly primitive conditions.[20] The word *bolster* for 'pillow,' which apppears in Old High German as *bolstar,* 'cushion,' appears in earlier cognate forms, represented by the Sanskrit *barhis,* with the meaning

---

[19] Schrader, I, 214, II, 273.
[20] *Ibid.,* p. 289.

'straw.' The word *bed* has been traced back to an earlier meaning of 'a place hollowed out to lie in,' a meaning one element of which appears in the cognate Latin *fodere*, 'to dig.' It should be noted that *stead*, in the English *bedstead*, originally meant 'place,' and that *bedstead*, therefore, seems to mean a place to lie rather than a framework to support modern comportable sleeping appurtenances.

One of the most striking sets of words in this connection is that dealing with parts of vehicles.[21] Not only the word, *wagon*, but the allied words, *wheel, axle, thill, lynch* (pin) and *yoke*, appear in cognate forms in various Indo-European languages, indicating the development of the vehicle in the primitive stage of Indo-European life. Among these cognate words is conspicuous the absence of a word for spoke, an absence affording ground for the interesting inference that the primitive form of wheel was solid in form.

Vague enough is our knowledge of life in the times before the preservation of written records. The most definite sources of information are the relics from primitive times which have been gathered in museums. Information from such sources, however, is admirably supplemented by information from the study of words. Indeed, a set of words gathered from the dictionary and properly arranged and labeled as to origin, may be made of itself to serve as a museum of archæology.

REFERENCES FOR FURTHER READING

O. SCHRADER, *Sprachvergleichung und Urgeschichte*, 3d ed. (Jena, 1906), English translation by Jevons; *Reallexicon der Indogermanischen Altertumskunde* (Strassburg, 1901). [Jena, 1906], English Translation by Jevons.

V. HELM, *Kulturpflanzen und Haustiere*, 8th ed. (Berlin, 1911), English translation by J. Stallgebrass (London, 1888).

---

[21] Schrader, p. 298.

H. Hirt, *Die Indogermanen* (Strassburg, 1905-7); *Deutsche Etymologie* (Munich, 1909).
J. M. Tyler, *The New Stone Age in Northern Europe* (New York, 1921).
H. H. Bender, *The Home of the Indo-Europeans* (Princeton, 1922).
G. M. Bolling, *The Home of the Indo-Europeans, Cath. Univ. Bulletin,* Vol. xiii, pp. 211-31.

CHAPTER XXII

WORDS AND CULTURE HISTORY

Words, as has been seen, in many instances, offer means of illumination by which one is able to penetrate the dimness of a prehistoric past. For the study of human culture within the historic period, also, words may often be made serviceable. As signs of ideas, words may be made to serve as sign posts, indicating not only the distance but the direction of human progress.

The names for the materials and implements connected with the art of writing have often been cited in this connection. Methods of writing in practice among the Teutonic ancestors of the English are revealed by the words used. The word *write,* it has already been remarked, originally meant 'to scratch' and indicates an early mode of writing by means of scratching on stone or metal or wood. That wood was a material used for records is known not only from other sources, but from the history of the word *book,* which is related in origin to the word *beech.* The custom of carving characters on pieces of wood and of reading the future by means of these has been alluded to in the preceding chapter. The English word *read* still retains as one of its meanings that of 'interpret,' as in *read a riddle,* a meaning associated with this early custom. The German word *lesen,* meaning 'to read,' goes back to the physical act on the part of the forecaster, of 'picking up' the bit of wood with the written character. German *Buchstabe,* 'letter,' meaning etymologically 'piece of beech wood,' goes back to the same custom. The corresponding English word, *bōcstæf,* did not survive the Anglo-Saxon period.

The influence of Roman culture is shown once more in the names of Latin origin that are now connected with the literary arts. *Paper* comes by way of French and Latin from the Greek *papyrus*, the name of an Egyptian plant, somewhat resembling broom-corn, from the pithy stalks of which were cut thin cross sections, which, laid in a layer, offered a place for written record. *Parchment* comes from *Pergamum*, the name of a city in Asia Minor in some way associated with sheepskin used for writing. *Vellum* goes back to a Latin word meaning 'calfskin' and is thus related to the modern word *veal*. The word *library* goes back to a Latin word *liber*, 'book,' which originally meant the 'inner bark of a tree,' indicating that primitive Roman writing material, before the use of papyrus was learned from the Greeks, was not unlike that of the early Teutonic peoples. The name of the Latin *stilus*, the pointed instrument used in writing on waxen tablet or on the bark of tree, appears in English *style*, but with changed meaning, having been shifted in meaning from implement in writing to manner of writing and then in turn to manner of thought in writing, and in most recent times to 'manner' of varied kinds, even to 'modish fashion.' The substitution of a painted mark for a scratched mark is indicated by the word *ink*, which goes back through French and Latin to the Greek word *eghauston*, whih meant 'burnt in,' a meaning surviving in *caustic* from the same source. With the application of writing fluid, other implements superseded the pointed *stilus*. The nature of one new instrument is indicated by the word *pen*, which is derived from the Latin *penna*, meaning 'feather.' The use of another implement in competition with the quill is indicated by the word *pencil*, which is derived from a Latin word *penicillus*, meaning 'little tail,' and indicates the use of a brush made of the tip of a tail in making written marks.

The word *page*, which, according to one explanation, goes

back to a Latin word meaning 'fasten,' brings up a suggestion of an early page made by fastening together strips of papyrus. The word *volume,* on the other hand, related to the idea of 'roll,' as in the case of the related words *evolution, revolution,* etc., brings up the picture of books written on rolls of sheepkskin or calfskin or papyrus.

The word *pamphlet* reflects the popularity of a twelfth-century Latin poem, *Pamphilet or Pamphilus, seu de Amore,* the name of which became applied to small books as a class. Similar in origin to *book* and *library* are the words *code* and *codex,* which go back to the Latin *codex* from earlier *caudex,* meaning 'tree-trunk.' The word *rubber* belongs in the class under discussion, because this name came to be attached to the substance of which the native name was *caoutchouc,* through the use of the substance in erasing written signs. This early use of rubber, though now a relatively minor one, has given the substance an English name not to be erased.

The group of words just considered will convey some idea of the richness of word study in suggestion regarding earlier customs. Let us for further illustration take for consideration some sets of words intimately related with everyday life, the names connected with the houses in which we live and the foods that sustain us. The word *house* itself belongs to English of the earliest period. Judged by the names for its parts the earliest English house was a simple structure. The word *wall* is of Latin derivation (Lat. *vallum*) and indicates indebtedness to the Romans for the art of masonry. The word *window,* of Scandinavian origin, meaning 'wind eye,' like its native English equivalent, *ēagthyrel,* 'eye hole,' indicates a small opening intended to afford chance for watching rather than to admit light. *Glass,* in the sense of plate glass, is relatively late in coming into use. *Door* and *latch* are native English words, although *latch*, as a noun, has not been cited earlier than the Middle English period.

The different stories of the modern house are relatively late in their origin. The word *story* itself is of Old French origin, with an interesting history given in an earlier chapter. The names for the parts of the house above and below the ground floor are relatively late and of foreign derivation. *Cellar*, derived through the French from the Latin *cellarium*, is cited with the meaning 'a set of cells for foods' as early as 1225. *Basement* from the French is, of course, much later. Its earliest citation with the meaning 'lowest story' is from 1730. For the upper story a name appearing in late Old English was *loft*, of Scandinavian origin, which is known in Scandinavian countries to have been an upper room reached by outside stairs. Another name for an upper room, a name which has become obsolete, is *soler*, of French origin, and meaning 'sun room' (Lat. *solarium*). For the space at the top of the house the words surviving in use are *garret* and *attic*. Both have interesting histories. *Garret* appears in Middle English with the meaning 'turret' or 'watch tower.' It comes from the Old French *garite*, meaning 'refuge,' 'sanctuary,' which is derived from the verb *garir*, 'to protect,' from which comes also the word *garrison*. The word *garret* carries one back to the defensive features of buildings in the late Middle Ages. The word *attic*, of much later origin, reflects the classical fashions of architecture prevailing in the seventeenth century, when the upper floor of houses had Attic decorative features. The word *attic*, referring to decorative features, pilasters and the like, on the upper part of a house, is cited as early as 1676; as the name for the upper story of a house, the word is not cited until 1817.

The use of the word *room* as a class name for apartments in a house, it has already been remarked, is relatively modern. The earliest cited instance of its use in this sense is from 1457. The generic term *room,* in accord with a well-known principle in language history, is later in origin than the specific names of individual rooms. In early English the earliest native names applied to particular rooms are *hall* and *bower.* The first of these words was applied to the principal, often the only room, under a roof, the center of domestic life, the room of the hearth and the dining table, the room in many cases used for sleeping. The word *hall,* meaning 'entrance room,' 'vestibule,' is not cited until 1663. The word *bower,* surviving in our day only as a name for a romantic conception, appears in early English as the name for the earliest form of private apartment, usually a sleeping apartment, whether under the same roof with the hall or forming a separate building. "Ful sooty was hir bour, and eek hir halle," says Chaucer, in humorous grandiloquence, of the widow's cottage of the fourteenth century, a house in which, possibly, a single room served for both hall and bower, and, besides, we are informed, afforded a perch for Chanticleer and his seven wives. An idea of the gradual evolution of more complex living arrangements may be gained by tracing the history of the names for the several apartments of a house. The name *kitchen* (O. E. *cycene*) makes its appearance late in the period before the Conquest, and like so many of the terms connected with cooking, as has been already shown, is of Latin derivation. *Closet,* as a name for 'private room,' the meaning surviving in the language of the Bible, is borrowed from the French in the fourteenth century. With the present-day meaning of 'side room' or 'repository,' it is not cited until after 1600.

The word *parlor,* of French derivation, makes its appearance in the thirteenth century as the name for a room in monastic establishments used for conference with people of the outer world. The relation of this use with the meaning of the French word *parler,* 'to speak,' is apparent. In the fourteenth century the author of *Piers Plowman* laments the withdrawal of lords and ladies from the more public *hall* to the private *parlor:*

> Elying is the halle vche daye in the wyke
> There the lorde ne the lady lyketh noughte to sitte
> Now hath vche a reule to eten bi him selue
> In a pryue parloure. . . . .

With the meaning familiar in American use, as the room *de luxe* in more humble dwellings, the word *parlor* makes its first appearance late in the fifteenth century (1469). *Buttery,* which comes from the Old French *boterie,* and originally meant a 'bottle repository' or 'place for liquor,' is cited with this meaning as early as 1389, but soon thereafter takes its present meaning. *Pantry,* also from the French (O. Fr. *paneterie*), originally meant a 'place for the storing of bread.' (*Cf.* French *pain,* 'bread.') It first appears in English about 1300. *Drawing-room,* which is a clipped form for *withdrawing room,* dates back only to the middle of the seventeenth century (1642), and the differentiation in the function of rooms is indicated by the appearance at about the same time of the special name *dining-room,* which has not been cited before 1600. The recent word *living-room,* which serves to express an American ideal of a comfortable home, has taken on some of the characteristics of the primitive hall.

The word *hearth* goes back to the earliest period, to a time when a fire, perhaps in the center of the common hall with smoke issuing through an opening in the roof, served not only to warm the occupant of the house, but to cook his food. In a later period the word *chimney* was applied to the fireplace in the wall of the room, a word later shifted by metonymy to its present meaning. It is interesting to note that the word *fireplace,* a hybrid compound, is not cited earlier than 1702.

The modern development of external features of the private residence also finds illustration in the history of words. The use of the word *veranda,* which appears in Spanish and Portuguese as early as the sixteenth century, and was possibly borrowed from one of these languages, was certainly reinforced by later borrowing from India through English relations with that country. *Porch,* borrowed in the Middle English period from the French *porche* (from Latin *porticus*), as the name for a covered approach or entrance, usually of great dignity, to church or public building, in American English has come to be applied to the less formal entrance to a private residence. In the same way *piazza,* the Italian name for 'public square,' in English was applied to the Covent Garden square, which was surrounded by a colonnaded passage, Italian in character. By confusion, or by conscious metonymy, the word came to be associated with the surrounding colonnade, designed by Inigo Jones, rather than with the square itself. In America the term came to be applied to the colonnaded entrances of private residences, and eventually has come to be used as practically synonymous with *veranda.*[1] *Balcony,* a related word, also of Italian origin, makes its first appearance in English early in the seventeenth century.

To *veranda, porch,* and *piazza,* three terms which in American use are practically synonymous, should be added a fourth word, *stoop,* hardly to be distinguished in meaning. This word is a contribution to the American vocabulary from the Dutch settlers of New York.

If one turns one's attention from the names of external features of a dwelling to the names for the furnishings of the interior, one will once more gain an impression of growing complexity in manner of living, at least of growing attention to creature comfort. In the Old English period,

---

[1] A. Matthews, *The Nation,* LXVIII, 416, quoted by Greenough and Kittred

mat, a word of Latin origin, was the name of a fabric woven of coarse material, used among other things as a floor covering. Later the word *carpet* was borrowed from the French (O. Fr. *carpite,* 'coarse cloth'). The earliest cited use of *carpet* as a name for floor covering is in the fifteenth century. Earlier than that it had been used as a name for covers of tables and beds. The derivation of the word from a late Latin verb, meaning 'to pick' or 'to pluck,' suggests that the earliest English carpet may have had points in common with the later rag carpet. The woven carpet, originating in the Orient, was first manufactured in England in the reign of James I. *Rug,* the other common name for a floor covering, is of Swedish derivation, from a word cognate with English *rough.* It appears in English first toward the end of the sixteenth century.

Bed, which appears in the earliest period of English, as already pointed out, goes back to an original meaning of 'a dugout place,' a meaning surviving in *river bed, flower bed,* etc., offering suggestions of a distinctly primitive form of life. The word *cot* is an Anglo-Indian word from the Hindustani *khat,* 'bedstead.' The word is cited with the meaning 'portable bed' from about 1850, but under the influence of folk etymology has become falsely associated with the word *cot,* abbreviated from *cottage,* and hence frequently appears in the combination *cot bed.*

The word *couch* is derived from the French in the Middle English period and comes ultimately from the Latin *con + locare,* meaning to 'place together.' The verb *couch* in isolated phrases like 'couch one's ideas' is close to the original meaning. *Settle,* the old English word for 'seat,' in the eighteenth century was modified to *settee,* possibly under the influence of an anglicized pronunciation of the French *tête-à-tête.* Later came *sofa,* an Arabic word, derived through the French, and first cited in English with the meaning 'lounge' from 1717. The word *lounge* came to be applied as the name for a form of sofa about 1850. *Davenport,* said to be from the name of the maker, is cited from 1845 on.

Settle has been mentioned as a word for 'seat.' Another old English word for seat is *stool,* restricted in meaning in modern English, of which *Stuhl,* the German cognate, still retains the original meaning, 'chair.' The evolution of the individual seat and the growing elaborateness in modes of furnishing is indicated by the borrowing of the word *chair,* which comes through the French from the Latin *cathedra,* 'seat of state,' 'throne,' and in French continues to retain the original meaning.

Stairs is of native English origin (O. E. *stæger*). The architectural adornment of *stairs* is indicated by the word *baluster,* from the Italian through the French and derived ultimately from a Greek word, meaning 'the flower of the wild pomegranate.' The word *newel,* borrowed from French in the Middle English period, meant originally 'the stone of a fruit.'

The word *oven* goes back to the Old English period and meant originally 'something hollowed out,' a meaning the appropriateness of which is discernible in the ovens connected with old fireplaces. Even the word *range* is associated with cooking as early as the end of the sixteenth century. *Stove,* as the name for a heating contrivance, is relatively modern. It is a native English word and meant originally a 'heated room' or 'bath room.' The cognate German word, *Stube,* has been differentiated to mean 'room' in general, and the Danish cognate *stue* has developed nearly the same meaning. In English the word has come to stand for the other element in the original meaning, the means of heating.

The name *table* is of Latin origin. Its original meaning was 'board,' used for games, for writing, and the like. Its earlier meaning appears in such phrases as 'turn the tables on' and 'the tables of the law.' At a comparatively early date, however, the name *table* came to serve in English as the name for a definite article of furniture with fixed support. The native English equivalent of *table* is *board*, which has taken a wide variety of meanings, the meaning of 'eating table' surviving only in phrases such as 'the festal board.'

The names of implements used in eating at the table may serve as milestones indicating social progress. The word *knife* is an old English word, though probably of Norse origin. The word *spoon* is a native English word, but meant originally 'a splinter of wood,' a 'chip.' Later it came to be used as a name for a hollowed piece of wood used for conveying liquids to the mouth, and later was applied as the name of similar implements of horn or metal. The word *fork* is an Old English word, but derived from Latin. It was used in the earliest period as the name for an agricultural implement. As a table implement its use has not been cited earlier than 1463. The introduction of *spoon* and *fork* mark definite stages in the refinement of manners.

Development in the direction of greater elegance in table manners is indicated by the word *porcelain*, through the French from the Italian name of a shell with polished surface, which in turn took its name from its resemblance in shape to a little pig (Ital. *porcella*). Originally made in China, it was introduced to Europe by the Portuguese and began to be manufactured in Europe early in the eighteenth century. The word *china* was introduced to England in the seventeenth century from India, where it was the name used for *porcelain*. The Indian form of the word, *chini*, as already mentioned, is reflected in the English pronunciation, 'chayney,' prevalent in the seventeenth and eighteenth centuries.

If the table as a fixed piece of furniture suggests improved modes of serving meals, improvement in the nature of the fare itself is vividly suggested by the enlargement in the vocabulary of foods. The words *bread* and *meat* go back to the earliest period in English, but each of these words has experienced an interesting shift in meaning. The word *bread*, as already shown, has changed functions with the word *loaf*. The word *meat* originally meant 'food' in general, a meaning which it retained in sixteenth-century English, as reflected in biblical phrase and which survives in such phrases as *meat* and *drink, sweetmeats,* etc. *Wheat, barley, rye,* and *oats,* as well as *bean,* go back to earliest English, and all entered into the composition of various early forms of bread. *Milk* and *fish* and *apple* and *beet,* and the last element in the word *turnip,* go back to the Old English period, which also did not entirely lack seasoning elements, as is indicated by the native words not only for *salt,* but for *leek* and *garlic.* *Mustard* also was used, but bore an earlier name, *senep,* derived from Latin, cognate with the German *Senf.*

The influence of Roman civilization on the life of early Teutonic peoples has already been commented on. To earliest English belong the words *butter* and *cheese,* both of Latin derivation, probably indicating improved Roman methods of milk culture. From the same source at this period came *wine* and *cherry, peach* and *pineapple, pear, pea* and *asparagus, ginger* and *pepper.*

But it is in the period following the Conquest that came about the greatest enrichment of the vocabulary of foods. The humble breakfast retained its native English name, but *supper* and *dinner* were borrowed from the language of the superior French-speaking class. Possibly an improved process of milling is to be inferred from the replacing of the native word *meal* by *flour,* the figurative name meaning literally the 'flour of the grain.' In some instances a French name merely superseded an earlier

English name, as in the case of *mustard*, which took the place of *senep*. The introduction also of such French names as *beef, pork, mutton,* and *veal,* for meats ready for use, as compared with the native English names *cow, swine, sheep,* and *calf* for the beasts whose flesh provides the meat, has provided a classical illustration of the relations existing between the French-speaking and the English-speaking elements in the population of England following the Norman Conquest. That, however, improvement in the cuisine followed the Conquest is attested by the introduction from French at this period of such words as *sauce, gravy, boil, fry, roast, broil, toast, pastry, pasty, soup, sausage, jelly, dainty.*[2] Enrichment of the *menu* is further suggested by importation of such names as *currant, orange, melon, olive, parsnip* (from O. Fr. *pastenaque,* Lat. *pastinaca,* influenced in form by the analogy of *turnip*), *lettuce, onion, cabbage* (at this time called *col*), *cucumber* (probably directly from Latin. First cited, 1430) and the new forms of spice, such as *clove, nutmeg,* and *cinnamon* (first cited, 1430). Most important of all is the word *sugar,* which first appeared in English in the Middle English period (earliest citation, 1289), derived through the French by Latin and Arabic or Persian routes, from India. Of uncertain, probably Celtic, origin is the important word *pie,* first cited in 1362.

The sentimental tendency to idealize the 'good old times' of the past is a familiar one. For the *bon vivant,* at least, quite substantial grounds for contentment with the later period in which it is our fate to live is afforded by a list of food names with the dates of their earliest appearance. The following list of words, with earliest date of cited use, is gathered from the Oxford Dictionary: *coffee* 1600 (introduced into England after 1650), *cocoa* (end of the sixteenth century), *tea* (mid. seventeenth century),

---

[2] Jespersen, *Growth and Structure,* p. 89.

buckwheat 1548, *banana* 1597, *molasses* 1582, *cauliflower* 1597, *artichoke* 1531, *celery* 1664, *apricot* 1551, *potato* (as article of food) 1663, *rice* 1234, *salsify* 1706, *allspice* 1621, *catsup* 1711, *chili* (sauce) 1662, *cantaloupe* 1839, *arrowroot* (commercial use) 1811, *compote* 1693, *jam* 1730, *marmalade* 1524, *macaroni* 1599, *maize* 1585.

The history of these words will reveal the extent to which the ends of the world have been laid under contribution in the provision of modern food. From Asia, the cradle of modern civilization, come, by routes more or less direct, words like *rice* and *ginger* and *cinnamon* and *sugar* and *coffee* and *tea*, as well as earlier knowledge of *peach* and *cherry* and *orange* and *ginger* and *pepper*. From Africa come the *banana* and *yam*. From America, opened up to Europeans in the fifteenth and sixteenth centuries, come *tapioca, chocolate, cocoa, potato, tomato* and *maize*.

Transformations in meaning are numerous. *Marmalade,* from the Portuguese *marmelada,* a 'conserve of quinces' (Latin *melimelum,* 'honey apple,' 'quince') is applied in French and English to conserves of other fruits. After its pattern is created the recent name *grapalade*. With changed processes the older names are applied to new products. Thus *pudding,* a word of uncertain origin, in the fourteenth century applied to a product like the modern stuffed sausage, in the sixteenth century takes its present meaning of savory suggestion. The word *porridge* is derived, under the influence of *potage,* from Middle English *porrey,* a name for a form of soup, the nature of which is indicated by the derivation of the word from the Old French *poree,* 'leek.'

Turning from the subjects of foods to that of fabrics, one finds a similar complexity in the English vocabulary. The expansion of the world's commerce finds expression in the variety of words for varied forms of cloth. Many of the fabrics bear names associated in some way with their origin, real or supposed. *Calico* (originally *calicut-cloth*) appears in English in the early seventeenth century and is associated with Calicut, a town on the Malabar coast. In British English, the name is now applied to a white cloth; in America it means a printed cloth, coarser than muslin. More modern is *madras*, first cited as late as 1900, also derived from the name of a city of India. *Chintz* comes from Hindustani *chint*. It makes its appearance in English in the early seventeenth century, in the form *chints*, influenced in form by such words as *quartz, coblentz*, etc. *Cretonne*, a fabric of similar nature, comes from *Creton*, a village in Normandy, and makes its appearance in English about 1870. Other oriental names are: *damask*, from Damascus; *astrakhan*, from a place of that name on the Volga; *afghan*, from the name of a native of Afghanistan; *fustian*, from Fostat (Egypt); *gingham* (about 1600) probably of Malayan origin; *gauze*, from Gaza; *nankeen*, from Nankin in China; *muslin* (about 1600) from Mosul; *cashmere* (early nineteenth century) from the name of a district in India; *serge* (end of fourteenth century) borrowed from the French and ultimately from Seres, the name of a Chinese people from whom in the Old English period had come the word *silk; mohair*, from an Arabic word meaning 'select,' 'choice,' in English modified in form by folk-etymology from supposed relation to the word *hair*.

From Peru in South America comes the word *alpaca*, first cited as the name of a fabric in 1838. The word, however, bears the imprint of Spain, since to *paco*, the Peruvian name of an animal, has been prefixed the Arabic form element, *al-*.

Probably of Russian origin is the word *crash*, which appears first about 1800. The weaving activities of northern France are reflected in a series of names. The names of the principal towns of the Hindenburg line appear in the words: *lawn* (from Laon, about 1400), *arras* (from Arras about 1400), *cambric* (from Cambrai about 1530) and *Chambray* (from the same town in our own day), and *lisle-thread* (from *Lille* about 1850). *Poplin* (about 1700) is so named because made in the papal town of Avignon. The name of a German city appears in the American *hamburg* (edging).

British activity in woolen weaving is reflected in British names for woolen fabrics. *Broadcloth* goes back to the end of the fourteenth century. *Worsted* bears the name of Worstead, a town in Norfolk known for weaving in the time of Chaucer. *Tweed* originated in a misreading of the word *tweel*, a dialectal form for *twill;* the new form of the name, however, associated the fabric with a country famous for its woolen industries. With the hills of the same country is associated *cheviot* (cloth) first cited from 1883.

The domination of France in matters of dress is expressed in names of the finer fabrics, the recent dates of which are in many cases a striking feature. For example may be cited, with earliest date of record in the Oxford Dictionary, words with obvious French forms such as *chenille* (1738), *foulard* (1864), *percale* (1621), *chiffon* (1876), *crêpe de chine* (1887), *georgette, voile.*

A fabric name with an interesting development in meaning is the word *canvas*, already cited. This cloth name, derived from the French, comes ultimately from the name of the material of which canvas is made, Latin *cannabis*, 'hemp.' The later use of *canvass* as a verb goes back to a method of examining certain substances in a canvas sheet. The name for this form of minute scrutiny has later come to be applied to examination at long range as in the case of a political canvass, very far removed in meaning from tossing in a sheet.

The realm of dress is ruled over by a capricious being perhaps not inappropriately given a name with feminine prefix, Dame Fashion. The history of the words that make up the English vocabulary of dress conducts one over a long route, through the wigs and furbelows of the seventeenth and eighteenth centuries, the doublet and hose, ruffs and farthingales of the age of Elizabeth, and the mantles and wimples and kerchiefs of the time of the Plantagenets, back to the tunic and girdle and hose and cloak, of Saxon England. The history of the terms in the vocabulary involved would obviously form a history of English costume.

The word *dress* itself has an interesting history, already alluded to. From a conjectured Latin form *directiare*, related to modern English *direct*, comes the Old French *dresser*. The original meaning was to 'set straight,' 'arrange,' a meaning still apparent in the English *dress* in such phrases as *dressed chicken* and *Right dress*, the military command. Associated with one's person, the verb came to mean to 'clothe oneself.' The English noun *dress* has become further specialized so as to apply only to a form of apparel of women.

Male attire of the present time has become generally standardized. The history of the names applied to men's garments shows that this standard form is the last stage in a long course of development. Take for instance the covering for the legs. In the early days of tunic and cloak, breeches and hose formed the principal leg apparel. The word *hose*, now applying only to stocking, goes back to the Old English period. In the two or three centuries leading to the sixteenth century, the hose covered the entire leg. The word *breeches*, which really is a double plural, since *breech* is already a plural in the class of words like *feet* and *geese*, goes back to the Old English period, where it was the name for a garment, in origin a loin cloth, but developed into a covering for the leg down to the knee. Certain wide breeches referred to as early as the time of Chaucer, and later much in evidence in the age of Elizabeth, bore the name *slops*. From Italy in the sixteenth century came the word *pantaloon*. The plural form, *pantaloons*, was applied as the name for a kind of breeches, of Venetian origin, in fashion in the period following the Restoration, and later as the name for "a tight-fitting kind of trousers fastened with ribbons or buttons below the calf" (earliest citation, 1798). The name is doubtless of slangy origin, applied by Italians to Venetians because the patron saint of Venice is St. Pantaleone and because Pantaloon (Ital. *Pantaleone*) is a stock type for Venetian in Italian comedy. The word *trousers* as a name for long, loose breeches makes it appearance at the end of the seventeenth century. First used by sailors, then by soldiers, since about 1820 trousers have been a standard garment in the uniform male dress which marks modern Western civilization.

With loose breeches came the need of supports, first named *braces* (O. Fr. *bras*, 'arm'), later called *suspenders* (chiefly United States, first cited 1810). Colored by homely humor is the provincial name *galluses, gallowses* (from *gallows*), first cited about 1730.

In an earlier chapter it was pointed out how one Teutonic word, coming through Old English to modern English, yielded *shirt*, coming through the Norse, yielded *skirt*. The word *coat* again offers illustration of how one word may be made to cover both upper and lower parts of the body. The word *coat* is probably of Teutonic origin (*cf.* O. H. G. *chozzo*, 'shaggy mantle'). The underlying meaning appears to have been 'cover' or 'shelter.' This word, absorbed into French, was borrowed from Old French into English in the fifteenth century in the sense of 'mantle' or 'tunic.' The modern form of coat fitted to the body with loose skirts dates from the reign of Charles II, since whose time the coat has undergone many modifications in *frock coat, cutaway coat, sack coat, overcoat,* etc.

In French the word survives as *cotte* meaning 'petticoat.' English *petticoat* (fifteenth century *pety cote*, 'small coat') applied to a garment worn under the armor, but as early as the fifteenth century was used for female attire, though not at first for 'skirt.' Older meanings of the word appear in *coat of arms, coat of mail, Joseph's coat,* etc.

The word *vest* goes back to the Latin *vestis* with the general meaning 'article of clothing,' 'outer garment.' In English the word sometimes expresses its original general meaning, but is more usually specialized to mean a man's body garment. In the time of Charles II, *vest* was the name of an ultra-fashionable garment described by a contemporary writer as 'a wide garment reaching to the knees, open before, and turned up with a facing or lining, the sleeves turned up at the elbows.'[3] Later the word was appropriated, particularly in America, as the name of a sleeveless body garment, a use of the word which has been much objected to. The specialization of the word to use in connection with male attire is not complete, since something of its earlier wide applicability is shown by its use to mean 'a knitted form of undergarment' and 'a form of women's outer garment.'

Waistcoat was a name applied in the Elizabethan period to a body garment for men, worn under the doublet and intended to show through its slashes. With the doublet succeeded by the modern coat, the word came to have its present usual meaning, preferred by many to the word *vest* which, in America particularly, is popularly used as a synonym.

The word *waist* has developed in meaning by successive stages from (1) an Old English word meaning 'growth,' to (2) a section of the human body, to (3) a belt or girdle worn about the waist, to (4) a garment worn about the waist. Names for specialized forms of waist adopted in

---

[3] R. Holme, quoted by Fairholt, 4th ed. II, p. 405.

modern English, are: *blouse,* of French origin, first cited as an English word in 1834, and *basque,* a word admirably illustrating the transitoriness of things under the rule of fashion, first cited in English in 1860, now obsolete or obsolescent.

Other words exhibiting the capricious nature of fashion are: *ruff,* the name for the full form of collar distinctive of Elizabethan costume; *frill,* first cited in 1591 as the name for an ornamental edging then in vogue, a word showing an interesting metaphorical shift from an earlier meaning either the 'ruffling of a bird's feathers in the cold'[4], or the mesentery of an animal[5]; *ruching,* a later ephemeral word for an ephemeral form of neck dress derived from the French *ruche,* meaning literally, 'bee hive,' and cited first in English in 1827.

Of the external features of men's apparel may be cited the *cravat,* which was a borrowed form of adornment adopted in France in 1636 from the Croats and bearing as a name the French name for Croatian (Fr. *cravate* 1652). The word first appears in English about 1700. *Necktie* is first cited by the Oxford Dictionary from 1838.

The word *shoe,* the native English word for foot covering, going back to earliest English, has been applied to foot dress of the most varied form, from the sandal-formed shoes of the early Saxons, to the extreme forms of fashion reached in later periods. The word *boot,* which first appeared in English about 1325, was of French origin and applied at first to boots worn by riders. In later times the words *boot* and *shoe* have become variously differentiated, the English distinction, as is well known, differing from the American.

Passing now from the subjects of elemental importance, house and food and clothing, to a consideration of other

---
[4] Skeat's *Etymological Dictionary* and *Century Dictionary.*
[5] Oxford Dictionary and Weekley.

elements in modern life, one finds on every hand words which serve to exhibit the nature of human progress. Let us bring once more into service the terms of color. It has long since been pointed out that there is no set of color names common to the Indo-European languages. Distinctions in color are later in origin than the time before the Indo-European peoples had scattered. Even the English names, *black* and *white*, are of later origin. They are not absolute terms. *Black*, which in English has supplanted *swart*, the common Teutonic word (*cf.* Germ. *schwarz*), goes back, it is thought, to an earlier meaning 'burnt,' and *white* goes back possibly to the idea of 'shining.'

Since the discovery of the aniline dyes in the nineteenth century, Germany has been the center in the dye industry. In earlier times the art of colors was developed in the Orient, as may be learned from the source of many of the important color names. The word *purple*, of Greek derivation, from the name of the shell-fish that afforded the dye, was known in Old English as the name of a purple garment; in the Middle English period the word was again borrowed, this time through the French, as the name of a color. *Scarlet*, of Persian derivation, was used in English as the name for a red cloth as early as 1250, and since about 1440 has been a color name. *Azure*, which appears about 1374 as the name for a blue dye, is also of Persian derivation. *Crimson* and its doublet, *carmine*, make their entry about 1440 and go back to an Arabic word *germazi*, the name of the scarlet grain insect. *Indigo*, as the name for a blue Indian dye, making its appearance in English about 1600, is obviously related to India. The form of the word is Portuguese, indicative of the part played by Portugal at that period in commerce with India. The native Indian name for the indigo plant finds its way into English by a land route through Persian and Arabic and

French, as the first element in the word *aniline,* used since about 1850.

It will be observed that these color names were in their origin names of cloths or of dye materials in which particular colors appeared. The use of these words as abstract names of colors is relatively late in each instance. Let us take for illustration the word *cardinal* once more. As an independent name for color, the first use of the word is surprisingly recent. It is not cited in the Oxford Dictionary until 1879. The origin of the color name, *cardinal,* is typical of the origin of most recent color names. The names are not absolute, but as has been shown in an earlier chapter, are derived from the names of things bearing the particular colors. In other words, they are similes. *Drab,* like several of the earlier names, takes its name from a cloth (Fr. *drap,* 'cloth'). It makes its appearance as an English cloth name about 1541. That the cloth was of hempen or woolen or linen material is indicated by the nature of the color to which the name became applied about 1686. *Maroon,* as an English color name, first appears at the end of the eighteenth century, and is borrowed from French *marron,* the literal meaning of which is 'chestnut.' In the same way *mauve,* which is introduced into English as late as 1859, is derived from the French name for the mallow plant of similar color. *Mauve,* like *magenta* and *solferino,* owes its origin, not to oriental commerce, but to the coal tar processes of dye manufacture, which are an achievement of modern chemistry. The names *magenta* and *solferino,* however, which come into use at the same time with *mauve,* do not originate in similes, but serve to commemorate great battles of the time when the color processes were discovered.

Color names serve not only to indicate the geographic sources of color processes, but from the dates of their earliest use, one may learn of the growing fineness of discriminating in colors which is a mark of advancing civilization. Civilization has, indeed, made a long march from the days when there were no color names to mark distinctions as fundamental as black and white, when it has arrived at distinctions of color shades like those indicated by the names cited. But these names do not mark the end of the process. Such modern color names as *honeydew, tomato, tangerine, pimento, pistachio, periwinkle, endive, oasis, Resolute, Olympic, Marathon, paddock, Pompeian red, Bedouin brown, Siberian squirrel, Maduro brown,* and *Nanking blue,* represent a stage of refinement attained in modern times at least in the feminine world.

Turning now to various human activities and taking up words more or less at random, one may find means of lighting up other features of human progress. In the field of finance for instance the word *bank* carries one back to the beginnings of banking in northern Italy. The word, of Teutonic origin, which came through the Old English *benc* to modern English *bench,* was adopted in Italian use, probably from the Teutonic Lombards of northern Italy, in the form *banco,* and applied as a name to a money changer's bench or table, the beginning of the modern bank. The Italian idea, with its Italian name, was borrowed by the other nations of Europe, yielding such words as French *banque,* Spanish *banca,* English *bank.* The Spanish further developed the idea by using the form *banco* as a name for a game of cards. From this word, through contact between English and Spanish in the western United States, came into American English the word with obviously related idea, *bunco.*[6]

If the word *bank* carries one back to Italy, the word *dollar* conducts one to eastern Europe, to Bohemia, where in the early sixteenth century the gulden, called the *Joachimsthaler,* was first coined, taking its name from the *thal* or 'valley' in which silver of especially high grade began to be mined at that time. The clipped form of the word, *thaler,*

---

[6] Greenough and Kittredge.

came into general use not only in Germany but in other countries, as in the Danish *rigsdaler*, Swedish *riksdaler*, and English *dollar*, first cited in 1553. The name came also to be used in English for the Spanish *peso*, used in Spanish America and British America as well. When an independent system of American coinage was instituted, the "Spanish milled dollar" was adopted in 1787 as the monetary unit. The influence of the famous silver coin, the product of a particular mine in central Europe, has been paralleled in striking fashion in the modern history of the Mexican dollar. This silver coin, driven, by the operation of economic law, from the country of its origin, circulated for a time in the United States, but was driven from there in turn, and eventually found its place in the commerce of eastern Asia. Here it has come to be a prevalent unit of value, and has been made the basis of value in recent Chinese coinage.

The word *finance* itself has an interesting history. The word goes back to the Latin word *finis*, 'end.' It appears in English in the Middle English period with the meaning 'fine,' 'forfeit,' or 'ransom,' a meaning which originates in the idea of 'settling up,' a meaning easily derivable from that of the Latin *finis*. Its modern meaning arose in French in the eighteenth century, especially in connection with the tax-farmers or *financiers*.[7] The word is now in general European use appearing in French *finance*, Italian *fianza*, Dutch *financie*, Danish and Swedish *finans*, German *Finanz*, as well as English *finance*. A similar sense development appears in pay, which comes through the French from the Latin root that appears in *pax*, 'peace' and its English derivatives, *pacify*, etc. *Assets* comes from an earlier form of the French *assez*, 'enough,' and applied originally to the part of an estate needed to pay the debts.

---

[7] Weekley, *Etymological Dictionary.*

WORDS AND CULTURE HISTORY 335

The history of municipal government is involved in the word *alderman*. The Old English word *ealdorman*, 'senior,' came to be used as a title of rank second only to that of king. Later, under Norman rule, with the development of the trade guild, the word *alderman* was revived in use as the name of the chief officer of a guild, and with the later development of municipal government from the guild organizations, came not only the use of the name *guildhall* for city hall, but the functioning of the board of guild *aldermen* as the city council.

Older occupations have yielded words which have been applied to new uses. From archery, now practically obsolete except as an adjunct to the golf course, comes *tackle*, the earlier name for 'arrow.' *Target* goes back to an earlier meaning, 'shield,' the mark for the arrow in more practical use. The common word *bend*, which is in origin a causative verb, derived from the earlier word *bind*, brings up an interesting picture, since it takes its meaning from the bending of the bow involved in binding its ends.

In conceptions associated with the old science of astrology originate a number of words now almost completely dissociated from their original use. Such words as *influence*, literally 'flowing in,' and referring to the forces coming from an ascendant star, *disaster*, 'evil star,' and the English word *ill-starred*, which has the same underlying meaning, call to modern attention the earlier beliefs regarding the relation of the stars to human destiny.

There are numerous other words which bring to memory older superstitious beliefs. *Butterfly* takes its meaning from the conception that witches and their kind, in the form of butterflies, steal milk (*cf.* Germ. *Milchdieb*, 'butterfly'.)[8] *Spell*, already discussed, recalls the earlier belief in the magic potency of certain forms of words. The same idea underlies *enchantment* and *charm* derived

---

[8] Hirt, *Etymologie*, p. 145.

through the French respectively from Latin *cantus,* 'song,' and *carmen,* 'song,' and revealing the earlier belief in the magic power of certain forms of song. *Glamour,* which is a corrupted form of *gramarye,* which in turn is a derivative of *grammar,* reveals the belief in the connection between magic power and word tricks. *Hoax* (from *hocus*), which makes its first appearance in English about 1800, illustrates the modern skeptical attitude toward magic word tricks, or *hocus pocus.* The word *prestige* has somewhat outgrown its earlier associations, but is derived through the French from the Latin *præstigium,* a 'deception' or 'illusion,' the plural of which *præstigiæ,* applied to juggler's tricks.

Older ideas regarding the constitution of the human body have left behind words which have been applied to modern conceptions, but which still serve to bring back memories of earlier stages of knowledge or at least of belief. It should be recalled that knowledge of so fundamental a fact as the circulation of the blood is comparatively modern. Its discovery was the achievement of William Harvey in 1628. It requires an effort of the imagination to conceive of the ideas in physiology prevailing before that date, but the history of certain words aids in conducting one back into the atmosphere of that interesting time. It was formerly supposed that the body was composed of solids, liquids, and aeriform substances. The belief in the aeriform substances called *spirits* has left vestiges in the language in such phrases as *high spirits, animal spirits,* and the like. The liquid elements in the body were called *humors,* and were supposed to be four in number: *blood, phlegm, bile,* and *black bile.* The *temperament* of a person (Latin *temperare,* 'to mix'), depended upon the mixture of these humors, and was *phlegmatic* or *sanguine* or *bilious* or *melancholy,* according as one or the other of the humors dominated. *Temper* retains its earlier meaning of mixture in such phrases as *temper of steel,* referring to the mixture of elements, iron, carbon, etc., in the composition of steel, and *ill temper,* literally 'ill mixture,' *good temper,* etc., referring to the mixture of humors in the body. The word *temper,* however, has in recent times come to be largely restricted to the meaning 'ill temper,' of persons. *Complexion,* meaning literally, 'weaving together,' was another term applied first to the combination of humors and then to the resulting 'disposition,' a meaning which the word retains in French. In English, by metonymy, the word has been shifted to mean the hue of the skin, the exterior sign of complexion taken in its original meaning.[9]

The older ideas prevailing regarding these terms appear in the following lines of Ben Jonson:[10]

> In every human body
> The choler, melancholy, phlegm and blood,
> By reason that they flow continually
> In some one part, and are not continent,
> Receive the name of humours. Now thus far
> It may, by metaphor, apply itself
> Unto the general disposition;
> As when some one peculiar quality
> Doth so possess a man, that it doth draw
> All his affects, his spirits and his powers,
> In his confluctions, all to run one way,
> This may be truly said to be a humour.
> *Every Man out of his Humour, Induction.*

Oddity, it appears, was associated with the idea of dominance of one of the humors. Hence the early use of the noun *humor* and the derived adjective *humorous.* In later English the word *humor* has been shifted so as to apply to a quality in the thought or language of a *humorous* person.

Older conceptions of physiology regarding the seat of

---

[9] Greenough and Kittredge, p. 30.
[10] Quoted from Weekley.

various emotions survive in the use made of the names for parts of the human anatomy. *Heart* and its derivatives are associated with the warm affections. *Courage, cordial* and their like, which go back to the Latin *cor*, 'heart,' originate in the same conceptions. *Spleen* and *splenetic* are associated with ill-temper, *kidney* with temperament in general, *stomach* with feelings as various as pity, courage, pride and wrath. *Pluck*, already mentioned, a butcher's collective term for heart, liver, and lungs, has become associated with the idea of courage, a use of a word strikingly paralleled in the case of a recently adopted colloquial synonym for 'stamina.' It is interesting to note that the Greek word *phren*, meaning 'mind,' goes back to an earlier meaning, 'diaphragm' or 'midriff.' The early nineteenth-century inventors of the science, or pseudo-science, of phrenology, in the name which they created for their new science, quite unintentionally, it must be supposed, brought their science into association with a discarded system of primitive thought regarding the seat of the human intelligence.

Some of the misconceptions of early medical science appear in the use of such words as *rheum* and *gout*. *Gout*, which is derived ultimately from the Latin *gutta*, 'drop,' was adopted in the Middle English period from the French, but applied to dropsy and catarrh as well as to gout, all of which were presumed to be due to a defluxion of the humors. *Sassafras*, in the medicinal virtues of which faith has by no means been entirely lost, comes from the Spanish, probably from the American Indian. The word has, however, been modified in form through the influence of Spanish *sassifragia* (Lat. *saxum*, 'rock' + *frangere*, 'to break'), assumed to be efficacious against stone in the bladder.

In numerous instances words have survived the customs or methods in which they originated. Such old names applied to new uses serve to bring to the memory departed

WORDS AND CULTURE HISTORY 339

features of life, and thus serve as links connecting the present with the past. Thus the word *ballot*, already mentioned, which comes from the Italian *ballotta*, diminutive of *balla*, 'ball,' brings to mind older methods of voting by means of little balls or bullets. This name for 'little ball' is now applied with no feeling of inappropriateness to the mammoth sheets used in exercising the modern rights of suffrage. The word *black ball* obviously finds an explanation with that of *ballot*.

The word *watch*, like the instrument which it names, may be made to indicate the passage of time. It goes back to the earliest English (O. E. *wæcce*, 'waking,' 'watch') and has developed through successives stages: (1) waking, (2) the looking out on account of which the waking state is maintained, (3) a period of time for watching, (4) a means of measuring time. In earlier times the name *watch* was applied to a candle marked into sections for measuring time. This use of the word appears in Shakespeare:

> Fill me a bowl of wine. Give me a watch.
> —"Richard III," V, 3, 63.

The modern instrument, however, was not unknown in Shakespeare's time.

The word *match*, the name of a means of starting a fire, had had a similar history, the course of which marks stages in the development of the ease and convenience which characterize modern modes of life. This word *match*, which is entirely unrelated to the word *match*, meaning 'mate,' originally applied to a 'wick' (O. Fr. *mesche*, 'wick'), which was also used in conveying flame. Formerly hemp, cotton, tow dipped in sulphur, paper dipped in niter, and touchwood, were used as matches. The old-fashioned paper lamplighter was a *match* in the older sense of the word. Later, splinters of wood tipped with sulphur were introduced. About 1830 the earliest form of friction match was introduced. In competition with *locofoco, lucifer, congreve, vesuvian, fusee, vesta,* the word *match* continued to be used as the name for various forms of the new device. The older meaning of *match* survives in phrases such as *matchboard, match-lock.*[11]

Many are the words which, like those cited, may be made to bring up pictures of features of life in earlier days. The word *stump speaker,* still applied to a political orator, suggests romantic scenes in earlier American history. The name *cowcatcher,* still applied in America to the pilot of a locomotive, brings up lively memories of conditions of life quite incongruous with modern ideas of speed and dignity. In the same way English terms of the railway, such as *coach, driver, guard, carriage,* and *booking office,* serve to recall the earlier days of the stage-coach.

The subject broached in the present chapter is obviously as big as the universe or at least as the human conception of the universe. Obviously a single chapter can not exhaust a subject of which an encyclopedia can offer only the elements. Enough, however, has been offered, it is hoped, to show the fascinating interest of the subject. The search for the sources of words reveals the different currents of influence which have contributed to modern life; the examination of changes in meaning undergone, not only exhibits interesting processes in thought, but affords much information regarding the successive stages passed through in arriving at the complexity of modern civilization.

---

[11] *Century Dictionary.*

CHAPTER XXIII

WORDS AND ROMANCE

'The romance of words' is a phrase which has gained wide currency of late. It has given the title not only to an interesting book about words, but to a series of syndicated articles running in the American press. In the case of many words the enthusiastic interest suggested by the phrase is well justified. Few romantic narratives can vie in interest with that of such a word as *bank*. Originally a humble Teutonic word, serving as a name for 'bench,' through adoption by the Lombard bankers of northern Italy, this word has eventually become the name for an institution which is the center of modern worldly power. Further, in Spanish guise, as *banco*, the name of a game of cards, the word journeyed with the Spanish to Western America, where it had an adventurous, not to say hazardous career, surrounded by all the romance of life in the Wild West. Even more romantic, if possible, is the story of the word *dollar* told in the last chapter. Of humble origin as the name for a coin produced from the silver of a Bohemian valley, the word has been exalted to the highest worldly position. Migrating to the western hemisphere, it served as the name for a Mexican coin which has come to be the unit of value in the commerce of China and the Far East. Adopted as the name for the unit of value in the coinage of the United States, it has attained almost divine honors as the symbol of human success, the supreme end of wordly endeavor, the 'Almighty dollar.'

The possibilities of romance in the subject of words are

obviously practically limitless. Unfortunately, not content with the record of authenticated facts, the amateur in word lore has, in many instances, allowed fancy to run amuck and has set in circulation many a story which will not stand the realistic tests imposed by a critical age. The word *quiz*, for instance, a word which is first cited in 1782, and which had a remarkable colloquial vogue in a variety of meanings around the beginning of the nineteenth century, was explained by an interesting anecdote. It was said to have been the creation of Daly, a Dublin theatrical manager, who made a wager that he could manufacture a word and put it into general circulation. Unfortunately for the story, which one is loth to discard, the known dates in the life of Daly, and in the history of the use of the word, do not permit its acceptance.

Roam, a word of obscure origin, making its appearance about 1330, has been associated with the wandering habits of pilgrims to Rome, so marked a feature of medieval life. Unfortunately the history of the sounds in the word do not permit the acceptance of this romantic explanation. The association of *roam* with Rome is believed to owe its origin to later punning proclivities.

The puritanic person, averse to profanity, in giving vent to his emotions, has had recourse to the phrase, 'tinker's dam,' because this expression has been provided with an innocent explanation as originating in a practice of the itinerant tinker, when mending holes in pot or kettle, of using bread molded in doughnut form about the hole and called a dam. Unfortunately ignorance is no excuse in the eyes of the law, and the critical lexicographer has left no grounds for defense of the expression since he has explained it as due to the "reputed addiction of tinkers to profane swearing."[1]

In the same way Hector, the Trojan hero, has recently

---

[1] *Cf. Atlantic Monthly*, Contributors' Column, May, 1920.

been freed from an unpleasant insinuation, since the verb *hector*, 'to bully,' has been shown to have no connection with the name *Hector* but to go back to an Old English word, *hecettan*.²

The explanation of proper names, always a treacherous subject, has given occasion to many a flight of fancy. Old story derives the name *Courtney* from *court nez*, 'short nose,' an epithet applied to the famous Guillaume d'Orange, who showed undaunted spirit when a Saracen sword had cut off his nose. In like manner *Percy* is derived from *pierce-eye*, referring to a treacherous exploit. In the same way the search for an explanation of the name *Lockhart*, gave rise to the story of the original Lockhart who took the heart of the Bruce to the Holy Land in a locked casket.³ De Quincey, in burlesque of this fascinating but unsound method of pseudo-science, tells with gusto of "a most agreeable madman," a traveling companion in the leisurely days of post-chaise, who gave an ingenious explanation of the name *Saxon*. The Saxons, according to this amusing explanation, "had no breeches and of course no silk stockings. They had however, *sacks*, which they mounted on their backs, whence naturally their name *Sax-on*. *Sackson!* was the one word of command, and that spoken, the army was ready.—Having no breeches nor silk stockings of their own, they intended, wind and weather permitting, to fill these same sacks with those of other men."

The romantic bit of culture history evolved from the name *Saxon*, thus gleefully recorded by De Quincey, turns to parody a form of story in earlier times turned to serious literary use. From the name *Britain* was evolved a story that connected the beginnings of British history with the fall of Troy, the connecting link being the hero Brut, a

² F. A. Wood, *Modern Language Notes*, 39, 208.
³ These three anecdotes from E. Weekley, *The Romance of Names*, p. 7.

descendant of Æneas, from whose name was formed the name *Britain*. To the same class of stories belongs that of Corineus, a companion of Brutus, who, according to the story, occupied and gave his name to *Cornwall*. French history was connected with Trojan story by means of the name *France*, from Francus, a son of Hector, and *Paris* from the Trojan hero of that name. In the same way *Lisbon* (*Olisipo*) was, according to story, built by Ulysses. Going the other nations still better, the Scots trace their ancestry to Scota, a daughter of Pharaoh.[4]

To come more close to home, the word *Yankee,* of obscure origin, has not daunted the fanciful. A bewildering number of ingenious explanations have been offered. It has been derived from the effort of the Indians to pronounce *Anglois,* the French name for *English*. It has been derived from *Eankke,* a word for 'coward,' in one of the Indian dialects, and from the Scotch *yankie* allied to *yanker,* meaning a great falsehood. It has been explained as a corruption of *Yorkshire*. It is said, again, to come from *Yankoos,* the name of a tribe of Indians whom the English conquered and from whom, "according to Indian custom," they took their name. It has been derived from *Jannekin,* a derisive name applied to the New Englanders by their Dutch neighbors. Imaginative learning has explained the phrase *Yankee Doodle* as derived from the Persian "*Yanghi Dunia*."[5] Still farther east fares the source hunter and finds the origin of *Yankee* in the Chinese phrase, "Yang jung," which in East Indian use was corrupted to "Yang Gee," which means 'you are a foreigner.' The theory advanced by a Chinaman is that this phrase "was first applied to New Englanders by English or Dutch sailors who had learned it in the Orient."[6]

Material illustrating this interesting form of pseudo-

---

[4] I. Taylor, *Words and Places,* p. 207.
[5] Elson, *The National Music of America,* p. 128.
[6] Newspaper story.

science is everywhere at hand. Anecdote and theory make up by their entertaining qualities what they lack in authenticity. Thus *poltroon* (Fr. *poltron*, Ital. *poltrone*, from *poltro*, meaning 'sluggard') is used to illustrate the antiquity of the methods employed by the modern 'slacker.' Fanciful learning derives the word from the Latin *pollice truncus*, 'one deprived of his thumb.'

Cootie, the new name for an ancient pest, until recently unrecorded in English dictionaries, standard or dialectal, provides the occasion for an uninteresting anecdote. A *poilu*, exhibiting one of the pests to an American soldier, used the French exclamation, *Ecoutez*, which was promptly misunderstood by the American as 'a cootie' and was adopted by him as a name for the unwelcome guest.

In harmony with the spirit of enterprise which characterizes the modern newspaper is the explanation that has been provided for the word *news*, as derived from the initial letters of the four words, *north, east, west, south*. Since, however, this explanation cannot apply to the French *nouvelles* and German *neuigkeiten*, which parallel the English *news* exactly, one is obliged, though with reluctance, to abandon it.

The search for an explanation of the convenient symbolic letters, O. K., has served as a stimulus to the humorous fancy. The symbols have been associated with the illiteracy which accompanied the rugged strength of Andrew Jackson. Another explanation is that the symbols originated in the 'hard cider' campaign of William Henry Harrison in 1840, when the farmers, desiring to express their true Whig qualities, floated a banner with the inscription, "The Farmers is oil Korrect." The initial letters were adopted as symbolic of crude honesty, and are said to have been placed over the door of the Sugar Grove House of Springfield, Ohio, by the proprietor, Dan Leffel, an ardent Whig.[7] This anecdote, in which lives the spirit of earlier American politics, admirably suits the character of the well-known symbols. Once again, however, science proves to be a joy dispeller. One has to abandon fiction for fact. The derivation recognized by the dictionaries for O. K., is from the word *okeh,* from the language of the Choctaw Indians and meaning 'It is so.' This explanation becomes officially sanctioned by the use of the signature "okeh W. W.," by a distinguished scholar who for eight years lived in the White House.

In the days not long before the war there emerged on human consciousness a mysterious word with powers of magic. This word, *jitney,* had the power to lead men to solicit the privilege of giving to the general public a motor car ride for the sum of five cents. Where did the word come from? A man of Scotch-American farmer extraction professed to be familiar with the use of the word by his father who came to Ohio in the early nineteenth century. A man in the grocery had heard of the word in Italy and felt sure of its Italian origin. A newspaper, however, says, "In Russia it used to signify a small coin corresponding to our nickel. The so-called jitney bus made its first appearance in Kansas City." Another authority, of equal weight with those quoted, derives *jitney* "from the corruption of a Japanese term for a small coin."

An old-time minstrel, the kind of a man qualified to give information on such subjects, gives to Louisiana the credit for the origin of the word. He derives *jitney* from the word *jetton,* a word anglicized from the French and meaning a small metal disc used in French gambling houses instead of checks. According to his anecdote, a minstrel troupe playing in Lake Providence, Louisiana, when it came to count up the receipts at the box office, found a quart or two of jettons of which negroes of the dis-

---

[7] Story told by Gen. J. W. Keifer.

trict had secured a supply at New Orleans or Baton Rouge, and which they called "jitneys." The word, according to this story, was taken up by members of the minstrel troupe and thus was started on its surprising career.

Still another story, not less circumstantial, derives the story from the name of "a trusty," named Jedney, who used to smuggle tobacco in to the prisoners at the penitentiary at Joliet, Illinois, and used to take a toll of half to pay for his risk. A colored boy who succeeded him in this humanitarian work continued his practice in the matter of taking toll, and from the pronunciation of Jedney in his expression, "You-all get a jitney's worth for dis here dime, 50-50," sprang the word *jitney,* meaning five cents.

The word *tip* is recorded in the dictionaries with a variety of meanings. Probably more than one word has fallen into the one sound mold. The word *tip* in the sense of 'a gratuity,' has been explained by the practice in old English inns of keeping in a conspicuous place a little box with the letters T-I-P, meaning 'to insure promptness.' This explanation is entirely too methodical to seem plausible to any one familiar with the capricious ways of words in colloquial language.

War-time mystery enveloped the armored device, the *tank,* which, developed from the American caterpillar tractor, played so conspicuous a part in the second half of the Great War, and war-time mystery was permitted to cling to the origin of the name. Popular imagination, however, did not fail in this case, and various explanations, more or less satisfactory, found their way into print. "Mr. Thomas Tank Burall," one learned, was the manager of a well-known firm of engineers in Norfolk, England. *Tank* was the maiden name of his mother, and "Tank" was the name applied to Mr. Burall by his friends. At the Royal Agricultural show at Derby in 1881, Messrs. Burrell (*sic*) the employers of Mr. Tank Burall, exhibited a "most novel engine," a ten-horsepower traction engine. Later Mr. Tank Burall conceived the idea of pattens for the wheels in order to overcome the difficulty of getting over plowed fields. The name *tank,* therefore, is eponymous, derived from the nickname of an English inventor.

But this explanation, satisfying to British complacency, was not alone in the field. Another journalistic account attributed the name to motorcycle drivers, from whose ranks the drivers for the new war machines were recruited. According to this explanation, motorcycle riders applied to their new vehicles the name *tanks* because of their striking resemblance to the tanks in their motorcycles.

Neither this lame explanation nor its rival contained anything offensive to the military censor, and both gained publicity. A more plausible story, however, is one which attributes the name to the gossips of the small English town where the new contrivances were built. The curiosity excited by the manufacture of the myterious new implement of war, was officially satisfied by the explanation offered, that a much needed new form of water tank was being provided for the fighting front. The name *tanks,* based on this conjecture, was satisfactory to the censor, and has become inseparably attached to the machine which it so little fits.

The word *humbug,* which made its appearance in the fashionable slang of the early eighteenth century, has of late been provided an anecdotic explanation which has found wide publicity in the American press. According to this account, the word is of Irish origin, from Irish *uimbog* (pronounced 'oombug') and meaning the soft, mixed metal that was used by James II in a base coin made at the Dublin mint. The worthlessness of this coin was such that it became synonymous with 'fraud' in such phrases as: "That's a piece of *uimbog,*" and *"Don't think to pass off your uimbog on me."*

The word *doughboy*, which, in a spirited competition, won a place for itself as the name for the American soldier in the World War, has stimulated the imagination of the amateur linguist. Its use has been traced back to the Civil War and has been explained as originating in the various shaped buttons provided for the overcoats of the troops. Because of the resemblance of these buttons to hard-tack, the soldiers became known as doughboys. Not without good reason, little content with this none too ingenious explanation, a recent writer has provided a rich variety of alternative explanations, wise and otherwise:

First. In olden times when infantrymen used to clean their white trimmings with pipe-clay, if caught in the rain the whiting would run, forming a kind of dough—hence the sobriquet 'doughboy.'

Second. The tramp of infantry marching in the mud sounds as if their shoes were being worked and pressed in 'dough.'

Third. From 'adobe' (mud) contracted 'dobie'—the idea being infantrymen are the soldiers who have to march in the mud; hence the expressions used in the early sixties and seventies in referring to infantrymen as 'dobie crushers,' 'dobie makers' and 'mud crushers.'

Fourth. However, some infantrymen think they are called 'doughboys' because they are always 'kneeded' (needed), while other old-time infantrymen think they are so called because they are the flower (flour) of the army.

Probably loyal infantrymen think this for the same reason that good artillerymen say they are called 'wagon soldiers' because they are the ones who 'always deliver the goods.' [8]

In America the word *crank* has come to be used with the meaning 'eccentric person' or 'person with one idea.' There is an interesting story regarding the origin of this use of the word. This story, which one would like to be able to believe, is that the use of the word originated in a famous saying of Donn Piatt regarding Horace Greeley, that he "is

---

[8] W. C. Hendrix, Knoxville *Journal and Tribune*.

like the crank of a hand-organ, continually grinding out the same old tunes."[9]

Journalistic story attributes the creation of *jazz* music to a blind newsboy of New Orleans. This boy, who endured existence under the unhappy name "Stale Bread," played the violin, and one day, under inspiration, divine or diabolic, found self-expression in a new kind of music to which the name *jazz* came to be applied. Another explanation, equally plausible, derives the word *jazz* from the name of an underworld negro, Jasbo Brown, whose manner of playing called forth excited cries of "jazz, Jasbo, jazz." Competing with these stories is the explanation of *jazz* as of African origin. This explanation has the support of learned opinion. Lafcadio Hearn reported the word *jaz* (*sic*) as common among the blacks of the South, with the meaning 'to speed things up,' 'to make excitement,' and adopted in Creole speech to mean a 'rudimentary syncopated type of music.' Does *jazz*, then, conduct one to the African jungle? In such matters even the learned are none too sure guides.

The adventurous amateur in the field of words is ever in danger of being tripped. There are obviously many pitfalls for the unwary. Along with the many words, however, concerning whose history there is so much uncertainty, there are hosts of words richly provided with romantic associations that are supported by authentic knowledge. The rewards of word study are like those of travel. Places visited by the traveler may be hallowed, or perhaps profaned, by memories of an historic past. In the same way many words, to one acquainted with their history, are rich in romantic memories of places and events, of peoples and personalities.

The name *dauphin* carries one back to the old province of *Viennois,* which later came to be called *le Dauphiné,*

---

[9] *Romance of Words,* Wheeler Syndicate.

'dauphiny,' from the surname of its lords who bore on their crest three dolphins in allusion to the origin of the name. The lordship of the province was ceded to the king on condition that his eldest son should always hold the title, *Dauphin of Viennois*, later shortened to *Dauphin*.

Less aristocratic is the origin of the name *jimson weed*, which is a popular corruption of *Jamestown weed*, which brings to memory the early settlement at Jamestown and the "weed said to have sprung upon heaps of ballast and other rubbish discharged from vessels."[10]

In *jingo* we have surviving a sailor's oath of the seventeenth century, supposed to be derived from a Basque name for God. The defiant meaning of the word has its origin in the use of the oath *by jingo* in a popular song which expressed the spirit of the Tory administration under Beaconsfield in the time of the Russo-Turkish war (1878).

The synonymous *chauvinist* is somewhat earlier in its origin. It made its first appearance in English about 1870, but had been in use in French for a considerable time. The word originated in the name of a French veteran soldier of the First Republic and Empire whose extreme patriotism was first celebrated and then ridiculed by his comrades. His name gained general fame through its use as the name of a braggadocio character in the popular vaudeville, *La Cocarde Tricoloré* (1830).

Somewhat different in character is the story which explains the origin of the phrase, *psychological moment*. This phrase, which is the English translation of the French *le moment psychologique,* conducts one back to the time of the Franco-Prussian War. The German war theorists of the time laid emphasis on *das psychologische Moment* (meaning 'momentum'), which must coöperate with the work of the artillery. This phrase the French made game of and adopted in mistranslation as a slang expression.

---

[10] Century Dictionary.

But it is words derived from proper names that are most alive with romantic interest. Names such as *Virginia, Louisiana,* and the *Philippine Islands,* derived from the names of persons, serve to link the present with glorious days in the colonial history, respectively, of England and France and Spain. Many common nouns are in this way linked with definite stories. *Stentorian, pandar, quixotic, mentor, boniface, lothario, maudlin,* and their kind, carry one back to old story, to old play, or to scriptural narrative. *Piazza* takes one to Covent Garden in London. *Palace* takes one to the Palatine hill in Rome, the site of the palace of Augustus. *Mausoleum* conducts one in memory to the famous tomb erected for Mausolus, King of Caria, and in the adjective *colossal* survives the memory of another of the Seven Wonders of the World, the Colossus at Rhodes. *Canter* introduces one to the company of the Canterbury Pilgrims. *Magenta* brings up the memory of the victory of the French over the Austrians in 1859. *Solecism* conducts one to Soli, a Cilician city associated, in the Athenian mind, with incorrect use of language. *Sardonic* conveys one to Sardinia, or rather to life among the Greeks who applied to a bitter laugh an adjective derived from the name of a Sardinian plant which had the property of distorting the face of the eater. *Lumber* is connected with memories of the Lombard bankers, whose rooms were crowded with disused articles serving as pledges for loans. Hence the name *lumber room* and the use of *lumber* in its meaning of 'useless furniture,' destined later, in American speech, to take on the meaning of 'sawed timber.' *Spruce,* a word of which an earlier form was *pruce,* takes one back to the time when the name *Prussia* was associated with elegance of dress rather than with militarism.

Various peoples and places have lent their names to qualities associated with them. The chaste elegance of the Athenian is expressed by the adjective *attic,* from the name of the province of which Athens is the chief city. The reputed dullness of the inhabitants of Bœotia has given rise to the use of *bœotian* as a synonym for 'stupid.' The simple life of Arcadia gives rise to the phrase *arcadian* simplicity. The sternness once associated with the Spartan is still expressed by the adjective *spartan;* his brevity in speech explains the origin of the expression, *laconic* brevity, from the name of the country, Laconia, which he inhabited. The traditional qualities of Trojan and Turk are held in memory by modern nouns. The savageness of the Hun is commemorated in the adjective *hunnish.* The kind heart of one Samaritan has forever associated the name of his race with charitable deed. The word *bugger,* which goes back to an earlier meaning of 'heretic,' recalls the earlier reputation of the Bulgarians for heresy, and the later development in meaning of the word reveals the detestation in which heresy was held in former times. The word *frank* goes back to an earlier meaning, 'free,' and is derived from the name of the Teutonic tribe, the Franks, the 'free' people. A picture different in kind is brought up by the word *slave,* which brings to memory the captive Slavs of Byzantine days. *Gothic,* from the name of the well-known Teutonic people, was formerly used as a synonym for 'barbarian.' In this sense, in the days of the prevalence of taste for the classical, the word was applied as an adjective to non-classical forms of architecture. With the rise in appreciation for medieval forms of architecture, the name *gothic,* which applied to it, has taken on new dignity. The habits of the Assassins, a tribe in Asia Minor in medieval times, has caused their name to be indissolubly linked with the idea of murder. In the same way the word *thug* perpetuates the reputation of the Thugs, a religious organization of India suppressed as late as 1835. The race of Tartars will ever find it hard to live down the reputation of their ancestors that survives in the use of their name as a synonym for 'cruel.' The noun *gasconade* serves to proclaim the boastful propensities proverbially attributed to the Gascon.

More personal are the memories associated with many words. The word *grog*, for instance, is a monument to the memory of the English Admiral Vernon of the eighteenth century. He was nicknamed "Old Grog," from his grogram breeches, and his nickname was transferred to the form of rum mixture which he was the first to dispense in the British navy. The gambling tastes of an Earl of Sandwich and his reluctance to leave the gaming table are kept alive to memory in the name applied to his form of quick lunch, the *sandwich*. A London hangman named Derrick, of about 1600, had the honor of having his name bestowed on the structure associated with his occupation. The grim humor in the transfer of the name to other meanings is readily apparent. The word *guy*, already discussed in an earlier chapter, carries one back to the seventeenth century and the panicky state of mind in the times of the Gunpowder Plot.

The irony of fate appears in the history of the word *dunce*. This word is derived from the name of one of the greatest intellects of the late Middle Ages in England, John Duns Scotus, who died in 1308. The followers of this schoolman bore the name *Scotists* down to the sixteenth century, when in the new age of the Renaissance, the contempt for the older modes of thought found expression in the names, *Dunsemen, Dunses*, applied to the older order. The transfer of the word to the general meaning of 'stupid person,' cited first in 1579, further exemplifies the generalizing process illustrated in the history of *guy*.

Namby-pamby commemorates the ridicule lavished by Pope and some of his contemporaries on the pastoral poet, Ambrose Philips.

Pasquinade as a general name for lampoon has its origin

in the name of an old statue, *Pasquino,* set up in 1501, and still standing in the Piazza Navonna in Rome. This statue at one time served as a place for displaying satirical posters. The statue itself is said to have taken its name from Pasquino, a tailor, or cobbler, or barber (accounts differ) of the fifteenth century, famed for his satirical powers.

The name of the early English saint, Ethelreda, in popular language became contracted to *St. Audrey,* and a popular fair held in her honor was called *St. Audrey's Fair.* The reputation of the character of goods sold at St. Audrey's Fair is kept in memory through the adjective *tawdry,* which is a contraction of *St. Audrey.*

The word *blue-stocking* calls to mind the intellectual coteries of other days, the social assemblies of the middle eighteenth century held at the houses of Mrs. Montague and others of her kind, where literary conversation was substituted for cards and gossip. The guests at these assemblies affected plainness of dress. From the blue-stockings of one of them, Mr. Benjamin Stillingfleet, was derived the term which was derisively applied to members of the social set, an earlier term for the modern 'high brow.' [11]

The memory of Sir Robert Peel survives in two common nouns. The Irish *peeler,* for police, goes back to the name for the force of Irish police established by him when secretary for Ireland (1812-18). The epithet *bobby,* bestowed on the London policeman, has its origin in the first name of Sir Robert, who, while Home Secretary (1828-30), improved the police system of London.

In many instances a type of weapon serves to commemorate an inventor whose name it bears. The *bowie knife,* which takes its name from the name of its inventor, Colonel James Bowie, a native of Kentucky, who died in 1836, is

---

[11] *Century Dictionary.*

alive with associations of days when law was not all supreme. *Gatling* and *shrapnel* and *maxim* are words derived from names of military inventors. *Big Bertha,* which war slang derived from the name of Bertha Krupp as the name for a cannon of large caliber, finds an interesting parallel in the history of the word *gun* itself which, according to one explanation, is derived in similar fashion from the Norse proper name *Gunnhildr,* first cited as the name for an 'instrument for propelling missiles' in 1339.[12]

Story material of this kind it would not be easy to exhaust. From the earliest times to the most recent we have instances of words associated with concrete individual and concrete act. From the costly victories of the Greek Pyrrhus comes the adjective *pyrrhic* in 'pyrrhic victory.' From the strategy of delay employed by the Roman Fabius against Hannibal we get *fabian* policy. From the name of Samuel Maverick, a Texas cattle ranger, and his habit of not branding his cattle, we have the word *maverick* applied to a variety of meanings, to an unbranded animal, and then, by abrupt transition not unusual in colloquial speech, to anything dishonestly obtained, or, used as a verb, to the meaning 'to seize dishonestly.'

Far-fetched, indeed, seem the meanings that have in many instances been derived from simple incident or from individual proper name. This romantic element in the history of words lends itself readily to burlesque. Let us, then, conclude the consideration of this subject with an admirable newspaper parody which gives the history of the word *viaduct*. "Once upon a time a girl named Sylvia, who was called Via for short, was riding on a load of hay, and when an overhead railroad bridge was approached, *Via ducked.*"

---

[12] But see article on this subject by T. A. Jenkins, *Modern Philology*, April, 1915.

REFERENCES FOR FURTHER READING

E. WEEKLEY, *The Romance of Words* (London, 1913).
GREENOUGH and KITTREDGE, *Words and their Ways in English Speech,* particularly Chapter xxvi.
R. C. TRENCH, *The Study of Words.*

CHAPTER XXIV

PLACE-NAMES

Many words, it is evident, have a romantic interest owing to their association with the names of particular places or particular persons. These proper names, in their turn, have their own interest, and in this, also, there enters the element of romance. Names such as *Yosemite* and *Himalayas* appeal to one through sheer beauty of sound. To euphony, however, is joined romance in the appeal of many names; the romance of simple sentiment in *Loch Lomond* and *Killarney,* that of sacred story in *Nazareth* and *Bethlehem,* that of idealized existence in *Avalon* and the *Hesperides,* that of remoteness and mystery in *Samarcand* and *Timbuctoo.* Places more near at hand are not lacking in this kind of appeal. Who is there that has not his *Carcassonne* that he vainly longs to see? Who is there that has not felt allurement even in the prosaic names sonorously proclaimed by a train announcer? Who has not felt the desire to promenade on the *Nevski Prospekt* (at least in earlier, happier days) on *Piccadilly* or the *Corso,* on *Unter den Linden* or the *Champs Elysées?*

Strangely fascinating are place-names, not only by their euphony, but by their romantic associations. But besides this special appeal which belongs to them, place-names have the kind of interest that attaches to other words; they introduce one to interesting features of history and exhibit interesting sides of human nature.

The study of English place-names has lagged far behind that of other elements in the English vocabulary. Indeed, the scientific study in this direction may be said to have begun only about twenty years ago. The twentieth century is now trying to make up for the neglect of earlier periods and to put at last on a scientific basis the study of place-names so long left the subject for fanciful conjecture and romantic theory.[1]

The tardiness in the study of place-names is in great part due to the special difficulty of the subject. Place-names offer the student greater difficulty than any other class of words, owing in great part to the fact that, more than most words, they have been subjected to the wear, and at times to the mutilation, that goes with use in popular speech. Like coins long in circulation, they have often lost their original markings. Let us take for illustration the name *York*. The ancient British name was *Eburācon*, probably from the name of a man, *Eburos*. On the tongues of the Teutonic Angles this British name became modified to *Evurōc*, which in turn underwent further modification, quite usual with the Angles, by losing its final syllable and taking on as an ending the Anglian word *wīc*. In this way the name came to the form *Eoforwic*, which seemed to mean 'Boar Town' (*eofor*, 'boar' + *wīc*, 'dwelling place'). Under Danish rule the name acquired a new pronunciation, indicated by the spelling *Iorvik*, which has later become contracted to the modern *York*.[2] Transformation like that in the case of *York* may be observed in the case of many names whose origin goes back to antiquity. The name of the German city *Mainz* is far removed from the earlier Latin form *Mogontiacum*, that of *Laon* from the earlier *Laudunum*. Even names of comparatively recent origin have often undergone striking change, particularly when adopted into the use of people speaking a different language. Thus the name *Chateau Vert*, meaning 'Green Castle,' given by the Anglo-Normans to an English place near Oxford, in

---

[1] A. Mawer, *English Place-Name Study* (London, 1921).
[2] H. Bradley, *English Place-Names, Essays and Studies by Members of the English Association*, Vol. I (Oxford, 1910).

English speech became transformed to *Shotover*. Numerous other instances of changes of this kind in the way of folk-etymology are to be met with in the case of the English transformation of French place-names in America dealt with later in this chapter.

A striking feature in place-names, especially in the names of physical features, is their permanency. The names often seem as imperishable as the lakes and mountains that they designate. In such names as *Skiddaw* and *Helvellyn*, *Thames* and *Clyde*, there is a seeming inevitableness, an absolute quality, such that it is hard to conceive of them as other than eternal. The superlative phrase 'old as the hills' seems often to apply. Indeed the drums and tramplings of three conquests have failed in most cases to dislodge the Celtic place-names from British mountains, lakes, and streams. The Celtic word which survives in Welsh *Bryn*, 'brow' or 'ridge,' if we may believe an old authority,[3] forms an important element in such names as *Brandon, Brendon, Birnwood, Braintree, Brinton,* and *Brancaster*. The Celtic *pen*, in modern Welsh meaning 'head,' transferred to mean 'mountain,' appears in such names as *Pen, Penhill, Inkpen, Pendleton, Penshurst, Penrith, Pendennis, Pembroke, Pentland,* and in its Gaelic form, *ben*, in the Highland names *Bennevis, Benlomond, Benmore*.

Throughout England there is hardly a river name that is not Celtic.[4] The Celtic *avon* 'river,' appears in the name of streams not only in Great Britain, but in France and Italy, preserving the memory of the earlier Celtic occupation of Central Europe. In England *Avon* is the name of several streams, including, besides the one flowing through Stratford, one in Gloucestershire, two in Hampshire, and others in Devon, Monmouth, and various districts of Scot-

---

[3] I. Taylor, *Words and Places*, pp. 146, 147.
[4] *Ibid.*, p. 130.

land. The Celtic *stour*, also, is the name applied to important rivers in Kent, Suffolk, Dorset, Warwickshire, and Worcestershire.[5] The Celtic word *uisge*, 'water,' which in anglicized form becomes *whisky*, also appears as the name for various streams. In the form *Esk* it applies to streams in Donegal, Devon, Yorkshire, Cumberland, Dumfries, two in Forfarshire, and two in Edinburghshire.[6]

Whatever may have become of the earlier Celtic inhabitants of Britain and continental Europe, the sites of their earlier fortified strongholds may be traced by the old names that still cling to them. The name *dun*, 'fortress,' may be found in places as far apart as *Carrodunum* on the Dneister and *Singidunum*, an old name for Belgrade, to *Dundalk*, *Dungannon*, etc., in Ireland. The duration of the Celtic occupation of France is attested by the numerous French place-names in which *dun* entered as an element, such as *Autun* (Augustodunum), *Laon* (Laudunum), *Lyons* (Lugdunum), *Verdun* (Verodunum). In Great Britain it appears not only in the Scotch *Dumfries*, *Dunkeld*, *Dumbarton*, *Dundee*, etc., but in English *Dunstable* and *Dunmow*.

As further evidence of the persistent quality of local names may be cited the numerous instances where the names have outlived the physical conditions that explain their origin. *Sandwich* 'sandy bay,' is now a mile and a half distant from high water mark, and *Stourmouth* is now four miles from the sea.[7] Concerning the earlier wooded character of the land, there survive mute witnesses in the numerous names, in which older forest terms such as *holt*, 'wood'; *weald*, 'forest'; *hurst*, 'grove,' and *den*, 'wooded valley,' enter as elements. Such names as *Bagshot* (hold), *Aldershot*, *Cotswold*, *Billingshurst*, *Penshurst*, *Arden*, are little more appropriate to modern conditions than are

---
[5] Taylor, pp. 132-134.
[6] *Ibid.*, p. 135.
[7] *Ibid.*, p. 236.

Primrose Hill to a residential section of London adjoining Regents Park, or *Shepherd's Bush* to a busy tramway terminal in West London.

While the physical features of a country are enduring and the mountains and lakes and streams hold fast to their earlier names, the human element in geography is subject to change. In consequence, in the names of inhabited places there does not appear the same degree of permanency. At the same time even temporary occupation of a country rarely fails to leave its record in place-names, so that the place-names often serve as monuments to the memory of the works and ways of a country's successive inhabitants. *London* and *Dover* are among the few names of towns that have come down without important change from the days of Celtic Britain.[8] *London* (anciently *Londinion*, Lat. *Londinium*), except for the loss of its ending, retains approximately the pronunciation which it had in the days when Cæsar first landed on the coast of Britain. There are, however, many place-names in which Celtic elements survive. The name of the Celtic god, *Lugus* (Irish *Lugh*), for instance, appears in the second element of *Carlisle*, contracted from earlier *Luguvalium*, to which has been prefixed the word *caer*, meaning 'city' or 'fortress.'

The nature of the Roman occupation of Britain is reflected in the nature of the place-names left behind by them. The sites of Roman military camps, *castra*, formed the sites of well-known cities, as indicated by the appearance of the word *castra*, in one of three modified forms, as the ending in such place-names as *Lancaster, Doncaster, Chester, Winchester, Leicester,* and *Worcester.* The Roman custom of constructing paved military roads in the provinces finds its record in the surviving names *Watling Street* and *Ermin Street,* and in such place names as *Stratford, Stratton, Stretton, Streatham, Stretford, Strealty,* in all

---

[8] Bradley, p. 19.

of which appears the element *street,* from Latin *strata via,* 'paved way.' The military walls, a feature of the Roman occupation of Britain, like the Roman paved ways, have left their traces not only in massive remains, but in a series of names of places in one way or another related to the walls, such as *Wallsend, Walbottle, Welton, Walltown, Thirlwall, Wallby.*

The Romans did not make a practice of inventing Latin names for inhabited places. Where a British name was not already provided, they seem to have followed the custom of adopting the name of a neighboring river. Examples of such names are: *Danum,* from the name of the river *Don,* from which has been formed modern *Doncaster* by the addition of the suffix *-caster; Deva* (now Chester), from the river *Dee;* and *Isca,* from the river *Exe,* from which is derived modern *Exeter* by the addition of the suffix *-caster.*[9]

The practice of the Angles and Saxons seems to have been often like that of the Romans. They frequently retained the older names. But they usually adapted the older words by the addition of a new element to the name, either *burh* (dative *byrig*), which in their language originally meant 'fortified place,' or '*wīc,* which meant 'dwelling place,' or more frequently *ceaster,* which they had borrowed from the Latin (*castra,* 'camp' or 'fortified place'). In this way were created such names as *Wintanceaster* (Winchester), *Eoforwicceaster* (York), *Exanceaster* (Exeter).

But in many instances new settlements were made by the Angles and Saxons, and there was not at hand a traditional name. In such cases they did not resort to sheer creation, but used the name of some conspicuous feature of the vicinity. Thus *Oxford* took its name from a neighboring ford for oxen (*oxena* + *ford*), while not far distant *Swinford* took its name from a ford for swine. Neighboring rivers also gave names to inhabited places, as in the case

---

[9] Bradley, p. 23.

of *Petherton* (older *Pedrida-tūn,* from *Pedrida,* an older form of the name of the *Parret* river) and *Cheltenham* and *Charwelton,* respectively, from *Chelt* and *Cherwell,* the names of streams, on whose banks the towns stand. Local agricultural interests provide place-names, as in the case of *Linacre* (O. E. *līn* + *æcer,* 'flax-field'), *Waddon* (O. E. *hwætedūn,* 'wheat down'), *Swinton* (O. E. *swīn,* 'swine'), *Shipley* and *Shipton* (O. E. *scēap,* 'sheep').[10] Local landmarks also provided names. *Oswestry* seems to be derived from a tree planted by Oswald or in memory of him. *Folkstone* (O. E. *Folcan stān*) takes its name from a stone probably erected in memory of *Folca*.[11] Local superstition explains *Dwaraden,* which comes from the Old English *dweorga denu,* 'valleys of the dwarfs.'[12]

But most frequently Anglo-Saxon place-names are derived from the names of persons. *Brighton* comes from earlier *Brihthelmestun,* meaning 'farmstead of Brihthelm.' The way place-names of this sort originate may be observed in the way in which American railroad stations often take their names from the names of nearby farmer or miller or keeper of supply store, and later form the centers about which grow up towns, which keep the names of the stations. The common use of personal names as sources for English place-names is illustrated by the frequency of the use of the syllable *-ing*. This ending, according to Canon Taylor,[13] enters as ending or medial element in the composition of the names of "more than one-tenth of the whole number of English villages and hamlets." This element, *-ing,* is in origin the regular patronymic suffix in Anglo-Saxon. For example, the *Scyldings* and the *Scylfings* in the *Beowulf,* are the descendants respectively of Scyld and Scylf. The prevalence, therefore, of this element in English

---

[10] Bradley, pp. 30, 32.
[11] *Ibid.,* p. 31.
[12] *Ibid,* p. 30.
[13] *Ibid.,* p. 82.

place-names indicates the origin of English villages and towns in family or tribal settlements. A conspicuous example of the kind of name under discussion is *Buckingham,* which by the addition of the suffixes, *-ing* and *-ham,* is derived from the personal name *Bucca.*[14]

Still another wave of migration into England is held in memory by place-names. The Norsemen, who for several centuries infested the coast districts of western Europe and who in the ninth and tenth centuries effected permanent settlements in England, Scotland, Ireland, and France, permanently blazed their trails of migration by the place-names left behind. Characteristic Scandinavian personal names, such as *Grim, Biörn, Harold,* and *Thor* appear in such place-names as *Grimsby, Harroby, Burnthwaite* and *Thoresby.*[15] The Norse origin of place-names is revealed also by the characteristic endings, *-by,* and *-thwaite,* and *beck,* and *dale,* in such names as *Ormsby, Whitby, Hacconby,* and *Hallthwaite, Finsthwaite,* etc. The ending *-thorp,* also, while common to native English and Scandinavian names, is more frequent in Scandinavian forms. With its variant forms, *-thorp* and *-trop,* it appears in such names as *Althorpe* and *Wilstrop.*[16]

The extent of Scandinavian immigration in various parts of Great Britain is fairly well registered by the character of the place-names. In Lincolnshire, for instance, a Norse center, there are about three hundred place-names bearing a Scandinavian mark, while to the south, in Buckingham, Bedford, and Warwick, little penetrated by Norse colonists, the Scandinavian names are only a scattering few.[17]

By the time of the Norman Conquest, the map of England was fairly well provided with names. Hence the Norman

---

[14] Bradley, p. 27.
[15] Taylor, *op. cit.,* p. 123.
[16] *Ibid.,* p. 105; Jespersen, *Growth and Structure,* p. 62 and Ch. vii.
[17] *Ibid.,* p. 200.

influence on place-names was relatively slight. The most striking change brought through the Normans consisted in the transformation of older names through their adaptation to a Norman pronunciation. The Old English *Searobyrig*, created in customary Anglo-Saxon fashion by shortening the British name *Soriviodūnon* and adding the ending, *-byrig*, in Norman speech became *Salisbury*. To the same influence must be attributed the form *Exeter* instead of *Exchester* and the shortened pronunciation of such names as *Leicester*, *Worcester*, and *Gloucester*.

The number of new names of Norman origin is comparatively small. There are a number of names given by them to newly established monasteries, such as *Beauvale*, *Beaulieu*, *Belvoir*, and *Beauchief*, which exhibit a new principle in nomenclature, that of expressing beauty of situation, and *Jorvaulx*, *Rievaulx*, and *Grosmont*. Other Norman names are *Pomfret*, *Grampound*, and *Richmond*.[18]

Let us now turn our attention to the place-names of North America. These names have been variously judged. They have been spoken of as "poetical, humorous and picturesque,"[19] and as "an incongruous medley of names, for the most part utterly inappropriate."[20] There are facts to support each of these characterizations. In any case, one who will take the time may find much that is diverting, as well as much that is solidly instructive, in an examination of a list of the place-names in the United States.

In the history of the place-names of the United States are repeated many of the features in the history of British place-names. The Teutonic conquerors of Britain made free use of the names already attached to the physical features of the country, and from these names also formed

---

[18] Bradley, *op. cit.*, pp. 38-40.
[19] R. L. Stevenson, quoted by Mencken.
[20] Taylor, *op. cit.*, p. 313.

names for families and for towns. In the same way European occupants of the United States found ready for their use native Indian names, which were not only retained in their original use as names for mountains and lakes and rivers, but were applied to new uses as names of cities and states. Indian names apply not only to four of the five Great Lakes, to the greatest river and most of its tributaries, and to the great mountain system of the East, but to twenty-five of the states and to many of the largest towns, including the one second in size. The distinctive value of these names is universally conceded. In æsthetic quality they range from the attractively ugly in *Massachusetts* and *Connecticut,* and the grotesque in *Canojoharie, Kalamazoo, Ypsilanti,* and *Skaneateles,* to the liquid beauty of *Minnesota, Ontario,* and *Wyoming.*

As in the case of Great Britain, the place-names serve as an index to much of the history of the settlement of the country. The kings and queens of England, from Elizabeth to George II, are honored in American colonial names from Virginia to Georgia. Names of English princes survive in *Cape Charles* and *Cape Henry,* of English queens in *Cape Ann* and *Maryland,* of English statesmen in *Halifax* and *Bolingbroke,* of English colonizers in *Raleigh, Baltimore, Delaware,* and *Pennsylvania.* Dutch names, such as *Hoboken, Brooklyn, Rhode Island, Schuylkill, Catskills, Yonkers,* and *Spuyten Duyvil,* tell a story of colonization from Holland. Names of French origin, such as *Cape Breton, Quebec, Montreal, Vermont, Champlain, Detroit, Sault Ste. Marie, Marquette, Fond du Lac, Joliet, La Salle, Terre Haute, Duquesne, St. Louis, Baton Rouge, Mobile,* and *New Orleans,* serve to mark the course of French colonizing activities. In the same way the Spanish part in American colonization is mapped out by place names: *Florida* (from *Pascua Florida,* Spanish for Easter, because discovered on Easter Sunday), *San Antonio, El Paso, Albuquerque, Santa Fe, Colorado,*

Pueblo, San Diego, Los Angeles, San Francisco, Oregon, Nevada, Montana. Less conspicuous, but by no means rare, are the names from other languages, such as the German *Muhlenberg* and *Rohrsburg* in Pennsylvania, *Schwartzburg, Naugart,* and *New Coeln* in Wisconsin, *Kassel* in North Dakota, and the Scandinavian *Alstad* (Wisconsin), *Flom, Upsala, Ibsen, Tegner* and *St. Olaf* in Minnesota, *Tagstad* and *Skjold* in South Dakota, and *Svea* in both North Dakota and Minnesota.

The task of the name-makers in America differed from that of their ancestors in Europe in that there existed a rich supply of European names to draw from. American lack of originality in name-giving has sometimes been criticized. Certain it is that free use has been made of the older ready-made store. More than six hundred American post-offices bear names with the prefix *New*. Old world names reappear with endless repetition. *London* appears in 11 states, *Paris* in 21, and *Berlin* (before the war) in 24. The names of many minor towns in Europe have American duplicates almost as numerous. *Bremen* appears in 8 states, *Genoa* in 14, *Florence* in 34, *Zurich* in 3, *Geneva* in 19, *Rotterdam* in 2, *Antwerp* in 2, *Amsterdam* in 4, *Harlem* in 7, *Hamburg* in 19, *Dresden* in 7, *Moscow* in 23. Even the Orient has been resorted to. *Cairo* appears in 12 states, *Calcutta* in 1, *Bombay* in 3, *Delhi* in 12, *Tokio* in 1, *Shanghai* in 1, *Pekin* in 7.

Antiquity has yielded a greater number of names, at least in proportion, than modern geography. *Babylon* appears in 1 state, *Nineveh* in 3, *Sparta* in 19, *Thebes* in 2, *Corinth* in 13, *Alexandria* in 13, *Athens* in 22, *New Athens* in 2, *Ravenna* in 5, *Rome* in 16, *Troy* in 29. Classical learning, or at least aspiration in that direction, is indicated by the name *Alpha* in 18 states; unfinished beginnings appear to be indicated by the smaller number of states (11) in which *Omega* appears.

PLACE-NAMES 369

Biblical lore is particularly in evidence in American nomenclature. The prominent names of Palestine are represented literally from *Dan* (Kentucky) to *Beersheba Springs*, Tennessee. The list includes *Bethel* (22 states), *Bethlehem* (12 states), *Bethany* (15 states), *Bethpage* (3 states), *Beulah* (17 states). The range of sentiment involved extends from *Paradise*, in 13 states, to *Hell Creek* in Colorado, from *Zion City*, in 14 states, to *Gahanna*, Ohio.

In the formation of new names for American places honor has been paid to the great personal names of all times and places. Biblical heroes are commemorated from *Aaron* in 4 states to *Zachary*, in Louisiana; classical heroes from *Achilles* (2 states) to *Zeno* (2 states). The names of poets are cherished. *Burns* appears in 11 states, *Addison* in 14, *Goethe* in 1, *Ibsen* in 1, *Hugo* in 3, *Racine* in 7. Statesmen, like Pitt and Gladstone and Bismarck, are widely honored, and military heroes from *Alexander* (14 states, not including the use of *Alexandria*) and *Hannibal* (4 states), to *Napoleon* (7 states) and *Wellington* (14 states). In fact hardly a hero of history or romance or mythology has been neglected. *Jupiter* appears in 3 states, *Juno* in 5, *Thor* in 1, *Woden* in 2. *Dido* is remembered in 3 states, *Lancelot* in 1, *Romeo* in 4, *Juliet* in 1, *Juliette* in 2.

American place-names have a further interest as affording an exhibition of American ideals and American sentiment. Not only has the Old World stock of names been freely drawn on, but new names have been applied, names which serve to express qualities esteemed or conditions aspired to. It is not surprising to find love of liberty registered in the use of *Liberty* as a place-name in 36 different states, *Independence* (26 states). Similar ideals are expressed in *Freedom* (11 states), *Freeman* (13 states), *Equality* (3 states), *Unitia* (2 states), *Amity* (12 states), *Union* (38 states). Energy and ambition are expressed by *Energy* (2 states), *Enterprise* (24 states), *Excel* (1 state),

Speed (4 states), *Excelsior* (11 states), *Money* (11 states), *Money Creek* (1 state), *Dollar* (2 states), *Backbone* (2 states), *Young Blood* (Alabama), *Young America* (2 states). Peace and concord find expression in *Philadelphia* (7 states), *Philanthropy* (1 state), *Fidelity* (2 states), *Concord* (28 states), *Peace* (6 states), *Fellowship* (2 states), *Harmony* (16 states). Homely sentiment finds expression not only in such abstract names as *Comfort* (5 states), *Felicity* (2 states), *Good Luck* (1 state), *Friendship* (12 states), *Lonely* (25 states), *Happy* (Texas), *Lonesome* (2 states), *Yellow Bud* (Ohio), *Friendly* (W. Va.), but in concrete names like *Goodnight* (2 states), *Bewelcome* (1 state), *Sweet Home* (3 states), *Twilight* (1 state), *Pleasant Valley* (W. Va.), *Sunshine* (7 states), *Sunnyside* (14 states), *Survive* (6 states), *Sunset* (9 states), *Morning Sun* (2 states). The Christian graces find expression in *Faith* (3 states), *Hope* (18 states), *Charity* (3 states), *Love* (3 states). It is reassuring to know that the seven deadly sins are represented only by *Pride* (2 states), unless *Ira* (4 states) is to be interpreted as 'wrath.'

Perhaps to be associated with sentiment in name-giving is the fondness for feminine names for places. Hardly a common feminine name is neglected from *Ada* (17 states) to *Zenobia Peak*, Colorado. The list includes 2 *Nellies*, 1 *Nell*, 1 *Maggie*, 7 *Alices*, 4 *Annas*, 9 *Mauds*, 3 *Libbys*, 5 *Evas*, 5 *Luellas*, 3 *Lucilles*, 8 *Ednas*, 8 *Ediths*, 9 *Ethels*, 4 *Amys*, 1 *Mary*, 1 *Sallie*, 2 *Sarahs*, 11 *Coras*, 7 *Emmas*, 1 *Emmalene*, and 1 *Emmalena*.

But the nomenclature is not dominated exclusively by virtue and sentiment and desire for euphony. The spirit of realism is alive in such names as *Bad Lands, Barren Forks, Bald Eagle, Bay Horse, Beehive, Beef Creek, Greasyridge, Flat* (2 states) *Yelk* (W. Va.), *Yell* (Texas), *Hard Times Landing*, and their like. The censorship of a fastidious geographical board is probably responsible for the disappearance of such boldly frank names as *Henpeck City* and *Louse Village* in California, as well as for many of the names such as *One Horse Gulch, Poker Flat, Greaser Cañon, Murderer's Bar, Fiddletown,* and *Dead Broke,* which appear in the writings of Bret Harte. A remarkable progress in culture, or at least aspiration for culture, is recorded in the change of the name of a Kansas village from *Wild Cat* to *Keats.* The change in sound is not great, but that in sentiment is fundamental. The same influences that have tamed the *Wild Cat* to *Keats,* and changed *Paddy's Run,* Ohio, to *Glendower,* have penetrated most of American nomenclature. But the careless humor and masculine quality of pioneer life still crops out here and there in such names as *Whynot* (3 states), *Jeff* (Alabama), *Fred* (Kansas), *Josh* (Georgia), *Baby Basket* (California), *Jamboree* (Kentucky), *Jingo* (Tennessee), *Zero* (Iowa), *Enigma* (Georgia), *Disputanta* (2 states), and *Hell Creek* (Colorado).

Lack of variety has often been urged in criticism of American place-names. Certain it is that not only do the European names *Berlin, Cambridge, Belmont, Burlington,* and their kind, appear in endless repetition, but words more distinctively American lose their distinctiveness through constant iteration. Not only do *Washingtons* and *Franklins* and *Jacksons* appear in wearisome numbers, but a name such as *Brooklyn* (a modification of Dutch *Breukelen*) is worn out by adoption in 21 states outside New York. The effectiveness of *Buffalo,* admirably American in quality, is spoiled by its application including compounds, in about 75 different places. Compounds with *Elk-, Bald-, Maple-, Beech-, Oak-, Red-,* and the like are open to similar objection. In many instances inventive power seems to have been entirely lacking. *Disputanta* is said to owe its name to lack of agreement on a name, and in a number of instances settlements have been named like streets by the use of numerals, as in the case of *Seven* (Tennessee), *Fourteen* (West Virginia), *Seventeen* (Ohio), *Seventy-six* (Kentucky and Maryland), *Ninety-six* (South Carolina).

There remains a word to be said about English names for foreign places and the Anglicizing of foreign names. For most foreign countries of prominence the English language has its distinctive name; *Italy* for *Italia*, *Spain* for *España*, *Holland* for *Nederlanden*, *Germany* for *Deutschland*, *Denmark* for *Danmark*, *Bavaria* for *Baiern*, *Prussia* for *Preussen*, *Saxony* for *Sachsen*, *Belgium* for *La Belgique*, *Norway* for *Norge*, *Sweden* for *Sverige*. The same is true of names for foreign cities. English has *Milan* for *Milano*, *Venice* for *Venezia*, *Florence* for *Firenzi*, *Leghorn* for *Livorno*, *Rome* for *Roma*, *Naples* for *Napoli*, *Waterloo* for *Vaterlo*, *Copenhagen* for *Köbenhavn*, *Vienna* for *Wien*, *Munich* for *München*, *Leipsic* for *Leipzig*, *Prague* for German *Prag*, Bohemian *Praha*, *Brunswick* for *Braunschweig*, *Cologne* for *Köln*, *Brussels* for *Bruxelles*, *Antwerp* for *Anvers*. In names like *Hamburg* and *Paris*, where the English and native modes of spelling coincide, the English pronunciation prevails. In the case of *Berlin*, however, the English pronunciation is mongrel, neither English *Bérlin* nor German *Bare-léen*, and in the case of minor towns like *Ypres*, *Rheims*, *Rouen*, *Calais*, *Havre*, English usage vacillates in an embarrassing manner. Logical consistency would justify the frank anglicization of all foreign names, that is to say, when the foreign spelling is kept, giving to the letters that make up the word, an English pronunciation. This practice is supported by French use and is one actually in English use in the pronunciation of the name *Paris*.

In the pronunciation of the foreign names which have been adopted into American nomenclature, there has been a similarly confusing vacillation in practice. In general

PLACE-NAMES 373

there has prevailed the disposition to anglicize or Americanize. *Harlem, Staten, Nassau, Hoboken*, of Dutch extraction, are thoroughly English, or American, in pronunciation. In other cases the Dutch name has been modified so as to fit into an English word mold, as in the case of *Breukelen* (Brooklyn), *Walle Bobht* (Wallabout), *Helle Gat* (Hell Gate), *De Kromme Zee*, 'crooked lake' (Grammercy), *Bouwerij* (Bowery).[21]

Spanish names have, in general, been easily assimilated. This is due in great part to the phonetic character of Spanish spelling. *Florida, Colorado, El Paso, Sacramento, San Francisco*, etc., lend themselves easily to American use. Spanish qualities, however, appear occasionally, as in the pronunciation of the *e* in *Santa Fe* and *San Diego*, the *i* of *Rio Grande*, the *n* of *Cañon*, the *J* in *La Junta* ('Hunta'), *La Jolla* ('Hoya'), *San Jose* ('Hosay'), etc.

French names, on the other hand, have proved an unending source of confusion and embarrassment. In eastern Canada, in the province of Nova Scotia, not only were the earlier French colonists transplanted, but the earlier French names have, for the most part, either gone out of use, or have been replaced, as in the case of *Port Royal* succeeded by *Annapolis* and *Acadia* by *Nova Scotia*. Farther west, in Canada and in the United States, the French names have shown remarkable vitality, from *Montreal* to *Mobile*, but they have undergone remarkable changes in their new environment. Most of them are now mongrel words, retaining generally a French spelling but practically never retaining a purely French pronunciation. *Quebec* is English in its first syllable, but French in its accentuation. *Des Moines* has a French silent *s* in *Des* and a French accentuation. The anglicization of *Montreal* extends only through the first two syllables. *Champlain*, on the other hand, has a French pronunciation of the initial consonant

---

[21] Mencken, p. 290.

and a French accentuation, combined with English vowel sounds. In *Baton Rouge* the first word has been anglicized, the second remains pure French. *Detroit, La Salle, Vermont, Joliet, Versailles, Terre Haute,* retain little French quality except in accentuation.

Embarrassment often arises from uncertainty on account of divided usage in the pronunciation of these French American names. Shall one, or shall one not, pronounce the *s* in *St. Louis* and *Louisville?* Shall one accent *New Orleans* on the last or the next to the last syllable? Shall one pronounce *Haute* in *Terre Haute* with the French vowel sound and silent *h*, or shall one follow popular use, by pronouncing *hut?*

About the only French names in America, in which the anglicization has been complete, are those in which the name has been recast in English written form as well as in sound. Earlier English handling of its French names in England established an interesting precedent. *Chateau Vert* in England became *Shotover, Leighton Beau-desert* became *Leighton Buzzard, Burgh Walter* became *Bridgewater, Beau Chef* became *Beachy (Head).* Not at all by conscious imitation of English method, but nevertheless governed by the same tendencies in popular etymologizing, American use has made some interesting transformation of French names. The somewhat grandiloquent *Bellevue,* probably of literary origin, which appears in 13 states, is transformed into *Bellvue,* Colorado, *Belvue,* Kansas, and *Belview,* Minnesota. *Smackover* is an Arkansas name from *Chemin Couvert. Picketwire* is the local name for the *Purgatoire* river in *Colorado.*[22] *"Bowsley"* is the characteristically English pronunciation of *Beau Soleil* in *Ontario.* Even *Bunker* in *Bunker Hill* is said to be a transformation of an earlier *Bon cœur.*[23]

---
[22] Mencken, p. 293.
[23] *Ibid.*, p. 274.

Half-breed names, that is to say, Indian names in French form, occur in numbers hard to determine. Such a word is probably *Miami,* the sounds of which appear in English form as *Maumee.* *Pickaway* in Ohio seems to be another instance of an English form given to the English pronunciation of a Franco-Indian *Piqua.* In Canada, where French names are more thickly strewn, such English transformations are frequent. *Les Cheneaux Islands* have become the *Snow Islands, Les Chats* and *Les Joachims* on the Ottawa River, have become the *Shaws* and the *Swartings.* *Chapeau Dieu,* an eminence near the head of the Bay of Fundy, has become *Shepody* Mountain. Most striking of all is the New Brunswick river with Indian name, *Quah-Tah-Wah-Am-Quah-Duavic,* which first received the shortened, probably French, form *Petamkediac,* which in turn was converted into English *Tom Kedgwick.*

American modification of inherited English names is often interesting. A dominant influence is that of the written form. This in time leads to the American pronunciation of elements silent in English pronunciation, the *w* in *Warwick, Norwich,* etc., and the *h* in *Chatham* and the like. Or in case the English pronunciation is retained, the spelling is often made to suit it, as in the case of *Wooster* which appears in 3 states for *Worcester* in 6, *Hartford* (also used in England) in 19 states for *Hertford* in 1, *Darby,* in 7 states for *Derby* in 13.

The modification in sound, to which even native English place-names have been particularly subject, makes it difficult in many cases to trace them back to their originals. It is a long way from *Ripon* to *In hripum,* from *Rochester* to *Hfrofeceaster,* from *Brixton* to *Egbrihtes Stān* (Egbert's stone), from *Knowsley* to *Kenulfes lēah,* from *York* to *Eoforwīc,* from scholastic *Oxford* to pastoral *Oxena ford.* The last word cited, offers striking illustration of the distance the modern world is removed from the conditions that fixed the names to places. Still more striking illustration is afforded by names to features in modern great cities. It requires effort of the imagination to connect busy *Holborn* in London with *burn*, the creek to which was once attached the name *Hol*, or *Fleet Street*, now associated with English journalism, with the *Fleet* stream which once crossed it at right angles, or the *Strand* with the bank of the Thames. Equally striking as illustrating the vicissitudes in the history of names and the slight relation existing between present names and the original name-giving conditions are the New York names already cited; *Gramercy Square* from *De Kromme Zee* 'the crooked lake,' from the Dutch name for a lake which is indicated on early maps of New York, and the *Bowery* from *Bouwerij*, the Dutch name for Peter Stuyvesant's farm, which occupied the site of the modern street.

REFERENCES FOR FURTHER READING

ISAAC TAYLOR, *Words and Places,* New ed. (London, 1882), (A classic work, but not representing the present stage of knowledge).

ISAAC TAYLOR, *Names and their Histories.* (Reprinted as Chapter xi in the Everyman Library edition of *Words and Places*).

W. BLAKE, *Etymological Dictionary of Place Names.*

C. E. JOHNSON, *English Words* (New York, 1891), Ch. xiv.

ERNEST WEEKLEY, *The Romance of Names* (London and New York, 1914), Chapters, xii, xiii.

W. G. SEARLE, *Onomasticon Anglo-Saxon* (Cambridge, 1897).

H. L. MENCKEN, *The American Language,* 1st ed. (New York, 1919), Ch. viii.

E. T. KER, *River and Lake Names in the United States* (New York, 1911).

United States Geographic Board, *Report* 1890-1916 (Washington, 1910).

F. W. LAWRENCE, "The Origin of American State Names," *National Geographic Magazine,* August, 1920.

CHAPTER XXV

PERSONAL NAMES

In England, as in other countries of Europe, the use of surnames did not become customary until late in the Middle Ages. Most Englishmen of the Anglo-Saxon period were content with a single name. A characteristic form for English names of the earliest period was a compound word. A frequently appearing first element in these compounds is *Ælf-*, meaning 'elf' or 'fairy,' appearing in such common names as *Ælfgar, Ælfgifu, Ælfheah, Ælfhelm, Ælfhere, Ælflæd, Ælfred, Ælfric, Ælfstan, Ælfwin,* and *Ælfthryth*. The use of this word suggests an attempt to propitiate the supernatural beings of an earlier faith, an attempt which in later times is paralleled by the seeking of saintly protection through giving to children the names of protecting saints. More frequently, however, the compound word is made up of names of qualities which the parent name-giver, with a degree of not unnatural sentiment, hoped to see realized in the character of his offspring: *Æthel-*, in *Æthelbald, Æthelberht, Æthelflæd, Æthelgifu,* and their kind, means 'noble,' obviously a desirable quality. *Ead-*, in *Eadberht, Eadgar, Eadgifu, Eadgyth, Eadhild, Eadmund, Eadred, Eadric, Eadsige, Eadweard, Eadwine, Eadwulf, Eadwig,* is probably to be associated with the adjective *ēadig*, meaning 'happy.' Other common elements are *beald*, 'bold'; *ecg*, 'edge,' 'sword'; *gōd*, 'good'; *wīg*, 'battle'; *sige*, 'victory'; *wulf*, 'wolf'; and such frequent suffixes as *beorht*, 'bright,' 'renowned'; *heard*, 'strong'; *here*, 'army'; *mund*, 'hand,' 'protection'; *rǣd*, 'counsel'; *wine*, 'friend'; appearing in such compounds as *Ecgberht, Sigebeorht, Gōdmund, Wig-*

heard, and their like. Less grandiose are such uncompounded names as *Cytel,* 'kettle'; *Brand,* 'sword'; *Rēad,* 'red'; *Wicga,* 'horse,' 'warrior'; *Wulf, Bœda, Ceol, Cutha, Offa, Duda, Hild* (a), *Hengest, Horsa, Ine, Tucca, Wini, Hudda, Wada,* etc., many of them probably to be explained as shortened or pet forms of longer names.[1]

As specimens of modern names, often greatly disguised, derived from this early stock, may be cited:[2] *Baldwin* (Bealdwine), *Winbolt* (Winebeald), *Herald, Harold, Harrod* (Hereweald), *Bardell* (Beorhtwulf), *Elmer* (Ælfmær), *Colvin* (Ceolwine), *Goddard* (Godheard), *Herbert* (Herebearht), *Herrick* (Hereric), *Hubert, Hubbard, Hobart, Hibbert* (Hygebeorht), *Wyman* (Wigmund), *Willard* (Wilheard), *Read, Reid, Reed* (Rēad, 'red'), *Kemp* (Cempa, 'warrior'), *Cobb* (Cobba), *Froude* (Froda 'prudent), *Tucker* (Tucca), *Dodd* (Dodda), etc., besides later *Jane, Jones, Johnson, Jennings,* etc.[4]

In English names, as in so many other things, a great change followed the Norman Conquest. Not only were law and education brought under new control, but in matters more directly subject to the sway of fashion, continental manners followed the conquering Normans into England. Fashion in dress underwent striking change under the influence of the newcomers, and the character of names, likewise, underwent change in the new social order. Many of the older stock of words, such as *Edwin, Edgar, Alfred* and *Ethel* were reintroduced into common use at periods considerably later. But for the time being, names of the Anglo-Saxon type were out of fashion. Henry I, who cultivated the support of the native English, and his queen Matilda, sister of Edgar Ætheling, were ridiculed by the Norman element under the Anglo-Saxon names *Godric* and *Godgifu.*

---

[1] Weekley, p. 73.
[2] *Ibid.,* p. 73.

The names of the new kind which were most widely used are said to have been *John, William, Thomas, Richard, Robert,* in the order given.[3] Of these *John* and *Thomas* are scriptural names, which in Anglo-Saxon England had in general only a literary use and had retained their full Latin form, but which among the Normans were early appropriated as personal names and in popular use underwent striking transformation in many instances. To this class belong *Andrew* (Lat. *Andreas,* O. E. *Andreas*), *Matthew* (Lat. *Mattheus,* O. E. *Mattheus*), *James* (Lat. *Jacobus,* O. E. *Jacobus*), names to whose common use as personal names we owe the origin of the expression 'Christian name.'

Of these Christian names probably the one most widely used is *John* (Lat. *Johannes,* O. E. *Johannes*). The familiarity with which it has been handled, since brought into popular use in various languages, is shown by the variety of forms that it has assumed: Italian *Giovanni* (derivative, *Zany*), modern French *Jean,* Welsh *Evan,* Scotch *Ian,* Breton *Yves,* Russian *Ivan,* Danish and Dutch *Hans,* Scotch-English *Shawn.* The derivatives of *John* and its feminine correspondent *Joan* are innumerable, including *Jane, Jones, Johnson, Jennings,* etc.[4]

The name *Thomas* owes its wide vogue to the popularity of the shrine of St. Thomas of Canterbury, the goal of popular pilgrimages. Not only the first part of the name has yielded derivatives such as *Thoms, Thomson,* etc., but the ending, a French clipped form in popular use, yields *Macey, Massie, Machin,* and *Masson.*[5]

The other three names of the five mentioned, are of Teutonic origin. The Middle High German form of *William* is *Willehelm,* in which may be seen the original meaning, 'helm of resolution.' In France the name as-

---

[3] Weekley, p. 58.
[4] *Ibid.,* p. 25.
[5] *Ibid.,* p. 59.

sumed two forms: *Guillaume*, which is still in French use, and the form with initial W-, used in the northeast of France, whence the English form is derived. The double form is paralleled in the double forms: *Gautier* and *Walter, Guy* and *Wyatt*. The widespread use of *William* in England in the centuries following 1066 A. D. is not hard to explain. Derived from *William* are such names as *Williams, Wills, Williamson, Wilson, Wilkin, Wilkins, Willett*, etc., as well as *Gilliam*, etc.[6]

The Teutonic forms of *Robert* and *Richard* appear in the Old High German *Hruodbert*, 'fame-bright,' and *Richart*, 'powerful,' names which will recall the Anglo-Saxon mode of name formation. *Richard* and *Robert* in familiar use gave origin to *Rick, Hick*, and *Dick*, and *Rob, Hob, Bob*, and *Dob*, respectively, from which in turn are derived such forms as *Ricketts, Hicks, Hixon, Dix, Dixon, Rich, Ritchie, Hitch, Higgs, Ditch, Digg, Robb, Robbins, Robson, Robinson, Hobbs, Hobson, Dobbs, Dobson*, etc.[7]

Almost as markworthy as the popularity of *John, Thomas, Robert, Richard,* and *William,* was the relative infrequency of names, like *Arthur, Charles,* and *George*. These names were familiar enough, the first two being the names of central figures in the two best known medieval cycles of romance and the third, *George* (Greek, *Georgos* 'tiller of the soil'), the name of England's patron saint; but all three owe the favor in which they have now come to be held, to later events, *Charles* and *George*, it is said, to the influence of the royal houses of Stuart and Hanover, and *Arthur* to the fact that it was the name of the Duke of Wellington.[8] *Frederick,* in the same way, is said to owe its popularity to the fame of Frederick the Great.

The period following the Conquest was marked by another innovation, the adoption of the use of surnames.

---

[6] Weekley, p. 63.
[7] *Ibid.*, p. 63.
[8] *Ibid.*, p. 61.

The development of surnames was a practical necessity. With the widening of interests from interests involving only a local community, to interests involving a whole country, and in our own day, to a considerable extent, the whole world, new means of distinguishing names have become more and more indispensable. The use of a second element in a name, a surname, for a time satisfied needs, but in later times additional means have been found necessary. The use of a third, or middle, name which was adopted in England in the eighteenth century, but which did not become frequent much before the nineteenth, has now become a general practice. This, one may come to realize, if he will consider the names famous in the literature of England and America from William Shakespeare and John Milton to Robert Louis Stevenson and H. G. Wells. In recent times, added power of distinction has been gained by supplementing the relatively restricted stock of given, or Christian, names by names drawn from the more widely varied list of surnames. The hyphenation of surnames in recent times has served the same purpose. It must be reckoned a remarkable achievement in language to have been able to supply names sufficient in variety for so long a time to serve the ever-expanding need of distinction.

In the period before the Conquest, individuals were not infrequently distinguished by the use of an epithet, as in the case of Edmund Ironsides, Æthelred the Unready, Edward the Confessor, etc. Such additional names, however, are not to be reckoned as surnames in the modern sense of the word, because they were not transmitted from generation to generation. Probably the earliest form of surname proper was the patronymic, the name derived from parent or ancestor. For instance, Alfred the Great was distinguished by the added name *Æthelwulfing*, 'son of Æthewulf.' In early Teutonic life this mode of naming was in use. Among the characters in the Beowulf story, Healfdene, Hrothgar, Heorogar, Halga, are designated as Scyldings, 'descendants of Scyld'; Wægmund, Ecgtheow, Weohstan, Wiglaf, and Beowulf are designated as *Scylfings,* 'descendants of Scylf.' The last four are also referred to as Wægmundings, since Ecgtheow and Weohstan were sons, and Wiglaf and Boewulf grandsons, of Wægmund. The suffix *-ing,* therefore, served to denote not only the immediate parent, but a famous ancestor more or less remote. It served in the formation of tribal designations, and if the use of surnames in the Anglo-Saxon period had been prevalent, would doubtless have been the distinctive suffix for surnames.

The patronymic surname is common in most languages. In Slavic languages it is familiar in the characteristic names ending in *-vitch.* In the Norman period the French word *fitz* (Mod. Fr. *fils,* 'son') served the same purpose and appears in such modern English names as *Fitzgerald, Fitzsimmons,* as well as *Fitz* and *Fitch.* Among Scotch and Irish the same function is accomplished by the familiar syllable, *Mac,* meaning 'relative.' Among the Welsh, *Map,* or in later forms, *Ap* or *Ab,* serve the same purpose. This element, in disguised form, enters into the composition of many common names of Welsh origin, such as *Pugh* (ap + Hugh), *Bowen* (ap + Owen), *Powell* (ap + Howell, Hoel), *Price* (ap + Rhys), *Pritchard* (ap + Richard), *Prothero* (ap + Roderick), *Blood* (ap + Lud), as well as in *Upjohn, Updike,* etc.[9] The Irish *O'* serves practically the same function as *Mac.*

Among Scandinavian peoples the patronymic suffix is *-son.* The surnames most used in Norway, Sweden, and Denmark are said to be respectively *Olson* (Olaf + son), *Anderson* (Andrew's son), and *Pedersen* (Peter's son). For the most part, to Norse source or to Norse influence

---

[9] Weekley, pp. 62, 66.

are to be attributed the names in *-son* so frequent in northern England and lowland Scotland as well as in the American Northwest, where the Scandinavian element in the population is so strong.

In the South of England the older genitive ending, *-s*, accomplishes a similar function. This mode of distinction is well enough known in large families of our own time, where the numerous Johns or Marys in a large family are distinguished by the added name of the parent, for example Tom's Mary as distinguished from Herbert's Mary, etc. To it are to be attributed in great part the many surnames ending in *s* frequent among the Welsh, such as *Jones, Williams, Hughes, Evans, Roberts, Edwards, Rogers, Harris,* etc.[10]

A second source of surnames is from the country or locality with which a man is associated. *Scott* is said to be an English name applied to Scotchman;[11] the reverse is of course true of the name *English*. *Cornish* and *Cornwallis* are names for natives of Cornwall, said to have originated in neighboring Devonshire. Names of provinces and towns find a like use as surnames, though usually much disguised in form. *Champneys* is a name applied to a native of Champagne. Other names of the kind are *Brett, Britton* (native of Brittany), *Picard, Power* (Picardy), *Loring* (Lorraine), *Bullen* (Boulogne), *Bloss* (Blois), *Loving* (Louvain), *Sessions* (Soissons), *Turney* (Tournay), etc. Place-names more purely local, which, serving first as a distinguishing addition to a name, have developed into surnames with or without the genitive '*s*, are *Ford, Bridges, Field, Craig* ('crag'), *Lake, Rivers, Creek, Brooke, Cairnes, Glenn, Dunne* and *Dun* ('hill'), *Hill,* etc. From the Old English *burh* (dat. *byrig*), meaning 'fortified place,' come *Burrows, Burroughs, Borrow, Brough, Burke,*

---

[10] Weekley, p. 46.
[11] *Ibid.*, p. 46.

Bury, Berry, Attlebury, etc. Many place-names, no longer familiar as common nouns in standard language, continue in use as proper names, such as *Peak, Pike, Peck* and *Pick,* variant forms of the name for 'hill-top'; *Law, Low, Lynn, Shaw, Holt, Hurst* and *Barrows,* all of them from words familiar in dialect or in the archaic language of poetry. More definite are the place-names appearing in *Tuttle* (Toot + hill), *Tyndall* (Tyne + dale), *Haywood* (Hay, 'hedge' + wood), *Radcliffe, Wycliffe, Doddridge, Bradshaw* ('broadwood'), *Crashaw* ('crowwood'), *Earnshaw* ('eaglewood'), *Renshaw* ('ravenwood'), *Schofield* ('schoolfield') and the like. The older northern form *yett* for *gate*, appears in *Yeats* and *Yates*. *Hyatt* is disguised *High* + *yett*. Dialectal variants of *Hedge* appear in *Hay, Haig, Haigh, Haw,* and *Hey*. Plural forms are *Hayes* and *Hawes.*[12] Countless instances of common place-names used as surnames will occur to any one. Some of the less obvious instances cited here, will serve to show how many such names live under disguise.

A third principal source of modern surnames is to be found in names of occupations. The number of names from this source is even greater than appears at first sight. There are *Smith, Butcher, Carpenter, Miller, Taylor,* and their like, now applied utterly without relation to occupation, but forming the most widely used type of surname. Besides these obvious instances there are numerous surnames from old forms of names of occupations the meanings of which are no longer always evident. The name *Chaucer,* 'shoemaker,' is an obvious instance. In this class may be included such early forms of name as *Hunt,* 'hunter'; *Day* 'dairyman'; *Webb,* 'weaver'; *Kemp,* 'warrior'; *Frick,* 'warrior'; *Wright* (originally 'worker,' O. E. *wyrhta*); *Brewster, Baxter and Webster,* names for the

---

[12] Weekley, Ch. XIII.

feminine brewer, baker and weaver, respectively; *Millard,* 'millward'; *Plummer,* 'plumber'; *Inman,* 'landlord'; *Ward,* 'guard'; *Firminger,* 'cheesemaker'; *Barker,* 'tanner'; *Chapman,* 'merchant'; *Clark,* 'scholar.'

Besides these more or less disguised occupational surnames, there are a large number of surnames derived from names of obsolete occupations, occupations which have gone out of use because there is no further use for the article produced or because modern methods of manufacture, based on the principle of division of labor, have proved too efficient to permit the survival of the early type of craftsman trained to the production of a single article. With the decline in the importance of archery has come about the disappearance of the arrowmaker whose name survives in the surnames, *Arrowsmith, Fletcher,* and *Flower* (O. E. *flā,* 'arrow'), *Boulter,* 'bolt maker,' and of the maker of bows whose occupational name survives in the variant forms, *Bowyer, Bower, Boyer.* Connected with the earlier art of cloth manufacture were the occupations whose names survive in *Fuller, Tucker, Shearer, Sherman, Walker.* To the same class of names are to be assigned, *Tyler* ('tile man'), *Chandler* ('candle maker'), *Hawker* ('itinerant salesman'), *Parmenter* ('parchment maker'), *Pilcher* ('maker of fur cloaks'), *Quiller* ('maker of quilted ruffs'), *Cutler* ('knife maker'), *Spooner* ('spoon maker'), *Collier* ('charcoal burner'), *Croker, Crocker* ('maker of crocks'), *Cooper, Cowper* ('maker of casks'), *Lorimer* ('bridle maker'), *Sellars* ('saddle maker'), *Parker* ('park custodian'), *Hayward* ('a guardian of the tilled fields,' literally 'hedge ward'), *Marshall* ('horse servant'), *Constable* ('stableman'), *Stuart,* Stewart ('steward'). In the name *Graves* two forms have coalesced: the O. E. *gerēfa* ('reeve') and *Greaves* from an earlier form for *Grove.* The same is true of *Howard,* which originates, on the one hand, as a variant form of *Hayward,* on the other hand, from *Harward,* a late form for earlier *Hereward.*[13]

A fourth general source of surnames is to be found in epithets or nicknames, the word nickname itself, from earlier 'an eke name,' originally being the equivalent of surname. The use of epithets in the Anglo-Saxon period, in such names as *Æthelred the Unready* and *Edmund Ironsides,* has already been referred to. The use of epithets in the succeeding period may be illustrated by the names of the successive kings: *William the Bastard, William Rufus* ('the red'), *Henry Beauclerc* ('fine scholar'), *Henry Plantagenet, Richard the Lion-Hearted, John Lackland, Edward Longshanks.* Of these, *Plantagenet* ('sprig of broom'), which Henry II inherited from his father, Geoffrey, Count of Anjou, became the surname of a long royal line.

The subject of nicknames and epithets is a treacherous one to handle. Their application is subject to every kind of caprice. The unessential quality is as likely as the essential to be the one to give the name. *Wolf,* as an epithet expressive of character, is not hard to understand. *Lovell* and *Lovett* are similarly explained since they are diminutive forms of the early French word for 'wolf.' *Drinkwater* probably was expressive of idiosyncrasy and is paralleled by the French equivalent, *Boileau. Dolittle* belongs to the same class. *Larned* represents an earlier pronunciation of *learned. Fairfax* had the meaning 'fair hair.' *Eames* comes from the genitive form of the old word *eme,* 'uncle.' Features of dress are expressed by *Capron* ('hood'), *Burden* ('staff'), *Motley* ('fool's costume'), *Gildersleeve.* Manner of speech is conveyed by *Purdy* and *Pardee,* from the oath *pardee,* of French origin. Shakespeare belongs in a class with *Wagstaff, Hurlbutt, Benbow* ('bend bow'),

---

[13] All these examples are cited from Weekley, *op. cit.,* Chapters XVIII, XIX.

Makepiece and *Lovejoy,* all of them imperative compounds. *Little* requires no comment, but *Stout* had a broader meaning, 'valiant'; *Seeley* meant 'happy,' 'blessed'; *Moody* meant 'courageous'; *Crook* and *Crum* meant 'crooked'; *Bolt* meant 'bold'; *Leaf* meant 'dear'; *Stow* meant 'big,' 'stout'; *Bragg* meant 'brave.'[14]

The original meaning of many names is hidden because of their French extraction, as in the case of *Burnett* (diminutive of *brun,* 'brown'), *Blunt* and *Blount* ('blonde'), *Gaylord* (*gaillard,* 'gay,' 'brisk'), *Prout* (*cf.* Fr. *Prud'homme*), *Power* ('poor'), *Follett* (diminutive of *fol,* 'mad'), *Curtis* ('courteous').

Many of the names of Celtic origin are interesting because the original meaning is so completely lost sight of, as in the Welsh *Gough* and *Roe,* both meaning 'red'; *Bain, Wynne* and *Gwynne,* 'white'; *Glass* and *Lloyd* and *Floyd,* 'gray'; *Sayce,* 'Saxon'; *Vaughan,* 'little'; and the Highland Scotch *Cameron,* 'crooked nose'; *Campbell,* 'wry mouth'; and the Irish *Kennedy,* 'ugly head.'

Probably no other kind of word is so subject to variation in form as personal names, due in part at least, to the fact that they have so little logical relation to the persons named, and hence drift in sound like a craft loose from its moorings. The variant forms of the name of *Shakespeare* are familiar enough. Dr. *Crown,* a writer of the seventeenth century, spelled his own name in six different ways: *Cron, Croon, Crown, Crone, Croone, Croune.*[15] Such variant forms as *Pierce, Peirce, Pearce, Pearse* and *Pears* are familiar to every one, all derived through the French *Piers* from the name of the apostle *Peter.* In the same way *Lea, Lee, Ley, Leigh, Legh, Legge, Lay, Lye,* are all derived from one place-name, the Old English word meaning 'meadow.'[16] The fashion of clipping names in familiar

---
[14] All these examples are from Weekley, *op. cit.*, Ch. XXI.
[15] *Ibid.*, p. 27.
[16] *Ibid.*, p. 28.

use, which has given rise to such a group of names as *Elspeth, Elsie, Eliza, Liza, Lisa, Lizzie, Beth, Bet, Bettie, Betsy*, etc., all from the name *Elizabeth*, is well known. When to full name or to shortened forms are added suffixes like the diminutives *-kin, -in, -ie, -ett*, etc., probably expressive of endearment, and the other suffixes *-son, -s, -man, -cock*, it is apparent that variation has practically no limits. To the variants of *Pierce* may be added *Perkins, Pierson*, etc. *Matthew* and its old French form, *Mahieu*, give rise to *Matthews, Mayhew, Mayo, May, Mee, Mayes, Mekins, Meeson*, and, sometimes, *Mason*. *Philip* gives rise to *Phillips, Philip, Phipps, Phelps, Filkins*, etc.[17] From *Bartholomew* come *Batty, Batten, Bates, Bartle, Bartilson, Bartlett, Badcock, Badman*. From Hugh and its diminutive *Huggin* come *Hewett, Hewlett, Howitt, Howlett, Hutchins*.[18]

The remarkable divergence in popular use from the original pronunciation of names gives rise to many new names hard to associate with the original forms. As examples of this class may be cited *Farrar* from *Farquhar, Mean* from *Meaghan, Meany* from *Mahoney, Calhoun* from *Colquhoun, Marshbanks* from *Marjoribanks, Mannering* from *Mainwaring, Beecham* from *Beauchamp, Warrick* from *Warwick, Beeton* from *Bethune, Car* from *Ker, Mills* from *Milnes, Marr* from *Meagher*.

The names of saints, due to familiar use, have been particularly subject to this kind of change. *Tolley* comes from *Bartholomew, Munn* from *Edmund, Tedman* from *St. Edmund, Tobin* from *St. Aubyn, Toosey* from *St. Osith, Toomer* from *St. Omer, Tooley* from *St. Olave, Selleger* and *Sellinger* from *St. Leger, Seymour* from *St. Maur, Sidney* from *St. Denis, Sinclair* from *St. Clair, Semark*

---

[17] Weekley, pp. 46, 86.
[18] *Ibid.*, p. 57.

from *St. Mark,* Semple from *St. Paul,* Simper from *St. Pierre.*[19]

Along with the natural unconscious tendencies toward change in pronunciation, later registered in changed spelling, must be reckoned the frantic striving for novelty, distinction, individuality. This spirit finds expression in forms of names of girls, often adopted by the girls themselves, such as *Alys, Edythe, Evelyn, Carolyn, Marye; Emmajeane, Evajeane, Donna, Gladelen, Gladene, Aleen, Karleene, Eunice, Nelle, Lorna, Thelma, Elaine, Marion.*

In the pronunciation of the names of foreigners one finds oneself in a predicament much like that in the case of foreign place-names. Down to times comparatively recent, names of foreigners have been anglicized in pronunciation, frequently in spelling as well. The great names of antiquity, sacred and profane, from *Confucius* to *Cæsar,* have taken English pronunciation. The same is true of the historic names of later times: *Charlemagne, Dante, Petrarch, Raphael, Titian, Galileo, Luther, Huss, Columbus, Cervantes, Gustavus Adolphus, Napoleon, Frederick the Great, Ney, Blücher, Schiller, Hugo, Swedenborg, Handel, Haydn, Mendelssohn, Mozart, Talleyrand, Metternich.* Down to recent times, only a small number of foreign names, such as *Goethe, Medici, Beethoven,* and *Chopin,* have failed in English use to take an English pronunciation. In our own times the situation is different. Attempt is made, in words like *Wagner* and *Maupassant,* more or less successfully, to give the pronunciation of the language to which the name is native. Is this because English has reached the saturation point? Or is it a form of pedantry? Even now almost any name that gains popular circulation inevitably takes the English stamp. Occasionally a name, not entirely popular, such as *Maeterlinck,* is made at home.

---

[19] Weekley, *op. cit.,* p. 34.

Would it not be an obvious gain if, as in the case of place-names, the learned should espouse the popular cause and apply English sounds to the pronunciation of foreign names? The reason for the hesitation and vacillation is doubtless to be found in the uncertain pronunciation of English letters, which prevents the arrival at agreement in the pronunciation of names with foreign spelling.

In the United States the problem of dealing with names of foreign extraction is an alive one. In the solution of the problem, however, considerable progress has been made through the assimilation of the foreign names. The assimilation usually comes about in one of two ways. The foreign name is fitted in pronunciation and spelling into an Anglo-Saxon form. Dutch names thus transformed are: *Reiger* to *Riker*, *Van Huys* to *Vannice*, *Van Siegel* to *Van Sickle*, *Haerlen* to *Harlan*. French names thus handled are *Caillé* to *Kyle*, *De la Haye* to *Dillehay*, *Dejean* to *Dishong*, *Soule* to *Sewell*, *Gervaise* to *Jarvis*, *Bayle* to *Bailey*, *Pebaudière* to *Peabody*, *Bon Pas* to *Bumpus*, *de l'Hotel* to *Doolittle*. German shifts of this kind are *Blum* to *Bloom*, *Reuss* to *Royce*, *Kuehle* to *Keeley*, *Stehli* to *Staley*, *Bauman* to *Bowman*, *Oehm* to *Ames*, *Furth* to *Ford*, *Kuntz* to *Coons* or *Kuhns*, *Jung* to *Young*, etc.[20]

In a great many cases, on the other hand, the foreign name is translated. German *Pfund* becomes *Pound;* *Schumacher*, *Shoemaker;* *König*, *King;* *Koch*, *Cook;* *Neuman*, *Newman;* *Steiner*, *Stoner;* *Schwartz*, *Black;* *Weber*, *Weaver;* *Sontag*, *Sunday.*

Jews have been particularly active in modifying their names, changing *Cohen* into *Cohn*, *Cahn*, *Kahn*, *Kann*, *Coyne*, and *Conn*, *Aaron* into *Aren* or *Ahren*, *Solomon* into *Salmon*, *Salomon* or *Solomsen*, shortening *Wolfsheimer* to *Wolf*, *Goldsmidt* to *Gold*, *Rosenblatt*, *Rosenthal*, etc., to

---

[20] Mencken, *The American Language*, p. 275.

Rose, translating *Schneider* into *Taylor*, *Schlachtfeld* into *Warfield*, *Reichman* into *Richman*.[21]

What might happen to a foreign name in America may be illustrated by the following anecdote of a resident of New Orleans:

> When he moved from an American quarter into a German quarter his name of *Flint* became *Feuerstein*, which for convenience was shortened to *Stein*. Upon his removal to a French district, he was rechristened *Pierre*. Hence upon his return to an English neighborhood he was translated into *Peters*, and his first neighbors were surprised and puzzled to find *Flint* turned into *Peters*.[22]

An examination of the proper names in the United States reveals some interesting facts regarding the race material that makes up the population. In New York City the fourth most common name is now *Murphy*, and the fifth most common is *Meyer*. *Cohen* and *Levy* come eighth and ninth in rank. Of the names *Smith, Jones, Williams,* and *Taylor*, which rank first to fourth in England, only *Smith* holds its place in the United States. Nine names come ahead of *Jones* in New York, and *Taylor* comes twenty-third. *Smith, Brown,* and *Miller*, which are the first three names, ranked by numbers, in New York, hold their places because their numbers have been recruited from German and Scandinavian sources, from the ranks of *Schmidts* and *Brauns* and *Müllers*.[23] Judging from proper names, the elements in the American melting pot are showing new proportions.

The brief consideration of proper names offered in this chapter will afford some realization of how the almost endless variety in names has been reached. Illogical, but on the whole successful, has been the method by which distinctive names have been found for millions of distinct individuals. The varied names arrived at, however, offer

---

[21] Mencken, p. 280.
[22] Quoted by Weekley, p. 199 note, from *London Daily Chronicle*, April 4, 1913.
[23] Mencken, *op. cit.*, p. 371.

many curious features. Hence almost any list of names may be made a source of information and of entertainment. There is to be noted not only the wide range in the sources, but particularly the humorous incongruity so often apparent between the physical or spiritual qualities of a person and the conventional, inherited name which he bears. These features are particularly apparent in lists of American names. In a limited list of about seven thousand names in the directory of a State University for 1919-20, in a city where the native-born American forms 93 per cent of the population, appear names of marvelous variety. The names of the different colors and of practically every common beast, bird, and fish appear. The list also includes *Ruble, Mark, Dollar,* and *Pound, Wolf* and *Lamb, Moon* and *Starr, Summer* and *Winter, Way* and *Means, Hand* and *Foote, Pen* and *Ink, Hill* and *Dale, Lock* and *Key, Salt* and *Pepper, Root* and *Branch, Flower* and *Weed, Rich* and *Poor, Shy* and *Bold, Short* and *Long, High* and *Low,* and *Knight, Earl, Marquis, Duke, Kaiser,* and *Pope.* Surely the ends of the earth are brought together in the words that form American personal names.

REFERENCES FOR FURTHER READING

E. WEEKLEY, *The Romance of Names* (New York and London, 1913). An instructive and at the same time entertaining book from which most of the illustrative material in the present chapter has been derived.

H. L. MENCKEN, *The American Language,* First ed. (New York, 1919).

W. BARDSLEY, *Dictionary of English Surnames* (Oxford, 1901).

W. G. SEARLE, *Onomasticon Anglo-Saxon* (Cambridge, 1897).

C. F. JOHNSON, *English Words* (New York, 1891), Ch. xv.

ROBERT FERGUSON, *English Surnames* (London, 1858).

G. M. YONGE, *Christian Names* (London, 1884).

M. A. LOWER, *Patronymica Brittanica* (London, 1860).

M. A. LOWER, *Essay on English Surnames* (London, 1842).

H. HIRT, *Etymologie,* pp. 306ff. (Munich, 1909).

CHAPTER XXVI

CHOICE OF WORDS

One of the most important results of the speech activity discussed in the preceding chapters has been the accumulation of a rich store of synonyms. The choice of words thus afforded is the principal source of the capacity of English for the expression of refinements of meaning. The bewildering variety of words, however, proves at times almost an embarrassment, and one of the sources of difficulty in gaining effective command of English lies in the very richness of its vocabulary.

By way of illustration of the complex variety of words that one is required to select from, let us take a collection of phrases involving the idea of group, or number.[1] One may speak of a *bevy* of quail, but in speaking of birds in general, the collective word called for is *flock*. In other instances still different words are called for, as exemplified by the following phrasal combinations: *Pack* of wolves, *gang* of thieves, *host* of angels, *shoal* of porpoises, *herd* of buffalo or cattle, *troop* of children, *covey* of partridges, *galaxy* of beauty, *horde* of ruffians, *heap* of rubbish, *drove* of cattle, *mob* of blackguards, *school* of whales, *congregation* of worshipers, *corps* of engineers, *band* of robbers, *swarm* of locusts, *crowd* of people.

The agreement required between the words in the phrases cited is like the concord required in inflectional endings in languages such as Latin. This concord in meaning, however, gives rise to the fault branded by the rhetorician as redundancy, since the words *gang, drove, congregation*, etc.,

---

[1] R. P. Utter, *Every-Day Words*, p. 61.

in their connotation have absorbed in part the meaning of the words accompanying them. The complexity in the choice, it is also to be noted, is like that which, as has earlier been pointed out, characterizes language in its primitive stages. From this complexity modern popular speech revolts. In the case of the meaning under consideration, for the variety of words, it substitutes one word universal in its application, the slang word, *bunch*.

But the method adopted in this instance by popular speech is not one to be commended. The use of one word as a general substitute for a group of words serves to blur distinctions that are useful. The evils resulting from a false economy of this kind are everywhere apparent. It is to be seen in the use of the word *allow*, which tends to supplant such useful words as *permit, consent to, concede, grant,* and *suffer*. This blurring of distinctions of meaning appears also in the use of the one word *anxious* for *eager, desirous, yearning, longing,* etc.; *furnish* for *supply, provide, afford, deliver, impart,* etc.; *claim* for *maintain, hold, affirm, contend,* etc.; *grab* for *snatch, catch hold of, grasp, clutch, seize,* etc.; *compel* for *make, require, force constrain,* etc.; *located* for *situated, settled,* etc.; not to speak of such words of general utility as the words *nice* and *fine* and *great* (slang for *magnificent*, etc.).

Somewhat similar to the tendency in popular language for one word to occupy the field to the exclusion of all others, is the tendency in literary language for certain words to acquire a special vogue which leads to the neglect of more varied means of expression. The fine word *strenuous* lost much of its sharpness of meaning through the excessive vogue established through the use of it by one man of unusual prominence and force. Other words of the literary vocabulary subjected to the wear resulting from excessive use are *inevitable, meticulous, grueling, gripping, compelling* (art). With these words may be joined certain words and expressions which belong to the threadbare type of language known as journalese. Under this head Sir Arthur Quiller-Couch brings verbs such as *obsess, recrudescence, envisage, adumbrate;* phrases such as *the psychological moment, the true inwardness, it gives furiously to think.* It gives pain to think that there has recently been published for practical guidance a collection of such petrified modes of expression under the title, *The Happy Phrase.*

If, then, useful distinctions of meaning are to be maintained, if threadbare forms of expression are to be avoided, how is one to be guided in a discriminating choice?

There was a time in the earlier history of the language when the problem of choice between alternative words was solved in a simple manner. If two or more words offered themselves, the difficulty of choice was evaded by the method of using both. This method, if it did not always yield precision, at least afforded a close approximation to the meaning. Besides, the two or more words gave to the expression a roundness of form which appealed to a rhetorical taste. This fashion of using two or more words in place of one made its appearance in the works of at least one writer before the Norman Conquest, but it was especially in vogue in the period around the year 1500. Caxton, in the prologue to his *Recueil des Histoires de Troye,* says of himself and his work:

> When I remember that every man is bounden by the *commandment* and *counsel* of the wise man to eschew *sloth* and *idleness* which is *mother* and *nourisher* of vices, and ought to put myself into virtuous *occupation* and *business,* then I, having no great charge of occupation following the said counsel, took a French book and read therein many *strange* and *marvellous* histories wherein I had great *pleasure* and *delight,* as well for the novelty of the same as for the fair language of French, which

was in prose so *well* and *compendiously set* and *written,* which methought I understood the *sentence* and *substance* of every matter.

In the writings of Lord Berners, a younger contemporary of Caxton, one meets such phrases as: "ancient acts, gests, and deeds"; "greatly admonish, ensigne, and teach"; "by the faults and errors of others to amend and erect our life." The same feature of style appears in the writings of Archbishop Cranmer, and, through his influence, became a conspicuous feature of the language of the English Book of Common Prayer.

It should be remarked in passing that this use of two or more words in place of one does not owe its origin to the bilingual character of the language and a consequent effort to use words representing both the French and the native English elements in the language. This interesting and much discussed hypothesis is unsupported. An examination of the French works translated by Caxton and by Berners reveals that the use of doublets is a feature even more conspicuous in the French originals than in their English translations.

The comparatively simple method of approximating to expression by the use of several words, in spite of a resulting dignity of tone and an appeal to the ear, does not commend itself to modern practice. The problem of modern style, to quote the words of Pater, is "the one word for the one thing." Governing modern taste is an underlying philosophic idea of an exact correlation between the world of language and the world of thought. For each element in thought language should offer an exact counterpart. Everyone will recall the martyrdom to this idea of "Sentimental Tommy," how he sacrificed his chances for the prize in composition because in the competition he spent his precious time in mental groping for the right word. He wanted a Scotch word that would signify how many people were in church. *Puckle* was nearly the word, but it did not mean so many people as he meant. Not content with nearly the word, to the great disquietude of his teacher, he consumed his time in the vain search for the right word, *hantle*.

The painful method adopted by the Scotch boy is the one that must be used by any one that aspires to a mastery of the resources of the language. How is one to be guided in one's choice?

In finding an answer to this question let us turn our attention to a single instance. Suppose the idea to be expressed is some phase of the general idea 'hinder.' A standard work on English synonymy[2] offers the following words to select from: *baffle, balk, bar, block, check, clog, counteract, delay, embarrass, encumber, foil, frustrate, hamper, impede, interrupt, obstruct, oppose, prevent, resist, retard, stay, stop, thwart.*

This list offers illustration of the variety of sources from which English words are assembled. *Balk* and *hinder* and *hamper* and *stay*, and, possibly, *clog*, are of native English origin. *Block* comes from early Teutonic through the French; *thwart* comes from the Norse; *stop* is probably a nautical term, meaning 'plug up,' from a Low German, probably Dutch, word, meaning 'tow'; *check* comes from the Persian through the French; *baffle, bar, delay, embarrass, encumber, foil, oppose, resist* and *retard* are from the French, though most of them are ultimately of Latin origin; *Frustrate, impede, interrupt, obstruct, prevent* and *act* (in *counteract*) are direct from Latin or formed in English from Latin elements. It will hardly be contended that the foreign origin of these words affects their value. One finds here further illustration of the fact already established in an earlier chapter that the source from which a word is derived has little to do with the practical use of the word.

More important than the variety of sources is the variety

---

[2] J. C. Fernald, *Synonyms, Antonyms and Prepositions.*

of figurative meanings underlying. This variety appears in *baffle*, with the earlier meaning 'ridicule' or 'hold up' for contempt; *balk*, O. E. *bealca*, 'ridge,' 'beam'; *bar*, 'barrier,' 'rail'; *block*, 'large piece of wood'; *check*, a word from the game of chess, in origin an oriental name for 'king'; *clog*, probably 'log of wood'; *counteract*, 'to act against' or 'neutralize'; *embarrass*, 'to put within bars'; *encumber*, 'to block up a way' (late Lat. *combrus*, 'barrier' or 'weir'); *foil*, a blend of two words, one a weaving term meaning literally 'to trample,' the other meaning 'to befool'; *hamper*, 'to fetter' or 'bind'; *impede* (first used by Shakespeare), 'to shackle'; *interrupt*, 'to break in on'; *obstruct*, 'to build up against' (*cf. construction*); *oppose*, 'to put against'; *prevent*, 'to come before'; *resist*, 'to stand against'; *retard*, 'to make slow'; *stay* (O. E. *stæg*, 'to support'; *stop*, 'to plug up'; and *thwart*, 'to cross.')

It would be the height of pedantry to make the etymology of words the sole criterion in determining their practical use. Frequently it has been shown, in earlier chapters, a word has shifted in meaning not once, but several successive times, so that the meaning finally reached may be several stages removed from the original, may in fact be precisely the reverse of that at the beginning. Moreover, it must be held in mind that in living speech the meaning of a word is greatly affected by the phrasal combination in which the word habitually appears.

Nevertheless, a knowledge of the etymological meaning is usually of practical value. In the writings of any literary artist one cannot fail to feel that the underlying meaning of the words used is present in the consciousness of the writer. In the case of the synonyms listed above, it may in most cases be assumed that the one who first introduced the word into English was alive to the underlying meaning. Furthermore, this consciousness of the original meaning must have determined the nature of the phrasal combina-

CHOICE OF WORDS

tions into which the word might be introduced, and in this way served to keep alive earlier distinctions. Among the synonyms cited, the original meaning still determines the phrases that may be entered into by such words as *bar* and *obstruct* and *thwart* and *block*. The underlying meaning is still distinctly apparent in such expressions as 'bar the way,' 'obstruct a movement,' 'thwart a purpose,' and 'block a passage.' In such phrases, also, as 'a military check,' 'financially embarrassed,' 'mainstay,' and 'stop gap,' the meaning is not far removed from the original. In other expressions, however, such as 'baffled plans,' 'feel embarrassed,' 'foil an attempt,' 'stay progress,' or 'sensible of a check' (rebuke), the original meaning is so far removed as to offer no practical guidance in the use of the words. The meaning of the word in such cases is determined by the phrase in which the word appears.

Conclusions entirely similar will be reached from an examination of the underlying meanings in the set of synonyms for *obstinate*. Along with *obstinate* (Lat. *obstare*, 'to stand against') are listed as synonyms: *decided*, 'cut off' (Lat. *caedere*, 'to cut'); *determined* (Lat. *terminus*); *dogged, firm, fixed* (Lat. *figere, fixus*, 'to fasten' or 'to make firm'); *headstrong; heady; immovable; indomitable* (*domitare*, frequentative of *domare*, 'to tame'); *inflexible* (Lat. *flectere*, 'to bend'); *intractable* (Lat. *tractare*, 'to handle'); *mulish; obdurate* (Lat. *durus*, 'hard'); *opinionated; persistent* (Lat. *persistere*, 'to remain standing'); *pertinacious* (Lat. *per* + *tenere*, 'to hold'); *pigheaded; refractory* (Lat. *re* + *frangere*, 'to break back'); *resolute; resolved* (Lat. *solvere*, 'to loosen,' 'separate into parts'); *stubborn* (apparently from *stub* and meaning 'stock-like'); *unconquerable* (hybrid formation from *un* + *conquer*, Lat. *quaerere*, 'to seek,' O. Fr. *conquerre*, 'to acquire'); *unflinching* (ultimately from Lat. *flectere*, 'to bend'); *unyielding* (O. E. *gieldan*, 'to pay,' 'to render').

A consideration of the words in these two groups will serve to convince that etymology, while by no means an exclusively determining factor in the choice of words, is still something by no means to be left out of account. The earlier meanings, although in many instances faded almost beyond recognition, must usually still be reckoned with if one is to avoid the discords of mixed metaphor.

Let us now take for consideration other groups of words. The two groups discussed are not entirely representative, since in them the native English language-forming activities have come little into play. The native element is represented in the second group only by *unyielding,* by the compound *headstrong,* and by the figurative words *dogged, heady, mulish, pig-headed,* and *stubborn,* in which, with the exception of the last, the simile is still sharply alive. In general, the lists are made up of ready-made words adopted into English with comparatively little change. It is for the most part only in the case of meanings, associated with strong feelings or elemental feelings that the English speech-creating faculties are quickened once more into action. Words associated with contempt or indignation, therefore, may serve to illustrate the native capacity of English for enriching its stock of synonyms from its own material The synonyms for such words as *blockhead* and *rascal* may be made to illustrate.

The list of synonyms for *blockhead* embraces words of all classes, in amazing variety, in the creation of which the debt to foreign languages is comparatively slight. A single list,[3] which might easily be amplified from colloquial sources, includes *simpleton; Bœotian; dunce* (sixteenth century, from the name of followers of Duns Scotus); *stupid* (Lat., meaning 'stunned'); *dolt* (sixteenth century, probably contraction of *dullard*); *dullard; ass; block; stick* (colloq.); *chump* ('log,' 'thick end,' colloq. or slang);

---

[3] F. S. Allen, *Synonyms and Antonyms.*

CHOICE OF WORDS 401

numbskull (*cf.* mod. slang *bonehead*); *stock* (rare); *dunderhead* (*cf.* Scotch *donnerd,* 'stupefied'); *blunderhead; blunderbuss; clod* ('lump of earth'); *clodpate; clodpoll; cods-head* (slang); *buzzard* (rare); *dotterel, lobster, shrimp, mullet-head,* etc.; *chucklehead* (chiefly dialectal); *coof* (Scotch); *pigsconce; oxhead; loggerhead; lunkhead* (Amer. slang); *woodenhead; hardhead; booby; doddypoll* (obsolete or rare); *cuddy* (Scotch); *idiot; dummy; driveler; mome* (archaic); *imbecile; foozle; saphead; jolthead* (rare); *wiseacre* (ironical).

The synonyms for *rascal* exhibit the same lively activity of popular invention. The list includes: *rascal* (applied in the sixteenth century also to lean deer); *rogue* (sixteenth century cant word for 'vagabond'); *scoundrel; blackguard* (sixteenth century, 'lowest menial of a large household'); *villain* (O. Fr.'serf'); *scamp* (originally cant for 'highwayman,' O. Fr. *escamper,* 'to decamp'); *miscreant* (rare or literary, literally 'unbelieving,' applied originally to Saracen foes of Christian); *sealawag* (colloq.); *scapegrace; rapscallion* (from earlier *rascallion*); *vagabond* (Fr. from Lat.); *reprobate; knave; imp* (O. E. *impa,* 'shoot' or 'graft'); *limb* (earlier *limb of Satan*); *sinner; varlet* (archaic); *shyster* (Amer. vulgar or cant); *spalpeen* (Irish); *scab* (vulgar slang); *skellum* (archaic or South Africa); *comrogue* (archaic); *canter* (archaic); *rautener* (obsolete).

The last two groups of words, so strongly charged with emotion, offer illustration, not only of the life in the English language, but of word distinction of another kind from those considered. Words, like people, have their class distinctions. The two groups of words form a mob. The mob is composed of slang words in their shirt sleeves, dialect words in homespun garb, archaic words in old-fashioned apparel, along with a few words in modern conventional attire. The problem of speech, like that of society, is one of grouping. Words, like people, are ill at ease out of their natural environment. The choice of words is like social tact. People must find their own social set; words must be adapted to the context.

From the discussion thus far may be gathered certain obvious conclusions. In the selection of words, the matter of source one may in general leave out of consideration. One must, however, take into account the relation between sound and sense. To take an extreme instance, it would obviously be impossible to apply a word with the sound of *buzz* as a name for the note of a flute. For much the same reason one cannot afford to fail to take into account the figurative meaning so frequently underlying. There must be harmony not only between sound and meaning but between the meanings of different elements in a phrase. A word must suit its context. There would, for instance, be obvious discord in speaking of a farm as *panning out*. Further, one cannot afford to ignore the class distinctions referred to, to combine the archaic with the neologistic slang and the dialectal with the aristocratic and elegant.

There remains one more extremely important consideration. In the choice of a word, one cannot afford to leave out of account those elements of meaning which are derived from association.

Qualities derived by association vary in nature. A word is affected by the kind of people with whose use it is associated. Words such as *chunk* and *chore* and *callate* (for 'expect'), expressive in themselves, are objectionable because of homely associations with the manner of speech of the uncultivated. Other words are affected by their association with certain occupations. Language, like romance, is aristocratic in tone. Words such as *balance* (for 'remainder'), *endorse* (for 'approve'), *posted,* (for 'informed'), are affected by their middle-class associations with the pursuit of gain. Still other words are affected by their phrasal associations. *Enormity,* already discussed, may be cited in

CHOICE OF WORDS 403

illustration. From constant phrasal association with the words *crime* and *offense*, it has absorbed into its connotation an element of meaning derived from these words. Other words of this class are the words *gang, herd, band,* etc., discussed above.

Let us consider a few additional instances of words that have absorbed elements of meaning from associations. The word *condign,* which by etymology means 'merited' or 'suitable' (Lat. *con,* 'with' + *dignus,* 'suitable' or 'becoming') has been indelibly affected through association with the word *punishment*. *Lengthy* can no longer be used with the innocent meaning, 'somewhat long,' because it has absorbed, through association, the meaning 'tedious.' *Visitation* in like manner may no longer safely be used as a substitute for *visit* as it was used by Chaucer and Shakespeare, because the word is now too vividly associated with affliction or calamity. The effect of different associations may be observed in the different meanings expressed by *heavy, weighty,* and *ponderous,* words which by etymology are nearly equivalent. Associations of this nature vary with different periods. *Companion,* for instance, which in the sixteenth century had been affected in meaning by association with the adjectives *base* and *vile,* in modern use has quite cleared itself of its old associations. *Fellow,* on the other hand, once associated with a dignity which it still retains in a few phrases, has become affected by associations undignified in character. In modern America the word *moonshine* has acquired associations which unfit the word for its earlier uses.

Associated meaning, unlike figurative meaning, may not be universal in character. Associations may be personal in character like those familiar to all in the case of special personal names. Hence a word objectionable to one may not arouse the same objectionable associations for another. Hence the violent personal likes and dislikes attached to certain words, for instance, the word *vittles*. Hence, also, the difference of opinion regarding certain words and the need of some standard to govern usage.

Nearly a century ago De Quincey deplored the lack of critical taste in the language of his time.

> We have [said he], no sufficient dictionary; and we have no work at all, sufficient or insufficient, on the phrases and idiomatic niceties of our language, corresponding to the works of Vaugelas and others for the French.
>
> Hence an anomaly not found perhaps in any literature but ours, that the most eminent English writers do not write their mother tongue without continual violations of propriety. With the single exceptions of Mr. Wordsworth, who has paid an honorable attention to the purity and accuracy of his English, we believe that there is not one celebrated author of this day who has written two pages consecutively without some flagrant impropriety in the grammar or some violation more or less of the vernacular idiom.

The words of De Quincey are hardly applicable at the present day. In the hundred years since these words were written, critical works dealing with the purity and propriety of words have not been lacking. Innumerable books on rhetoric and English composition have given attention to the subject. Negative directions are always easier to give than positive ones, or in any event are easier to put in definite form. Hence the number of *don'ts* which, beginning in the critical age of Addison and Swift, have in the nineteenth century, with ever increasing frequency, come to be applied to different words. Not only men of letters in critical writings, and grammarians and rhetoricians in their treatises, have taken a hand in the attempt to prune the inelegancies from our speech, but editors of our periodical literature have joined in the effort. In American journalism it is a prevailing practice with every newspaper and literary journal of prominence to have "style books" or

CHOICE OF WORDS 405

"style sheets," a prominent feature of which is a list of words to be avoided by contributors.

Some of these lists offer interesting information regarding puristic tendencies and also regarding the popular tendencies against which purism has to contend. Let us take for consideration two of these lists of proscribed words. First let us take the well-known list prepared by William Cullen Bryant about the middle of the nineteenth century when he was editor of the New York *Evening Post:*

Above and over (for "more than")
Artiste (for "artist")
Aspirant
Authoress
Beat (for "defeat")
Bagging (for "capturing")
Balance (for "remainder")
Banquet (for "dinner" or "supper")
Bogus
Casket (for "coffin")
Claimed (for "asserted")
Collided
Commence (for "begin")
Cortège (for "procession")
Cotemporary (for "cotemporary")
Couple (for "two")
Darky (for "negro")
Day before yesterday (for "the day before yesterday")
Début
Decease (as a verb)
Democracy (applied to a political party)
Develop (for "expose")
Devouring element (for "fire")
Donate
Employé
Endorse (for "approve")
En Route
Esq.
Graduate (for "is graduated")
Gents (for "gentlemen")
Hon.
House (for "House of Representatives")
Humbug
Inaugurate (for "begin")
In our midst
Item (for "particle, extract or paragraph")
Is being done, and all passives of this form
Jeopardize
Jubilant (for "rejoicing")
Juvenile (for "boy")
Lady (for "wife")
Last (for "latest")
Lengthy (for "long")
Leniency (for "lenity")
Loafer
Loan or loaned (for "lend" or "lent")
Located
Majority (relating to places or circumstances, for "most")
Mrs. President, Mrs. Governor, Mrs. General and all similar titles

Mutual (for "common")
Official (for "officer")
Ovation
On yesterday
Over his signature
Pants (for "pantaloons")
Parties (for "persons")
Partially (for "partly")
Past two weeks (for "last two weeks," and all similar expressions relating to a definite time)
Poetess
Portion (for "part")
Posted (for "informed")
Progress (for "advance")
Quite (prefixed to "good," "large," etc.)
Raid (for "attack")
Realized (for "obtained")
Reliable (for "trustworthy")
Repudiate (for "reject" or "disown")
Retire (as an active verb)
Rev. (for "the Rev.")
Rôle (for "part")
Roughs
Rowdies
Secesh
Sensation (for "noteworthy event")
Standpoint (for "point of view")
State (for "say")
Taboo
Talent (for "talents" or "ability")
Talented
Tapis
The deceased
The United States as a singular noun
Transpire (for "occur")
Via (for "by the way of")
Vicinity (for "neighborhood")
Wall street slang generally ("bulls, bears, long, short, flat, corner, tight, moribund, comatose," etc.)
Which (with a noun, as "which man")
Wharves (for "wharfs")
Would seem (for "seems")

If one searches for an explanation of the aversion felt toward the words in this list, one will find the reasons varied. Some of the words were felt as new, and new words in all periods have aroused opposition. Ben Jonson cites as new words in the language of his rival Marston, apparently with disapproval, the words: *clumsy, inflate, spurious, conscious, strenuous, defunct, retrograde,* and *reciprocal.* Benjamin Franklin, at the end of the following century, objected to *improved, noticed, advocated, progressed, opposed.*[4] New words with their sharper colors have the

---

[4] Brander Matthews, *Parts of Speech*, p. 159.

effect of new threads worked into an old fabric whose colors have been softened by time. Or is the aversion to new words to be explained by the fact that speech is made up of formed phrases and the new words have not become fitted into phrases that are usual? Among the words felt as new in 1850 were *aspirant, bogus, donate, reliable, standpoint, taboo, talented.*

Another ground of objection to words in the list was the disregard shown for refinements of distinction in form and in meaning. Such words as *graduate, last, located, mutual, in our midst, partially, quite, reliable* and *transpire,* in the senses objected to, either did violence to some principle of word structure which attention to formal rule in language had caused to be felt as important, or in the case of *last, partially, mutual, quite, transpire,* effaced distinctions of meaning which belonged to the refinements of cultivated speech.

In the case of other words aversion was felt for a vulgar form of grandiloquence conspicuous in journalistic style, a quality appearing in such words as *banquet, commence, inaugurate, devouring element, jubilant, ovation, portion,* or for a no less vulgar timidity about calling a spade a spade in such words as *casket* and *decease.*

More potent still as a reason for objection was the nature of the underlying figurative meaning. Ground for this objection is apparent in such words as *bagged* and *beat.* But the most conspicuous set of objectionable words in the list is the set of terms from the language of law and commerce figuratively turned to more general meanings, words whose associations render them objectionable in general use. The taint of commercialism is plainly evident in such words as *balance, endorse, item, loan, parties, posted, realized,* and *repudiate.*

Let us take one more list of this kind, a list of "words

to be avoided," which appears in the "Style Sheet" of the *Century Magazine:*

above or *over* for *more than*
affair for *thing*
aggravate for *annoy*
aggregate for *total*
along these lines, hard lines
anxious for *desirous*
balance for *remainder*
bogus for *spurious*
call attention for *direct attention.*
claim for *assert*
center around for *center in* or *upon*
commence for *begin*
conscious for *aware*
couple for *two*
cultured for *cultivated*
date back to for *date from*
dived for *dove*
donate for *give*
he was given a dinner for *a dinner was given to him*
indorse for *approve*
fall for *autumn*
from whence for *whence*
inaugurate for *establish, institute*
individual for *person*
infinite for *great, vast*
in our midst for *among us*
in spite of for *despite*
in the last analysis
last for *latest*
less for *fewer*
liable for *likely*
materially for *largely*
mutual for *common*
notice for *observe*
on behalf for *in behalf*
onto for *on* or *upon*
partially for *partly*
party for *person*
past two years for *last two years*

'phone for *telephone*
position for *place, office*
practically for *virtually*
prior to for *before*
propose for *purpose*
proven for *proved*
providing for *provided*
quite for *something of*
rarely ever for *rarely* or *hardly ever*
realize for *obtain*
section for *region*
some ten miles for *about ten miles*
spend for *pass*
standpoint for *point of view*
start for *begin*
subsequently for *afterward*
transpire for *happen*
universal for *general*
vest for *waistcoat*
vicinity for *neighborhood*
viewpoint for *point of view*
wire for *send a telegram*
would seem for *seems*

One will observe in this list a number of words from the earlier list of Bryant, words against the use of which the purist is obliged to maintain his struggle. One will observe also additional words, either new words, such as *viewpoint*, *phone* and *wire*, or words in popular use lacking in distinction because, as in the case of *vest*, associated with vulgarity of social class or, as in the case of such words as *aggravate* or *anxious*, with the more serious form of vulgarity springing from inability to feel shades of distinction in meaning, or as in the case of *along these lines*, or *hard lines*, insensibility to qualities associated with words. One will observe also the absence of many words that appeared in the earlier list. In some instances such as *gents*, *secesh* or *tapis*, the victory of purism has been so complete that the objectionable words no longer need to be pointed out. In a smaller number of instances, such as *reliable, leniency, talented, jeopardize,* and *taboo,* the words have apparently become so firmly established that further objection does not exist, or if urged, would be vain.

Unceasing has been the attempt in modern times to regulate the use of words. Among the ranks of the purists probably the most conspicuous figure has been that of Richard Grant White, whose objections to certain words have exerted an appreciable influence, and whose lists of objectionable words compiled about a half century ago, still form the basis for similar lists in use with various modern publishers. His point of view may best be expressed in his own language: "Reason always wins against formal grammar or illogical usage." "The authority of eminent writers, conforming to, or forming the usage of their day . . . does not completely justify or establish a use of words inconsistent with reason or out of the direction of the normal growth of language."

Opposed to the position of White is that of the most influential students of language of the present day. An opinion prevailing at the present time is that the use of words is determined by the prevailing usage of cultivated people and that the ability to use words properly is to be gained, not from reason or logic or from the study of etymology, but from an alert feeling for the shades of meaning of language in actual use and a sensitiveness for the associated meanings that attach themselves. Theoretical considerations are obliged to yield before the facts of prevalent use.

An instructive illustration of the way in which theory is compelled to yield before practice is offered by the experience of A. S. Hill, perhaps the leading rhetorician of the generation just passed. The gradual yielding of purism before the tide of prevailing usage is registered in successive editions of his rhetorics published in 1878, 1892, 1895 and 1902. Among the words discussed in his books as of questionable propriety, one finds, among changes arising from the invention of new words, such examples as *cablegram, agriculturalist, brainy, an elective, an editorial, curios, to clerk, to deed, to launder, to boycott;* among changes caused by reviving old words, *back of* for *behind, clever* for *good-natured, eat* for *ate;* among usages brought about by the force of analogy, *in our midst, onto, meet with, try and, one . . . his* for *one . . . one's;* among doublets blurred by disregarding distinctions in meaning, *alone* and *only, aware* and *conscious, confess* and *admit, oral* and *verbal;* among doublets arising from the free use of technical or dialectic words, *wage* and *wage-fund, to depreciate, campus, to umpire, to referee,* and *lumber* for *timber.* Though Professor Hill, at one time or another, criticized these expressions severely, in his latest edition he accepted them as being in more or less good colloquial use; and in a few instances, such as *to boycott, to meet with, to depreciate, to launder, to try and, lumber, a verbal message,* and *confess* for *admit,* he gave them literary rank.[5]

[5] Elizabeth Colton, *Modern Language Notes*, November, 1910.

CHAPTER XXVII

WORDS PAST AND PRESENT

The contrast between modern English and English in the earlier stages of its development hardly needs further to be pointed out. Old English, or Anglo-Saxon, the English of Alfred the Great's time, to be understood, must be learned as one learns a foreign language. English even of the Middle English period, the English of Chaucer, is hardly intelligible, except to the specialist, without the aid of a glossary. The differences within the Modern English period, which begins about 1500, are not so strikingly apparent but are nevertheless real, and a realization of their existence is of incalculable importance to one who will rightly understand the literature of centuries preceding our own.

The language of Shakespeare, for instance, is farther from modern English than is sometimes realized. If Shakespeare himself were to recite his verse before a modern audience, his pronunciation would hardly escape ridicule. The hearer would inevitably be reminded of the pronunciation associated with farcical humor in the speech of the stage Irishman. Shakespeare's words, while somewhat less unfamiliar, nevertheless convey their full and precise meaning only to the instructed. For a precise understanding of his language, specialists have found it necessary to compile glossaries in bulk comparable to the lexicons used in studying foreign languages.

In order to illustrate in short space the difference between his use of words and that of to-day, let us take a few words from a single one of his plays. In *King Lear* we meet with the phrase "fretful elements" (III, 1, 4). The older meaning of *'devour'* (O. E. *fretan*) is still an element in the meaning. The adjective has not yet been restricted to nursery use. In "all germens spill at once" (III, 2, 8), the obsolete word *germen* (Lat. *germen*, 'sprout, 'germ') is accompanied by *spill* in an obsolete meaning (O. E. *spillan*, 'to destroy'). In "thrilled with remorse" (IV, 2, 73), we meet with an earlier use of *thrill* (O. E. *thyrlian*, 'to pierce'). The word has not yet been limited so as to apply exclusively to the piercing effect of exciting emotions. In "on flickering Phœbus' front" (II, 2, 110) we meet with the original meaning of *front* (Lat. *frons, -tem*, 'forehead'). In "horrid thunder" (III, 2, 41) *horrid* has not yet become restricted to its modern trivial use. "Smug bridegroom" (IV, 6, 184) exemplifies the use of *smug* in the sixteenth century when the word first made its appearance in English, with the meaning 'trim,' 'spruce.' The later degeneration in the word is striking. In "fast intent" (I, 1, 33) the native English word *fast* (O. E. *fæst*) retains its original meaning, which survives in a few modern expressions such as 'fast asleep.' In "taking airs" (II, 4, 166) the word *taking* has the meaning 'bewitching,' in a malignant sense. The word in later use, like the word *bewitching*, has been elevated in use through the loss of the suggestion of malignancy. With this change the word appears in modern expressions such as 'taking manners' and 'taking appearance.'

The Shakespearean words just cited, exemplify, for the most part, the survival in Elizabethan English of earlier English words with meanings that have since been modified. The difference between Elizabethan English and present-day English is perhaps even more strikingly apparent in the case of the classical words which, under Renaissance influence, were in the sixteenth century crowding into English. It was not until the end of the seventeenth century that these imported words were sifted, and only gradually have those retained settled into phrasal combinations that have determined their later meanings in English. In the sixteenth-century English, in words of classical derivation there is frequently still apparent a surviving consciousness of the etymological meaning, a consciousness which has been lost in later use. *Curiosity* (I, 1, 5), meaning 'painstaking,' has not arrived at its later meaning of 'inquisitiveness' but is nearly related in meaning to its Latin original. The same surviving consciousness of the original meaning appears in a great number of words. *Enormous* (II, 2, 171) means 'extraordinary' (Lat. *e* 'out of' + *norma,* 'rule'). It has not yet become restricted to the modern meaning, 'extraordinary size.' *Diffidences* (I, 2, 155) means 'suspicions' (Lat. *dis* + *fidere,* 'to trust'); the word had not yet narrowed to its later meaning of 'self-distrust.' *Mortified* (II, 3, 15) means 'deadened' (Lat. *mortificare,* 'to cause death'); it has not yet become specialized so as to apply exclusively to a state of feeling. *Dejected* (IV, 1, 3) means literally 'cast down' (Lat. *de* + *jacere,* 'to throw'); like *mortified,* it has not yet become restricted in application to personal feeling. *Provoke* (IV, 4, 13) means literally 'call forth' (Lat. *pro* 'forth' + *vocare,* 'to call'); it has not yet become restricted to the calling forth of anger. In like manner *continents* (III, 2, 53) means literally 'containers,' not yet restricted to its modern geographical use, and *impertinency* (IV, 6, 159) means 'irrelevancy' (Lat. *in,* 'not' + *pertinere* 'to pertain') without the modern acquired meaning of 'sauciness.' The phrase *upon respect* (II, 4, 24) means 'after consideration' or 'after reflection' (Lat. *re* 'again' + *specere* 'to look at'). It is to be noted that the later development of meaning to 'deferential consideration' is closely paralleled in the history of the words, *consideration* and *regard.*

WORDS PAST AND PRESENT

For an understanding of the Authorized Version of the Bible the same degree of importance is to be attached, as in the case of Shakespeare, to an appreciation of the difference between the language of three centuries ago and that of to-day. To one who will escape downright heresy in his interpretation, a knowledge of the original Greek or Hebrew is hardly more important than a knowledge of Elizabethan English.

In some ways the language of the King James Bible is less far removed from present-day use than is that of Shakespeare. This is true because in many instances the modern use of words has been determined by the phrasal combinations into which they entered in the English Bible. Nevertheless differences from modern use are everywhere at hand in Biblical language. Like the language of Shakespeare, the language of the King James Bible preserves many a fossil form of speech. Like a geological stratum, it serves to preserve the remains of many a word elsewhere extinct. Good old Anglo-Saxon uses of words survive in phrases like the following: *meat and drink* (O. E. *mete* 'food'); *fowls of the air* (O. E. *fugol*, 'bird'); *give up the ghost* (O. E. *gāst*, 'spirit'); *the quick and the dead* (O. E. *cwic*, 'alive'); *wax warm* (O. E. *weaxan* 'to grow'); *stand fast* (O. E. *fæste*, 'firm'); *sore afraid* (O. E. *sār*, 'very,' like German *sehr*); *exceeding wroth* (O. E. *wrāth*, 'angry').

In the reading of the Bible, a failure to appreciate the changed meanings of words in our day, may easily lead the unwary from the strait and narrow way of true belief. Let us consider a few expressions that exemplify the changes in meaning that have come about. Both *anon* and *by and by* still retain their earlier meanings in such expressions as "he that heareth the word, and *anon* with joy receiveth it" (Matt. 13:20) and in the following verse, "when tribulation or persecution ariseth because of the word, *by and by* he is offended." These words have not yet degenerated under the influence of habitual exaggeration in statements regarding promptness, but retain their earlier meaning of 'at once.' *Outlandish* has not yet arrived at the meaning 'bizarre,' but still retains its etymological meaning 'foreign,' as in the expression, "even him did *outlandish* women cause to sin" (Neh. 13:26). *Naughty* has not yet reached the meaning 'ill-behaved' as applied to children, but retains its original meaning of 'good for naught' exemplified in the assertion, "the other basket had very *naughty* figs (Jer. 241, 12).

The changes that have affected words, have in many instances deprived biblical expressions of the dignity that was once theirs. In this way many biblical phrases, if the words are taken in their modern meaning, appear to be slangy or at least highly colloquial and subject to irreverent interpretation. For example take the expressions: "I am a *smooth* man" (Gen. 27:11); "away with such a *fellow*" (Acts 22:22); "lest he be *full* and deny thee" (Prov. 30:9); "He cometh *skipping* upon the hills (Songs of Solomon, 2:8); "were passed *clean over* Jordan" (Josh. 3:17); thou shalt *bestir thyself* (II Sam. 5:34); "I am escaped with the *skin of my teeth* (Job, 19:20).

As in Shakespearean language, also, there are frequently appearing instances of classical derivatives, words of recent introduction not yet assimilated to English use, but retaining their earlier meanings. As instances of words of this class may be cited such words as *conversation* in the sense of 'conduct,' *overcharge* meaning 'overburden,' *provoked* meaning 'called forth,' *instant* meaning 'urgent,' 'importunate,' *congregation* meaning 'assembly,' *determined* meaning 'limited,' *convenient* meaning 'fitting.' In the sentence, "For that which I do, I *allow* not" (Rom. 7:15), where *allow* has an earlier meaning, 'praise,' to read the modern meaning into *allow* would be to convict St. Paul of special privilege. On the other hand his injunction,

"Be careful for nothing" (Phil. 4:6), where *careful* has its etymological meaning 'full of care' or 'anxious,' if followed with the modern meaning of *careful,* would lead on the road to destruction.

The instances cited from Shakespeare and the Bible will serve to convey an idea of the extent to which words have changed in meaning within the Modern English period. In the case of the words cited, one may observe in operation many of the semantic principles discussed in preceding chapters. But the difference between modern English and that of earlier periods is not to be explained solely by natural tendencies inherent in the nature of language. Deeper forces have shared in the work. In the growth of the English language within the four centuries of the Modern English period, may be seen outwardly expressed the expansion of the human intelligence which is the most important outcome of the Renaissance movement. A recent writer in a most illuminating manner has shown how during the modern English period, beginning with the sixteenth century, the English language has expanded in response to the intellectual growth of the race.[1]

Under the influence of the Renaissance, beginning with the sixteenth century, there came a new way of looking at the universe. Knowledge, which the Middle Ages had looked upon as a traditional heritage authoritatively interpreted by the church, came to be sought from new sources. Nature came to be looked upon as an open book to be attentively read and studied. The new conception of knowledge as something expansible is registered in language by such words as *theory, theorize,* and *theoretical. Theory* in its modern meaning of a 'supposition explaining something' is first cited in the Oxford Dictionary from 1638. *Theorize* is cited from 1638; *theoretical,* with its modern meaning, from 1652. The attitude of the early humanists toward

---
[1] L. P. Smith, *The English Language* (New York, 1912), Ch. ix.

earlier modes of thought is further illustrated by their use of the word *dunce,* discussed in an earlier chapter.

The natural science of the Middle Ages had been directed toward learning things of symbolical meaning or of immediate practical utility. The lore of beasts was assembled in medieval bestiaries for the sake of the symbolical light it might throw on things of the spirit. The knowledge of precious stones was cultivated because of the magical powers stones were believed to possess, a form of superstition even yet not extinct. Plants were studied for their medicinal virtues, from which many plants took names which they still bear. The heavens, in their turn, were studied for the information the stars might afford concerning human destinies. The chemical relations of substances were studied in the search of a method by which baser metals might be transmuted into gold.

To such ill-directed efforts the new era brought an end. The medieval lapidarist was succeeded by the mineralogist, the herbalist by the botanist, the alchemist by the chemist, the astrologer by the astronomer. Pure science, devoted to the assembling and classification of facts, succeeded the earlier science interested solely in the symbolical or magical properties of things. The dates of the first use of the names of various modern sciences affords an idea of the time of this transformation. In the Oxford Dictionary the word *astronomy* is cited from as far back as 1205, but it is there confused in meaning with astrology. On the other hand, *chemistry* is not cited until 1646, *botany* until 1696, and *mineralogy* until 1690 (*mineralogist* 1646). One is brought to a realization of the substantial progress in knowledge resulting from the new intellectual activity, when one calls to mind that the circulation of the blood was first discovered in 1635 and the law of gravitation in 1685. The new mode of thought, and the resulting realization of the order prevailing in nature, of the domination of natural law and the way by which nature's secrets are to be learned, find their outward expression in new words. *Orderly,* in the Oxford Dictionary, makes its appearance in 1477, *orderliness* in 1571. *Observe* and *observation,* referring to the act of giving attention, appear respectively in 1559 and 1557. *Method* appears in 1586, *system* in 1638, *systematic* with its modern prevailing meaning not until 1790, *natural history* in 1567, *distinguish* in 1561. *Experiment,* in the meaning 'ascertain' or 'establish by trial,' appears as early as 1481, but *analyse* not until 1601 and *analysis* not until 1667. *Synthesis* is cited as a logical term in 1611, as a *chemical* term in 1733. *Classify* and *classification* do not appear until the end of the eighteenth century, respectively 1799 and 1790, and *arrange,* as a military term in use since the fourteenth century, does not appear with the meaning 'put in order' until the dawn of the nineteenth century (1802).

Modern times are dominated not only by the idea of a natural order but by that of progress. Interest in the present is, to be sure, engrossing enough, but along with it goes aspiration for the future. Progress is the watchword in the world of mechanics and in the world of politics. In the world of plant culture and of animal culture, improvement of type is an aim constantly in mind. Such modern words as *eugenics* and *superman* indicate aspiration for development even in the human species. So dominant is the modern idea of progress that it is not easy to conceive of a state of mind which regarded the state of the world as a fixed state. Yet the history of English words bears witness to the development from the earlier way of thinking.[2] It has been pointed out that of the series of words for progress, *advance, amelioration, development, improvement, progress* and *evolution,* not one was used with its present meaning in English before the sixteenth century.

---

[2] Smith, *op. cit.,* p. 224.

The present writer well remembers his feeling little short of astonishment at the discovery that the word *selfish* does not appear in English until the seventeenth century. Against pride and envy and avarice and the other four Deadly Sins, the church from early times waged persistent war. But not until the seventeenth century (1640) is what may be regarded as the most universal human fault singled out by means of this seemingly indispensable adjective, first alluded to as of the "Presbyterians' own new mint." The word, however, illustrates another feature of human development which has characterized the period covered by modern English. This feature is the ever increasing interest in self-analysis, culminating in the modern general engrossing interest in psychology and her younger sister, psycho-analysis. The ever increasing interest in personality and in personal emotion is registered in language in the ever increasing number of names for conceptions of this nature. Making their first appearance in the sixteenth century are *loneliness* 1586, *to entrance* 1599, *fancy* 1581. In the seventeenth century first appear *lonely* 1607, *lonesome* 1647, *depression* (of spirits) 1665, *ennui* 1667, *chagrin* 1656, *agitation* (mental) 1605, *to divert* ('entertain') 1662, *enliven* ('make cheerful') 1626, *entertain* ('amuse') 1625, *amuse* ('entertain') 1631, *fascinate* ('hold spellbound by delight') 1651, *disgust* 1611. Of eighteenth-century origin are *constraint* (of feeling) 1706, *embarrassment* 1774, *sentimental* (of persons) 1749, *sentimentalist* 1793, *interesting* ('engaging attention') 1768, *disappointment* (state of feeling) 1756, *bore* (verb and substantive) 1750, *funny* 1756, *fun* ('amusement') 1727, *genius* ('natural ability of exalted type') 1749, *egoism* 1722, *self-centered* (of persons, unfavorable sense) 1783, *homesick* 1798. Of nineteenth-century origin are *to excite* ('move to strong emotion') 1850 and *excitement* (mental agitation) 1856. In the twentieth century have been set in circulation—how many? Certainly most of the technical vocabulary of modern psycho-analysis.

The opening of eyes to the facts of existence and the efforts made to interpret these facts, has led to immense progress in all the natural sciences. The distance progressed from the fixed ideas of the medieval mind is marked by such words as *intolerance* 1765 and *open-minded* (not cited in the Oxford Dictionary). The direction as well as the extent of this progress is indicated by the dates of the first registered appearance of such words in the field of chemistry as *chemistry* 1646, *acid* 1646, *alkaline* 1667, *analysis* (chemical) 1667, *molecule* 1794, *atom* (chemical) 1819, *ion* 1834, *electron* (chemical unit) not yet recorded in the Oxford Dictionary, *aluminium* 1812, *bromine* 1826, *cyanide* 1826, *aniline* 1850, *argon* 1894, *radium* (not in Oxford Dictionary). *Physics* (in place of older *natural philosophy*) first appears in 1715. Other terms indicating the nature of progress in the field of physics are *atom* (natural philosophy) 1650, *gravitation* (physical) 1645, *electricity* 1646, *adhesion* 1645, *actinic* 1844, *chromatic* (colors) 1835, *cathode* 1834, *anode* 1741.

Growing precision in medical knowledge is indicated by the series of words *consumption, phthisis,* and *tuberculosis,* elsewhere cited, as well as by such modern technically precise words as *anemia* 1738, *aphasia* 1867, *amnesia* 1878. More recent progress in medical science is registered by such words as *antiseptic* 1751, *disinfectant* 1837, *vaccinate* 1803, *anesthetic* 1848, *serum* (as a therapeutic) 1876, *bacteriology* 1884, *adenoid,* (adj.) 1873. (The noun *adenoids* is too recent for the Oxford Dictionary.) The modern point of view in the world of science is indicated by such words as *scientist,* first recorded from 1840, and *specialist,* in a general sense recorded from 1842, but as applied to medicine first recorded in 1856.

That modern times are not lacking in thought activity

nor in inventive creation, is indicated by the hosts of new names which, as set forth in an earlier chapter, are requiring constant expansion in English dictionaries. Nor do the older sources of word material show signs of exhaustion. Foreign importations, and new creations from native and from classical elements as well, are represented in the swarms of new words that modern speech activity is driven to adopt to express the new features of modern life. An impression regarding some of the currents of influence that are contributing to modern progress as well as of the nature of modern speech activity may be gained from such modern words as *agnostic* 1870, *airplane, airedale* 1886, *Anzac, atoll* 1842, *ball-bearing, barrage* 1918, *benzoate, blimp, blow-out* (of a tire), *blue-print, blurb* 1922(?), *brain-fag, cinema* (which in England has survived in competition with *kinetoscope, animotoscope, biograph, cinematograph,* and *movie), coaster* ('low round tray') 1887, *co-ed, cold-wave, chop-suey, croquet* 1858, *cyclone* 1848, *death-trap, denatured* 1878, *dreadnaught* (naval), *dynamite* 1867, *fire-drill, flivver, futurist* (in art), *gunman* ('robber'), *hangar* 1852, *heckle* (English use) 1880, *imperialism* (spirit of empire) 1881, *kindergarten* 1852, *kodak* 1890, *linoleum* 1878, *linotype* 1888, *loganberry* 1900, *lorry, lyddite* 1888, *mackintosh* 1823, *mercerize* 1850, *multimillionaire, omnibus* 1829, *opportunist* 1876, *periscope* (of submarine) 1899, *pogo* 1921(?), *press-agent, protoplasm* 1849, *push-button, radio-gram* 1896, *sabotage, slacker* 1898, *slide-valve, slot-machine* 1892, *sloyd* 1825, *slum* 1825, *slush-fund, swank* (general use begins after 1900), *thermos* (bottle) 1909, *third-rail, triplane, ukulele, vitamine, week-end, whippet,*[3] *wire-tapping, wood-pulp, yegg* 1903.[4]

[3] The dates of earliest citation in the Oxford Dictionary are given as far as available. Of the words in this list, the only ones appearing with their latest development in meaning in the 1893 edition of *Webster's International Dictionary* are *agnostic, atoll, benzoate, croquet, cyclone, dynamite, imperialism, kindergarten, linoleum, omnibus, opportunist, protoplasm,* and *slum.*

[4] 1903 *Century Supplement.*

What an atmosphere of modernity is created by such words! They serve to conduct one into the modern era which, because of its contrast in so many ways with the era just passed, has not inappropriately been called "The New World." We may well conclude our survey of the subject of English words with a consideration of the use of words which expresses the spirit of "The New World" in which we are living.

The spirit that governs the use of words to-day may, perhaps, be best exhibited by contrast with the spirit of the Victorian Age. One should recall the puristic spirit that dominated during most of the nineteenth century, the opposition to the use of words at that time new, such words as *talented, environment, reliable, jeopardize,* and *aspirant.* Emerson, we are told, used *potentially* with apology and only hesitatingly such words as *nescience* and *uncouth.* In the search for freshness of expression, nineteenth-century writers followed the commendable practice of searching the dictionaries. Browning is said to have "enlarged his poetic vocabulary by a diligent study of Johnson." Ruskin, we are told, "assured the late Sir James Murray that he read the first part of the Oxford Dictionary from beginning to end." Robert Louis Stevenson, also, so alert in his watch for new modes of expression, in expressing his pleasure derived from this same dictionary, burst forth: "I have the new dictionary; a joy, a thing of beauty, and bulk. I shall be raked i' the mools before it's finished; that is the only pity; but meanwhile I sing." [5]

Throughout the Victorian age prevails the feeling that we of the present are guardians of an inherited language and that it is our duty to preserve this language in its classical purity. "When a language has been cultivated,"

---
[5] Letter to W. E. Henley, 1883.

says Cardinal Newman, "and so far as it has been generally perfected, an existing want has been supplied, and there is no need of further workmen. In its earliest times, whilst it is yet unformed, to write in it at all is almost a work of genius. It is like crossing a country before roads are made communicating between place and place. The authors of that age deserve to be classics both because of what they do and because they do it. It requires the courage and force of a great talent to compose in the language at all; and the composition, when effected, makes a permanent impression on it."

From the spirit of the Victorian Age, thus expressed, the present age is in active revolt. Everywhere one may see evidence of a feeling that literary forms and literary phraseology that have become commonplace must be superseded. Classical forms of verse are succeeded by free verse; classical diction is succeeded by a diction more directly expressive of the life of the immediate present. The vogue, at least temporarily, has passed for what has been called "the over-appareled art" of Tennyson and his contemporaries, who have been called the "race to whom literature was a gesture of gentility and not a comprehension of life." There is a revolt also from a dominant intellectual quality in language. In some instances words used exclusively as tools of the intellect have become fringed with associations scientific in nature. Let us take a single striking example. The word *female,* which writers of a century ago, Charles Lamb, for instance, might use for 'woman,' is now the exclusive tool of science in the discrimination of sex. In other instances, the generalizing process has gone so far that words have become quite removed from the world of the senses. There is at present an insistent demand for words associated with "direct and concrete experience," as Walter Pater has expressed it, in place of words that have become "abstractions which are but the ghosts of bygone impressions."[6]

Sounds of revolt are to be heard on all sides, Ford Maddox Hueffer, referring to the days of his collaboration with Joseph Conrad, says that "in those days Mr. Conrad's unceasing search was for a New Form for the novel, mine for a non-literary vocabulary." That Mr. Conrad, too, was alive to the need of a renewed sharpness to expression is shown by his complaint regarding "the old, old words, worn thin, defaced by ages of careless usage."[7] In similar vein has been pointed out the disadvantage at which the literary artist stands in relation to the musician. The musician has at his command pure tones uncontaminated by associations clinging from use in earlier combinations. With the word artist, when he undertakes to convey his impressions, the situation is different. "For the names he uses are the names neither of these things nor of his vision of them, but of a thousand blunted perceptions and half obliterated memories. He cannot, like the musician, invent an expression never used before. He must take the shabby old names of things and by a trickery that threatens always to make an artifice of his art, seek to lend them some freshness and immediacy and sting."[8]

If such are the ideals of the modern world, how are these ideals reflected in the practice of modern writers? Older members of the present generation will easily recall the startling effect on the literary world produced by Kipling's early writings. Here was something new in matter, revolutionary in manner. Different, yet like, was the effect produced by the early writings of Maurice Hewlett. Mr. Hewlett, in his recreation of medieval scenes, ransacked early literature and popular dialect for words fresh in color. To the same purpose he created new words and

---

[6] *Marius the Epicurean*, Ch. viii.
[7] Preface to *The Nigger of the Narcissus*.
[8] *The Nation*, Nov. 3, 1920.

turned old words to new uses. The literary world of the time was startled to attention by the use of such words and expressions as: *longanimous, smouldering* night, *scourged* forward (rode fast), *vair* (fur), *picksome* mood, *meinie* (company), *dreadful* of (fearing), an *inchmeal stalker, bliaut* (surcoat), a *shatter* of hoofs, the *gules* of August (dog-days), *orotund* (*ore rotundo*), *flacking* (waving) arms, *keening* (weeping), King John a *puddock,* a maid with a *placket.*

The liberties taken with language by Kipling and Hewlett, so startling in their day, have in our day ceased to be novel. Such practices have ceased to be in any way exceptional. Writers such as H. G. Wells are modern not only in mode of thought, but in mode of expression. New words, and old words newly applied, have become frequent features. For instance, in one of Mr. Wells's earlier books,[9] appear such expressions as "the bare brown *surround,*" "somewhere, *somewhen,*" *duologues, chummed* ('brought jaws together'). Reflecting the modern spirit of American literary independence there appears in the writings of many Americans a similar conscious disregard for the older proprieties. In the most widely read of recent American novels[10] appear such expressions as *wage-hogging, babycentric* (wife), *oozed out* (of a room). Such departures from purism, however they might have seemed a generation ago, create no consternation in our day. From the pages of some of the most positive and vigorous modern writers might be selected words with far greater power to shock.

A generation ago Walter Pater in describing the literary aims of an advanced type of young Roman in the age of Marcus Aurelius, spoke of his purpose in language of "asserting, so to term them, the rights of the *proletariate* of speech." Events in recent times have given to the word

---

[9] *The New Macchiavelli.*
[10] *Main Street.*

proletariat a connotation that did not attach to it in Pater's time. If we dissociate from this word its later acquired meaning, then Pater's phrase will serve to express a spirit apparent in the use of words prevailing to-day. New words are required for the expression of modern thought. The dictionaries which are the repositories of words used by earlier generations do not always afford the needed means of expression. Various technical vocabularies provide new words, but for the expression of the concrete realities of everyday experience, it is often necessary to resort to the proletariat words of living modern speech, to the homely words of local dialects, to the vulgar creations of colloquial speech, including slang. The debt of modern language to these lower forms of speech has perhaps been sufficiently dwelt on in the early chapters of the present book. The debt of such writers as John Masefield to popular forms of speech has been pointed out. A like debt may be pointed out in the case of another much admired modern stylist. The language of Joseph Conrad is alive with modern idiom. On the pages of his novels one meets with such words as: *spotted* (for 'observed'), *fuss, dun* (verb), *funk, dry up, bilge* (for 'rot'), *jim jams* ('delirium tremens'), *point-blank, off my chump, hard case, a rise out of me.*[11]

Not only is modern English characterized by the introduction of new words and the assertion of the rights of the 'proletariate' in speech, but older words are used in new ways. Modern literary style is characterized by a straining after new expressiveness. Perhaps as part of the art learned in college courses in writing, the verb is made to accomplish the function of adjective and verb combined. For instance, "Fetzy's Hungarians . . . *were sighing* out a wonderful waltz," "They *threaded* their way to their seat," "Oh, how fine! *pæaned* she," "Presently a waltz

---

[11] All from *Lord Jim.*

faded out."[12] Much the same quality apppears in such expressions as *buzzed down* ('motored').[13] "They were *snorting* out of West Bowlby."[14] "A twilight like blue dust *sifted* into the shallow fold of the—hills," "A *crisping* frost had already stamped the maple trees," "A *pattern* of wild geese—*wavered* against the serene, ashen evening," "With the *drooping* of day—," "Mr. Polder *gloomed*." "James Polder was perceptibly *fogged*."[15] "The low-lit causeway that *slinks* from West India Dock Road," "short curls, *chiming* with the black and scarlet,"[16] "He *creaked* to his feet," "he *fumbled* for sleep," "*minced* into the safety of the living-room."[17] The straining after new effects, which appears in some of these expressions, is of the kind associated formerly with verse-composition rather than with prose.

Dominating the literature of the present day is the spirit of realism. The scientific spirit of the nineteenth century has led to a fresh observation of fact which it is the function of literature to record. Literature presents hitherto neglected nooks and corners and substrata of life in the form of language that belongs to this new subject matter. Furthermore, the 'close-up' kind of picture demanded calls for a minuteness in expression not in keeping with the dignity of language hitherto cultivated. Realism in some instances, in the language of poets such as Lindsay and Sandburg, reaches barbarism. The rubbish heaps of language are raked for startling effects. The barbaric love of the primitive leads to the use of words new and old describing primitive emotions in primitive language hitherto not tolerated.

Sympathy must be expressed for the yearning of the

---

[12] *Queed.*
[13] *If Winter Comes.*
[14] A. Huxley, *Chrome Yellow.*
[15] J. Hergesheimer, *The Three Black Pennys.*
[16] Thomas Burke, *Limehouse Nights.*
[17] Sinclair Lewis, *Babbitt.*

present day for freshness of expression, for a more immediate relation, like that in music, between form and meaning, for a language means of exhibiting the 'close-up' view of life which modern taste demands. The lengths, however, to which it is permissible to go must be left to individual taste. Furthermore, the nature of words, as revealed in the preceding chapters, is not such as ever to permit the entire realization of the aspiration for immediacy of expression. Language is a heritage from the past. The meanings of words have been colored by associations. Hence, meanings must often be expressed by indirection, by the use of the links of association between word and meaning created by past use. There is, however, no ground for despair. New means of expression will be created in the future as in the past. But in the future, as in the past, artists able to play on the strings of the association will be able by means of words to convey the most subtle of thoughts, to call up or record the most delicate and most elusive of emotions.

Truly varied is the character of the language that expresses the spirit of a people in the succeeding stages in its history. Strange to modern English-speaking peoples seems the language of five hundred years ago. But if we go back five centuries, we find Chaucer, whose language is so different from our own, already marveling at the strangeness of modes of speech earlier than his own. His words express his sense of marvel and at the same time illustrate anew the shifting values of words.

> Ye knowe eek, that in forme of speche is chaunge
> With-inne a thousand yeer, and wordes tho
> That hadden prys, now wonder nyce and straunge
> Vs thinketh hem; and yet they spake hem so
> And spedde as wel in love as men now do;
> *Troilus and Criseyde,* II, 22-26.

WORD INDEX

abate, 228
abbreviate, 203
abominable, 188
abound, 228
abridge, 203
acorn, 183
acquaintance, 195, 198
acre, 93
admission, 200, 234
adulterate, 286
adventure, 189
advise, 189
afghan, 325
aggravate, 408, 409
aggravating, 245
agony, 227
ail, 198
alderman, 335
allow, 416
alpaca, 325
alto, 208
aluminum, 307
ambition, 236
among, 256
analysis, 419
ancient, 262
anemone, 224
anguish, 237
aniline, 332
anon, 94, 282, 415
anxious, 408, 409
apparition, 262
apple, 303
arcadian, 353
Arctic, 188
ardent, 228

around, 256
arrange, 419
arras, 325
arrive, 252
Arthur, 380
asparagus, 182
aspirant, 405, 407
ass, 299
assassin, 353
assault, 189
assets, 334
aster, 224
astrakhan, 325
astronomy, 418
asylum, 287
atheist, 271
attic, 200, 246, 315
attic (adj.), 352
Auburn, 199
auburn, 208
auction, 200
awful, 196
awfully, 255
awkward, 213, 236
avenue, 272
Avon, 360
azure, 331

bachelor's button, 239
bad, 204
balcony, 318
ballot, 295, 339
baluster, 212, 320
bank, 333, 341
barberry, 184

barter, 237, 291
base, 281
basement, 315
bashful, 285
bask, 200
basque, 330
be, 256
bead, 237
beam, 91, 238
bear, 297-8
beautiful, 276
bed, 310, 319
beech, 301, 312
behave, 200
bellows, 93
belly, 93
bend, 227
benignant, 190
bereaved, 262
berry, 73, 303
bestir, 416
best wishes, 197
Big Bertha, 356
bilious, 336
bird, 96, 236, 250
bishop, 258
black, 331
bleacher, 225, 241
bleeding-heart, 225
blouse, 291, 330
blue-stocking, 355
blunder, 204
blunderbuss, 183
board, 91, 211, 321
boast, 200
bobby, 355

WORD INDEX

bob white, 240
bœotian, 353
bogus, 405, 407
bolster, 309
book, 234, 235, 312
boor, 284
boot, 330
borrow, 92, 236
botany, 418
boudoir, 291
boulevard, 272
bounce, 234
bower, 316
Bowery, 373, 376
bowie knife, 355
boycott, 411
boyish, 290
braces, 328
bray, 287
bread, 92, 238, 308, 322
breeches, 309, 327
bridge, 200
brief, 203
brilliant, 252
bristle, 290
Britain, 343-4
broach, 228
broadcloth, 326
bronze, 305
brood, 204, 227
buckle, 212
buckwheat, 184
bugger, 353
bunch, 394
bunco, 333
bureau, 214, 234
business, 154
busk, 200
but, 95, 281
butcher, 252
butter, 251
buttery, 182, 317
butterfly, 335
buttonwood, 235
buxom, 234

buzzard, 183
by and by, 282, 415
by-law, 187

cab, 225
calculate, 204
calico, 200, 324
calm, 233
cambric, 325
camel, 299
camel's-hair, 295
camera, 200
can, 94
candidate, 236-7
cannon, 263
canter, 352
canvas, 326
canvass, 212
capital, 205
caoutchouc, 314
cardinal, 200, 210, 230, 332
care, 196
career, 226
careful, 417
carmine, 331
carol, 263
carpet, 319
cash, 263
cashmere, 325
cat, 299-300
catch, 203-4
catsup, 184
cattle, 263
cauldron, 184
causeway, 184
cease, 209
cellar, 315
cemetery, 269
chafe, 233
chain, 208
chair, 320
challenge, 208
chamberlain, 289
chambray, 325

chance, 253
chap, 254
character, 205
charge, 222
charity, 283
charm, 265, 335-6
chauvinist, 351
cheap, 93, 200, 270, 286, 290
check, 228
cheese, 308
chemistry, 418
cherry, 303
cheviot, 326
chevron, 214
chicken, 236, 250
chief, 205
childish, 285, 290
chimney, 317
china, 321
chintz, 325
chivalrous, 289
churl, 284
cinder, 154
city, 296
civil, 289, 296-7
classify, 419
clear, 195
climate, 236
cloak, 223
clock, 224
clumsy, 213, 236
coal, 246
coat, 328
cobalt, 307
cockroach, 184
cocoa, 323
cocoanut, 225
code, 234, 314
codex, 314
coffee, 323
cogitate, 204
coin, 233
cold-slaw, 183
colossal, 252
columbine, 224

WORD INDEX 433

commencement, 209
commit, 200
common, 281
companion, 403
complexion, 337
comprehend, 203
conceit, 200, 246, 257
concentrate, 200, 246
concert, 200
concrete, 227
condition, 281
coney, 250
congregation, 416
considerable, 200
constable, 289
consumption, 72
contemptibles, 290
continent, 414
contrite, 225-6
convenient, 416
conversation, 416
convert, 259
cootie, 345
copper, 305
cordial, 338
corn, 200, 257, 258
Cornwall, 344
corpse, 257
correspondence, 200
cot, 319
couch, 319
could, 189
countenance, 245
counterfeit, 286
country-dance, 183
courage, 338
course, 253
court, 288, 296
Courtney, 343
cowcatcher, 340
crank, 349
crash, 325
crater, 226-7
cravat, 330
crawfish, 185
crayfish, 185

crazy, 269
crescent, 246
cretonne, 325
crimson, 331
crooked, 204
crop, 93, 234
crystal, 226
cucumber, 323
curate, 200
curious, 198
curiosity, 286, 414
currants, 303
currency, 263
curtail, 183
cutlet, 183

daft, 287
daisy, 224
dam, 342
damask, 325
dame, 276, 282
damson, 303
danger, 236
dapper, 284
daub, 208, 286
dauphin, 350
deal, 96
debt, 188
decency, 271
deer, 236
degraded, 281
dejected, 414
deliberate, 204
delusion, 204
demijohn, 184
deranged, 269
derrick, 225, 354
desire, 208, 233
diffidence, 414
dilapidated, 228
dining-room, 317
dinner, 322
disaster, 335
disease, 269
disparage, 228

dispatch, 200
distinction, 291
distinguish, 228, 419
ditty, 287-8
do, 256
doctor, 200
dog, 206, 226, 242, 298
dollar, 333-4, 341
donate, 405, 407
donkey, 190, 299
door, 314
double, 200
doubt, 188
doubtless, 282
doughboy, 349
doughty, 284
Dover, 362
drab, 230, 251, 332
drawing-room, 317
dress, 200, 209, 245, 327
drunk, 271
dumps, 200
-dun in place-names, 361
dunce, 354

easel, 225
effectives, 200
elegant, 197
eliminate, 227
elocution, 284
embarrass, 228, 229, 397 ff.
emblem, 237
emolument, 228, 296
enchantment, 265, 335
endure, 203
engine, 257, 258
enjoy, 209
enormity, 244, 246, 260, 287, 402-3
enormous, 259-60, 414
episcopal, 258
error, 228

WORD INDEX

ethical, 204
etymology, 265
eugenics, 419
evil, 204
exaggerate, 228
examine, 204
execute, 257, 263
experiment, 419
explore, 237
exult, 228

Fabian, 356
fabric, 237
fair, 281
faith, 133
fall, 200
fame, 291
family, 238
fare, 200, 234
farmer, 284
fast, 203, 208, 236, 413
fastidious, 238
fathom, 93, 238
fault, 189
fear, 145
fearful, 146
feature, 245
fee, 264, 296
feel, 252
fellow, 254, 403, 416
female, 424
ferment, 238
ferret, 226
fiddle, 287
fiend, 96, 262
finance, 334
fine, 209
fir, 73
fireplace, 317
fish, 72
flag, 209
flash, 37
flatter, 223
flavor, 238
flour, 226, 322

flourishing, 222
fob, 200, 234
foot, 42
Ford, synonyms for, 44
forest, 242
forfeit, 208
fork, 321
fowl, 96, 261
France, 344
franchise, 237
frank, 353
Frederick, 380
free, 297
freedom, 195
freethinker, 271
fresh, 199
fret, 285
fretful, 413
frill, 227, 291, 330
front, 205, 233, 252, 413
frontispiece, 205
frugal, 195
fry, 287-8
fund, 263
funny-bone, 197
fustian, 48, 325

gadget, 254
gallant, 289
gallowses, 225, 328
gaoler, 145
garble, 286
garret, 315
gasconade, 354
gate, 200
gatling, 356
gauze, 325
gentleman, 276
George, 380
geranium, 225
germen, 413
ghost, 261
gibbridge, 48

gigantic, 252
gillyflower, 184
gingham, 325
glad-eyed, etc., 197
glamour, 336
glass, 314
gold, 306
good, 204
good-bye, 85
good-hearted, 282
Gothic, 289, 353
gout, 338
govern, 226
graduate, 405, 407
Gramercy Park, 373, 376
grandiloquent, 282
grandiose, 282
grasp, 203-4
grass, 96, 199
gravelblind, 187
green, 209, 251
grenade, 227
greyhound, 186
grieve, 199
grog, 354
gun, 356
guy, 254, 354

had better, 85, 86
had rather, 85, 86
hail, 213
halcyon, 188
hall, 316
halo, 223
ham, 95
hamburg, 326
hammer, 305
hamper, 229
hand, 205, 207, 240
handkerchief, 209
hap, 198
hard, 92, 234
hazard, 253
head, 205, 240

WORD INDEX

heal, 96
healthful, 196
healthy, 196
hearse, 224
heart, 338
hearth, 317
heartsease, 225
heaven, 259
heckle, 253
hector, 342-3
hell, 259
henna, 231
hiccough, 183
hide, 200
hideous, 197
hoard, 95, 262
hoax, 336
Holborn, 376
hoe-down, 183
hold up, 193
hollyhock, 184
holy, 205
homely, 281
honey, 251
horrid, 197, 413
horror, 196
horse, 206, 298
hose, 327
hound, 96, 236
humbug, 348
humor, 337
hunger, 148
hunnish, 353
hurt, 236
hustle, 253
hybrid, 223

ice-water, 197
idiot, 263
ill-starred, 335
influence, 335
immodest, 271
immoral, 271, 280
impassive, 209

impede, 229
impertinency, 414
impertinent, 271, 280
implicit, 245
inappreciable, 244
Indian corn, 246
indignant, 271, 280
indigo, 331
indolent, 271, 280
indulge, 200
industrious, 195
ineffable, 244
infidel, 271
ink, 313
innumerable, 244
inquisitiveness, 286
insane, 280
insanity, 269
insolent, 280
instant, 416
instigate, 228
integrity, 204
intellect, 203
intended, 227
invaluable, 209
investigate, 204
iris, 223
iron, 306, 307
irritate, 227
isinglass, 183
island, 189

jaunty, 183
jazz, 350
jeopardize, 405, 410
jerk, 234
Jewish flag, 225
jimson weed, 351
jingo, 351
jitney, 346
John, different forms of, 379
journal, 209
joy, 96

keen, 93
ketchup, 184
key, 208
kidney, 338
kitchen, 316
knave, 91, 96, 285, 289
knife, 321
knight, 91, 212, 289

labor, 196
laborious, 195
lack, 198
laconic, 353
lady, 276
lady-slipper, 225
language, 233
Laon, 359
lark, 186
last, 203, 262
latch, 314-5
lawn, 185, 325
lead, 309
learn, 194
leer, 93, 233
leg, 269
lengthy, 287, 403
leniency, 405, 410
library, 234, 313
lief, liefer, 85
like, 198
liquor, 189, 262
Lisbon, 344
lisle-thread, 326
list, 198
livery, 200
living room, 317
loaf, 92, 238, 308, 322
located, 405, 407
Lockhart, 343
loft, 315
London, 362
long, 198, 203
looking-glass, 197
loth, 198

Louisiana, 352
low, 281
lozenge, 211
lumber, 352
luxurious, 195

madras, 325
magazine, 223
magenta, 332, 352
magnificent, 291
maid, maiden, 96
maiden-hair, 225
maintain, 228
Mainz, 359
majesty, 289
mammoth, 251
manure, 234
manuscript, 209
marmalade, 324
maroon, 230, 251, 332
marshal, 289
mat, 319
match, 200, 221, 246, 339
mausoleum, 352
mauve, 332
maverick, 356
maxim, 356
may, 94
mean, 281
meat, 262, 322
medal, 237
mediocre, 223
melancholy, 336
menial, 285
mere, 243-4
metal, 305
methinks, 198
method, 419
Methodist, 290
middling, 281
mighty, 255
mineralogy, 418
miniature, 235, 252
minster, 132

minute, 203
mirth, 96
Mister, 276
mohair, 185, 325
molar, molest, emolument, 214
monastery, 132
mongoose, 185
mouth, 203
moral, 204
mortified, 414
muscle, 226
mushroom, 184
musket, 223
muskrat, 185
muslin, 325
must, 94
mustard, 322
mutual, 406, 407

naked, 269
namby-pamby, 354
nankeen, 325
naughty, 285, 416
necktie, 330
need, 198
needs, 83
nephew, 154
nervous, 209
new-laid, 280
news, 209, 345
nice, 197, 208, 210
nickel, 307
not, 277
nursery, 222

observe, 419
of, 95
oil, 251
O. K., 345-6
on, 95
orchestra, 238
orderly, 419
ordinary, 281

other, 84
ought, 44
outlandish, 416
oven, 320
overcharge, 416
owe, 44
Oxford, 363, 375

page, 313
palace, 352
palliate, 224
pamphlet, 314
pansy, 224
pantaloons, 328
pantry, 182, 317
paper, 312
paraphernalia, 255
paradise, 263
parchment, 313
parlor, 316-7
parsnip, 190
partially, 406, 407
pasquinade, 354
passive, 209
pate, 287-8
patter, 225
pay, 236
pea-bouncer, 240
peach, 303
peasant, 284
pecuniary, 228, 296
pedant, 285
pedicure, 271
pediment, 184
peeler, 355
peevish, 285
pen, 212, 221, 313
pencil, 212, 313
perceive, 203
perch, 221
Percy, 343
period, 203, 238
perplexed, 227
persecute, 263
person, 248, 253-4

WORD INDEX

pester, 212, 228-9
petticoat, 329
phaeton, 225, 283
Philippine Islands, 352
phlegmatic, 336
piano, 200
piazza, 318, 352
pickaxe, 184
pierce, 260
pig, 250
pipe, 207, 257, 258, 263
pitcher, 295
plain, 281
plainly, 243
plant, 234
platform, 187
platinum, 307
play, 92, 246, 258
play (stage), 200
please, 223
pleasure, 189
pluck, 291, 338
plum, 303
plunge, 253
pocket-book, 212
poise, 200, 257
poltroon, 345
ponder, 204
poplin, 326
porcelain, 212, 321
porch, 318
porridge, 324
posy, 238
potboiler, 225
Presbyterian, 258
prestige, 291, 336
pretty, 276, 278
priest, 132, 258
primrose, 184
prisoner, 195
progress, 419
proper, 248
proposition, 254
provisions, 263

provoke, 414
provoked, 416
prude, 283
pudding, 324
puerile, 285, 290
puny, 252
purple, 230, 301
purse, 212
pussyfoot, 225
psychic, 203
psychological moment, 351
pyrrhic, 356

Quaker, 290
quaint, 198
questionable, 281
quick, 93, 203, 204
quince, 303
quiz, 342

rabbit, 96, 187, 236, 250
radical, 287
range, 320
rapid, 203
rash, 290
ravel, 209
read, 293, 312
recalcitrant, 228
receipt, 188
redstart, 185
reek, 262
reflect, 204
regal, 288
rehearse, 228
reindeer, 185
reliable, 406, 407, 410
remacadamizing, 161
repent, 198, 200
respect, 414
rest, 200
result, 228
revolution, 263

rheum, 338
rhyme, 189
riband, 183
rich, 91
Richard, 380
rifle, 200
right, 204
rime, 91
rind, 287-9, 290
ringleader, 288
rivet, 229
roam, 342
Robert, 380
rogue, 189
romance, 214
room, 259, 315-6
roost, 221
rosemary, 184, 224
roster, 225
rubber, 200, 246, 295, 314
ruche, 224
ruching, 330
rue, 96, 198
ruff, 330
rug, 319
ruminate, 204
rustic, 284

salary, 225
saloon, 272
saltcellar, 186
salute, 212
salvation, 258
sanctimonious, 283
sandblind, 187
sandwich, 354
sardonic, 352
sassafras, 338
sauce, 244
Saxon, 343
scallop, 222
scandal, 228
scarlet, 331
scavenger, 286

WORD INDEX

scene, 212, 253
schedule, 237
scissors, 189
scrofula, 223
scruple, 228
scrutiny, 228
scurrilous, 283
season, 203
second, 203
secure, 196
sedulous, 237
seethe, 262
selfish, 420
self-made, 195
self-starter, 195
seminary, 222
seneschal, 289
senile, 285
sentence, 238
serge, 325
service, 291
servile, 285, 291
settee, 319
Shaker, 290
shall, 256
shinplaster, 225
shirt, 328
shoe, 330
short, 203
Shotover, 360
should, 94
show, 92, 195
shrapnel, 356
sick-bed, 197
silk, 325
silly, 382
silver, 306
sincere, 237
skirt, 328
skylark, 186
skyrocket, 229
slave, 353
slavish, 285
slops, 328
smug, 283, 413
snuff, 257

solecism, 352
solferino, 332
socialist, 287
socket, 238
soon, 94, 282
soothe, 238
sop, 223
sore, 255
sovereign, 183
Spartan, 353
specious, 283
spell, 92, 265, 335
spill, 96, 262, 413
spleen, 338
splendid, 291
spoon, 321
sport, 200
spruce, 352
spurn, 222
squire, 212, 289
stagnate, 223
stairs, 320
stamp, 214
standard, 186
standpoint, 406, 407
stare, 262
starved, 200
steel, 309
steward, 289
stimulate, 223
sting, 95
stink, 270
stomach, 241
stoneblind, 187
stool, 320
stoop, 318
story, 237, 315
stove, 320
stout, 290
straight, 204
strenuous, 42, 394
stump, speaker, 340
stunned, 228
stupid, 286
sturdy, 290
style, 212, 313

subject, 188
subtle, 188
sugar, 323
sullen, 286
superb, 197-8
superman, 419
supper, 322
sure, 196
surround, 183
suspenders, 328
sward, 290
swing, 91
sycamore, 235
system, 419
synthesis, 419

table, 236, 320
taboo, 293, 410
tackle, 335
take, 206
taking, 413
talented, 406, 407, 410
tank, 347
tansy, 224
target, 335
taste, 235
taupe, 231
tawdry, 355
tea, 323
tease, 212, 253
temper, 336-7
temperament, 336
temperature, 200
test, 238
the more, the better, 84
theory, 417
thigh, 241
thing, 248, **254**
thirst, 198
throw, 252
thug, 353
tile fish, 77
tinsel, 283

WORD INDEX

tip, 347
titanic, 252
titmouse, 185
token, 261
tongue, 189
Tory, 290
trammel, 212, 228-9
transpire, 245, 406, 407
tree, 91, 238, 249, 250, 302
tremendous, 244
trend, 223
tribulation, 225-6
trousers, 328
true, 204
try, 253
tuberculosis, 71
tuberose, 184
tulip, 225
tumbler, 209
tungsten, 307
turn, 252
turtle, 186
twain, 85
tweed, 185, 326
tyro, 253

unravel, 209
unspeakable, 244
urbane, 289
urchin, 223

vaunt, 200
vegetable, 234
vellum, 313
Venus, 215
veranda, 318
verdict, 188
very, 255, 282
vest, 329, 409
victuals, 189, 287
viewpoint, 409
vile, 286, 290
villain, 285, 287
Virginia, 352
virtue, 205, 209, 291
visitation, 287, 403
volume, 234, 314
vulgar, 281
wag, 95, 246, 260, 287

waist, 329
waistcoat, 329
wall, 314
want, 198, 233
warn, 195
was, 256
watch, 339
week, 203
Welsh rabbit, 187
wench, 285
Whig, 290
whilom, 84
white, 331
whole, 189

whore, 190
wicked, 205
will, 256
William, 379, 380
win, 91, 215, 234
window, 314
wiseacre, 183
wish-bone, 197
with, 95
wold, 208
wolf, 297
woodchuck, 185
wool-gathering, 204
work, 196
working-clothes, 197
worry, 237
worship, 282
worsted, 326
worthy, 282
wretch, 252
write, 312
writhe, 95
wrong, 204

Yankee, 290, 344
yard, 92, 233
year, 203
yes, 277
yield, 92
York, 359
youthful, 240

zest, 253

SUBJECT INDEX

Ade, George, 51
Adverb forms, 83, 84
Adverbs, flat, 193
African metaphor, 220
Africa, words from, 147
Agricultural names, 304
Air service, slang of, 56, 57
Allen, E. A., 134
American creation of names, 27; influence on English, 35; food names, 324; language, 23; surnames, 391; variation from English, 33-35; words transmitted by Spanish, 148
Americanisms, 30, 31, 32, 33
America, words from, 147
Anglo-Indian dialect, 18
Anglo-Irish, 20
Anglomania, 35
Anglo-Saxon, 82, 83, 412
Anglo-Saxon Chronicle, 279
Anglo-Saxon names disguised, 378; personal names, 377; place-names, 363-5
Antiquity represented in American place-names, 368
Antonomasia, 230
Arabic words, 144-6
Archaic survivals, 97
Archimedes, 178
Architectural terms, 71
Argot, 37
Æschylus, 299
Asia, source of various foods, 324
Aspects of ideas, 199
Asquith, H., 68
Associated meanings, 244 ff., 260, 270, 402-4, 425, 429

Atlantic Monthly, 67
Auchinleck, Laird of, 14
Australian creation of names, 170; dialect, 18, 20; slang, 52
Autocrat of the Breakfast Table, 64, 218

Back-formations, 177
Back slang, 54
Bacon, 173
Baedeker, 13
Barnes, Wm., 20
Barrie, Sir Jas., 280, 282
Baseball slang, 46, 51
Battledore, 46
Bear, names for, 266
Beast-names, 297-300
Belgium, 6
Bender, H. H., 297
Beowulf, 2, 279
Berners, Lord, 396
Bible, 4, 117, 234, 415-7
Biblical words and phrases, 98; element in American place-names, 369
Bird names, 300
Black, Hugh, 68
Blackwood's Magazine, 66
Blends, 165, 166
Blood, circulation of, 336
Bloomfield, L., 219
Bobolink, variant names of, 17
Body, slang names for parts of, 60
Borrowing of place-names in America, 368-9
Boston, 157

SUBJECT INDEX

Boundary between slang and legitimate speech, 66
Bradley, H., 140, 142, 163, 359, 364, 365, 366
Braid, Dr. James, 179
Bréal, M., 202
Bret Harte, 43, 371
British war slang, 53, 54
Bronze Age, 305
Browne, Sir Thos., 157
Browning, 423
Bryant, W. C., 405
Bunyan, J., 169
Burgess, Gelett, 165
Burlesque etymology, 356
Burns, 12

Caedmon, 2
California, 43, 176; 'forty-niners,' 30
Cambridge, 3
Card-table language, 47
Carlyle, 178, 218
Carroll, Lewis, 166, 177
Caxton, 395
Celtic words, 139, 140; place-names, 360-1
Century Dictionary, 73, 76
Century Magazine Style Sheet, 408-10
Changed meanings in native words, 89 ff.
Chaucer, 1, 3, 4, 6, 9, 40, 124, 166, 412, 429
Cheke, Sir John, 115, 158
Chemical terms, 77
Childhood, words associated with, 285
Children's use of words, 219, 221
China, words from 146-7
Chinese, 7
Chivalry in modern youth, 61
Choice between native and borrowed words, 161, 162
Christian names, 379; specialization of words, 79, 90, 258-9

Church terms, 71
Cicero, 10
City names, 150
Civilization of the South penetrating Northern Europe, 107
Class distinction in words, 401-2
Classification, lack of, 248-250
Clemenceau, 178
Clipped words, 50, 176, 177
Clothing terms, 309
Coaching terms surviving, 340
Cockfighting, 46
Cognates, 294, 297, 300, 301, 302, 309
Color names, 230, 331-3
Colton, E., 411
Combination of native and foreign elements, 160, 161
Commercial associations, 402, 407
Competition between native and Scandinavian words, 101, 102
Compounds, 167-176; modern creations, 170, 171, 175, 176; in Old English, 111, 112
Comte, 178
Concatenation, 210, 216
Connotation, 248
Conrad, Joseph, 67, 425, 427
Conscious volition in determining meanings, 218-9, 239, 246
Contamination of meaning, 287
Craps, slang of, 46
Cynewulf, 2

Daisy Ashford, 244
Dame Quickly, 181
Danish Conquest, 100
Darwin, 178
Dates of introduction of various foods, 323-4; first use of technical names, 77, 78, 418 ff.
Death, avoidance of direct reference to, 268
Deference to British usage, 34, 35

SUBJECT INDEX 443

Degeneration, 280 ff.
Dennis, C. J., 20, 53
Denotation, 248
De Quincey, 63, 157, 343, 403
Dialect, source of slang, 50; words adopted into Standard English, 20, 21; Dictionary, 14
Dicing terms, 47
Dickens, 63
Dick Whittington, 300
Disguised compounds, 87, 167, 168
Divergent development in meaning: English and German, 89, 90; English and French, 135; English and Italian, 141
Divinity, names for, 267
Dixon, George, 47
Domestic animals, 298-300; fowls, 300-1
Doublets, 101, 131-4, 152, 167, 388
Dress, terms of, 71, 72, 326-330
Drug store slang, 45
Duns Scotus, 354
Dutch words in English, 103-5; in American English, 25; place-names in America, 373
Dwelling, names for, 309

East-Midland, dialect of, 2, 3, 12, 13
Echoic words, 163, 164
Education filling words with meaning, 71
Elevation of meaning, 288 ff.
Elizabethan English, 103, 168, 413, 415; creation of words and phrases, 168, 169; slang, 39, 40
Elson, L., 344
Emerson, O. F., 116, 117
Emerson, R. W., 218
English, non-literary forms, 8-11; source of name, 82
Ervine, St. John, 21

Eskimo words, 148
Etymology as a guide in the choice of words, 398-9, 400
Euphemism, 264 ff.; value of, 270, 271
Evening Post, 405
Excessive use of certain words, 394-5

Fabrics, names for, 324-6
Fading of slang, 65
Fairholt, F., 329
Fairies, names for, 266
Falconry, 46
Far-fetched figures in slang, 65
Farmer and Henley, 41, 51
Fashion in dress, 326 ff.; in names after the Conquest, 378
Fencing terms, 46
Fernald, J. C., 397
Field, Eugene, 20
Flat adverbs, 84
Flemish, 82
Flicker, variant names of, 17
Flower names, 74, 294
Folk-etymology, 180-190
Food names, 308, 322-4
Foreign names in English use, 372-5; personal names, 389-90; element in American place-names, 367-9
Forest trees, 302
Formula representing elements in a word, 243
Fossil survivals, 84 ff., 97
France, Anatole, 10
Franklin, Benjamin, 31, 406
French, literary language, 5; element in English, 122 ff.; words of varied origin 128 ff.; words in American English, 25; specialized in meaning, 262; changed in form, 180, 181; terms of cuisine, 323; names for fine fabrics, 326;

place-names in America, 373-5; sounds in English, 180
Frisian, 82
Fritzsche, 178
Frontier life reflected in American words, 29
Fullerton, Hugh, 51

Galsworthy, John, 67
Genius of the Language, 164
Germanic sources of English, 82
German, literary, 5; borrowing of words, 149; words related to English, 81, 82, 89, 90; words in American English, 25, 26
Gibbon, E., 116
Gibbs, Sir Philip, 67
Girls' slang, 62
Glass blower slang, 45
Gothic, 83
Gower, 3, 124
Grammar, objections to, 10
Grandiloquence, 407
Greek element, 117 ff.; early Christian terms, 118; early science, 118; scientific terms, 118, 119; personal names, 119; amount of debt, 120; source of technical words, 76
Greek, modern, 7, 8
Greenough and Kittredge, 117, 118, 159, 186, 197, 215, 253, 254, 256, 268, 277, 289, 318, 333, 337
Group names, 249, 343

Half-breed place-names, 375
Hardy, Thomas, 178
Harvey, G., 288
Hauptmann, G., 19
Hazlitt, 62, 162
Hearn, Lafcadio, 350
Hebrew words, 144
Henry, O., 43, 49, 51

Hergesheimer, J., 428
Hewlett, Maurice, 67, 425, 426
High-brow, 42
High German words in English, 105
Hill, A. S., 410-11
Hindustani words as source of slang, 53
Hirt, H., 254, 290, 302, 304, 306, 335
History reflected in American place-names, 367
Hobson-Jobson, 180
Hoffman, H. A., 119
Holland, literary language of, 6, 82
Holmes, O. W., 179
Homeric times, 299
Homonyms, 153, 154
Hotten's *Slang Dictionary*, 60
House, names for parts of, 314 ff.
Hueffer, Ford Maddox, 425
Humor, 225; in place-names, 371
Hungarian words, 144
Huxley, A., 428
Huxley, T. H., 178
Hybrids, 171, 172; compounds, 102
Hyperbole, 264, 272 ff.; value of, 273; grades of intensity, 274; effect of, 275; American propensity, 279

Icelandic, 83
If Winter Comes, 428
Incongruity between names and places, 375-6
Indebtedness of European languages to Latin, 105
Indian words, 24, 25, 148; place-names in America, 367; use of words, 220
India, words from, 146
Indo-European, 294, 297, 301, 302, 303, 304, 305, 306, 308

SUBJECT INDEX

Inflections in earlier English, 83 ff.
Innuendo, 260, 281, 296
Interior of house, 318
Interurban railroad terms, 45
Irish element in American English, 26, 27
Irony, 260, 281
Italian, literary, 6; words in English, 140-142

Japan, words from, 147
Jean Paul, 218
Jenkins, T. A., 356
Jespersen, O., 107, 128, 142, 150, 170, 220, 221, 250, 323
Jews, names of, 390-1
Johnsonese, 158
Johnson, Samuel, 9, 117, 158, 159, 175
Johnston, H. H., 21, 67
Jonson, Ben, 4, 337, 406
Journalese, 158, 222, 345

Kennings, 221
Kentish dialect, 3
King George, 68
King's English, 23, 68
Kipling, R., 21, 279, 425, 426
Kroesch, S., 204

Lake District, 13, 15
Lamb, Chas., 424
Landmarks in place-names, 364
Latin in English: earliest words, 107, 108; through Britons, 108; Christian influence, 109; Old English period, 109-111; after Conquest, 113; influence of Renaissance, 114; technical words, 116; amount of borrowing, 116, 117; words of slangy origin, 38

Latin, vulgar, 10
La Tour Landry, 243
Law terms, 79, 124
Legitimate expressions become slangy, 40, 41
Lewis, Sinclair, 426, 428
Lindsay, Vachel, 32, 428
Listener, part of, in determining meanings, 240
Lloyd George, 68
Locality as source of names, 383-4
Logic, 191
London dialect, 3, 6
Loss of words, 86, 91, 168, 172, 173
Lost distinctions, 407, 409
Lost meaning in surnames, 387
Lowell, 20, 22, 24, 32
Low German, 19, 103, 104

Macaulay, Rose, 67
Magic power in words, 265
Mahan, Admiral, 178
Main Street, 426
Mark Twain, 43
Masefield, John, 21, 427
Mathematics, 250
Matthews, A., 318
Matthews, Brander, 242, 406
Mawer, A., 359
Mead, L., 178
Mechanics, terms of, 75, 76
Medical terms, 421
Meillet, A., 6, 254
Mencken, H. L., 25, 26, 27, 32, 143, 169, 373, 374, 390, 391
Metaphor, 202 ff., 218 ff.
Metonymy, 232 ff.
Middle Ages, 417, 418
Middle names, 381
Military terms, 79
Milton, 9, 157
Mineral names, 305 ff.

Misuse of classical words, 157, 158; of technical language, 79
Modern words, 422; literary use of words, 424 ff.
Modification of English names in America, 375
Money, slang names for, 60; synonyms for, 277
Monotony in American place-names, 371
Moore, George, 19
Motion picture slang, 44
Motor-car language, 44
Motor transport slang, 56
Muddling through, 191, 200
Müller, Wilhelm, 19
Murray, Sir J. A. H., 11, 163, 164, 172, 177, 423

Napoleonic wars, 66
Nation, 425
Native element in technical words, 75, 76; words specialized, 261; substitutes for Latin derivatives, 115
Nature of Scandinavian derivatives, 102
Naval slang, 56
New creations, 164-166, 177, 178
New England dialect, 24
Newman, Cardinal, 424
New words, aversion to, 406-7, 409
New York, dialect, 15
Niceforo, A., 266, 267
Nicknames, 386-7
Nomenclature of plants and birds, 28, 29
Norman Conquest, consequences of, 123 ff.; contemptuous attitude, 90, 284; influence on place-names, 365-6
Norway, literary language of, 7
Norwegian, 83
Novelty sought in personal names, 390

Objectionable uses, 245
Objections to words, 404-11
Obsolete occupations as source of surnames, 385
Occupational names, 384-6
Ohio dialect, 15, 16, 19
Oliphant, K., 169, 170
Onomatopoetic words, 163, 164, 215
Orchestra slang, 45
Oxford, 3

Paradoxical changes, 208-210
Parody words, 50
Parts of speech, shifts, 191-3
Pater, Walter, 2, 396, 424-5, 426, 427
Patronymic names, 381-3
Pearl, 106
Peddlar's French, 48
Permanency of place-names, 360, 361, 362
Personal feelings, 420
Personal names as place-names, 369, 370
Philippine words, 148
Phrasal associations, 244, 245
Physiology, old conceptions, 336-8
Piddington, H., 179
Piers Plowman, 124, 317-8
Place-names as surnames, 383-4
Plant names, 17, 73, 74, 79
Poetic vocabulary in Old English, 81
Poetry, 226, 231
Political life, vocabulary of, 31; slang, 44, 45
Portuguese words, 143
Pound, L., 178
Precision from use of technical terms, 72
Prefixes, 171-175
Prescott, F. C., 218, 221
Primero, 47
Primitive language, 248-9

Prince of Wales, 68
Profanity, 41, 42
Progress, words associated with, 419
Proletariat words, 426-7
Pronunciation of foreign names, 389-90
Propriety, 404 ff., 411
Provençal, 5, 19
Pugilistic slang, 47, 63
Purism, 35, 115, 172, 410-11
Purity, 404 ff.

Queed, 428
Quiller-Couch, Sir Arthur, 162, 395

Race track slang, 47
Radiation, 207, 216
Railroad terms, 34, 44
Ralph Roister Doister, 40
Realism in American place-names, 370-1
Reason for English borrowing, 150-1
Recent expansion of technical vocabulary, 78
Reeve, Chaucer's, 20
Reformation, 4
Relation between sound and meaning, 163, 164
Renaissance, 417
Renewal of life in language, 275-6
Renewed metaphors, 229
Reuter, Fritz, 19
Repplier, A., 300
Restaurant slang, 45
Revolt of youth, 59
Riley, Whitcomb, 20
Romance in place-names, 358
Roman civilization, 304; culture, 313; place-names, 362-3
Romantic associations, 350 ff.

Rural life, words associated with, 284-5
Ruskin, 173, 423
Russian literary language, 6; words borrowed, 143-4

Saints' names as personal names, 388-9
Salisbury, 366
Sandburg, Carl, 32, 428
Sanskrit, 294
Santayana, G., 218
Scandinavian place suffixes, 100; elements in dialect, 102; place-names, 365
Schauffler, R. H., 67
Schrader, O., 295, 299, 300, 306, 309
Science, beginnings of, 418; development of, 421
Scotch, 1, 15
Scott, Sir W., 12, 178
Sea-craft, 250
Sea terms, 71, 79
Sentimental Tommy, 396-7
Sentiment in American place-names, 369-70
Seventeenth-century slang, 40
Shakespeare, 4, 9, 10, 19, 39, 40, 41, 117, 168, 172, 173, 412, 415, 416, 417
Shaw, G. B., 178
Shifts of meaning in native words, 91 ff.
Sill, Dr. A. T., 178
Simile, 218, 231
Skeat, W. W., 12, 13, 104, 127, 130, 138, 140, 142, 215, 328, 330
Slang, meaning of word, 37, 38; antiquity of, 38-40; contribution to Latin, 38; definition, 43; in other languages, 51; created in war, 53 ff.; student, 58; of youth, 59 ff.; of girls, 62; objections to, 62 ff.

Smith, L. P., 114, 125, 166, 417, 419
Sounds, changes, 87; relation to meaning, 402; Scandinavian derivatives, 100, 101
South African dialect, 18; war, 164
South Seas, words from, 147
Spanish, literary, 6; derivatives, 142-3; in American English, 25; place-names in America, 373
Speaker, meaning determined by, 240
Specialization, 257 ff.
Spenser, E., 20, 288
Spices, names of, 323
Sporting slang, 46-48; sources of, 50-51
Squeamishness, 267
Stages in generalization, 250
Standard English, rise of, 1-5
Standard of taste, 404
St. Augustine, 178
Stephens, James, 21, 217
Stevenson, R. L., 366, 423
Stone Age, 305
Stories connected with names, 352
Strunsky, S., 278
Student slang, 58 ff.
Style books, 404
Suffixes, 171-175; -ie, -y, 175, 176
Superstition in place-names, 364
Surnames, 377, 380-1
Survival of older English words in New England dialect, 24; in other dialects, 97, 98
Swedish, 83
Synecdoche, 232 ff., 246
Synonyms, 393, 395 ff.

Taboos, 266 ff.
Tardiness in study of place-names, 358-9

Taylor, I., 344, 360, 362, 365, 366
Taylor, Jeremy, 157
Technical words become popular, 79
Tennyson, 117, 424
Teutonic, 293, 303, 306, 307, 309, 312, 313
Theater slang, 44
Thieves' jargon, 48, 49
Thomas, names derived from, 379
Toller, T. N., 110, 304
Transformation of foreign names, 390; of English place-names, 375-6
Timidity in American language, 34
Translation of foreign names, 390
Trench, Archbishop, 17, 117, 169, 173, 226, 288
Tropes, 202 ff.
Turgenev, 178
Turkish words, 146
Twelfth Night, 217
Two words in place of one, 395-6

Unconscious tendencies, 219, 220, 246
Understatement, 277 ff.; English propensity, 278-9
Utter, R. P., 393

Value of native element, 158, 159; of borrowed words, 155-7, 159, 160
Variation of forms in personal names, 387-8
Varied sources of English words, 397
Vehicle, parts of, 310
Victorian period, 21; euphemism, 269; ideals, 423, 424
Vulgar Latin, 130

Walpole, Horace, 173
Walpole, Hugh, 21
War slang, British, 53, 54; American, 54; special vocabularies, 55-57; French, 57, 58; German, 58
Webster, Noah, 31, 32
Weekley, E., 47, 223, 224, 237, 238, 253, 272, 277, 287, 330, 334, 337, 343, 378, 379, 380, 382, 383, 384, 386, 387, 388, 389, 391
Weeks, R., 160
Wells, H. G., 174, 426
Wessex, dialect of, 1, 2
White, R. G., 410
Whitman, Walt, 20
Wight, Isle of, 13
Wilson, Woodrow, 68
Winter's Tale, 40

Wither, George, 226
Wittman, E., 177
Women, use of hyperbole, 274
Wood, F. A., 343
Woodpecker, variant names of, 17
World War, 164, 180
Wörter und Sachen, 295
Wright, Joseph, 14
Wundt, 217, 219, 243, 278
Wycliffe, 1, 3, 40, 124

Yeats, W. B., 19
Yorkshire dialect, 3
Youth, source of slang, 59 ff.

Zoölogical terms, 77